THE
BLACK
LEDGER

HOW TRUMP BROUGHT PUTIN'S DISINFORMATION WAR TO AMERICA

ROBERT WALDECK

© 2020 COBRA Y CRÁNEO, INC.

TO MY MOTHER AND FATHER

TABLE OF CONTENTS

Introduction by Casey Michel: i
     What *The Black Ledger* Tells Us about
     Trump, Russia, Ukraine, and Impeachment

Preface: The Singularity Disappeared   ix

Prologue: Manafort Agonistes   xviii

BOOK I: FROM SMALL THINGS

Chapter 1: "All Decided in the Back Room"   2

     "That Money We Have Is Blood Money"
     "The Tanks, the Propaganda, the Agents, Provocateurs"
     A Defeat for the Dukes

Chapter 2: Revenge Rules the Soul of the Fool   42

     The Fall of Viktor Shokin
     The Fears of Andrii Artemenko

Chapter 3: "A Genius Killer"   62

     "Putin's Political Brain"
     "Ted Cruz Says Putin Is a Bully"
     "Criticize Hillary and the Rest (Except Sanders and Trump)"
     "Someone Has Your Password"
     "I Have Already Experienced the Power, I Know Its Taste and Price"
     "Don't Even Talk to Your Dog about It"
     "This Whole Thing with Russia"
     "For Immediate Release"

Chapter 4: A Secret Peace — 107

"The Greatest Danger Is In Washington, D.C."
The Death of the Warlord Motorola
"An Incredible Piece of Shit"
Birth of the Burisma Disinformation Campaign against Joe Biden
"A Very Minor Wink"
"I'm Not Coming through the Gold-Gilded Lobby of the Trump Tower"
"Can You Call Me?"
"I Have Never Met Viktor Vekselberg"
Peace Plans Bloom
Ukraine Reformers Strike at the Nasirov Back Channel
"Prepare a Visit to Kharkov by the Former Mayor of New York, Rudy Giuliani"

Chapter 5: "Somebody Gave an Order to Bury the Black Ledger" — 175

"What's Holding You Back is Corruption"
"Ain't Bragging if You Can Do It"
"Declare a Public Relations War on the FBI"
Kurt Volker Gets Back in the Game
"The Mother of All Fake News"

Chapter 6: "A Story that Is Pretty Untold" — 192

"Mockingbird 10.30.17"
"It Is Not Their Brief to Have an Opinion on the National Security or Foreign Policy"
"No One Can Continue Investigating Them"
"We Have Crossed the Rubicon, This Is Lethal Weapons"

Chapter 7: The Fatal Stain — 210

"This Phony Cloud"
"Junior Varsity Gamesmanship"
"He Called My Late Mother a Bitch"
People Are Not Always Who They Appear to Be on the Internet
War and Peace: Washington, Munich, Kyiv, Moscow
Substance-33
"Perhaps Some Bad Judgment, Inappropriate Meetings"
The 195th Richest Man in Ukraine
"They Were Operating Off of a Pre-Social-Media—Pre-Fragmentation-of-all-Media Strategy"
"He Starts His Game"
The "Long-Awaited Weapon"

BOOK II—THE ZELENSKYY AFFAIR

Chapter 8: A Name to a Face — 244

A Classified State Department Assessment—The Secret Memo
The Origins of Congressman-1
"It's Clear that Our Superiors Are Trying to Create Obstacles"
"At Our Quiet Direction"
It's Good to Put a Name with a Face
"Gay Parade on Blood"
"The Black Ledger Was Always Involved"
Servant of the People
Such Respect for a Brave Man!
Don't You Think that It's Kind of Stupid for Two Straight Men to Be Carrying Perfume for Ladies?
"They Will Start a Hundred Investigations"

Chapter 9: The Desperate Circus — 269

"I Actually Know the Guy Vaguely from Years Ago"
The "Secret Mission"
"A Big, Fat, Fishing Expedition Desperately in Search of a Crime"

Chapter 10: "I Will Do Big Practice in English" — 294

"Dad, They Say Zelenskyy Is the President"
"Remember These Two Names: Lev Parnas and Igor Fruman"
"Give Me Ninety Days"
"Gordon, I Think this Is All Going to Blow Up"

Chapter 11: Stray Voltage — 318

The Favor
"The Final Question Comes from Jill Colvin with *Associated Press*"

Chapter 12: A Scandal of Major Proportion — 336

"We Happen to Have the Man in the Middle Tonight"
"You're One Lucky Guy"
"I Want to Add this Investigation Is Continuing"
"Have You Ever Heard of the Black Ledger?"

Acknowledgments — 370

About the Author

Notes

CAST OF CHARACTERS

THE PRESIDENTS

> Barack Obama, 44th President of the United States

> Donald Trump, 45th President of the United States

> Vladimir Putin, 2nd and 4th President of the Russian Federation

> Viktor Yanukovych, 3rd President of Ukraine

> Petro Poroshenko, 4th President of Ukraine

> Volodymyr Zelenskyy, 5th President of Ukraine

THE VICE PRESIDENTS

> Joseph R. Biden, Vice President of the United States

> Michael Pence, Vice President of the United States

THE RUSSIAN OLIGARCH

> Oleg Deripaska

THE PROSECUTORS

> Robert Mueller, US Special Counsel

> Karen Greenaway, Supervisory Special Agent, Federal Bureau of Investigation

> Yuriy Lutsenko, General Prosecutor's Office of Ukraine

> Serhiy Horbatiuk, Chief, Special Investigations Division

Artem Sytnyk, National Anti-corruption Bureau of Ukraine

Nazar Kholodnytsky, Special Anti-corruption Prosecutor's Office

Viktor Shokin, General Prosecutor's Office of Ukraine

Viktor Trepak, First Deputy Chairman, Security Service of Ukraine

THE REFORMERS

Sergii Leshchenko

Daria Kaleniuk

Vitaly Shabunin

THE DISINFORMATION MACHINE

The Internet Research Agency

Cozy Bear (GRU), aka. the Dukes, APT29

Fancy Bear (FSB), aka. APT28, Pawn Storm

Wikileaks

Unit 29155 (GRU)

THE LAWMAKERS

Andrii Artemenko, MP, Radical Party of Oleh Lyashko

Oleksandr Onyshchenko, MP, People's Will

Andriy Derkach, MP

Representative Adam Schiff, D-CA

Representative. Devin Nunes, R-CA

Senator Mark Warner, D-VA

Senator Richard Burr, R-NC

THE POLITICAL TECHNOLOGISTS

Paul Manafort Jr.

Vladislav Surkov

THE FIXERS

Rudolph W. Giuliani

Lev Parnas

Igor Fruman

Michael Cohen

Roger Stone

Felix Sater

Daniel Vajdich

Boris Lozhkin

Roman Nasirov

THE DIPLOMATS

Kurt Volker

Marie Yovanovitch

GORDON SONDLAND

WILLIAM TAYLOR JR.

GEORGE KENT

REX TILLERSON

THE PARTY OF REGIONS AND THE OPPOSITION BLOC

YURIY BOYKO

DMYTRO FIRTASH

SERHIY LYOVOCHKIN

RINAT AKHMETOV

THE CIVIL SERVANTS

JOHN BOLTON

FIONA HILL

WHAT THE BLACK LEDGER TELLS US ABOUT TRUMP, RUSSIA, UKRAINE, AND IMPEACHMENT

BY CASEY MICHEL

In the summer of 2019, a single phone call—and a single whistleblower complaint from a concerned American listening to a sitting president sell out his country—tripped up an administration like few similar disclosures had ever done before. Due to the call between US president Donald Trump and Ukrainian president Volodymyr Zelenskyy, in which the American president asked for a "favor" of unprecedented proportions, Americans watched the first impeachment in the country's history brought on the ground of national security.

When the dust had settled on Trump's impeachment, one thing was clear: Trump had not only become just the third American president ever impeached by the House of Representatives, but he was the first American president to try to strong-arm a foreign government for "dirt" on a political rival. And the American president had specifically targeted a Ukrainian government that lay prone, chewed apart by a revanchist Russia, which was looking to America for stability and security and any help Washington could provide—a position Trump took full advantage of for political gain.

The details of Trump's impeachment, for those trying to follow either in the US or Ukraine, remained hard to untangle. Murky allegations, confusing narratives, and outright fabrications spun out wildly from Trump and his supporters, defending a president unlike any America had ever seen. The whole affair was a confused, sordid mess—a mess that *The Black Ledger: How Trump Brought Putin's Disinformation War to America* masterfully unravels, and lays out in all of its seamy, surreal detail. There was Trump's team in Ukraine, cornering Ukrainian officials with the president's self-serving demands. There was a bevy of corrupt Ukrainian oligarchs aiming, like Trump, to thwart Joe Biden's path to the Democratic nomination, and quite possibly, the presidency. And there was Trump's lawyer, Rudy Giuliani, imploding on national television, dismantling his legacy as a putative American hero. All of these diffuse threads were aimed at getting the Ukrainian government to open a fabricated investigation into Biden—the man who had led the Obama administration's anticorruption efforts in Ukraine, making untold enemies along the way.

For many Americans, that's where the story began and ended: Trump making unprecedented demands of a weak foreign government, and watching it all fall apart after his cronies began letting their secrets slip. The entire affair seemed to explode out of nowhere—few in the US had paid much attention to Ukraine following Russia's 2014 invasion of the former Soviet republic—and by early 2020 it seemed to have been wrapped up in the bow of Trump's impeachment.

But there was always something else, a shadowy stalking horse, behind Trump's impeachment saga that pointed in a different direction, one that few Americans had paid much attention to in the previous years. After all, it's not like this was Trump's first foray with controversy in the post-Soviet space. The first half of his term as president was dominated by a separate round of unprecedented revelations: of a campaign that had welcomed help from Russian operatives, that had benefited from Russian operatives' spreading of disinformation in social networks and via third-party websites, that had flirted with an entire range of pro-Russian policies, from lifting sanctions to recognizing Russia's claims in southern Ukraine. The investigation from Special Counsel Robert Mueller's office into the Trump campaign and Russian interference revealed the extent of these efforts, and the lengths to which Trump campaign operatives—several of whom were prosecuted for their efforts—willingly aided the interference and pushed it through the process.

The details of that campaign, and the full writ of Mueller's findings, had dropped only a few months before Trump's fateful conversation with Zelenskyy—which itself came only one day after Mueller's congressional testimony. Both of them involved a Russian government that had upended the post-Cold War order. Both of them involved a tangle of crooked post-Soviet figures specializing in dirty money, kleptocracy, and disinformation campaigns.

Could there be a connection between the two? Could Russia's 2016 campaign to help Trump and Trump's later efforts to force the Ukrainians to do his bidding actually be part of a single, larger story? Were these two sides of the same coin? And if so, how—and why?

These are some of the questions the book in your hands seeks to answer.

★ ★ ★

In *The Black Ledger*, Robert Waldeck presents the most thorough examination of this story—of its twists and turns, of its characters and connections—that has yet been published. Waldeck melds his understanding of the law and graduate degree in European history with extensive knowledge of the region, building his narrative upon a vast body of research, as indicated by the more than 2000 source notes you'll find at the back of the book. He packages his findings in a brisk run-through with details both new and overlooked, offering a coherent narrative, a coherent story, and a coherent set of facts about how Trump ended up as the only US president impeached during his first term in office.

Because, without providing any spoilers, there is one clear answer to the questions posed above. Not only are the Mueller report and Trump's Ukraine-related demands part of the same story—two sides of the same coin, indeed—they're part of a broader narrative that stretches back even further than Trump's unexpected rise to the presidency. That story involves many of the characters that grew close to Trump's campaign, most especially figures like convicted criminals Paul Manafort and Rick Gates, as well as the story of a pro-democracy revolution in Ukraine that toppled a post-Soviet goon named Viktor Yanukovych in 2014. It involves the efforts of anti-corruption crusaders in Ukraine who tried to trace the dirty money networks that had propped up Yanukovych's regime, and which found its way to paid-off lobbyists and white-shoe law firms in Washington, exposing the rot at the heart of America's political establishment along the way.

And it involves, most especially, one item in particular: the aptly named Black Ledger, from which the book takes its name. This ledger—which actually comprised hundreds of documents, detailing payments to and from the crooked Yanukovych regime and all of its enablers—haunts the entire saga that has played out over the past half-dozen years. From Yanukovych's overthrow to Russia's brutal invasion of Ukraine, from the staffing of Trump's campaign to the Russian efforts to aid Trump's election, from so-called "peace plans" in Ukraine—that would have been advantageous to

Russia—to the voices convincing Trump that Ukraine could open up an investigation into Joe Biden and possibly tilt the 2020 US presidential campaign his way, the Black Ledger has affected everything we've watched unspool in the Trump era.

It is the connective tissue for a series of seemingly divergent events that have influenced events in the US time and again, but which many Americans never even realized existed. Touching campaigns and revolutions, invasions and impeachments, the Black Ledger has always been there. And now, thanks to Waldeck's insightful book, we know why.

* * *

There's another thing worth mentioning before you dive into Waldeck's book. Even with the close of impeachment—and even with everything that's followed since, from the pandemic to the recession to an election unlike any other—the story of the Black Ledger isn't over yet. With the outcome of the Democratic primary, where voters selected Joe Biden as the party nominee, the story of the Black Ledger has simply reached its latest phase. Biden, after all, has long been one of the targets not only of Trump, but of those who want to see a return to thuggish rule in Ukraine, and elsewhere in Europe. Corrupt post-Soviet oligarchs fearing extradition to the US loathe Biden, and their American lawyers have been only too happy to help Trump target the former vice president. An entire right-wing media ecosphere, buoyed by far-right conspiracy theorists across social media, has helped inflame the allegations spawned by the revelations in the Black Ledger.

And while the anti-democratic efforts of corrupt post-Soviet figures seem to have receded somewhat since the close of impeachment, they're actually not through yet. They're peddling fabricated "tapes" of Biden, claiming that he actually helped entrench corrupt rule in Ukraine, and placing Biden and Democrats at the heart of some transnational conspiracy —one that just so happens to fit with the Kremlin's broader designs. These conspiracists and sycophants have carried the legacy of the Black Ledger well into 2020. And there's little reason to think they'll stop anytime soon. After all, they nearly succeeded time in getting Trump to implement one of the bogus "peace plans" they peddled, lifting sanctions, absolving crooked figures, and returning Russia to the stature the Kremlin feels it deserves in the post-Soviet space, no matter the cost. Just because they were caught doesn't mean that their efforts will stop anytime soon.

As Gordon Sondland, one of the key administration players in Trump's schemes, said about the president's efforts, "Everyone was in the loop. It was no secret." And now, thanks to *The Black Ledger*, you can see just how all-encompassing that loop was, and who was connected to it—and how everything from the past several years, from Russian interference efforts to the Mueller probe to Trump's remarkable impeachment, is part of the same story. And how all of it traces back to a single ledger uncovered in Ukraine all those years ago.

New York City

August 2020

Introduction, © 2020 Casey Michel

PREFACE: THE SINGULARITY DISAPPEARED

In 1999, David Bowie sat down with Jeremy Paxman on BBC's flagship program, *Newsnight*. Paxman asked him if he would have gone into music if he were still young. The superstar musician said no—instead he would get involved with the internet. Bowie told Paxman that the internet "carries the flag for the subversive and possibly rebellious and chaotic and nihilistic..."

Paxman was skeptical, remarking that on the internet "anyone could say anything" and that there was nothing cohesive about it in the way that say, the 1960s youth revolution was cohesive.

"Oh, absolutely," agreed Bowie:

> because I think that we, at the time, up until at least the mid-70's, really felt that we were still living under the ... guise of a single and absolute created society, where there were known truths

and known lies and there was no kind of duplicity or pluralism about the things that we believed in. That started to break down rapidly in the 70's and the idea of a duality in the way that we live, in, in, there is always two, three four, five sides to every question, that the singularity disappeared and that I believe produced a medium such as the Internet which absolutely establishes and shows us that we are living in total fragmentation. I don't even think we've seen the tip of the iceberg, I think the potential of what the Internet is going to do to society, both good and bad is unimaginable, I think we're actually on the cusp of something exhilarating and terrifying.[1]

Bowie was prophetic. In the post-Soviet sphere, the breakdown of the singularity of the U.S.S.R. became a nursery for a new politics of disinformation based on living in fragmentation. This politics combined off-the-books funding from oligarchs with the creation of new realities based on plausibility, not truth. The historian Timothy Snyder described how its architects did it: "first spread fake news themselves, then claim that all news is fake, and finally that only their spectacles are real."[2] These "concepts and practices moved from east to west," Snyder argued. They have been a feature of the American political landscape since 2016.

Thus the politics of disinformation burst onto the American scene. In a world where any randomly present cell phone camera could discredit a cover story, political truth needed only internal and emotional consistency. These rules now dominate our politics.

On May 17, 2018, Donald Trump's recently fired secretary of state, Rex Tillerson, gave the commencement speech at the Virginia Military Academy.[3] Quoting from Chapter 8 of the Gospel of John, he repeated "You shall know the truth, and the truth shall make you free" *three* times during his speech. Tillerson pointed out the new danger:

> An essential tenet of a free society, a free people, is access to the truth. A government structure and a societal understanding that freedom to seek the truth is the very essence of freedom itself. "You shall know the truth and the truth shall make you free." It is only by fierce defense of the truth and a common set of facts that we create the conditions for a democratic, free society, comprised of richly diverse peoples, that those free peoples can explore and find solutions to the very challenges confronting the complex society of free people.
>
> If our leaders seek to conceal the truth or we as people become accepting of alternative realities that are no longer grounded in facts, then we as American citizens are on a pathway to relinquishing our freedom. This is the life of nondemocratic societies, comprised of people who are not free to seek the truth.[4]

This book is about exactly that—how a political struggle between pro-Russian and pro-Western forces in Ukraine seeped into the politics of the United States, and how political disinformation techniques from that conflict infected American politics as a result.

The Black Ledger, a set of documents linking Putin-controlled oligarchs and Trump's campaign manager with a $4 billion dollar bribery and influence scheme to keep the former Soviet republic tied to Russia, was an impediment to Putin's preferred settlement of the conflict: a swap of Russian-occupied areas in Ukraine's east for recognition of his annexation of Crimea. It also provided the most compelling evidence that Paul Manafort, Jr. had been an agent of influence of the Russian Federation for a decade, a fact that could prove fatal to any Trump re-election bid.

The Black Ledger, uncovered during the 2014 revolution that deposed Ukraine's pro-Russian president Viktor Yanukovych, detailed a disinformation and bribery scheme that was only a rumor in Ukraine until a corrupt prosecutor named Viktor Shokin went after the wrong man, the State Security Service's Viktor Trepak. In revenge, Trepak handed the documents to anti-corruption investigators and alerted the press to their contents in May 2016.

This book details how Putin's goal in the 2016 election interference scheme was to reverse the outcome of the 2014 Euromaidan revolution in Ukraine by electing a friendly Donald J. Trump. The goal was Putin's but the plan was Paul Manafort's: raise Hillary Clinton's negatives amongst White voters in the upper Midwest.

The tool to do that was a set of Clinton emails stolen by Russia's GRU. Days after Trump hired Manafort, the GRU launched its attack on Democrats. The result was a Trump victory based on raising Clinton's negatives by directing the campaign narrative to her emails. A Harvard study showed that media coverage of Clinton's emails far outstripped any other issue.

The August 2016 revelation that Paul Manafort's name appeared in the Black Ledger did more than push the architect of Trump's victory off the podium, it also exposed the underside of Vladimir Putin's long term efforts to control Ukraine. The revelation tied Trump to Putin politically and created a major impediment to Russia's designs upon Ukraine.

No one was better positioned to know what Manafort was doing than Ukrainian President Petro Poroshenko, who doubtless monitored Manafort's former associates in Ukraine. Facing the potential disaster a Trump Presidency for Ukraine, Poroshenko moved sharply towards peace in the closing days of the 2016 US presidential campaign. He secretly agreed to the broad outlines of a peace with Russia, swapping Russian-annexed Crimea for the return to Ukraine of areas of the Donbas region then under Moscow's control. This peace would surely anger Ukrainians and potentially spark a new revolution in Ukraine, which required Poroshenko to conceal his plans. The parties hid the exchange of Crimea for Donbas and announced only that they were implementing the stalled peace deal, known as the Minsk Protocols.

Poroshenko hoped to get the best deal for Ukraine in this secret peace. The day the parties announced they had agreed to implement the Minsk

Protocols, the Ukrainian president opened a backchannel to Trump associates.

Unbeknownst to Poroshenko, that backchannel came with a dubious gift for Trump—disinformation in the form of false allegations from a Putin ally that linked Poroshenko to a fantastical set of corruption allegations with potential 2020 candidate Joe Biden and his son Hunter. The peace was derailed in March 2017 when a key player in the back channel between Trump and Poroshenko was indicted in Ukraine, risking exposure of both Trump and Poroshenko. The secret peace was put on hold.

Poroshenko moved to cultivate Trump. The two men, convinced they had put the danger of revelation behind them, agreed again to go forward, jointly working to eliminate the opponents to the plan in Ukraine and the US. But those opponents refused to sit still. At the same time, Trump faced the Mueller investigation. In the summer of 2017, Trump allies launched a disinformation campaign to combat it in the US and Ukraine.

As ties between Poroshenko and Trump deepened, US investigators plumbed the depths of the connections among Trump, Russia, and Ukraine. By spring 2018, Trump faced four separate investigations into his links to Russia, two in Congress, one from Special Counsel Robert Mueller, and a grouping of separate FBI counterintelligence investigations. The president and his allies increased their reliance on the politics of disinformation to derail these investigations. As Manafort continued to advise attacks on the FBI, the FISA warrants against Trump associates, and the Steele dossier, the

House Permanent Select Committee on Intelligence became the weapon of choice for the Republicans seeking to use disinformation help Trump to push back against the tide.

The fall of 2018 brought a dark turn of events for Trump and his supporters. While Manfort ostensibly agreed to cooperate with Mueller, Democratic electoral fortunes increased, After the Democrats won a House majority in the midterm elections, Trump dispatched Giuliani, Lev Parnas, and Igor Fruman to dig up dirt on potential Democratic presidential candidate Joe Biden and discredit the upcoming Mueller Report.

The following spring, Attorney General Bill Barr was able to dilute the impact of the Mueller Report. Trump moved to assure his reelection via the politics of disinformation. Working with dubious sources in Ukraine, Rudy Giuliani sought to discredit the Black Ledger, the Ukrainian reformers, and the State Department front channel and its main voice, US ambassador to Ukraine, Marie Yovanovitch.

Latching on to the 2016 Russian disinformation operation involving Trump's 2020 opponent Joe Biden, Giuliani used Manafort-inspired tactics to obtain information supporting a false narrative regarding Biden and Ukraine. Public servants and reporters exposed this second act, resulting in Trump's impeachment in 2019. The carefully husbanded Biden-Burisma disinformation was used as a defense in House impeachment hearings. They melted in the white heat of the inquiry, likely limiting their future usefulness and impact.

The operatives who sought to borrow the new politics of disinformation from Russia and Ukraine also sought to fund it using new money-laundering techniques from the former Soviet Union designed to hide the role of the political beneficiaries of the disinformation.

When seen through this prism, the Mueller investigation, the efforts to craft a peace, and the politics surrounding the Russia Affair, finally come together into a coherent whole. Mueller's primary effort for two years was to prove legally that Trump was changing US-Ukraine policy to pay back the Russians for their help in the election. Manafort lied about the peace plan to prevent Mueller from doing just that. Mueller's interest in Michael Cohen centered around his role regarding the peace plan after the interference campaign. US ambassador to Ukraine Marie Yovanovitch was targeted because she was dangerous to the disinformation campaigns as a fact witness to the deals with Poroshenko, and dangerous because of her contacts with Ukrainian reformers. Those reformers had gone after Trump associates in Ukraine at inconvenient times. They had also provided information on Trump's Ukrainian dealings to the US State Department, information that made its way to Congress and Robert Mueller.

In the words of one of the participants, Andriy Derkach, "since 2016, Ukraine has been at the center of domestic politics and the political confrontation of its strategic partner, the United States" and the result has been a "series of international scandals and corruption, in which some representatives of law enforcement and diplomatic bodies of the two countries are mired."

So far Trump, Putin, and their Ukrainian allies have maneuvered to prevent the American public from becoming aware of the Black Ledger. Republicans, led by Trump associate Rudy Giuliani, are trying to prepare their base for revelations about the Black Ledger by continuing to make accusations about it. Democrats, led by Adam Schiff, prepared the country for its revelations by impeaching President Trump for acts relating to Ukraine. The press has tried to reveal as much as their sources will allow.

The Black Ledger has remained unknown to most Americans. Until now.

PROLOGUE:
MANAFORT AGONISTES

On August 14, 2016, Steve Bannon took over the Trump 2016 campaign. The plan was to retain the Campaign Chairman, Paul Manafort as a figurehead. But Manafort had bad news. The *New York Times* was about to run an expose on his time as a political consultant for pro-Russian politicians in Ukraine.

The next day, August 15, 2016, was a Monday. On that day's *New York Times* front page the top left column carried the headline "Secret Ledger in Ukraine Lists Cash for Trump Aide." A subheadline read: "Benefiting from Powerful Interests, While Mixing Business and Politics." Underneath appeared a photo of Paul Manafort Jr., campaign manager for Republican presidential nominee Donald Trump.

The piece was written by Andrew E. Kramer, the *Times*' Moscow bureau chief. It had appeared online the evening of the 14th. The article reported that a secret ledger of cash payments linked Manafort to "a corrupt network" that Ukrainian anti-corruption investigators said "was used to loot Ukrainian assets and influence elections" to help "Mr. Manafort's main client, former president Viktor F. Yanukovych."

The article described the documents as "handwritten ledgers" which showed that Manafort had received $12.7 million in undisclosed cash payments from Yanukovych's "pro-Russian political party." Kramer added that investigators from the National Anti-Corruption Bureau of Ukraine said the payments were "part of an illegal-off-the-books system, whose recipients also included election officials." The *Times* had linked the Trump campaign to a Russian scheme to use disinformation and bribes to exert controlling interest in its neighbor, Ukraine through its covert support for the pro-Russian Party of Regions.

This was not the time for the Trump campaign to be linked to Russia. The candidate, based on his own statements, had been considered to be unusually pro-Russia and personally admiring of Vladimir Putin. Trump's final primary opponent, Ted Cruz, had attacked his ties to Russia, and in June 2016, the Democratic National Committee announced that it had been hacked by state actors from Russia. For weeks, email messages from this hack had been released by hackers and WikiLeaks, the radical transparency organization run by Julian Assange. Trump's convention performance three weeks earlier, had been dogged by questions about his ties to Russia.

The morning that the *Times* article was published, Steve Bannon asked Manafort about the Black Ledger. Manafort told him he had known about the story for two months but did not explain how. At first, Bannon advised Trump to hang on to Manafort. Trump asked Bannon to explain the story about the payments.

Manafort and his long-time business partner Rick Gates fought a losing battle to mitigate the damaging effects of the story implicating Manafort. Four days after the *New York Times* story broke, Manafort called his partner Rick Gates to meet at Trump Tower. Manafort was then asked to come to a Trump family meeting.

BOOK I:
FROM SMALL THINGS

This war of opinions, or of categories, as Lafayette termed it, is in truth commenced, and Americans, if they will but use common observation, cannot but feel that a neglect to notice, and provide against the consequences of that settled, systematic hostility to free institutions so strongly manifested by foreign powers, and which is daily assuming a more serious aspect, will inevitably result in mischief to the country, will surely be attended with anarchy if they wake not to the apprehension of the reality of this danger.

Americans, you indeed sleep upon a mine.

"Brutus" (Samuel F. B. Morse),
Foreign Conspiracy against the Liberties of the United States, *1835*.

CHAPTER 1:

"ALL DECIDED IN THE BACK ROOM"

Paul Manafort's, and by extension Donald Trump's, link to the Black Ledger, stretched back more than a decade. The term "Black Ledger" was a translation of the term "Black Cash Books" coined by eager headline writers in Ukraine to describe a set of documents recording a bribery and disinformation scheme that Manafort's prior client, Viktor Yanukovych, who was the president of Ukraine from 2010 to 2014, undertook to secure and hold power. It included records of payments and documents related to the influence campaigns that Manafort and others undertook in Ukraine for the benefit of the Russian Federation.

In 2004, when Yanukovych first ran for president of Ukraine, his Party of Regions was caught attempting to rig the vote count by Western election observers.[5] Russia had been involved in it all, helping Yanukovych stuff ballot boxes and intimidate voters and election monitors. Worse, Yanukovych's opponent Viktor Yushchenko was poisoned with dioxin weeks before the election.[6] These efforts to rig the election failed. As a news anchor went on television to announce a Yanukovych victory, the sign language interpreter defiantly signed: "I address all deaf viewers. Yushchenko is our President. Do not believe the Electoral Commission. They are lying."[7]

Armed with data from Western election monitors, Yushchenko and his political ally, Yulia Tymoshenko, sent orange-clad supporters en masse on to the Maidan, the central square of Kyiv, to protest the announced election results. The political upheaval that followed was called the Orange Revolution. Protestors on the Maidan forced a new, fair election that Yanukovych lost. Yushchenko was elevated to the presidency and Tymoshenko became prime minister of Ukraine.

Discovery of Russia's deep involvement in Ukraine's 2004 election, and their interference on behalf of the Party of Regions, created what one report called "severe blowback" for Russia.[8]

Paul Manafort then worked as a political consultant on retainer for aluminum oligarch Oleg Deripaska, a Putin ally.[9] Deripaska rose to become a billionaire during the "aluminum wars" in 1990s Russia.[10] Fellow Russian oligarch Mikhail Khodorkovsky said "there were so many murders that I refused to go into this business" and forbade his associates from getting into a deal to buy an aluminum smelter. "Don't go out there" he told them, "I need you to stay alive."[11] Deripaska's company, Rusal, was the largest aluminum company in the world until overtaken by a Chinese firm in 2015.[12] Deripaska—in the words of Volume V of the comprehensive US Senate Select Committee on Intelligence (SSCI) report on the Russian interference campaign, released in August 2020—"acted as a proxy for Russian State and Intelligence Services."[13]

Soon after the Orange Revolution, Deripaska ordered Manafort to rehabilitate Yanukovych and the Party of Regions in Ukraine on behalf of the Russian government.[14] On June 23, 2005, Manafort and his partner Rick Davis sent Deripaska a strategy memo for what Manafort called "our program."[15] It was to be a broad system of political, lobbying, and legal efforts to restore the Party of Regions to prominence in Ukraine.[16] The memo outlined a strategy to "subtly influence the perceptions" of the West to provide "an acceptable explanation for actions by governments not totally in concert with Western thinking."[17]

The memo outlined the purpose of the plan:

> to create . . . the protections needed to ensure the avoidance of Orange Revolutions becoming acceptable in the West. The key is to understand the West and to use their tools to deal with the specific problems in ways that the West believes is in concert with them. Rather than attacking the West, the correct strategy can be created to embrace the West and in so doing restrict their options to ferment [sic] an atmosphere that gives hope to potential advocates of a different way.[18]

Manafort was confident of the plan's success in Ukraine and argued in his memo this method could be used beyond Ukraine: "We are now of the belief that this model can greatly benefit the Putin Government if employed at the correct levels with the appropriate commitments to success."[19] The plan was approved.

In fact, Manafort was also running influence campaigns for Deripaska in Central Asia, Cyprus, Georgia, Guinea, Montenegro and elsewhere in Europe, the purpose of which was to advance Deripaska's business interests and political influence. [20] These interests also coincided with the interests of Vladimir Putin and Russia.

The Russian state put its assets behind the Deripaska efforts. When a Deripaska-preferred candidate in the West African country of Guinea was shot during an election campaign, one of the oligarch's associates tied to the Russian military intelligence agency known as the GRU directed that a ship of the Russian Navy be sent there to intimidate anyone trying to interfere in Deripaska's attempts to manipulate local politics so he could corner the aluminum deposits there, one of the largest in the world.[21]

These efforts were full-spectrum. Deripaska would financially back candidates and then hire Manafort to provide on-the-ground consulting for those candidates.[22]

These were paid for in ways that disguised the operations. Deripaska introduced Manafort to "Dr. K," Kyprios Christomides, a Cypriot who specialized in creating offshore entities there.[23] Those entities paid Paul

Manafort $25 million in 2008 alone. Manafort learned the ropes of offshore funding from Dr. K. He would utilize those methods in the decade to come. The Party of Regions payments for Manafort's services came from Cypriot accounts.[24]

Paul Manafort was a premier agent of influence for the Russian state. For these efforts he was paid tens of millions of dollars.[25]

In diplomatic cables sent to Washington, US ambassador to Ukraine for the George W. Bush administration, William Taylor, described Manafort's efforts on behalf of Yanukovych as an "extreme makeover."[26] Assisting Manafort in this effort was Konstantin Kilimnik, who worked as translator, guide and fixer for the American in Kyiv.[27] Kilimnik had started as a translator for the GOP-backed International Republican Institute (IRI), one of two nonprofits supported by the major US parties to help spread democracy outside the US. He was fired by IRI for moonlighting for Manafort in the aftermath of the 2004 election.[28]

According to Volume V of the SSCI report, Konstantin Kilimnik is a "Russian intelligence officer."[29] Kilimnik is five foot three, loves Western craft beers, and speaks Swedish, English, and Russian.[30] Manafort described him as "a powerful little dude."[31]

Paul Manafort Jr. had always broken political rules. The son of a Connecticut politician who resigned under a cloud of bribery allegations, Manafort once ran the campaign of his childhood friend Roger Stone for the presidency of the Young Republicans so effectively that Stone's opponent quit before the election, complaining "it's all been scripted in the back room."³² Manafort's 1976 convention defense of President Ford from the Reagan insurgency gave him a reputation as a master of GOP presidential delegate rules. Manafort became a high-roller in Republican circles following his 1980 work on Ronald Reagan's election campaign.

As campaign strategist in charge of the south, the Connecticut-born Manafort ran Reagan's plan to once and for all break the lock the Democrats had held over the South for more than 100 years. There Manafort broke the rules involving the Republican Party and the South, organizing Reagan's infamous speech at the Neshoba County Fair in Mississippi where the GOP nominee sounded themes of white grievance with leadership in Washington.³³

Manafort's political gifts clustered around division, in the US and Ukraine.³⁴ His power was to see that division in polling and put a story around it. His partner Konstantin Kilimnik explained to a reporter: "Manafort is a guy who can merge, you know, strategy and messages into something that will work for victory."³⁵ "I've seen him work in different countries," Kilimnik continued, "and . . . he really does take seriously his polling and can spend, you know, two weeks going through the data, and he'll come [up] with the best strategy you can ever have."³⁶

These talents helped Manafort rise. An old television clip of the Nickelodeon game show "What Would You Do?" preserved on YouTube from the early 1990's illustrated his ascent.³⁷ As Manafort looked on, his wife was called up to compete with another woman in a little game with the host, Marc Summers, later of "Double Dare" fame. "I'm going to play Monty Hall here," he announced before asking the women to produce their purses. As Summers asked about what was inside their handbags, Kathy Manafort laughingly admitted that she carried her husband's wallet in her purse. Summers could not resist. He pulled out the wallet, quipping: "Yeah, that's a big wallet, things are obviously going well for your husband there, aren't they, huh?" As Manafort looked on laughing, Summers opened the wallet and bellowed with mock surprise: "Sir, how many American Express Cards does one person need?[38] Summers showed the audience that Manafort's wallet held gold, silver, and corporate Amex cards.

Those badges of success came from his norm-breaking innovations in the business of politics. Professionally, Manafort and his childhood friend Roger Stone were part of two interdependent firms. The first, Stone, Manafort, Black and Kelly, was a firm that lobbied government officials. The second, Black, Manafort, Stone and Atwater, provided political and election consulting for those same government officials.[39] But the big money the firms were making came from overseas, representing figures like Angolan guerrilla leader Jonas Savimbi and Philippine dictator Ferdinand Marcos.[40] These clients had access to the wealth of the places they controlled and a need to burnish their reputations in Washington.

Although Manafort focused on international clients in the years after 1984, he did not give up entirely on domestic ones. One of these US clients was Donald Trump.[41] Manafort represented Trump in front of Congress, pushing back on Indian casinos. Trump famously testified as part of this effort that "nobody likes Indians as much as Donald Trump" but that "there is no way Indians are going to protect themselves from the mob."[42] Stone said it succinctly: Manafort was "charming, entertaining, well-tailored and he certainly understands power and how it works."[43]

★ ★ ★

With charm, entertainment, good tailoring and an understanding of power and how it works, in 2005 Paul Manafort began executing Deripaska's plan to rehabilitate Yanukovych. Yanukovych's party, the Party of Regions, was centered in the Russian-speaking southeast of Ukraine. It had been described as representing "Russophone Ukraine and [bringing] together pan-Slavists, ex-communists, trade unionists, oligarchs, former Soviet functionaries, and red directors (industrial managers during the communist era)."[44]

Over time, Manafort became closer to Yanukovych and other Party of Regions figures. He began to drift from the direct control of Deripaska and into the orbit of Russia's clients in Ukraine as Ukrainian oligarchs began to pay him.[45] Manafort's work was valuable, as the Party of Regions gained a significant number of seats in Ukraine's parliament, the *Verkhovna Rada*, in the 2006 elections.[46] Yanukovych became Prime Minister of Ukraine. His comeback was on the way.

Unlike Western political parties, the Party of Regions lacked a budget or a political action committee because the oligarchs who controlled the Party and paid its bills did not trust one another to pull their weight. Instead, various individual oligarchs would pay for the work on a project-by-project basis.[47] According to Rick Gates, these oligarchs would "pass the hat" to pay for Manafort's services.[48] Every project had its own vehicle to receive payments.[49]

The men paying these bills were oligarch polticians like Rinat Akhmetov and Dmytro Firtash, who moved between the Ukrainian Parliament, called the Verkhovna Rada, the government and business and footed the bill for the party's political fixing needs. This meant bribes. These bribes were paid because control of Ukraine's political levers was worth billions of dollars. Events preceding Yanukovych's second presidential run displayed the value of that control and why he would spend millions to hire a strategist like Manafort.

The system required accounting for which oligarch had paid for which project. Between late 2004 and 2014, between thirty and fifty oligarchs paid for various aspects of the Party of Regions political work.[50] Thus the Black Ledger was born, made up of sheets tallying financing and spending for the Party of Regions by the oligarchs who funded the work behind the scenes. The man tasked with controlling the Party of Regions finances and keeping the Black Ledger was Yevhen Geller.[51] His name was on more entries than any other. Geller was paid like many others—via contracts his companies were awarded by the Ukrainian state.[52]

Control of political power in Ukraine was worth billions of dollars. Vladimir Putin provided those billions to oligarchs behind the Party of Regions. After laundering the funds through New York real estate, they used them to bribe judges, police, and elections officials. Those payments were recorded in the Black Ledger and associated documents, kept under lock and key in the Party of Regions' headquarters on Lypska Street in Kyiv and at the mansions of government officials.

As the 2010 Ukrainian presidential election approached, a dispute over the price of natural gas broke out between Ukraine and Russia. This dispute would be the prologue of the scheme that created the Black Ledger. At 11:48 a.m. on New Year's Day 2009, an engineer pressing a button at a Gazprom compressor station in Kursk, Russia, turned off the flow of gas from Russia to Ukraine, and by extension, Western Europe.[53] For several years prior to 2009, such gas crises erupted in Ukraine during the wintertime when Russia decided to cut off supplies in disputes over prices.[54]

Every cubic meter of gas that left Russia and Kazakhstan for Ukraine and the rest of Europe, was controlled by a middleman, the primary oligarch behind the Party of Regions: Dmytro N. Firtash.

Yulia Tymoshenko, the prime minister of Ukraine, had determined to solve the gas cutoff crisis once and for all by cutting Firtash out of his middleman position. The fact that it would provide Tymoshenko a political win on her signature issue—reducing utility costs to Ukrainians—was all the better for her. The votes of the millions of Soviet-era pensioners who were dependent on the price of natural gas would power her own campaign for the presidency in 2010.

Firtash was so suspicious of Tymoshenko's plans that just prior to the shutoff, in December 2008, he showed up at the US Embassy in Kyiv, asking to speak to the ambassador, William Taylor. In an unusual meeting at the US Embassy he explained his fears of a Tymoshenko-Putin deal and tried to paint a sympathetic picture of himself.

Taylor recounted the scene in a cable home. Firtash told Taylor he was a "simple person who grew up in the village of Synkiv" who had to get permission from the head of the Russian mafia, Semion Mogilievich, to even enter business.[55]

With a partner, this "simple person" cornered the lucrative Kazakhstan-to-Ukraine gas market in the early 2000s becoming its sole vendor, he recounted to the American ambassador.[56] Firtash had also cornered the transit rights for Russian gas through Ukraine to Western Europe.[57] He made a fortune with these ploys.

Firtash's fears regarding Tymoshenko were well-founded. To solve the gas standoff, Tymoshenko went to Moscow and hammered out a deal with Putin that cut out Firtash because he owed Gazprom $1.7 billion for 11 billion cubic meters of gas he had purchased, which he was holding in Ukraine for later sale to countries in Eastern Europe.[58] Tymoshenko agreed on behalf of

Ukraine's state-owned gas monopoly Naftogaz, to pay the debt owed by Firtash in exchange for the 11 billion cubic meters of gas.[59]

Cut off from his main source of income, on March 24, 2009, Firtash filed an arbitration case against Naftogaz at the Arbitration Institute of the Stockholm Chamber of Commerce, a group that oversaw business disputes in Europe.[60] In countries with a weak rule of law like Ukraine and Russia, large contracts like the one between Naftogaz and Firtash stipulated that disputes would be settled by the institute.

However, before Firtash's arbitration could be heard, Manafort's "extreme makeover" made the case moot: Yanukovych was elected president of Ukraine on January 17, 2010. Firtash's friend Yuriy Boyko became energy minister and another friend, Serhiy Lyovochkin, became the head of the new presidential administration—a powerful position, the equivalent of the chief of staff to the president in the United States.[61]

Using bribes and following a motto coined by his prime minister, "the ancient human instinct of fear has to be activated to a much greater degree again," Yanukovych and his party began their rule by bribing the police, prosecutors, and election officials, and taking control of the mechanisms of the judiciary and the state.[62]

Within two months of taking office, Yanukovych declared success in a program of "coordinating" government, which observer Alexander Motyl likened to dictatorship.[63] Motyl, calling Manafort's extreme makeover "a con," predicted the new Ukraine: "dispersal of demonstrations by means of force and, if need be, violence. The harassment, persecution, and possible "disappearance" of opposition leaders in general and of outspoken national-democratic and nationalist leaders in particular. Particular targets: Yulia Tymoshenko."[64]

The "coordination of government" included Naftogaz, which Yanukovych gave over to his Party of Regions colleague, Yuiry Boyko. The company was promptly purged and before long conceded the arbitration case in Stockholm to Firtash.[65] The compensation to be paid to Firtash was 12.1 billion cubic meters of natural gas, with a market price of approximately $3.5 billion.[66] This represented more than half of the gas production in all of Ukraine and went from the taxpayers' pockets to Dmytro Firtash personally.[67] Profits began to roll in for Firtash and his associates again. Prior to the 2009 deal, Firtash's company had regularly brought in three-quarters of a billion dollars in profit per year.[68] Prodigious cash flows began again in earnest.

Russian government documents record sales of 20 billion cubic meters of gas at below market prices from Russia's Gazprom to Dmytro Firtash between 2009 and early 2014.[69] Firtash then made a $3 billion profit by selling the gas at market prices in Ukraine and Europe.[70] These below-market gas sales cost the Russian state-controlled Gazprom $2 billion in profits that it would have received in arms-length transactions.[71] This was the cost of Putin's foreign influence operations in Ukraine.

At the same time, Putin-affiliated bankers loaned $11 billion to Firtash to purchase a commanding stake in Ukraine's fertilizer and chemical industry.[72] The purchases made Firtash the fifth largest fertilizer producer in Europe.[73] Coupled with the $3.5 billion in the Stockholm award, Putin and his associates had sent Firtash more than $18 billion over five years.

Firtash was not the only member of the Party of Regions who was profiting from control of government. Oligarch Mykola Zlochevsky, the minister of ecology, was responsible for allocating oil and gas leases to private companies. He also owned the largest independent oil and gas company in Ukraine, Burisma Holdings.[74] While minister, Zlochevsky had given out lucrative gas licenses to several different shell companies that were subsidiaries of Burisma.[75]

To keep control of the billions harvested by Firtash and Zlochevsky, the Party of Regions engaged in large-scale bribery and disinformation operations. Using funds provided by Firtash and other oligarchs, Yanukovych bribed judges and police to imprison his former political opponents, many in revenge for the deal that had cut out Firtash. Tymoshenko and Yuriy Lutsenko, the former interior minister under Yushchenko, were imprisoned and tried on trumped-up charges.[76] At the same time, oligarchs funded foreign disinformation and influence operations directed by Manafort.

Putin used this corruption of Russian state assets to create a network of clients in Ukraine centered around the Party of Regions. His clients included politicians and oligarchs like Firtash, Serhiy Lyovochkin, Gennady Kernes, and Yuriy Boyko, all who served as Ukrainian government officials while continuing to own large corporations.

Worldwide, Russia used a carrot-and-stick approach with groups like the Party of Regions, co-opting local elites by offering them less than savory deals while threatening them with the revelation of negative information, known as "kompromat."[77] It was a pattern that would repeat itself, first, across the former Soviet Republics and later, the world.

Imprisoned by this system, former prime minister Tymoshenko sought to trace the funds that paid for it to win her freedom. From her prison cell in Ukraine, Tymoshenko hired a former assistant US attorney, Kenneth F. McCallion, to file a class-action lawsuit on her behalf and for "John Does 1–10" against Dmytro Firtash and "John Does 1–100 on April 26, 2011."[78]

The suit, filed in the Southern District of New York, alleged that Firtash had skimmed gas profits and laundered the proceeds in the US, then sent the money back to Ukraine to be used in a large bribery and influence scheme to help Yanukovych regain and remain in power, while imprisoning Tymoshenko and the other plaintiffs as retaliation for her reversal of Firtash's favorable deal with Naftogaz.[79] An amended complaint added Paul Manafort, placing him at the center of the scheme:

> [Manafort] played a key role in the defendants' conspiracy and racketeering enterprise by assisting Firtash to become a major "investor" and silent partner in defendants CMZ Ventures

(sometimes referred to as "ZMC Investors"), Group DF and their affiliated companies, through which Firtash and his associates were able to money launder a large portion of the funds that Firtash, Group DF and RUE were skimming from numerous Gazprom/Naftogaz natural gas transactions, as well as the windfall payments and profits worth approximately $3.5 billion.[80]

Tymoshenko's complaint alleged that the monies from the Stockholm award "were used to pay off political figures and government officials in Ukraine" who imprisoned her and others and that Manafort allowed "Firtash to utilize the various US based companies to facilitate Firtash's money laundering" in the United States."[81] Tymoshenko also named Serhiy Lyovochkin and Yuriy Boyko as codefendants in the Amended Complaint.[82] In short, Tymoshenko's Amended Complaint alleged the laundered money went to pay the bribes listed in the Black Ledger.

According to the suit, thirty-three separate US entities set up by Manafort laundered the funds Vladimir Putin sent to Firtash and the other oligarchs behind the Party of Regions.[83] The skimmed gas profits funded sham real estate deals, primarily in New York City real estate, where Firtash would go through all the steps to buy a building and back out at the last minute, using the return of escrow monies from banks to launder the funds.[84]

The suit alleged that a one-time protégé of Fred Trump—Donald Trump's father—Brad Zackson was a partner in these deals.[85] Zackson had been so successful as an agent for Fred Trump that the developer sent a limo to collect the man who was renting all of his units.[86] Impressed, Fred Trump Jr. hired Zackson on the spot to run rentals for all his Queens apartment buildings.[87]

To facilitate the scheme, Tymoshenko's complaint alleged, Firtash had obtained control of a bank in Ukraine, Nadra Bank, which he used to send half a billion dollars to New York banks for the sham real estate deals.[88] By placing these funds in US banks and appearing to engage in real estate transactions, the money was kept from scrutiny by Ukrainian law enforcement.[89]

Zackson suggested to his partners that they include Fred Trump's son Donald in the scheme, though no evidence has yet surfaced tying Trump to Firtash's efforts in New York.[90] These deals were under US federal criminal investigation, the complaint alleged.[91] This investigation later was transferred to the Special Counsel, Robert Mueller.[92]

These laundered funds, Tymoshenko's complaint explained, were used for political tasks. One task stood out: defending Yanukovych's jailing of his political opponents. The prosecution of Tymoshenko and the other political opponents was wedded to an international disinformation and political influence campaign run by Paul Manafort.

Manafort married emerging techniques of Russian political disinformation to American political organizing, along with sophisticated efforts to align the Republican Party in the United States with the Party of Regions in Ukraine.93

In a remarkable 2011 proposal, Manafort advised Yanukovych to create an alternate explanation and analysis of the Ukrainian president for political audiences within the United States. Manafort's plan centered around attacks in the American press on then secretary of state Hillary Clinton's opposition to President Yanukovych. It was explicitly aimed at undermining the lawful foreign policy of the United States by turning the question of US policy towards Ukraine into a partisan political issue in the US. It has been so ever since.

By this time, Paul Manafort had a "mythic status" in Ukraine, and using "large teams" of ten or fifteen expatriates, was "flying around with a 747 with an advance team and things like that."94 Every step of the way he was accompanied by Konstantin Kilimnik, identified as a Russian intelligence officer in Volume V of the SSCI report.95

Unsurprisingly then, Manafort's proposal to solve Yanukovych's foreign problems was executed. The plans sought to subvert America's largely bipartisan foreign policy regarding Ukraine by inducing conservatives in the US to view that policy through the prism of partisan politics. The Republican Party would be aligned with the ruling pro-Russian Party of Regions in Ukraine. By making Obama's foreign policy toward Ukraine a new center of partisan strife, Manafort would try and limit the US government's ability to conduct foreign policy detrimental to his client by raising the political costs for it inside the United States.

Accordingly, the influence plan included a blog on the US website *RedState* and an article on the right-wing site *Breitbart* by conservative bomb-thrower Ben Shapiro.[96] A federal law, the Foreign Agents Registration Act, required Americans representing foreign entities and governments to register with the US government. Manafort did not register this activity as lobbying in the US, an act that could facilitate hiding the income from the IRS.

The payments in the Black Ledger went to all manner of persons, including some in the United States. Larry King, the avuncular US talk show host, was listed in the Black Ledger for having interviewed Yanukovych's prime minister in 2011 as part of the disinformation campaign. News reports stated King received $225,000.[97] US lobbyists Vin Weber and Tony Podesta also had payments listed to their firms in the ledger.[98]

The two lobbyists, Weber and Podesta, were hired to work on a project known as the "Habsburg Group," a collection of discarded European statesmen who would spin their commentary and analysis in favor of Yanukovych in the media and in international policy circles.[99] Disinformation needed messengers and there were plenty of former heads of state seeking riches. True to the Party of Regions funding model, oligarch Serhiy Lyovochkin paid them for the Habsburg Group project.[100]

But Manafort also executed an even more dubious scheme to use Skadden, a white-shoe US law firm, to advance Yanukovych's interests inside and outside of Ukraine. The firm worked on two projects relating to Yanukovych's persecution of his former election opponent Tymoshenko. The first involved a report justifying her arrest and conviction to policy makers in the US.[101]

The second, far more secret project involved helping obtain those convictions in the first place. Skadden advised Yanukovych's Prosecutor General's Office on twenty-one separate criminal cases filed against Tymoshenko.[102] Skadden lawyers coordinated directly with the efforts of Yanukovych's prosecutor general, Viktor Pshonka.[103] Skadden's retainer was $4 million.[104] Documents later revealed that a third party, oligarch Viktor Pinchuk, paid Skadden for the work.[105]

A third Skadden project contemplated another prosecution of Tymoshenko which never occurred.[106] While Skadden wrote its report justifying the prosecution, it was not disclosing its involvement in the criminal actions filed against her by Yanukovych's prosecutor general.

The complex disinformation operations Manafort deployed on behalf of Yanukovych had been pioneered by Putin's visionary political technologist Vladislav Surkov. Manafort added old-fashioned foreign influence peddling and GOP partisan politics to the mix.

Originally from the theater world, Surkov started in public relations working for the first generation of post-Soviet oligarchs in Russia.[107] From business, Surkov shifted to politics, working first for Russian president Boris Yeltsin and then his successor, Putin.[108] In 1999, Putin made him deputy chief of staff.[109] By 2008 Surkov was appointed first deputy chief of staff to President Medvedev when Putin spent a presidential term as prime minister while continuing to retain ultimate power in Russia.[110]

Political technologists such as Surkov and Manafort were using what one observer, Peter Pomerantsev, called "the new Russian name for a very old profession: viziers, gray cardinals, wizards of Oz."[111] Surkov described himself as "the author, or one of the authors, of the new Russian system."[112] Perhaps he was: Surkov would meet weekly with the heads of the television channels, ordering them to attack some and defend others, defining how President Putin was to be presented, and setting the language and categories in which Russians thought and felt.[113] Networks would pick a theme such as oligarchs, America, or the Middle East and insinuate a conspiracy existed while actually saying very little.[114]

"The brilliance of this new type of authoritarianism is that instead of simply oppressing opposition, as had been the case with 20th-century strains, it climbs inside all ideologies and movements, exploiting and rendering them absurd," observed Pomerantsev.[115] (As an example, Surkov published a novel under a pseudonym and then wrote a review under his own name panning the book. Later he would praise it.)[116] It was not a surprise, then, that the Party of Regions also paid its opponents as a means of control. The Black Ledger even included payments to Svoboda, a political party that was in opposition to Yanukovych.[117]

Surkov saw this hall of mirrors as part of a larger system that he called "Sovereign Democracy" or "Managed Democracy."[118] Putin used it effectively within Russia. He would soon export it. His response to accusations of Russian influence operations summed up Russia's attitude: "Foreign politicians talk about Russia's interference in elections and referendums around the world. In fact, the matter is even more serious: Russia interferes in your brains, we change your conscience, and there is nothing you can do about it."[119]

To pass these messages on to the Russian people, Putin associates launched a sophisticated disinformation campaign in 2011, a year when Putin's approval rating dipped sharply.[120] After protesters had used the internet to spread their message during a wave of protests, the Russian president sought to turn the tables and use the Internet for his own benefit.[121]

A company known as the Internet Research Agency (IRA) was set up to feed content on behalf of the Russian government to its own citizens.[122] Like the disinformation operations in Ukraine, it was funded by a Russian oligarch, the Putin-connected Yevgeny Prigozhin. The IRA would start by advancing Russia's narratives in Russia, then move on to Ukraine and finally the United States.[123]

These disinformation schemes were paid for in ways familiar to Russian oligarchs—sham business deals and loans that hid the real purpose of the funds. One payment to Manafort was evidenced by a contract between Yanukovych and Manafort that purported to pay the American $750,000 to sell a thousand computers to a company registered in Belize that banked in Kyrgyzstan.[124]

Unusual deals like Manafort's "sale" of those thousand computers were the norm in these new transnational political influence operations. Unlike US off-the-books political activities, the payment methods for political influence operations often derived from advanced money-laundering techniques pioneered by Russian organized crime.

These techniques were known as the "Russian Laundromat." A laundering party would enter into a sham transaction for a loan to complete a business deal. In one version, the deal would inevitably go bad, the laundering company would sue, and get a friendly court to order the money returned. Now the launderer had clean money, a court-ordered payment on their books.[125]

Such a process could also be used to hide payments of surreptitious activity. A business would "loan" money to a person they were paying to take actions they wanted hidden. After the deal went "bad" lawsuits to "get the lost money" could be used as a defense against showing intent to commit the crime of money laundering—if the suspect was laundering money, why would they pay lawyers to sue to get the money back?

Despite the disinformation campaigns and the firehose of cash from Putin, problems began to mount for the Party of Regions in 2013. In June of that year, Dmytro Firtash, the major source of the party's funds, was secretly indicted by a federal grand jury in Chicago.[126] The indictment described Firtash as a member of the "upper-echelon of organized crime."[127]

The indictment alleged that the management consulting firm McKinsey had recommended that aircraft manufacturer Boeing obtain permits to mine titanium in India for its make-or-break 787 Dreamliner To get the permits, McKinsey proposed using the financier and leader of the group that controlled the titanium, Dmytro Firtash. He owned a titanium smelting plant in Ukraine and had a deal to mine between 5 and 12 million pounds of Indian titanium per year.[128] Firtash used his Nadra Bank to structure the finances.[129]

McKinsey's PowerPoint presentation plainly told Boeing executives how Firtash was going to get the rights to mine the titanium: "traditional business practices (bribes)" to Indian government officials.[130] The Foreign Corruption Practices Act, or FPCA, forbid US companies from paying illegal foreign bribes. Rarely has a FPCA case been this well documented.

The lead agent on the Firtash case was FBI Supervisory Special Agent Karen Greenaway.[131] Greenaway spoke fluent Russian and had worked for years in the Bureau's Transnational Organized Crime Unit.[132] In 2014 she moved exclusively to one of the Bureau's new International Corruption Squads.[133] Her presence would soon become ubiquitous when it came to FBI investigations of Ukrainian and Russian corruption.

US prosecutors filed a sealed indictment against Firtash under which American authorities planned to request his arrest by Austrian authorities when the oligarch visited Vienna.[134] The Obama administration planned on arresting him in late 2013.[135]

But the secret indictment of Firtash was the least of the problems that faced the Party of Regions. Prior to Yanukovych's 2010 win, Ukraine had been one of the three largest recipients of aid from the International Monetary Fund (IMF).[136] But once Yanukovych became Ukrainian president in 2010, his policies resulted in a cutoff of IMF funds to the country. A big source of the friction between the West and Yanukovych was the jailing of his two political opponents Yulia Tymoshenko and Yuriy Lutsenko.[137]

Manafort's efforts to deploy the Skadden report and the Habsburg Group to limit the fallout from Yanukovych's jailing of his opponents failed.[138] The EU made signing of any potential economic agreement conditional on the release of Tymoshenko and Lutsenko and demonstrated its resolve by ordering its officials to boycott the Ukrainian portion of the UEFA Euro 2012 soccer tournament in Kyiv.[139]

Yanukovych's problems with Western Europe deepened into a crisis when he was faced with the decision on signing an association agreement with the European Union in 2013. Putin wanted Ukraine to join his emerging Eurasian Economic Union and turn away from Europe. Putin pressed on Ukraine's businesses, and in September threatened the Russia-based chocolate plants of Ukrainian oligarch Petro Poroshenko if Kyiv persisted in seeking to sign the EU Association Agreement.[140]

Faced with this pressure, Yanukovych wavered between Russia and the West as his attempts to sign a trade deal with both groups at the same time failed.[141] Yanukovych next released Lutsenko and stated he planned to sign the EU agreement in November 2013, but talks broke down under intense pressure from Russia.[142]

Many in Ukraine wanted EU membership and made their voices heard. At the end of November 2013, small demonstrations in Kyiv by protesters who favored the EU agreement burgeoned into rallies of 100,000 on the Maidan.[143] Manafort flew out of Kyiv in November.[144] By early December, Kyiv city hall was occupied by protestors and 800,000 regime opponents demonstrated on the Maidan.[145]

During the protests, the US aligned itself with the protestors. Senator John McCain dined with opposition leaders and US deputy secretary of state Victoria Nuland appeared on the Maidan on December 5, 2013, handing out cookies to protestors.[146] Three days later, protestors on the Maidan toppled the statue of Vladimir Lenin, long a symbol of Russian domination of Ukraine.[147] The following day, Vice President Joe Biden, delegated by President Obama, telephoned Yanukovych, warning him against a violent crackdown.[148]

The protestors were largely young, and many were activists who had experience in the West.[149] Leaders of the reform movement on the Maidan included Daria Kaleniuk, a lawyer who had used a Fulbright Scholarship to study at Chicago-Kent School of Law.[150] In 2011, Kaleniuk and activist Vitaly Shabunin formed the Anti-Corruption Action Center NGO with the motto: "Corruption always has a name."[151] These groups flocked to the Maidan.

But one of the men who had been coming to the Maidan regularly was far from being known as a reformer. Oligarch and former holder of top government posts Petro Poroshenko, considered a man of the establishment, joined the protesters and gave speeches from the stage.[152]
Poroshenko, who owned Ukraine's most popular news channel, also brought television cameras to the Maidan.[153] His extensive holdings in confections and manufacturing were typical of a post-Soviet oligarch who had benefitted unfairly from the breakup of Soviet state companies. Unsurprisingly, the Ukrainian public had long considered Poroshenko to be corrupt.[154] But on the Maidan, Ukraine's "chocolate king" was remaking himself in real time in front of the cameras and reporters he brought with him.[155]

On December 17, Yanukovych moved decisively to Putin. He signed an economic deal reducing gas prices and Ukraine's debt, which prompted the EU to break off talks.[156] As 2014 began, protestors occupied government buildings in Western Ukraine despite a law banning protests that was passed and then repealed by the Rada, which began to turn, along with public opinion, against the president.[157] Matters were coming to a head in Kyiv.

"THAT MONEY WE HAVE IS BLOOD MONEY"

At the end of December 2013, the fascist Russian legislator Vladimir Zhirinovsky had made a harsh prediction on Russian television regarding the growing protests in Kyiv. He claimed that following the end of the Sochi Olympics, things were going to get worse:

> Today, our client in Kiev is the respected Viktor Fedorovich Yanukovych. He will show you the heat when the Olympics ends. You will learn what Yanukovych is. Now he fell ill just in case. And then a voice will be heard: "Do not spare the cartridges!" And we will give cartridges. Instead of money, we will give cartridges.[158]

The Sochi Olympics were due to close on February 23, 2014.

On February 14, 2014, the protests turned violent.[159]

The Party of Regions had planned for a crackdown on what came to be known as the EuroMaidan protests with the help of top Russian operatives put up in hotels in Kyiv.[160] From the US, Manafort advised Yanukovych. A private text conversation between Manafort's daughters implicated him in the crackdown plans: he "killed people in Ukraine . . . knowingly" in conjunction with the "revolt."[161] Manafort's daughter saw him communicating with the Ukrainian government about the response to the protests with his "shady email" where he exchanged messages by use of webmail draft functions. She claimed it was "a tactic to outrage the world and get focus on Ukraine," and told her sister "that money we have is blood money."[162]

The result of Putin's help, Manafort's advice, and Yanukovych's need, were Operations "Wave" and "Boomerang." The regime positioned police snipers on buildings and activated plans to engage in military-style clearing of the streets with armed police.[163] On the morning of February 18, members of the Yanukovych administration met with special operations police, illegally issuing them riot gear and providing them with cash payments.[164] Phone records would later show dozens of phone calls between leaders of the public safety ministries and the police in the early hours.[165]

These plans would not be enough to save Yanukovych. On the 18th, police fired live ammunition from rooftops overlooking the surging Maidan crowd below, killing thirty-one people.[166] Late on the evening of the 18th, Vice President Joe Biden called Yanukovych. The readout from the Vice President's office said that Biden had told the Ukrainian president that his government had a special responsibility to de-escalate the situation.[167] In a subsequent memoir Biden recounted he went further: he told Yanukovych "to call off his gunmen and walk away."[168]

That same day, a few blocks away, 300 protesters equipped with metal bats, pipes and "at least 20 Molotov cocktails" approached a house on Lypska Street in Kyiv.[169] The house was the headquarters of Yanukovych's pro-Russian Party of Regions.[170] On the second floor, the headquarters offices had a special, secure room behind a metal door. Inside the secure room were some of the documents that would later be called the Black Ledger.[171] As a result of the break-in, someone obtained the documents. They ended up in the hands of the Security Service of Ukraine.

Protesters breaking into the homes of Party of Regions leaders found more documents floating in a small lake near Yanukovych's boat house, disposed of there to make them unrecoverable, and hidden in a secret compartment in a hot tub in the house of the prosecutor general.[172] These detailed the payments and the work that had been undertaken. Activists scanned and posted some of the documents to a Yanukovychleaks.org website.[173]

By February 20, video of police shooting protestors with live ammunition had circulated worldwide and eighty-eight people had been killed by police in the prior forty-eight hours.[174] On February 22, the situation came to a head.[175] As the Rada voted to impeach Yanukovych, his Interior Ministry announced it was going over to those on the Maidan. A press release from the ministry lionized the protestors its police had shot from the rooftops days earlier: "We bow our heads in memory of the dead," it read.[176] Yanukovych fled Kyiv for a Party of Regions meeting in Kharkiv that he never attended, then escaped to Moscow.[177]

"THE TANKS, THE PROPAGANDA, AGENTS, PROVOCATEURS"

Unlike what occurred in the Orange Revolution, Putin would not stand by again as Yanukovych was ejected from power. While the EuroMaidan was energizing Kyiv and Western Ukraine, in the Crimea and Eastern Ukraine, strongholds of pro-Russian and pro-Yanukovych sentiment, people expressed alarm. As the crisis in Kyiv deepened in early December, the State Council of the Autonomous Republic of Crimea convened an emergency meeting where they called on Yanukovych to "restore public order."[178] As a result of the huge protests in Kyiv, on February 2, 2014, the Crimean Parliament announced that it was establishing a working group to consider amendments to the Crimean constitution and reached out to Putin requesting he guarantee Crimean autonomy.[179]

After Yanukovych fled for Russia on February 22, Putin huddled that night with his advisors. "We ended at about seven in the morning," he later said. "When we were parting, I said to my colleagues: we must start working on returning Crimea to Russia."[180]

Five days later, on February 27, gunmen wearing uniforms without insignia seized the Crimean Parliament and government buildings.[181] Deputies voted in a new government.[182] When accused of sending the heavily armed soldiers without insignia to storm the Crimean Parliament, Putin provided an alternate explanation: the men were local defense forces who bought their uniforms at stores.[183]

On March 3, the Russian ambassador to the United Nations, Vitaly Churkin, told a meeting of the UN Security Council that Ukrainian president Viktor Yanukovych had written a letter appealing "to the President of Russia Vladimir V. Putin to use the armed forces of the Russian Federation to re-establish the rule of law, peace, order, stability and to protect the people of Ukraine."[184] Photos showed Churkin holding up the letter to display it to the assembled members of the Security Council.[185]

On March 11, the Crimean State Council declared itself independent.[186] On March 15, Russian troops invaded Crimea on the basis of the Yanukovych letter.[187] The following day, the Crimean government held a referendum on the question of whether Crimea should be part of Russia.[188] The vote was reported by Russian media as in favor of making the change in Crimea's status.[189] More Russian troops poured in and Ukrainian forces prepared to withdraw in the face of the vastly superior Russian army.[190] One aide to German chancellor Angela Merkel summed up Putin's actions: "It's just so twentieth century—the tanks, the propaganda, the agents, provocateurs."[191]

But the Russian efforts were actually very twenty-first century. Putin had tapped media wizard Vladislav Surkov to lead the efforts to place Crimea under Russian control and to manage the two client states set up in the Donbas, the Luhansk Republic and the Donetsk Republic.[192] Surkov launched a disinformation campaign in Ukraine and Russia regarding the operation.

* * *

The efforts to justify Russia's 2014 invasion of Ukrainian territory utilized the Internet Research Agency, created in 2011, to provide Putin with a disinformation machine for Russia.[193] It flooded social media and web comment sections with anti-Maidan content in Russia and Ukraine.[194]

The West would not stand still as Putin moved on Ukraine. On March 21, the acting Ukrainian leadership met with EU leaders and signed the political provisions of the EU-Ukraine Association Agreement.[195] At nearly the same time, the US. and the EU imposed crushing sanctions on Russia, including targeted sanctions on individuals associated with Putin.[196] He responded by incorporating Crimea as a region within Russia.[197] The struggle for Ukraine was just beginning. The sanctions and the conflict remain to this day.

While the revolutionaries consolidated their power in Kyiv, a small protest movement flared up in April in the Donetsk and Luhansk regions. Pro-Russian Yanukovych supporters occupied government buildings in the cities of Donetsk and Luhansk, located in Ukraine's two easternmost oblasts, adjacent to the Russian border.[198] As militias were formed by locals, Ukrainian government forces learned that armed Russians were amongst those fighting them.[199] Again, soldiers in uniforms without insignia led the charge. They were from Russia.

Russia's attack on Ukraine's sovereignty occurred while it lacked an elected president. The elections were rescheduled for May 25, 2014.[200] A leading candidate emerged: Petro Poroshenko, the same oligarch who had used his own television network to reinvent himself as a reformer on the Maidan during the Revolution.[201] He proposed a justice system "that defends the right of every citizen" as his campaign gained steam.[202]

When a reporter asked him during the campaign about being "a part of the past," Poroshenko provided his own alternate explanation: "On the 20th of February, we had a new country."[203] His reinvention was complete, his past rendered irrelevant by his appearances on the Maidan. But Poroshenko's path to the presidency was not assured—a potential opponent was a formidable competitor, the world-famous "Dr. Ironfist," Vitaly Klitschko, one of the greatest heavyweight boxers of all time.[204] Standing six feet seven inches, Klitschko had knocked out a staggering 87 percent of his opponents in his career, second only to Rocky Marciano.

But Klitschko would never step into the ring, as Poroshenko was apparently not above the backroom deals he claimed were over. On March 25, 2014, the Party of Regions politician Serhiy Lyovochkin brokered a meeting between Poroshenko and Klitschko in Vienna with Dmytro Firtash.[205] Firtash was stuck in Vienna, out on $174 million bond posted by a Putin ally, following his March 12 arrest on the US bribery charges.[206] He sought revenge against Poroshenko's presidential opponent Tymoshenko who had stripped him of his gas transit rights five years previously. Flight records show that Paul Manafort was also in Vienna that day.[207]

A deal was arranged. Klitschko would stay out of the presidential race and run for mayor of Kyiv in 2015. Porohsenko's allies would work together in the snap election Poroshenko planned for if he won the presidency.[208]

Four days later, Rick Gates, Paul Manafort's right hand man, sent an email to Tad Devine, a Democratic strategist who had worked with Manafort and Gates, to help Yanukovych, pitching work for Poroshenko's Presidential campaign.[209] Devine responded, suggesting to Gates that "a powerful introduction of PP [President Poroshenko] could resonate in Ukraine the way our campaign in Serbia resonated with voters."[210] Gates replied: "We are ready to take on this project."[211] The PowerPoint presentation Gates attached to the response included a series of pro-Russian talking points.[212] During an FBI investigation in September 2014, Manafort told the Bureau he was working for Poroshenko.[213]

Vice President Joe Biden, tasked with reaching out to the new powers in Kyiv, met with candidate Poroshenko on April 22.[214] On May 25 Poroshenko secured an outright majority, electing him the new president, the first time a candidate had done so in the first round.[215] The celebrity candidate, boxer Klitschko, went on to win the Kyiv mayoralty in 2015.[216] Although ostensibly on the opposite side of the political divide in Ukraine, Serhiy Lyovochkin put Konstantin Kilimnik in charge of Klitschko's election effort. Kilimnik selected American political consultant Sam Patten to advise Klitschko and Lyovochkin paid the American consultant's bill.[217]

After the Maidan and the election of Poroshenko to the presidency, the former leaders of the Party of Regions were at a loss. In October 2014, Poroshenko called the snap elections he planned in April to create a parliamentary majority for his presidency.[218]

Manafort returned to Ukraine to help the remnants of the pro-Russian contingent in the Rada. Now being paid by Lyovochkin, Manafort suggested the Party of Regions adopt a new strategy of uniting anyone opposed to Poroshenko in a loose grouping he called the Opposition Bloc.[219] The discredited oligarchs were surprised by Manafort's wizardry—their new party received twenty-nine seats in the 450-seat Rada and the immunity from criminal prosecution that went along with it.[220] The new party was financed by the same group of pro-Russian oligarchs that had financed the old Party of Regions: Lyovochkin, Akhmetov,[221] and Dmytro Firtash.[222]

A DEFEAT FOR THE DUKES

As Poroshenko schemed to obtain the presidency of Ukraine in 2014, a hacker from the Joint Sigint Cyber Unit, a collaborative unit involving the Dutch intelligence agency Algemene Inlichtingen- en Veiligheidsdienst (AVID) and Dutch military intelligence penetrated a Moscow computer network belonging to Cozy Bear, a renowned Russian intelligence hacking operation.[223] Cozy Bear, also known as APT29 or the Dukes, was thought to work for one of two Russian intelligence agencies, the Sluzhba vneshney razvedki Rossiyskoy Federatsii, (SVR) or the Federal'naya sluzhba bezopasnosti Rossiyskoy Federatsii (FSB) or both.[224]

The Dutch hackers gained near-complete penetration of Cozy Bear. They even obtained access to the security camera network at the door to the suite and recorded video of the Russian intelligence officers entering it and matched the videos with photos of known agents of the SVR.[225] The Joint Sigint Cyber Unit had penetrated one of the most malicious groups of computer hackers on Earth, and learned it was staffed by Russian spies.

In November 2014, the Dutch detected Cozy Bear hacking into US State Department servers.[226] The US National Security Agency quickly opened a direct line to the Joint Sigint Cyber Unit.[227] With the access obtained, Cozy Bear hackers sent a spear phishing email message to a White House staffer using a spoofed state.gov email address.[228] The staffer, followed the instructions in the email and went to change his password at a fake Russian website. The NSA worked in real time to control the damage and close the vulnerabilities.[229] The NSA stopped Cozy Bear before they were able to get to President Obama's personal BlackBerry.[230] One observer called it the worst hack of US government computer systems in history.[231]

Another Russian intelligence agency, the Main Directorate of the General Staff of the Armed Forces, also known by its Cold War acronym GRU, ran a part of another group of hacking operatives known as Unit 26165.[232] A second GRU unit, called Unit 74415, worked with Unit 26165.[233] Units 26165 and 74415 were Fancy Bear, a politically oriented GRU hack and dump unit, tasked with obtaining derogatory information on targets and spreading it to others for political gain.[234]

Fancy Bear was also known as APT28, Sofacy, Pawn Storm, Strontium, Tsar Team, and Sednit.[235] The GRU hackers had a backdoor exploitation program designed to allow access to a penetrated network on command. Both the Russians and Western intelligence services called the program X-Agent. Security firms knew the backdoor as "kazak" from a name that appeared in documentation often left in X-Agent code.[236] Kazak, it turned out, was Captain Lieutenant Nikolay Yuryevich Kozachek of the Russian Navy, a member of Fancy Bear.[237]

Like the origin of the IRA's influence campaign, Putin was first the victim of hack-and-dump operations. A group describing themselves as the "Russian Anonymous" pulled off a series of hacks against the Russian government. They reveled the existence of pro-Putin troll farms centered in a pro-Putin youth group during the 2011 Russian unrest. The group used uploads of hacked material to expose Putin's operation.[238] The group, also known as "Humpty Dumpty" leaked Putin's 2013 New Year's speech hours before he addressed the nation, hacked the Twitter account of the Russian prime minister to announce a fake resignation, and leaked documents linked to the Internet Research Agency.[239]

Soon, Putin was using hack and dump himself, with a new twist. A blogger, known as Hell, began leaking documents hacked from the personal accounts of dissident Alexey Navalny. After German authorities caught Hell,

Russian bloggers suggested that "Hell is not a master hacker but merely acted as a conduit for stolen materials spoon-fed to him by individuals with ties to Russian authorities."[240]

In 2014 and 2015, as Russia was in conflict with Ukraine, Fancy Bear began hacking Ukrainians, including politicians and media personalities, in a wide-ranging campaign that also attacked journalists and others worldwide.[241] In 2015 AVID's Joint Sigint Cyber Unit in the Netherlands detected that Cozy Bear had successfully hacked the Democratic National Committee.[242] The Russians were playing for keeps.

In August 2015, the FBI telephoned the DNC's IT director and told him they believed the DNC that had been hacked by foreign actors.[243] In a follow-up call, the FBI told him "the actor is probably an entity known as DUKES."[244] Over a series of calls over the following months, the FBI gave the DNC information about suspicious IP addresses that they thought were being used to possibly penetrate the DNC's servers.[245] The DNC did not find anything suspicious in its logs, frustrating the FBI.

But the GRU did more than just hack computers in its efforts to advance Russian state interests. Major General Andrei V. Averyanov commanded the agency's Unit 29155.[246] He was known as "Director 1."[247] It is headquartered in Moscow, at the 161st Specialist Training Center.[248] The unit has apparently existed for more than a decade and its mission is, according to US intelligence officials, to destabilize the West.[249] In 2015, Unit 29155 attempted to poison a Bulgarian arms dealer.[250] The two men used the aliases of Pavlov and Fedotov.[251] Western intelligence services only learned of the unit's existence after a 2016 coup attempt in Montenegro that sought to restore Oleg Deripaska's influence there.[252] Unit 29155 waited for orders to fulfil its purpose to destabilize the West.[253]

CHAPTER 2:

"REVENGE RULES THE SOUL OF THE FOOL"

An object that conveys the gravity and authority of the presidential office in Ukraine is the *Bulava*, a gilded silver mace.[254] On May 25, 2014, Petro Poroshenko won the right to wield it in the first round of balloting.[255] One observer aptly described the mace as particularly "heavy" at the time he took office.[256] Three fundamentally interrelated problems made the *Bulava* especially weighty: economic stagnation, endemic corruption, and Ukraine's hybrid war with Russia.

Addressing the hybrid war came first. Poroshenko released his peace plan in June 2014.[257] It included "measures to decentralize power and early local and parliamentary elections," unfavorable terms for Ukraine that perhaps reflected the power differential between it and Russia.[258] But in the post-EuroMaidan atmosphere, demonstrations of national resolve were required. Pavlo Klimkin, Ukraine's new foreign minister, appeared in front of the EU in late June to push the Poroshenko peace plan. When a reporter at the press conference that followed asked questions in Russian, Klimkin responded only in Ukrainian.[259] Putin came under international pressure to approve a peace deal.

The war continued despite the peace overtures of summer 2014. In June, a Buk anti-aircraft missile launcher, No. 731 of the Russian Army's 53rd Anti-Aircraft Missile Brigade in Kursk, was put on a transporter and driven across the border into separatist territory.[260] Satellite imagery captured the convoy en route to the launch area.[261] The launcher then shot down two Ukrainian troop transports.[262]

The next month, the same Russian Buk anti-aircraft missile launcher sat in separatist-controlled territory, when—according to intercepts—its operators mistakenly shot down Malaysia Airlines Flight 17 flying from Amsterdam to Kuala Lampur, killing all 298 people aboard.[263] A GRU general was heard on radio giving the order.[264]

Despite this setback, Ukrainian forces began effectively clearing the militias from the area in August looking to end the conflict.[265] Putin was not about to let that happen. As the Ukrainian operation began to seize its objectives in the separatist areas, large Russian Army mechanized formations crossed the Ukrainian border and counterattacked, throwing the Ukrainian army back and ending its chances of taking control of the Donetsk area.[266] The war entered a stalemate in August.

While the hybrid war raged, Ukraine's economic problems remained unsolved. One of the first acts Poroshenko took as the new president of Ukraine was to sign the economic provisions of the Ukraine-European Union Association on June 27, 2014.[267] With threats of retaliation, Russian was able to postpone the new free trade portions of the agreement until 2016.[268]

The Ukrainian state needed more than an agreement with the EU to solve its economic problems—it desperately needed funds to continue operating. The International Monetary Fund had not engaged Ukraine from 2011 to 2013.[269] A 2010 loan had been the last for Ukraine until after the Maidan revolution in 2014.[270]

To help solve its economic problems, the Ukrainian government requested an IMF loan of $15–20 million in March 2014. This would be a key to unlocking aid from the European Union and the United States.[271] In the talks, the IMF wanted three things to complete the deal: a change in the subsidy level for natural gas, a crackdown on corruption, and Ukrainian Central Bank support to float the nation's currency freely on world currency markets.[272] Ukraine agreed. $1 billion in US aid guarantees from the Obama administration followed.[273] When it came time to set the interim aid on a more permanent footing, Poroshenko agreed to keep these provisions in the permanent deal.[274]

Peace talks continued. The primary vehicle to discuss peace was the Trilateral Contact Group (TCG), set up to seek a peace in May 2014. After the war became stalemated the TCG met regularly in Minsk, the capital of nearby Belarus.

The TCG's Ukrainian delegation was led by former Ukrainian president Leonid Kuchma.[275] As a candidate for the Ukrainian presidency, Kuchma had run on closer relations with Russia.[276] Kuchma was also connected to the country's richest oligarchs. His son-in-law, the billionaire Viktor Pinchuk, owned Interpipe, LLC, a manufacturer of steel pipe and had been the third party who paid for the Skadden contract to persecute Tymoshenko.[277]

Critics alleged Pinchuk made money through his connections to Kuchma. During Kuchma's presidency, in 2004, Pinchuk teamed with Rinat Akhmetov of the Party of Regions, to buy the state steel company Kryvorizhstal for only $800 million, despite offers of over a billion dollars from other interested parties.[278]

Pinchuk had also served two terms in the Rada. He owned the most expensive home in London, which he paid £80 million for in 2008.[279] To move around the world, Pinchuk leased a gray-blue-and-white Bombardier Global Express 6000, registered in Austria under the tail number OE-IDO.[280]

Pinchuk and his aircraft OE-IDO were closely tied to the peace negotiations led by his father-in-law Kuchma.[281] Since nearly the beginning of talks, the members of the Trilateral Contact Group had used the jet to travel to and from Minsk and other locations where negotiations were occurring.[282] From the start, Victor Pinchuk was close to the peace negotiations between Ukraine and Russia.

A second structure for peace negotiations was called the Normandy Format, created when Poroshenko and Putin met for the first time on the sidelines of the D-Day commemoration ceremonies on June 6, 2014, a day prior to Poroshenko's swearing in.[283] The parley included Germany and France as international partners.

In September 2014, Kuchma hammered out a deal with Russia which had provisions that were highly disadvantageous to Ukraine. Known as the Minsk Protocols, its terms included an exchange of prisoners and a 30 km buffer zone between Russian and Ukrainian forces.[284] Observers declared it a "truce in name only."[285] The Minsk Protocols envisioned a decentralization process that would end up giving Putin's proxies in the occupied areas more powers and an election in those districts *prior* to Ukraine taking control of the area with its troops.[286] Those areas were to have special status under Ukrainian law. The Minsk Protocols were silent on Crimea.

The special status law required by the Minsk Protocols was so onerous that Poroshenko had it passed in a special closed session of the Rada on September 16, 2014.[287] The law, with its deference to Putin's interests in East Ukraine, was instantly despised by Ukrainians. Only a third of Ukrainians supported it and 62 percent of them, pollsters said, thought it would not bring peace.[288] Putin signed the treaty, but never committed to following it.

★ ★ ★

As Ukraine sought peace in early 2015, Dmytro Firtash claimed in his extradition hearing that his arrest had been political persecution for his pro-Russian stance in Ukraine. Records produced at the hearing showed that the US had held off extradition to try and keep Yanukovych from signing an economic deal with Putin in late 2013.[289] Lyovochkin testified in the hearing about the Poroshenko-Klitschko meeting in March 2014, admitting that Firtash wanted Poroshenko to prevail over his arch-enemy Tymoshenko.[290] The judge ruled in Firtash's favor, denying extradition.[291] The Americans appealed and Firtash remained trapped in Vienna.

The international politics that so interested the judge in Firtash's extradition hearing went on. Victor Pinchuk's interest in those politics was evidenced by his Yalta European Strategy Conference (YES). Since 2004 he had hosted the gathering, called YES for short.[292] In 2014, the venue had been moved from Yalta, in the Russian-occupied Crimea, to Kyiv.

YES played a large role in drawing Western attention to Ukraine. It was usually well-attended because the top panelists and speakers were well paid. In 2015 presidential candidate Donald Trump spoke. Pinchuk paid Trump's foundation $150,000 for a twenty-minute presentation from the candidate.[293] Doug Schoen, Pinchuk's US lobbyist, set up the speech.[294]

Dealing with Russia's shadow war in Donbas must have been foremost in Poroshenko's mind when he sat down with the *Wall Street Journal* in July 2015, five months after Minsk II. He was blunt about what he sought from the US: "We're looking for just 1,240 Javelin missiles" linking the missiles to

Ukraine's surrender of 1,240 nuclear weapons in a three-way treaty with the US and Russia in the 1990s.[295] The Raytheon FGM-148 Javelin is designed to defeat the armor of Russian-made tanks by autonomously flying to its target, elevating itself, and driving itself into the tank's thinner top armor.[296] Javelins were potent politically and militarily.

But the economic and military problems Poroshenko faced could only be solved if the corruption that Russia used to maintain a hold on Ukrainian elites could be broken. Like almost all other post-Soviet states, Ukraine suffered from endemic corruption from its founding—corruption used by Russia to further its aims.

Poroshenko took steps in in the fall of 2014 to reduce corruption. In October, he shepherded reforms through the Rada: the 2014 Anti-Corruption Package.[297]

The package set a deadline to move the investigation functions of the General Prosecutor's Office to a new agency, the State Bureau of Investigations, an attempt to end years of abuse. It also brought to life the National Anti-Corruption Bureau of Ukraine (NABU), the brainchild of the Anti-Corruption Action Center's Daria Kaleniuk, to investigate cases and the new Specialized Anti-Corruption Prosecutor's Office to prosecute them.[298] A third agency, the National Agency on Corruption Prevention, monitored public servants and maintained a database of "e-declarations" where government officials would declare their holdings openly on the Internet to avoid conflicts of interest.[299]

To help solve these problems, anti-corruption funding and financial aid flowed in from Ukraine's new Western partners, with US aid focusing particularly on corruption and civil society measures. By 2015, economic aid from the US aid had nearly doubled and $49 million of that funding package was earmarked for civil society organizations.[300]

The West also sought to help Ukraine prosecute specific cases against Yanukovych and his associates who had looted funds from the Ukrainian state. NABU and the Prosecutor General's Office were working with the FBI to get the money back. Those efforts began in March and April of 2014 and were led in Ukraine by FBI supervisory special agent Greenway.[301] But from nearly the beginning, the FBI had problems with the General Prosecutor's Office.[302] But at least now there was progress.

The biggest of these was Burisma. In April 2014, when Mykola Zlochevsky tried to move some of his ill-gotten gains from Burisma into the UK from Cyprus, the UK seized the funds.[303] Ukraine's General Prosecutor's office opened a case against Zlochevsky and Burisma.

In response, the company hired a series of new board members with international experience and reputations. One of those people was the vice president's son Hunter Biden who the board hoped could help them obtain overseas investors.[304] A nonexecutive director, Hunter Biden was also tasked with obtaining a law firm to help the company get investments from American companies.[305] The younger Biden joined the company in May.

* * *

The anti-corruption moves occurred as a second Minsk peace conference was scheduled for February of 2015. Minsk I had failed when Russian-backed separatists retook the Donetsk airport from the Ukrainians in bloody winter fighting in January 2015.[306] Poroshenko had vowed not to negotiate with separatists he deemed war criminals.

This time, prior to the conference, the leaders of the Donbas separatists began dying in a spate of attacks. On January 1, 2015, separatist Alexander Bednov, known by his nom de guerre, "Batman," was killed in a machine gun attack on a minibus in which he was traveling.[307]

On January 23, Yevheniy Ishchenko, a Russian separatist commander, was shot to death in an ambush.[308] Ukraine would never have to negotiate with Ishchenko or Batman. A pattern began to emerge—separatists that Ukraine did not want to negotiate with often died violently prior to negotiations between Russia and Ukraine about the Donbas.

Minsk II opened in February, and French president François Hollande later said that German chancellor Angela Merkel wrote the agreement. Just as with Minsk I, the proposal included an election in separatist-controlled areas *prior* to the arrival of Ukrainian troops.[309] Minsk II also failed, largely because Russia again sought to sabotage the agreements.[310]

The West was split on arming the Ukrainians, with Angela Merkel strongly against arming Ukraine, and the White House, represented by Vice President Joe Biden, arguing the Ukrainians had a right to defend themselves.[311] The terms Russia sought involved special decentralized status for the Donbas, something observers felt Poroshenko could never get a majority of the Rada to back in a full peace treaty.[312] Poroshenko was forced to accept the elections prior to Ukrainian control of the province being established.[313] But the war continued while the internal problems of Ukraine also continued on. Another meeting would not occur until October of 2016.

THE FALL OF VIKTOR SHOKIN

Ukraine's progress on corruption began to slow in early 2015. The problems began in February with the appointment of Viktor Shokin, the godfather of one of Petro Poroshenko's children, as prosecutor general of Ukraine.[314]

US officials accused Shokin's office of accepting a $7,000,000 bribe to forget to file documents in time in the Burisma case, interfering with what was now a joint US-UK effort to seize the funds Burisma chairman Zlochevsky had in Cyprus.[315] The US spent half a million dollars on the effort.[316] In response, US ambassador to Ukraine Geoffrey Pyatt and Deputy Secretary of State Nuland urged Biden to make the latest US loan guarantees conditional on the firing of Shokin.[317] By this time, Obama had deployed Biden to Ukraine.[318] Pyatt called out Shokin by name in a 2015 speech, decrying the prosecutorial failure with Burisma.[319]

Shokin's problems deepened with the so-called Diamond Prosecutors case. Poroshenko had asked the US to help him reform Shokin's Prosecutor General's Office (PGO). The US Embassy provided a grant for a program to set up an Inspector General's Office within the PGO, designed to catch corrupt prosecutors. The new office was staffed with experienced prosecutors from Georgia, who had successfully fought Russian corruption in their country and importantly, lacked ties to monied interests in Ukraine.[320] The funds were actually sent to the Organization for Economic Cooperation and Development, known as the OECD, a Paris-based international intergovernmental organization that had been involved in helping Ukraine fight Russia since 2014.[321]

The new Inspector General's Office the US helped stand up found a witness in mid-2015 who said that he had paid a $200,000 bribe to two prosecutors in the General Prosecutor's Office to stop harassing his company; one of those he bribed was Kyiv regional deputy prosecutor Oleksandr Korniyets.[322] The Inspector General's Office asked Viktor Trepak, the deputy head of the State Security Bureau, to set up surveillance on the two men.[323] The wiretaps resulted in an arrest in July 2015, and a search of Korniyets's home turned up an envelope of loose diamonds which a jeweler testified had been illegally seized from him.[324][325] The press dubbed the pair the "Diamond Prosecutors."

Unbeknownst to the experienced Georgian prosecutors with no ties to Ukraine, Korniyets used to be Viktor Shokin's driver, and Shokin had given him the job in Kyiv.[326] Shokin systematically sought revenge as Poroshenko stood by, firing the Georgian prosecutors and pushing Trepak out over a period of months. Little did Shokin know the unintended effect that firing

Viktor Trepak would have on world events for the next five years. From small things, big things came.

By the time NABU started work in October of 2015, anti-corruption reforms were running out of steam.[327] NABU was "charged with prevention, discovery, termination, investigation and solving corruption-related offences."[328] The new agency received technical advice from the FBI, based out of the US Embassy.[329] According to the State Department, by November of 2017, FBI support had contributed to the opening of 333 criminal cases, 207 notices of suspicion, and 108 indictments in corruption-related cases.[330] FBI agent Karen Greenaway played a key role in helping NABU begin to tackle public corruption in the country.

But for all of its investigative efforts, convictions eluded NABU because under the 2014 Reforms Package, it was reliant on prosecutors to bring its cases to court. This was the responsibility of the Specialized Anti-Corruption Prosecutor's Office, which began work in September 2015.[331] But its new head, Nazar Kholodnytsky, was seen as less independent of Poroshenko than NABU; Kholodnytsky praised Poroshenko in interviews and refused to open a case against the president when a company owned by him was involved in the Panama Papers exposé.[332]

As Ukrainian reformers saw anti-corruption reforms lose steam, they began to push for Shokin's removal in the fall of 2015.[333] In November, Trepak, first deputy head of the Security Service of Ukraine submitted his resignation, saying he could not remain because of Shokin.[334] Trepak hung on until the new year, when he was dismissed by the Rada in retaliation for his actions in the Diamond Prosecutors case. Shokin's actions in pushing out Trepak would end up revealing the Black Ledger to the world a few months later.

In December 2015 Joe Biden, who continued to run the Ukraine situation for the Obama administration, came to Ukraine and agreed to Pyatt's plan to push for Shokin's removal with Poroshenko.[335] In 2017, Biden would describe his December 2015 meeting with Poroshenko in stark terms:

> I remember going over, convincing our team, our leaders to—convincing that we should be providing for loan guarantees. And I went over, I guess, the 12th, 13th time to Kiev. And I was supposed to announce that there was another billion-dollar loan guarantee. And I had gotten a commitment from Poroshenko and from Yatsenyuk that they would take action against the state prosecutor. And they didn't.
>
> So they said they had—they were walking out to a press conference. I said, nah, I'm not going to—or, we're not going to give you the billion dollars. They said, you have no authority. You're not the president. The president said—I said, call him. (Laughter.) I said, I'm telling you, you're not getting the billion dollars. I said, you're not getting the billion. I'm going to be leaving here in, I think it was about six hours. I looked at them and said: I'm leaving in six hours. If the prosecutor is not fired, you're not getting the money. Well, son of a bitch. (Laughter.) He got fired.[336]

To emphasize this blunt anti-corruption message, Joe Biden gave a speech in front of the Rada on December 9. He told the assembled legislators that the protestors on the Maidan had "paid the ultimate price of patriots the world over. Their blood and courage delivering to the Ukrainian people a second chance for freedom. Their sacrifice—to put it bluntly—is now your obligation."[337] The vice president laid out the stakes: "When Russia seeks to use corruption as a tool of coercion, reform isn't just good governance, it's self-preservation."[338]

Ukraine did get the message from Joe Biden. Poroshenko, in control of the Rada, marshaled the votes needed to remove his own prosecutor general. Shokin was dismissed by a vote of the Ukrainian Parliament on March 29, 2016.[339]

But the Prosecutor General's Office continued to push back against the US. The same day Shokin was fired, the deputy prosecutor general wrote to Ambassador Pyatt, alleging misuse of US funds by the head of the Inspector General's Office of the PGO.[340] George Kent responded for the US Embassy on April 4, asserting the US "rejected allegations" that the funds had been misused, and that the efforts of the PGO to investigate these funds "appears to us to be an attempt to intimidate" those inside the PGO who were trying to reform the institution.[341] Thus were born false allegations that would explode three years later in Washington.

The firing of Shokin certainly created difficulties for Poroshenko: "veteran observers of Ukrainian politics said that the prosecutor, Viktor

Shokin, had played an important role in balancing competing political interests, helping maintain stability during a treacherous era in the divided country's history."342 Tymofiy Mylovanov, the president of the Kyiv School of Economics, pointed out the new dangers Shokin's firing brought to Poroshenko's balancing act between pro-Russian and pro-Western factions: "There are prices the new political establishment has to pay. How do they pay? They guarantee some security for their opponents' business interests."343 The hardest part of Poroshenko's Russian problem involved keeping the pro-Russian oligarchs who had served as kingmaker for him happy. Now Poroshenko was without Shokin and needed someone else for that job.

Poroshenko then turned to another godfather of his children, Yuriy Lutsenko, to take Viktor Shokin's place as prosecutor general. As a young Rada deputy, Lutsenko had started out supporting the Orange Revolution in 2004 and became a key supporter of the new president, Viktor Yushchenko.344 Yushchenko appointed him interior minister in 2005.345

In 2010, Lutsenko backed popular politician Yulia Tymoshenko against Yanukovych for the Ukrainian presidency.346 When Yanukovych won, he imprisoned Lutsenko along with Tymoshenko.347 While in prison, Lutsenko claimed to have studied the Buddhist *Dhammapada* and said that after his pardon, he was determined to follow the Buddha's teaching: "I read that revenge ruins the soul of the fool," he told an interviewer, "the same way a diamond breaks the cliffs from whence it came . . . I decided not to seek revenge."[348]

After receiving a pardon in 2013, Lutsenko began to lead opposition to Yanukovych. When the first EuroMaidan protests broke out in late 2013, Lutsenko was on the square and beaten by police.[349] At the time, reformers such as the Anti-Corruption Action Center's Daria Kaleniuk believed he was with them in their efforts to end Ukraine's endemic corruption.[350]

Lutsenko had originally returned to the Rada, this time as the head of the majority Poroshenko faction.[351] While there, he worked diligently to pass the 2014 Package of Reforms passed by the Rada that fall, but reformers soon suspected that Lutsenko's commitment to anti-corruption was "not as a great believer," but as a duty to Poroshenko.[352] US officials began to suspect that Poroshenko himself was committed to reform only as a form of *pokazukha*, Ukrainian meaning "just for show."[353]

After Lutsenko had served in Parliament for two years, Poroshenko required his services elsewhere—in the General Prosecutor's Office, to replace Shokin. The Rada passed a law removing the requirement that the prosecutor general be a lawyer and he was duly approved on May 16, 2016.[354] The US was not happy with Lutsenko's appointment.[355] Yuriy Lutsenko now held the same position as Viktor Pshonka, the man who had put him in prison a few years earlier.

Although he had loyally supported Poroshenko while others pushed for Shokin's removal, Lutsenko started his tenure as prosecutor general by making statements about transforming the Soviet-era apparat he controlled within a year's time.³⁵⁶ But he soon turned against the reformers. US chargé d'affaires in Kyiv, George Kent, described Lutsenko's attitude about reform succinctly: "because of [NABU's] initial effectiveness, which I think surprised a lot of people, it then became a target of people in places of influence, because it had been effective. And one of the people that was looking to destroy NABU as an effective bureau was Yuriy Lutsenko."³⁵⁷ Kent summed up Lutsenko: "he was bitter and angry at the Embassy for our positions on anti-corruption. And so he was looking for revenge."³⁵⁸ Revenge ruled the soul of Yuriy Lutsenko.

One of Lutsenko's first acts as prosecutor general was to retain the investigative staff that had served under Shokin.³⁵⁹ Amongst these subordinates was a man charged with prosecuting two sets of cases with huge political value, the head of the PGO's Special Investigations Department, Serhii Horbatiuk.³⁶⁰ Both sets involved former president Yanukovych directly: the cases which covered the shootings ordered by Yanukovych during the EuroMaidan Revolution, and the cases involving corruption around the former Party of Regions president.³⁶¹ Unlike Lutsenko, Horbatiuk had a reputation as a "reformist official."³⁶² Unlike Lutsenko, he worked to prosecute these cases. Soon, he would be handed the biggest case of his career: The Black Ledger.

THE FEARS OF ANDRII ARTEMENKO

Andrii Artemenko, a member of the Ukrainian Rada, was a fan of Donald Trump and saw himself as a future Trump-like leader of Ukraine.[363] Artemenko was a member of the right-wing Radical Party of Oleh Lyashko, who nominated the commanders of Ukrainian volunteer battalions against the Russian incursion to the party list for the Rada.[364] Artemenko was firmly opposed to the Russian incursion in Ukraine.

At the same time, Artemenko saw the dangers of a Trump-like presidency for Ukraine. In February 2017, he explained the background of his peace initiative to the Ukrainian publication *Strana* in an article entitled "Andrey Artemenko: Trump Is the Only Person in the World Whom Poroshenko Is Afraid Of." Artemenko explained to *Strana* that during the run up to the US election, he had told his colleagues in the Rada that:

> this was at a time when, as we recall, everyone in Kiev was pouring mud on Trump, and Ukraine . . . I said then—people, what are you doing? If Trump becomes president, it will have dire consequences for US-Ukrainian relations. And already at that time I began to establish channels of communication with the team of Donald Trump.[365]

According to the interview, Artemenko spoke about his concerns with "dozens" of other members of the Rada from all factions and they supported his plan.[366] In the spring of 2016, Artemenko was a one-man back channel for Ukraine to Trump.

On February 1, 2016, Artemenko attended a panel discussion at Manor College, a small institution associated with the Ukrainian diaspora in the Philadelphia suburbs. The panel, entitled: "Ukraine 2016: A Stability Dialogue at Manor College" included Curt Weldon, a former GOP congressman, the Ukrainian-American oligarch Alexander Rovt, former George H. W. Bush official Bruce Weinrod, and Representative Marcy Kaptur, in addition to Artemenko.[367]

The speakers at the Manor College event all seemed to urge support for Ukraine in its fight against Russia.[368] Weldon had lost his seat in Congress a decade earlier amidst a Department of Justice investigation of his actions regarding Russian interests represented by his daughter.[369] According to Artemenko, he, Rovt, and Weldon "drafted" a peace plan for Ukraine and Russia, which Artemenko later dubbed the Rovt-Weldon plan.[370]

Later in 2016, Artemenko told *Reuters* that he discussed the plan with Trump associate Felix Sater, at Sater's Long Island home.[371] Also present was Trump Organization lawyer Michael Cohen.[372] Artemenko told Ukrainian outlet *Hromadske* that he had known the Trump lawyer since Cohen founded a business in Ukraine.[373] Artemenko also stated that he had discussed the plan with Sater and Cohen in early 2016.[374]

The plan itself, according to *Reuters*, would result in the lifting of US sanctions against Russia upon withdrawal of their forces from Eastern Ukraine, but keep Russia's control of Crimea intact.[375] Critically, the plan took the pro-Ukrainian position that the transfer of control of the border in the rebel-held areas to Ukraine must happen *prior* to any nationwide referendum on special status for the Donbas.[376] This stood in contrast to the plans put forward by Putin. Despite Artemenko's work, going into the 2016 US presidential election, there was no peace to be had in the now two-year-old war between Russia and Ukraine.

CHAPTER 3:

"A GENIUS KILLER"

On November 8, 2016, Donald Trump was elected president of the United States.[377] Although the Democratic candidate, Hillary Clinton, won the popular vote by nearly 3 million votes, she lost the Electoral College vote 304–227.[378] She lost Pennsylvania and its twenty electoral votes by 44,292 votes out of 6,165,478 votes.[379] Trump's successful journey to his improbable victory had many progenitors.[380]

His path to the presidency was as unusual as Trump himself. Donald John Trump was the son of a Queens builder and developer, Fred Trump Jr.[381] Fred's father, born Friedrich Trump in Kallstadt, Germany, had come to the United States in the nineteenth century and opened a restaurant that catered to working men and the sex workers they frequented.[382] Friedrich changed his name to Frederick and undertook business ventures as far north as the

Yukon Territory of Canada.[383] Eventually, Donald's grandfather eventually settled in Queens, where he died of influenza during the epidemic of 1918.[384]

Frederick Trump's son, Fred Trump Jr.[385], was thus left fatherless at age twelve.[386] The younger Fred Trump, like his father, kept his eye out for the main chance. After Fred Jr.'s home-building empire collapsed in the Great Depression, he then bought the distressed assets of another real-estate empire and began a development career that would create what his son Donald would later call the Trump Organization.[387]

Donald Trump moved the Trump Organization into Manhattan from Queens.[388] At first the Trump Organization empire grew, but by 1990, he was in deep debt due to personal guarantees on many of his investments.[389] Worse, he was involved in litigation over his fortune with his soon-to-be ex-wife, Ivana.[390] But the banks agreed to save Trump. Much of the wealth from his father's trust would be signed away, but Donald Trump would survive, although diminished.[391]

Trump's decreased business fortunes did not dissuade him from an abortive 2000 presidential run for the Reform Party nomination. His campaign, run by Roger Stone, never made it past the exploratory stage. But Trump did get a taste of campaigning, doing real events in front of real voters.[392]

Stone himself remains one of the enigmas of modern American politics.[393] The son of a New York state well-digger, he became a conservative in high school. Stone's interest in Republican politics was so great that he left

George Washington University to work on Nixon's 1972 campaign and never returned to college. In the 1970s, Stone was known for dressing in custom-made suits, of which he owned more than a hundred. While working on the Bob Dole presidential campaign in 1996 scandal, ads Stone took out in swingers' newspapers seeking partners caused his dismissal from the campaign; the unpleasantness swept him out of electoral politics and into representing referendum holders across the country.[394] One of Stone's political aphorisms seemed to sum him up perfectly: "admit nothing, deny everything, launch counterattack."[395]

By the time of the Orange Revolution in Ukraine in 2004, Trump was looking for overseas deals in places where his credentials were not dented. One of the people helping him was Felix H. Sater. Sater's parents, seeking to escape prevalent anti-Semitism in the USSR, emigrated to Brighton Beach, Brooklyn, in the early 1970s.[396] Sater had been a successful stockbroker when, at age twenty-seven, he was imprisoned for his violent role in a bloody bar fight.[397] Sater's firm, Bayrock Capital, was a partner in several Trump projects.[398] According to one investor, "It seemed that Mr. Trump relied heavily on Mr. Sater's opinion on certain markets."[399] One of those markets was the former Soviet Union. In the early 2000s, Sater assisted Trump in a search for business in the Ukraine.[400] In 2006, Donald and his daughter Ivanka traveled to Ukraine to discuss building a golf course in the former Soviet republic, part of a larger drive to seek business in the former USSR.[401] In 2008, Donald Trump Jr. also tried to drum up business there.[402] Proposed developments included a golf course in Kyiv and a resort in Yalta, in the Crimea.[403]

Ultimately, Donald Trump only had one known business relationship in Ukraine. In 2006, he sold the Ukrainian rights to his Miss Universe pageant to oligarch Oleksandr Onyshchenko.[404] During this period, according to Onyshchenko, the two became friends, bonding, the Ukrainian said, over their love of the "beautiful."[405] In February 2009, Trump's son Eric traveled to Kyiv to judge that year's Miss Ukraine pageant.[406] Onyshchenko continued his business relationship with Trump until 2015, when Trump sold off the rest of his ownership in the Miss Universe pageant.[407]

But Oleksandr Onyshchenko was not who he seemed. Newspaper reports identified him as Oleksandr Radzhabovych Kadyrov, reputed to have been a gangster and a pimp at various times in his checkered career.[408] In the late 1990s, he changed his name to his mother's maiden name and began gas trading.[409] Onyshchenko had closer ties to Donald Trump than any other Ukrainian oligarch.[410]

Onyshchenko was originally elected to the Ukrainian Rada as a representative of the pro-Russian Party of Regions of disgraced former president Viktor Yanukovych. While serving as an MP, he allegedly used a company under his control to engage in a series of natural gas skimming transactions.[411]

Onyshchenko was also an equestrian who represented Ukraine as a rider in the Beijing Olympic games. After the EuroMaidan revolution in 2014, he became a deputy for the People's Will Party, in opposition to President Petro Poroshenko.[412] He often appeared on Russian TV to criticize Ukraine.[413] The one-time gangster and pimp had made it big.

Trump also wanted deals in Russia and with Russians. For years, much of his money had been made selling real estate and apartments to Russians with money of dubious origins. American real estate was a perfect way to launder money. Trump went all in—a 2019 analysis of his business showed that Trump had made eighty-six all-cash sales to persons from the former Soviet Union. The total haul was $109 million.[414]

Michael Cohen explored real estate deals in Russia for Trump. The big project, a "Trump Tower Moscow" was still being discussed when Trump ran for president in 2016.[415] The only lender who would work with Trump by this point was Deutsche Bank, a bank so deeply involved in Russian money laundering that in 2019 it had to report one of its own deals with Russians as suspicious.[416]

Cohen worked with Sater on the Trump Tower Moscow deal. When Trump announced his run for the presidency, Sater was ecstatic and linked the deal to the election in a series of emails. "Our boy can become president of the USA and we can engineer it," wrote Sater.[417] "I will get all of Putins [sic] team to buy in on this, I will manage this process," Sater expounded.[418] Sater told Cohen that "I will get Putin on this program and we will get Donald elected." He promised to get Putin to praise Trump's business acumen.[419] Sater boasted of his ties, and claimed that he'd arranged for Ivanka Trump to sit in Putin's chair when she visited.[420] Sater asked for one thing: the post of US ambassador to the Bahamas, "That my friend is the home run I want out of this," wrote Sater.[421] It appeared the Russians saw opportunity in a Trump presidency.

* * *

Trump's opponent was former First Lady, Senator, and US Secretary of State Hillary Clinton. For three years the Republicans attacked her about the fatal 2012 assault on a US State Department facility in Benghazi, Libya. A year out from the election, they finally got their angle—on March 2, 2015, an article appeared saying that Republican House investigators had learned that Clinton had used a personal email server based in her home while Secretary.[422] Clinton told the press that no classified information was on the server in her home.[423]

In July, those claims blew up when the State Department Inspector General announced that a random sample had determined that classified information *had been* stored on the server.[424] The Inspector General for the Intelligence Community filed a referral with the FBI, which began a full investigation.[425]

"PUTIN'S POLITICAL BRAIN"

Alexandra Chalupa, a lawyer and daughter of Ukrainian immigrants feared the influence of Russia on the Trump campaign.[426] In 2014, Chalupa was doing pro bono work for a client interested in the EuroMaidan Revolution and learned that Paul Manafort had played a key role in Yanukovych's extreme makeover. She also became interested in Donald Trump's links to Manafort.[427]

Unfortunately for Paul Manafort, she was also a consultant for the Democratic National Committee. When Trump declared for the presidency, she became suspicious, and watchful of the new campaign. In January 2016, months before Manafort joined up with Trump, Chalupa told a senior DNC official that she believed Trump was closely connected to Russia and that Paul Manafort would eventually be involved in his campaign.[428] She told superiors at the DNC that Manafort was "Putin's political brain for manipulating US foreign policy and elections."[429]

What Alexandra Chalupa did not know was that a lot of informed people close to Russia also thought that Paul Manafort would be Trump's campaign manager. When GOP lobbyist Sam Patten met with his new client Serhiy Lyovochkin in Kyiv, the Party of Regions stalwart asked him if Trump was going to hire Paul Manafort. Patten thought the idea was fanciful.[430] Patten was therefore surprised when Konstantin Kilimnik told him that Kilimnik believed it "likely" that Manafort would be Trump's campaign manager.[431]

Paul Manafort began reaching out to the Trump campaign for work in January 2016.⁴³² At a January 30, 2016, meeting with Trump confidant Tom Barrack, Manafort asked Barrack to try and get him onto the Trump campaign.⁴³³ Barrack obliged, bringing Manafort up twice in February to Trump.⁴³⁴

On February 29, Manafort emailed Barrack with a set of talking points for Trump.⁴³⁵ Barrack wrote out an email addressing "Donald," and attached the talking points. In the email he said Trump should be hired because "Manafort is a genius killer." Tom Barrack sent that email to Trump's longtime personal assistant Rhona Graff, Ivanka Trump, and Jared Kushner, attaching the talking points and two strategy memos that Manafort had drafted for Trump.⁴³⁶ Ivanka Trump promised to show it to Trump after Super Tuesday and printed out a copy of the email from Barrack and attached a note that said: "Daddy, Tom says we should get Paul."⁴³⁷

Super Tuesday was March 1, 2016. Ten days later, Major Boris Antonov of the GRU, at the orders of Vladimir Putin authorized Fancy Bear to attack the Hillary Clinton campaign.⁴³⁸ The technical side of the hack and dump operation was run by Unit 26165.⁴³⁹ Fancy Bear now waited for the time to launch the hack.

As Manafort tried to get onto the Trump campaign, Chalupa, unaware of how prophetic she was, began digging into his backstory in Ukraine as part of her duties at the DNC. She had met with Ukrainian embassy officials in March, including the Ukrainian ambassador to the US, who was not concerned, because he believed Trump would not win the nomination.440 After informing her superiors at the DNC of Manafort's past, she was again encouraged by her superiors at the DNC to work on the issue.441

Chalupa did not know it, but after being carefully briefed by Tom Barrack and told that Manafort would be "non-paid," the candidate was convinced. According to Barrack, Manafort offering to work for free "were the magic words."442 On the evening of March 16, Donald Trump personally called Manafort and asked him to run the delegate process for him.443 Manafort emailed Barrack that evening: "You're the Best!" read the subject line. "We are going to have so much fun and change the world in the process" Manafort told him.444

"SOMEONE HAS YOUR PASSWORD"

On March 19, 2016, at 11:28 a.m. Moscow time, the Russians struck. Using a secret email address stolen from a 2008 Clinton staffer who had clicked on a spear phishing email in an earlier attack, Fancy Bear sent an email message targeting top Clinton 2016 staffers, including John Podesta, Chair of Hillary Clinton's 2016 presidential campaign.445

Six minutes later, the message arrived in Podesta's inbox.446 The email message was titled "Someone Has Your Password" and looked like it came from Google and urged the user to change the password on their Gmail account.447 Whoever was using Podesta's account clicked through the link to a page that looked like the login page for Google and clicked on the change password link twice.448 It was a website set up as a ruse by Unit 26165 and it recorded the login information the user keyed into the fake Google site.449 The Russian government now had a backdoor into Podesta's email account. For months thereafter, Fancy Bear had access to 50,000 email messages from Podesta's account alone.450 Dozens of other staffers were also targeted.

On March 28, Manafort's hire was announced. Immediately after the public announcement, Konstantin Kilimnik emailed Sam Patten to rub it in that he was right and Patten was wrong about Paul Manafort running the Trump campaign.451

Manafort wasted no time in getting in contact with the members of the Opposition Bloc in Ukraine. The day after the formal announcement, he emailed Gates with instructions to send five personalized memos he had drafted to special recipients including three to key Opposition Bloc members and one to Oleg Deripaska. Gates was to forward them to Kilimnik for translation.452

By early April, one of Manafort's daughters had revealed in a text message that their mother Kathy Manafort had told her that "Dad and Trump are literally living in the same building and mom says they go up and down all day long hanging and plotting together."453

Manafort was also plotting with Konstantin Kilimnik, the Russian intelligence agent he worked with in Ukraine. On April 10, he sent an email message to Kilimnik, asking him if "our friends" had seen the coverage related to Trump joining the Trump campaign. "Absolutely. Every article." replied Kilimnik.[454]

Manafort emailed back "How can we use to get whole?" and then followed up with "has OVD [Deripaska] operation seen?"[455] Kilimnik then discussed a range of potential outcomes in Ukraine.[456] It appears that political outcomes in Ukraine were related to the Trump campaign in the minds of Paul Manafort and Konstantin Kilimnik.

On April 22, Kilimnik told an associate that Paul Manafort had a "cunning plan" to defeat Hillary Clinton. Kilimnik said that with Manafort's help, Trump would win.[457] When the associate emailed back to express concern about the collaboration with the American, Kilimnik told him that Manafort was a very good strategist and that "there could be surprises, even in American politics."[458] Kilimnik reiterated that Manafort believed in Trump and that he could win. The reason was "they had a cunning plan to screw Clinton."[459]

"TED CRUZ SAYS PUTIN IS A BULLY"

Before Trump could reach a point where he would need a delegate manager, he would have to win the Republican nomination. His ties to Russia became an issue as the field was reduced to himself and Ted Cruz soon after Manafort joined the campaign.

In the primary, much, if not most of the Republican party was opposed to his candidacy. Despite this, coming into the final stages of the primaries he led in delegates and in the polls over a winnowed field. Among the few still opposed to Trump was Paul Singer, owner of the *Washington Free Beacon*, a conservative website.[460]

Singer was a major Republican donor and concerned about Trump. In 2015, he hired a private intelligence firm, Fusion GPS, to do opposition research on Trump.[461] The firm turned to an old hand, Christopher Steele, the former head of the Russia desk at MI6, the British foreign secret service agency.[462] Steele went to work finding information on Trump on his connections to Russia.

Steele had maintained many personal connections in Russia and Ukraine. He had previously done work for Russian oligarch Oleg Deripaska for his lawsuit to connect monies he believed he was owed by Paul Manafort.[463] At the same time, between late 2013 and January of 2016, Steele provided to the US State Department, free of charge, a series of reports he had written for clients on the Russia-Ukraine situation and other issues in the region.[464]

In April 2016, Trump's victory in the Republican primary seemed impossibly far away, despite his lead with delegates and in the polls. Senator Ted Cruz trailed him and had just won Wisconsin. Trump needed to win two-thirds of the delegates going forward to obtain the nomination outright.[465] A contested convention could be fatal, given Trump's Russian baggage.

To defeat Trump, Cruz presented himself as a fierce opponent of Vladimir Putin and Russia. As part of his strategy, Cruz had taken on help from a hard-line GOP Russia hand, Daniel Vajdich.[466] Vajdich had worked in Republican foreign policy circles for years and served as top Europe staffer for Senate Foreign Relations Committee chair Bob Corker, and as a senior fellow at the Atlantic Council, a pro-engagement US think tank.[467] Vajdich began his work for Cruz with an op-ed in *National Review* where he argued that "Ted Cruz says that Putin is a bully and that the American president must negotiate with him only from a position of strength."[468]

As part of the strategy to highlight Trump's ties to Putin, in mid-March, Vajdich sent out an email calling on "GOP Russia hands" to join a new Cruz-sponsored "Russia Working Group."[469] Some were not impressed by the strategy. Kurt Volker, a former US ambassador to NATO, was concerned that anyone who took sides against Trump would be shut out of his foreign-policy team at a time when he would need such help.[470]

When polling showed Cruz that Trump was likely to win the New York primary, Cruz switched to a contested convention delegate strategy.[471] As the delegate strategy loomed large, Trump was frustrated because his outsider effort lacked someone with the ability to master delegate math. Trump complained that Cruz was trying to "steal" the nomination through an "absolutely rigged" system.[472] A disaster in the Colorado caucus underlined the danger for Trump, as organized Cruz supporters wearing bright-orange clothing handed out Cruz sample ballots while a handful of unprepared

Trump supporters handed out ones riddled with errors.[473] With his Colorado win, Cruz stayed alive.

In response to the threat of a contested convention, the Trump campaign announced Manafort's addition as delegate guru on March 29. He would "bring the needed skill sets to ensure that the will of the Republican voters, not the Washington political establishment, determines who will be the nominee for the Republican Party" crowed the announcement.[474]

On April 19, Trump won delegate-rich New York, and in the winner-take-all GOP primaries, he was then firmly in the lead for the nomination.[475] After winning 111 of the next 118 delegates, Trump was suddenly within striking distance of the nomination, only twenty-eight delegates away from locking it up.[476] On May 26, the *Associated Press* called the race for Trump.[477] Cruz's contested convention strategy had failed.

"CRITICIZE HILLARY AND THE REST (EXCEPT SANDERS AND TRUMP)"

Yevgeny Prigozhin, owner of the Internet Research Agency, could also be counted among the creators of Trump's victory. His boss, President Vladimir Putin, favored Trump over Cruz. In May 2016, employees at the IRA arranged a birthday surprise for their boss, who turned fifty-five on June 1. The employees recruited Americans to take photos of themselves holding signs reading "Happy 55th Birthday Dear Boss." One was even photographed in front of the White House.[478]

The employees were able to do this because they had spent the better part of two years infiltrating US social media and directed unwitting Americans to complete the ruse. The section dealing with these activities was known as the "translator department." The translator department started in April 2014, just as the Ukraine crisis heated up.[479] In mid-2014, the IRA sent employees to the US to take photographs of the United States for social media posts and to do research.[480] It was an IRA influence operation typically used on smaller countries. This time it was scaled up to the size of a superpower.

By February 15, 2016, IRA internal documents began discussing the operation that would seek to influence the election in favor of Donald Trump and against Hillary Clinton.[481] "Main idea:" one document read: "Use any opportunity to criticize Hillary and the rest (except Sanders and Trump—we support them)."[482] Agency personnel created fake social media groups for real and fictional organizations representing various stripes of US activism, from securing the border to opposing police violence towards African Americans.[483] Americans who interacted on those pages did not know it was all a part of a Russian government influence operation originating seven time-ones ahead of them in St. Petersburg, Russia.

The IRA moved from social media posting to advertising. The agency bought more than 3,500 advertisements, spending more than $100,000 with Facebook, ensuring a wide reach.[484] Individual social media accounts run by the IRA had follower counts in the hundreds of thousands: "United Muslims of America" had 300,000, "Being Patriotic" had more than 200,000, and "Don't Shoot Us" had 250,000 followers.[485] At least 29 million and as many as 126 million Americans viewed content originated by the agency during the 2016 campaign.[486]

* * *

The Russians rushed to inform the Trump campaign of what they had. They tapped an associate, Maltese academic and former diplomat Joseph Mifsud, to look for contacts in Trump's orbit.[487] In March 2016, a member of Trump's unusual foreign policy team, George Papadopoulos, was in Italy.[488] While there, Mifsud took an interest in him after learning he was on the Trump campaign.[489] Mifsud, known for speaking out in favor of Putin in international settings, informed Papadopoulos that he could get "dirt" on Hillary Clinton and discussed a meeting between Trump and Putin with Papadopoulos.[490]

On April 19, via a virtual private network (VPN) set up for secure communications between the Clinton Campaign and the DNC, Unit 26165 accessed the DNC network.[491] The Russians now had penetrated the two most important computer networks controlled by the Democratic Party.

On April 26, Mifsud revealed to the young Trump associate what the Russians had on Hillary: thousands of email messages.[492] The message Mifsud gave Papadopoulos, and by extension the Trump Campaign, was unambiguous: the Russians had thousands of Hillary emails, and they were going to use them to help Trump via anonymous releases through a third party. Russia wanted Donald Trump to know that they were responsible for their release.

The very next day, Donald Trump gave a major foreign affairs speech on at the Mayflower Hotel in Washington, DC. In it, Trump laid out a vision for his Russia policy: "I believe an easing of tensions and improved relations with Russia—from a position of strength—is possible. Common sense says this cycle of hostility must end. Some say the Russians won't be reasonable. I intend to find out. If we can't make a good deal for America, then we will quickly walk from the table."[493] The Russian ambassador to the United States, Sergei Kislyak, attended the meeting and was alleged to have met in a side meeting with then senator Jeff Sessions, the head of Trump's foreign policy committee.[494]

The Russians moved to prepare the information obtained for release. On April 19, 2016, using Bitcoin, Unit 26165 bought a domain using an anonymizing service, selecting "dcleaks.com" as the name.[495]

GRU Unit 74455 ran the influence side of the Translator Project.[496] By June, the unit was publishing some of the stolen Clinton documents to pages on the DCLeaks domain.[497] Unit 74455 then promoted the material through a set of Facebook accounts they controlled.[498]

Days later, Papadopoulos slipped up. After a chance meeting with a political counselor for the Australian High Commission in London, Papadopoulos agreed to meet with Alexander Downer, the Australian high commissioner to the United Kingdom.⁴⁹⁹ The pair met over gin and tonics in London on May 10. There, the American indiscreetly revealed that the Russians were going to anonymously release "information" that would damage Hillary Clinton.⁵⁰⁰ Downer drafted a cable to his government the next day, documenting the discussions and forwarded it up the chain of the Australian Foreign Office.⁵⁰¹

"I HAVE ALREADY EXPERIENCED THE POWER, I KNOW ITS TASTE AND PRICE"

Back in Ukraine, Viktor Trepak was angry about his firing and about corruption in the country.⁵⁰² Poroshenko had confirmed his dismissal on April 14, 2016.⁵⁰³ Trepak decided to do something about it. On his way out the door of the Security Service of Ukraine, he collected the documents seized from the Party of Regions that had been found at the party's headquarters on Lypska Street and in the compounds of the president and the prosecutor general in 2014.⁵⁰⁴ He conceived of a plan to release the information and provide it to the independent investigators of NABU.⁵⁰⁵

On April 27, 2016, Alexandra Chalupa spoke at the Library of Congress to a conference of sixty-eight investigative journalists from Ukraine.⁵⁰⁶ She had been invited to speak about some of her investigations into Paul Manafort,⁵⁰⁷ and had invited investigative reporter Michael Isikoff to attend.⁵⁰⁸ The Ukrainian journalists informed her that something that had "a big Trump component" was going to "hit in the next few weeks."⁵⁰⁹

Chalupa's main role remained as director of Ethnic Engagement for the DNC. As she had begun digging deeper into Manafort, she started getting messages from the Yahoo Mail security team.[510] These warnings stated: "We strongly suspect that your account has been the target of state-sponsored actors."[511] She told a colleague, "Since I started digging into Manafort these messages have been a daily occurrence on my yahoo account despite changing my password often."[512]

A big thing had come from the small thing of Shokin's revenge-fueled firing of the Security Service of Ukraine deputy head Viktor Trepak. On May 27, 2016, Trepak took what would become known as the Black Ledger to the National Anti-Corruption Bureau of Ukraine.[513] Artem Sytnyk, its director, opened four cases based on the documents. One of these was a criminal case opened on May 30 against the sitting head of the Central Election Commission, Mykhailo Okhendovsky, for accepting $165,000 in bribes while acting as the commission's head under President Yanukovych.[514]

Trepak then went to the offices of the newspaper *Dzerkalo Tyzhnia* ("Weekly Mirror") and revealed that he had taken a large number of documents from the Security Service of Ukraine that implicated the Party of Regions in a systematic bribery scheme of the Central Election Commission, the Ukrainian Supreme Court, and the Constitutional Court, and other key areas of the government, with a total price tag of $4 billion over five years.[515] The documents, Trepak told *Dzerkalo Tyzhnia*, showed that Yanukovych had committed sophisticated electoral fraud in 2010 when he won the presidency.⁵¹⁶ According to Trepak, many current officials were implicated in the documents, which ran over 800 pages.⁵¹⁷ When asked about the consequences of his actions on his career, Trepak said, "I have already experienced the power, I know its taste and price." ⁵¹⁸

On May 30, 2016, Artem Sytnyk of NABU confirmed that on the 27th, Trepak had provided the "black cash books" to the bureau.⁵¹⁹ On May 31, MP Sergii Leshchenko gave a press conference where he revealed that in February, he had received twenty-two pages of the ledger in an envelope sent to his legislative office.⁵²⁰ Sytnyk gave a press conference on June 2 detailing the next steps in the investigation of what reporters began calling the Black Ledger.⁵²¹ For months, the story reverberated in the Ukrainian press as lawmakers and others were publicly called in to testify.

Radio Svoboda's investigative group *Skhemy* ("Schemes") ran a series on the Black Ledger, naming Geller its paymaster and noting that a $500,000 payment had been made to Ukraine's Central Election Commission.⁵²² The Schemes' piece included a denial from Geller.⁵²³

Paul Manafort knew immediately what the Trepak revelations in the Ukrainian press meant. In August, when Steve Bannon asked Manafort when he knew the release would be coming, he told Bannon that he had known about the documents for two months.⁵²⁴

After joining the campaign, Manafort did not waste time getting into contact with Konstantin Kilimnik, who in April had learned details of new

Opposition Bloc leader Yuriy Boyko's recent visit to Moscow where he met with high-level Russian officials.[525]

On May 5, 2016, Kilimnik flew to Washington, DC.[526] Gates put him on a red-eye train to New York for a May 7 meeting with Manafort.[527] Manafort insists that the pair only discussed the situation in Ukraine and the United States, and that Kilimnik only mentioned that Boyko told him about a turnout plan for local elections in the eastern zone of Ukraine where the Opposition Bloc had its base.[528] Local elections, which pro-Russian politicians were expected to win, was the centerpiece of Russia's peace plan for Ukraine.

Manafort detailed Trump's path to winning the election. He explained the states in which he had a chance to pull off a win. He fully expected that Kilimnik would pass this information on to their shared contacts in Ukraine and elsewhere.[529] Manafort then directed Gates to send Kilimnik Trump campaign internal polling data and other campaign updates.[530] Gates then sent the information via encrypted chat application.[531]

On May 19, 2016, Manafort was promoted to Trump campaign chair, but in reality he was its campaign manager and his deputy, Rick Gates, became deputy campaign manager.[532] Thus, in the words of author Timothy Snyder, the campaign manager for the last pro-Russian president of Ukraine became the campaign manager for the first pro-Russian president of the United States.[533]

After Manafort took the helm, it did not take long for the Russians to make a direct approach to the campaign. "On June 9, 2016, senior representatives of the Trump Campaign met in Trump Tower with a Russian attorney expecting to receive derogatory information about Hillary Clinton from the Russian government."[534] The meeting occurred because a Russian contact of Donald Trump Jr. had emailed the son of the candidate and told him "Crown prosecutor of Russia . . . offered to provide the Trump Campaign with some official documents and information that would incriminate Hillary and her dealings with Russia"[535] Manafort, Kushner, and Don Jr. were all at the meeting.[536] Participants indicated the meeting included discussions about some donations to the Clinton campaign that came from supposedly "illegal activities in Russia."[537]

"DON'T EVEN TALK TO YOUR DOG ABOUT IT"

The FBI had been trying to convince the DNC that they were under cyberattack for months. On April 18, they learned that a second foreign actor, Fancy Bear, had also been inside the DNC network for some time.[538] It was Fancy Bear that was running the hack-and-dump operation, not Cozy Bear. Still, the Clinton operation did not see the problem in its server logs.[539] The FBI repeatedly asked for the server logs. Tamene kicked the request upstairs.[540]

The FBI finally took a major step. They called the DNC's General Counsel.[541] Within days the FBI was authorized to see the logs and Tamene discovered the Fancy Bear operations within the DNC network, eight months after having been informed of Russian hacks by the FBI.[542]

The Clinton campaign brought on a computer security contractor, CrowdStrike.[543] Tamene later told investigators the Russians had "potentially everything . . . they could delete things, they could copy things, they could exfiltrate things."[544] It appeared there was no evidence that Fancy Bear or Cozy Bear knew that they had both had access to the DNC servers.[545]

Clinton was especially vulnerable on issues of computer security. In late May, the US State Department's inspector general released a report sharply critical of her use of a private server to conduct government business while Secretary of State.[546] The FBI investigation into her use of the server continued.[547] Issues surrounding emails and hacking were extremely politically sensitive for the Clinton campaign.

On June 10, 2016, more than 100 staffers met for an all-hands meeting at DNC headquarters in Washington, DC, where they were instructed to bring all of their campaign electronics.[548] The staffers thought they were all being fired.[549] DNC COO Lindsey Reynolds stepped up to address the crowd: "What I am about to tell you cannot leave this room. Don't even talk to your dog about it."[550] After hearing a briefing on the Russian intrusions, all staff members were required to turn in all their devices.[551]

On June 14, the DNC announced that it had been hacked by state-sponsored actors from Russia.[552] The GRU responded the next day by creating an alternate explanation—using a WordPress blog, a new personality, Guccifer 2.0, wrote a post saying that he was a Romanian hacker who had hacked the DNC.[553] GRU officers then posted doctored documents stolen from the DNC and the Democratic Congressional Committee on the Guccifer 2.0 blog.[554] Posing as Guccifer 2.0, GRU officers passed documents to the website the *Smoking Gun* and others.[555] These releases would continue until August.[556]

After Trump clinched the nomination, Paul Singer was no longer paying for Fusion GPS's opposition research.[557] Hillary Clinton's law firm, Perkins Coie, hired them to continue their work against the new nominee.[558] On June 20, 2016, Steele provided Fusion with his first report. It was a stunner. Steele stated that the Russian government had been working for years to cultivate Donald Trump, and that his inner circle was accepting intelligence information from Russians to hurt Hillary Clinton.[559] In early July, Steele, alarmed by what he saw, contacted an old friend, FBI Agent Michael Gaeta.[560] Gaeta immediately moved the information up his chain of command.[561] The report would languish in the bureau's New York Field Office until September, long after a separate FBI investigation of Russian election interference had been opened.[562]

Yet another parent of Trump's win was Wikileaks. In early June, Roger Stone told members of the campaign that he was in contact with Wikileaks and that the organization would leak documents damaging to Hillary Clinton.[563] Stone called Gates and told him that something "big" was coming and that it had to do with a leak of information.[564] He told Gates that he thought that WikiLeaks had Clinton emails.565 Manafort and Gates repeatedly pressed Stone for a release date for them. Donald Trump expressed frustration that they had not yet been released.566

On June 14, 2016, members of Unit 74455 used the Twitter account for DCLeaks to communicate with the WikiLeaks Twitter account via direct message.567 "You announced your organization was preparing to publish more Hillary's emails [sic]," a message read.568 "We are ready to support you. We have some sensitive information too, in particular, [sic] her financial documents. Let's do it together. What do you think about publishing our info at the same moment? Thank you."569

On June 22, WikiLeaks contacted the Guccifer 2.0 account on Twitter, asking to preview documents so as to give Assange time to review them prior to the Democratic Convention.570 On July 14, 2016, GRU officers sent Assange a link to an online group of documents it had obtained from the DNC.571

On July 5, 2016, FBI director James Comey spoke in front of cameras at FBI Headquarters in Washington, DC.572 Comey told assembled reporters that "Although we did not find clear evidence that Secretary Clinton or her colleagues intended to violate laws governing the handling of classified information, there is evidence that they were extremely careless in their handling of very sensitive, highly classified information."573 Clinton appeared to be off the hook, at least legally.

The Trump campaign continued with its efforts to find out about what Assange had and when he was going to release it. In a telephone call with

Trump and Cohen, Stone told Trump that he had just gotten off the phone with Assange and that the release of information was a couple of days away.574 Trump responded, "Oh good, alright."575

"THIS WHOLE THING WITH RUSSIA"

During the election, one Trump supporter was not doing well. On June 15, 2016, the special anti-corruption prosecutor announced that he was sending the results of a NABU investigation into criminal gas skimming by Oleksandr Onyshchenko to Lutsenko's General Prosecutor's Office (PGO) for the purpose of obtaining an arrest warrant.576 On July 1, 2016, prior to a vote in the Rada to strip Onyshchenko of his parliamentary immunity, he fled to Russia on his private jet. Reports stated four FSB agents accompanied him and set him up in a village for the well-off near Moscow.577 Eventually he would end up in London where he filed an asylum case.578

The week before the opening of the Republican National Convention (RNC) on Monday, July 18, in Cleveland, Ohio,579 the National Security Committee of the Republican Platform Committee met in the city to finish part of the party's platform that would be introduced the next week.580

At that meeting, perhaps as a vestige of Cruz's contested convention strategy, Diana Denman, a Cruz delegate and Platform Committee member from Texas, proposed a platform amendment that proposed maintaining or increasing sanctions on Russia for its invasion of Ukraine and to provide for lethal weaponry to Ukraine.581 She was approached by J. D. Gordon, Director for National Security for the Trump campaign, who told her that he had "called New York" and that he had discussed the issue with Donald Trump personally and that the language regarding arming Ukraine with lethal weapons had to be stripped from the platform.[582]

Kilimnik would later tell associates in Ukraine that he played a role in tabling the amendment.[583] CNN's Jim Acosta reported from the RNC that Gordon told him that in March Trump had discussed Ukraine at a Republican National Security Committee meeting, which took place in the then-unfinished Trump International Hotel in Washington. Per Acosta: "Gordon says Trump said at the meeting . . . that he didn't want to go to 'World War Three' over Ukraine."[584] Whether because of Trump or Kilimnik, the platform language was later softened from lethal weaponry to "appropriate assistance."[585]

Russian ambassador Kislyak visited the convention where he met with J. D. Gordon and others.[586] Gordon would later deny discussing the Trump campaign helping the Russians.[587] Trump's acceptance speech on July 21 at the convention did not mention Russia.[588] But, the night before, Mike Pence had accused Obama and Clinton of "feigning resets with Russia" in his acceptance speech.[589]

Kislyak was not the only foreign government official present. Andrii Artemenko, present in Cleveland, continued with his one-man back channel to the Trump campaign on behalf of Ukraine.[590]

But Russia was not the only country reaching out to the Trump campaign at the convention. Valeriy Chaly, the Ukrainian ambassador to the United States reached out through a State Department official Frank Mermoud, who introduced Manafort to the diplomat.[591] Chaly was upset about the change in the platform regarding lethal assistance to Ukraine.[592] After a few minutes of discussion with Manafort, Chaly was mollified.[593]

The night of Trump's acceptance speech, the *New York Times* ran an interview with Trump, stating that the candidate had "explicitly raised new questions on Wednesday about his commitment to automatically defending NATO allies if they are attacked, saying he would first look at their contributions to the alliance."[594] In the spin room after Trump's speech, Manafort tried in vain to argue that Trump had not said that and provided an alternate explanation to *Mother Jones*'s David Corn: that the reporters made up the quotes.[595] The *Times* responded by publishing a transcript a few hours later.[596] It showed that in response to David Sanger asking him if NATO allies could count on us to come to their military aid if attacked by Russia, Trump had replied, "Have they fulfilled their obligations to us? If they fulfill their obligations to us, the answer is yes."[597]

The next day, July 22, 2016, three days before the 2016 Democratic National Convention, WikiLeaks released 20,000 emails stolen from the DNC by the Russian government.[598] The Trump campaign sprang into action. On July 25, Stone sent an email to far-right writer Jerome Corsi. "Get to the head of Wikileaks," directing him to the Ecuadorean Embassy in London where Assange had been holed up for years avoiding prosecution on sex-crimes charges in Sweden.⁵⁹⁹ "Get the pending Wikileaks emails."⁶⁰⁰

The Trump campaign certainly wanted more of everything the Russians had to offer. After WikiLeaks released the documents, Trump told Cohen, "I guess Roger was right."⁶⁰¹ Trump then ordered Manafort to stay in contact with Stone.⁶⁰²

Manafort and Gates followed up with Stone in a conference call after the release. Manafort told Stone the candidate wanted him to keep in touch with Manafort and he also ordered Gates to stay in touch with Stone.⁶⁰³ Stone also repeatedly told Bannon he had contact with WikiLeaks.⁶⁰⁴

At a press conference in South Florida days later, Trump openly mused about Russian hacking assistance for his campaign: "Russia, if you're listening, I hope you're able to find the 30,000 emails that are missing. I think you will probably be rewarded mightily by our press. Let's see if that happens. That will be next."⁶⁰⁵ Trump later claimed he was joking when he said this, though many who heard that excuse found it unpersuasive.⁶⁰⁶ Trump deflected questions about his campaign's involvement in the email hack. "This whole thing with Russia" was a "total deflection," "farfetched" and "ridiculous."⁶⁰⁷ Russia did not consider it ridiculous. Hours after Trump's press conference, Fancy Bear attempted to hack into the servers for Hillary Clinton's personal office.⁶⁰⁸

The appearance of the WikiLeaks release also spurred the Australian government into action. On July 26, Alexander Downer contacted the US charge d'affaires in London, Elizabeth Dibble, about an "urgent matter."[609] Downer told Dibble about his meeting with Papadopoulos.[610] Dibble called the FBI's legal attaché in London and provided them with the information she had just learned.[611] The material was sent to the Philadelphia Field Office of the FBI.[612] The Philadelphia Field Office forwarded it to the Counterintelligence Division of the FBI.[613] Its head, Bill Priestap discussed it for several days with colleagues.[614]

As a result of those discussions, on July 31, 2016, exactly 100 days prior to the election, the FBI opened the first of four investigations that would dog the Trump presidency for four years, a counterintelligence investigation into the Russian operation to influence the 2016 election. The opening agent gave it a code name taken from the Rolling Stones' song "Sympathy for the Devil": Crossfire Hurricane.[615] Two agents were dispatched to London to interview Downer.[616]

The same day the FBI opened Crossfire Hurricane, Roger Stone emailed Corsi asking for a phone call in the next few days.[617] Corsi, who was in Europe, replied to Stone via email on August 2: "Word is friend in embassy plans 2 more dumps. One shortly after I'm back. 2nd in Oct. Impact planned to be very damaging."[618]

Meanwhile, Steele continued feeding Fusion GPS with explosive material. A second report from Steele, dated July 19, detailed the level of knowledge the Trump campaign had about the stolen emails. They knew the WikiLeaks releases were coming from the Russian government.[619] Liaison work for the operation, Steele stated, was centered in two individuals, Paul Manafort and Carter Page, a member of the same foreign affairs advisory council Papadopoulos belonged to.[620] The report stated plainly that Carter Page met with Igor Sechin and that what Russia sought was an accommodation in Ukraine, with sanctions on Russia being lifted.[621] On July 26, Steele submitted another report. It described, in general, the offensive hacking operations of the Russian government and efforts to penetrate the computer servers of Western institutions and governments.[622]

In late July a curious item was mentioned in the Dossier Report #97. Steele stated that a Trump associate told him that the information flow between Trump and Putin went two ways.[623] Trump provided information to Putin, Steele reported, via former Soviet emigres who transmitted the information to Russian consular officials in DC, New York, and Miami.[624] The cover for these exchanges was "pension disbursements."[625] There is no Russian Consulate in Miami.

On July 30, Steele submitted an additional report to Fusion GPS. He described Kremlin infighting regarding the effects of "elephant in a china shop black PR," which some feared would blow back on to Russia.[626]

Manafort also continued his contacts with the Russians. He ordered Gates to send polling data to Opposition Bloc supporters Akhmetov and Lyovochkin via Kilimnik.[627] Kilimnik provided Manafort with briefings on the situation in Ukraine and about Opposition Bloc meetings with the Russian government.[628]

On July 29, 2016, Kilimnik sent an email to Manafort from Moscow.[629] He referred obliquely to Yanukovych as the "guy who gave you your biggest black caviar jar," and then said that the deposed Ukrainian president had several important messages for Manafort. The messages all revolved around a peace plan for Ukraine.[630] Kilimnik wanted a meeting. Manafort emailed back, "Tuesday is best."[631]

That weekend, Trump appeared on ABC's Sunday morning show *This Week with George Stephanopoulos*. The host came right to the point: "What exactly is your relationship with Vladimir Putin?"[632] Trump claimed to never have spoken to or met Vladimir Putin.

Stephanopoulos turned to Ukraine. "Vice President Biden told me this week that Vladimir Putin wants to beat Hillary and Madeline Albright said that your victory would be a gift to Putin. And they're pointing to things like your statements . . . softening the GOP platform on Ukraine, even considering softening sanctions and recognizing Russian annexation of Crimea," Stephanopoulos added.[633]

After a lengthy exchange, Trump laid it out:

> But, you know, the people of Crimea, from what I've heard, would rather be with Russia than where they were. And you have to look at that, also. Now, that was under—just so you understand, that was done under Obama's administration. And as far as the Ukraine is concerned, it's a mess. And that's under the Obama's administration, with his strong ties to NATO. So

with all of these strong ties to NATO, Ukraine is a mess. Crimea has been taken. Don't blame Donald Trump for that.634

Donald Trump actually had a well-thought out view on Ukraine. It happened to be that of Vladimir Putin: Ukraine's ties to NATO were bad and it was a mess.

* * *

On August 2, 2016, the Russians made clear their price for the help. That evening, Kilimnik met with Gates and Manafort at the Grand Havana Room, a private club in Manhattan, only days after the Russian had visited Moscow.635 Kilimnik got to the point—the Russians wanted Trump to support a peace plan for Ukraine. "Kilimnik talked about a peace plan that would create a semi-autonomous [region] in Eastern Ukraine"636 Manafort recalled. "Yanukovych would get elected to head Eastern Ukraine" Manafort later told Robert Mueller, "and then reunite the country as its leader."

Manafort understood that the peace plan was really a "backdoor" way for Putin to maintain his hold over Eastern Ukraine.637 The key to the plan in Ukraine was former president Yanukovych, who would run the new area as Russia's proxy.638 Trump's help as mediator was the key in the international sphere.639 Yanukovych was asking Manafort to run his second "comeback campaign."640 Manafort laughed at the idea but later admitted that had he accepted a job to run a "comeback" for Yanukovych, Kilimnik would have asked him to ask Trump to support the plan.641

Kilimnik, an experienced opinion pollster himself, wanted to know one thing: Could Trump win? Manafort walked him through the polling and explained that voter bases in blue-collar Democratic-leaning states like Wisconsin, Michigan, Pennsylvania, and Minnesota were a place where Trump could find the votes to win.[642] Manafort explained further:

> Because Clinton's negatives were so low [sic]—if they could focus on her negatives they could win the election. Manafort discussed the Fabrizio internal Trump polling data with Kilimnik, and explained that Fabrizio's polling numbers showed that the Clinton negatives, referred to as a 'therm poll,' were high. Thus, based on this polling there was a chance Trump could win.[643]

Kilimnik, a veteran of years of political work around the world with Manafort, knew exactly what the data meant.[644] Gates understood this information was going to be shared with the members of the Opposition Bloc in Ukraine.[645] Gates and Manafort left separately from the club so as not to let any media watching them become aware of their connections to Kilimnik.[646] There is no doubt that Kilimnik thought Trump would win.

Stone then went into action establishing personal contact with those who could provide the emails. First, on August 4, he dined with Assange in the Ecuadorian Embassy in London.[647] Around the same time in August, Stone began communicating with Guccifer 2.0 as well.[648] He also asked Randy Credico, a radio talk show host, to pass on a specific request—any emails from the period when Clinton was secretary of state.[649] Credico agreed to pass them on to an attorney who had regular contact with Assange.[650]

Assange then appeared on the Dutch television show *Nieuwsuur*. In response to a question of whether or not WikiLeaks "sat on" material, Assange strangely chose to focus on the risks taken by the whistleblowers he alleged sent WikiLeaks materials.[651] He then turned to an alternate explanation for a source of the leaks, mentioning Seth Rich, a DNC staffer who was killed in a botched robbery in Washington, DC, on July 10.[652]

When asked if Rich was a source, Assange demurred, saying he was "suggesting our sources take risks," and then stated that the organization did not comment on sources.[653] That same day, WikiLeaks tweeted out a $20,000 reward for information on Rich's killer.[654] Assange, originally a fighter for transparency, was now a purveyor of the politics of disinformation.

Meanwhile, Steele continued submitting reports to Fusion GPS. The FBI interviewed him in Washington. On August 10, his new report indicated the Kremlin email leak strategy was to turn young people who had supported Senator Bernie Sanders in the primary against Clinton as the nominee.[655] It credited the idea of going after Sanders voters as originating with Carter Page.[656]

By the late summer of 2016, the Trump campaign had an entire campaign strategy ready to go surrounding the anticipated WikiLeaks disclosures.[657] Corsi knew that the emails would be released by Assange and that some came from John Podesta, Clinton's campaign manager.[658]

By August 14, Roger Stone and the military officers of Unit 74455 were in direct communication: On that date Twitter handles associated with both Stone and Guccifer 2.0 began communicating through direct messages.[659] Stone reached out to congratulate the Guccifer 2.0 personality for being reinstated by Twitter.

Steve Bannon was brought onto the Trump campaign on August 14. The expectation was that Manafort would remain a figurehead.[660] But Manafort had bad news—the next day the *New York Times* was going to reveal his connections to the Black Ledger.[661]

Late that evening, the *New York Times* revealed the existence of the Black Ledger and the fact that it contained records of millions of dollars in payments to Manafort from his time working with Yanukovych and the Party of Regions.[662] Three days later, the Ukrainian Reformers stepped in—the National Anticorruption Bureau of Ukraine released a statement confirming Manafort's name appeared in the Black Ledger, and attached nineteen pages of the ledger that detailed disbursements to Manafort.[663]

But a story in Ukraine doomed the last-minute efforts to keep Manafort in his position. On August 19, Sergii Leshchenko and a colleague at *Ukrayinska Pravda* ran a story that showed pages from the Black Ledger detailing twenty-two separate payments to Manafort.[664] It revealed the names of MPs and some foreigners who also received money from the Party of Regions.[665] The specific line items and photographs were a problem. Manafort was called into a "family meeting" of the Trumps. There, he was told that the information in the reports was too damaging.[666] Manafort denied the stories.[667]

Manafort resigned the day of the NABU press conference. Bannon and Kellyanne Conway took leading roles in the campaign. The day after Manafort resigned from the campaign, Kilimnik emailed Sam Patten to tell him that Manafort "continued with Trump" and floating a plan to sue journalists who wrote articles against them.[668]

One day after the revelation of the Black Ledger, on August 16, 2016, Trump held a campaign rally at the Erie Insurance Arena, in Pennsylvania. In his remarks, Trump specifically vowed to prevent the loss of jobs at the local General Electric locomotive plant: "we see what's happened with General Electric where they're cutting way back. Not going to happen."[669] Trump continued: "And you know why they're cutting back, it's one reason. Because we don't take care of our miners and we're not producing coal."[670] Trump mentioned General Electric and coal repeatedly in his speech.[671]

Trump then deployed a trademark of his politics: disinformation. He wondered aloud if "donors of Crooked Hillary" would want to stop production of locomotives at the Erie plant.[672] "Crooked Hillary" Trump mused, did not know what to do, but he did.[673] And "if she did, she couldn't do it anyway because her donors don't want to do it. There's reasons," he conspiratorially insisted.[674]

While Trump crisscrossed the country holding rallies, Fusion GPS continued to receive regular reports from Steele about Trump's relationship with Russia. After Manafort resigned, Steele reported that Yanukovych had informed Putin that he had indeed paid kickbacks to Manafort as alleged, but he claimed that the payments were untraceable.[675] According to Steele's report, Putin was concerned that the payments were traceable and felt that "for them, it remained a point of political vulnerability and embarrassment."[676]

Five times during August, Stone publicly acknowledged that he was in communication with Assange and WikiLeaks.[677] On August 21, he tweeted out that it was now "Podesta's time in the barrel"[678] He maintained indirect communications with WikiLeaks for the next two months.[679] Soon, he learned that in early October WikiLeaks would be releasing a second tranche of emails. He relayed the information to associates of the campaign.[680]

In mid-September, Steele submitted a new intelligence report. It described division within the Kremlin, with the senior foreign policy hands advising caution, and the intelligence services arguing that the operation was successful and should go ahead full steam.[681] The goal of the operation, stated Steele, was to shift US policy in the area of Ukraine and Syria.[682]

While in a limo with Richard Gates on September 29, Trump was briefed on the upcoming disclosures by telephone.[683] After the pair got on the campaign plane, Donald Trump turned to Gates and revealed that more releases of damaging information were coming.[684]

As if to highlight to Ukraine the danger of a Trump presidency, on October 6, 2016, two men were spotted on security cameras lugging a large, long rolled up item on the bicycle path of the Manhattan Bridge between the Lower East Side and Downtown Brooklyn.[685] Around 1:20 p.m. they unfurled a huge banner on the span, close to the Manhattan side.[686] The banner was a photograph of Vladimir Putin, with the word "Peacemaker" underneath.[687] Police never caught the pair.[688] The first social media accounts to highlight the stunt, came, predictably, from the IRA.[689]

"FOR IMMEDIATE RELEASE"

"For Immediate Release," the press release read, "The US Intelligence Community (USIC) is confident that the Russian Government directed the recent compromises of emails from US persons and institutions, including from US political organizations."[690] The intelligence community was announcing that Russia was interfering in the presidential election. The release continued: "Recent disclosures of alleged hacked emails on sites like DCLeaks.com and WikiLeaks and by the Guccifer 2.0 online persona are consistent with the methods and motivations of Russian-directed efforts."[691] It was early on October 7, 2016.[692]

But due to events ten years in the past, the Trump campaign would scarcely have time to respond. Roger Stone had information for Jerome Corsi —a videotape of Donald Trump making crude and sexist remarks about women was about to be released to the public. Corsi suggested that Stone tell WikiLeaks to immediately release the Podesta emails.[693]

Corsi told a conference call with the staff of right-wing tabloid *World Net Daily* that a tape featuring Trump making crude remarks was about to leak, and he urged the online site's staff to reach Assange immediately to have the Podesta emails released.[694] [695]

It turned out that the tape of Donald Trump on a hot mic making a series of lewd comments about women had been sitting in the vaults of NBC Universal's television show *Access Hollywood* for years.[696] Three days earlier, a staffer for the show had remembered the tape and a producer went to dig it up.[697] NBC debated for days what to do with the tape, finally making a decision on the morning of Friday, October 7.[698] *Access Hollywood* prepared a story to air on Monday, the day after the second presidential debate.[699]

Fate would not spare Trump the weekend. A source called the *Washington Post*'s David Fahrenthold, whose relentless pursuit of Trump's finances would later win him the Pulitzer Prize. The source asked him if he wanted to watch previously unaired footage of Donald Trump.[700] Within minutes, the reporter was on the telephone with NBC, *Access Hollywood*, and the Trump campaign.[701]

Hope Hicks burst into a debate prep session for the candidate with Rudy Giuliani, Chris Christie and Kellyanne Conway. Hicks showed Jason Miller an email from Fahrenthold and the campaign went into damage control mode.[702] The team pushed back, demanding a copy of the tape, but settled for a rough transcript.⁷⁰³ NBC readied a story for air, as the *Post* raced to get its tip on the internet, a race Fahrenthold won, at 4 p.m.⁷⁰⁴⁷⁰⁵

As negative reactions to Trump's lewd and offensive comments poured in, WikiLeaks and the Internet Research Agency (IRA) sprang into action to try and save his candidacy. Within an hour, WikiLeaks released the first of the Podesta emails stolen by the GRU.⁷⁰⁶ The Translator Department was actually ahead of the game. In preparation for their own October surprise, the tweets at the IRA peaked the day before.⁷⁰⁷ The Russians moved quickly to draw attention to the Podesta release.⁷⁰⁸

As many Republicans prepared to jump ship, one stood up for Donald Trump. That Sunday, Rudy Giuliani appeared on all four Sunday morning national news programs.⁷⁰⁹ Donald Trump never forgot it.⁷¹⁰

Meanwhile, Trump was paying special attention to Pennsylvania. A critical component of his campaign strategy was promoting coal and fracking in gas country. Nowhere was this more important than Luzerne County. On October 10, 2016, Trump held a rally in Luzerne's largest city, Wilkes-Barre. While there he again deployed the politics of disinformation, quoting from a story in Russian-backed *Sputnik News* blaming Hillary Clinton for the deaths of Americans in Benghazi.⁷¹¹ To a roaring crowd, Trump declared "I love WikiLeaks."⁷¹²

In an October 26 appearance on Fox News, Rudy Giuliani made a cryptic statement regarding the campaign: "I think he's [Donald Trump] got a surprise or two that you're going to hear about in the next few days. I mean,

I'm talking about some pretty big surprises."[713] Two days later Comey wrote to Congress indicating that the FBI had found Clinton emails on a laptop belonging to disgraced ex-congressman Anthony Weiner which required additional investigation.[714] Giuliani appeared later that day on a radio show, claiming that the letter went out because of "the pressure of a group of FBI agents who don't look at it politically."[715]

Steele's reports to Fusion GPS continued. In October, he reported that earlier that month, Michael Cohen had met with Russian officials in Prague in order to "clean up the mess" that resulted from the revelation of Manafort's prior work for Yanukovych.[716] On October 31, David Corn of *Mother Jones* broke the first story about what would eventually be known as the Steele dossier.[717]

On Friday, November 4, four days before election day, Comey appeared before Congress and informed the nation that the FBI had not changed its conclusion regarding Clinton after searching the laptop.[718] One of the concerns later cited in the decision to reveal the reopening of the investigation was that FBI personnel in New York, close to Giuliani, were suspected of leaking information about the Clinton Foundation and would leak this, too, damaging the bureau's reputation, if the discovery of the laptop had not been made public.[719] In fact the information about the discovery of the laptop *had* been leaked at least to Republican congressman Devin Nunes of California, who admitted as much on Fox News.[720]

Days later, Trump's eventual general election victory went through Pennsylvania. Erie County in the northwestern part of the state was key to that effort. In 2012, Obama had carried Erie County by sixteen percentage points.[721] That fall, union workers at Erie's General Electric Locomotive Division plant told Pennsylvania State Senate Democratic incumbent Sean Wiley that they were voting for Trump.[722] Trump would end up carrying the county by two percentage points.[723] A few days after the election the *New York Times* ran a long story entitled "How Erie Went Red," emphasizing the role of the General Electric plant in Trump's victory, and the job losses which had hit Erie hard.[724] As one observer put it "they didn't finish the job" referring to the Clinton campaign's losses in Erie and in coal country around Wilkes-Barre.[725]

Butler County, home of Westinghouse Electric, provided another shock for political observers in the Keystone State. There, the results indicated Trump had motivated thousands of new voters to go to the polls. In Butler in 2012, Obama had netted 28,550 votes to Romney's 59,761.[726] In 2016, Hillary Clinton got 34 more votes there than Obama had, 28,584.[727] But Trump got 64,428 votes in Butler County. In Butler alone, Trump had added nearly 5,000 votes to the GOP total for the state. In Luzerne County, home of Wilkes-Barre, Trump managed a 25,000-vote swing over Obama's 2012 result.[728] The 30,000 votes in Butler and Luzerne counties together accounted for two-thirds of Trump's margin in Pennsylvania.

Three people were responsible for Trump's battleground states strategy that paid off in Pennsylvania: Wells Griffith, Matt Mowers and Brian Jack.[729] Jack came from the Ben Carson campaign to handle delegate selection issues.[730] Griffith, who had long worked in Republican circles, was responsible for key states like Ohio and Pennsylvania.[731]

But if one person could be called the architect of Trump's victory it was Paul Manafort. His plan to draw attention to Clinton's emails to drive up her negatives worked spectacularly. A report by Harvard's Berkman-Klein Center did the math: "Donald Trump succeeded in shaping the election agenda. Coverage of Trump overwhelmingly outperformed coverage of Clinton. Clinton's coverage was focused on scandals, while Trump's coverage focused on his core issues."[732] Nearly 70,000 sentences were written covering Clinton's emails by US journalists, far outpacing all other issues covered.

The report also measured the number of references in the press about the candidates' positions on issues vs. references regarding candidate scandals. References to Clinton scandals came in first by a wide margin, with over 100,000 references.[733] Trump had slightly more than 40,000 references involving scandal. References to positions on Clinton's issues came in fourth place, with less than 40,000 appearances. Trump received nearly 80,000 references to his positions on issues.[734]

On election night, Griffith and Jack awaited returns in the Trump Tower war room.[735] By 9:30 p.m., the campaign learned that Pennsylvania was turning their way.[736] "Holy shit, we might have won this thing," thought

Mowers as the count dragged on into the night.[737] At 2:30 a.m. Wisconsin was called for Trump.[738] He would be the forty-fifth president of the United States.

Six people at the Trump Tower election party were noticed by a French reporter. The group sat around praising Trump. She felt them interesting enough to add to her piece on the celebration for *Le Figaro*. They were three men from Florida, accompanied by their "very made up spouses." They told the French reporter they were friends of Trump. One, from Boca Raton, told the reporter he was an insurer. His name, he said, was Lev Parnas.[739]

CHAPTER 4:

A SECRET PEACE

Lev Parnas's presence at Trump's election-night party was neither happenstance nor a coincidence. It was the result of events months earlier, which took place thousands of miles away. In September 2016, Ukraine and Russia agreed to an outline for peace: Crimea for the Russian-occupied parts of the Donbas, with the remaining details to be worked out. In October, the Normandy Format partners came together and initiated the process by which Ukraine and Russia would implement the Minsk Protocols. Such a peace would be so disadvantageous for Ukraine that the Ukrainian public might again take to the Maidan to stop the government from signing it. The world, wrapped up in the surreal drama of the Trump-Clinton battle, scarcely noticed as a specific framework for implementation of the Minsk Protocols was announced.

"THE GREATEST DANGER IS IN WASHINGTON, DC"

While the election raged on in the United States, there was a change of the guard at the US Embassy. Marie Yovanovitch became ambassador. Born in Canada, she was the daughter of Jewish refugees from the former Soviet Union.⁷⁴⁰ Yovanovitch had served as the US ambassador to Kyrgyzstan and Armenia prior to her posting to Ukraine.⁷⁴¹ Ambassador Pyatt left his post in Kyiv on August 18, 2016.⁷⁴² Yovanovitch presented her credentials in Kyiv on August 29.⁷⁴³

The policy of the United States when the ambassador arrived was "that strong anti-corruption efforts must form an essential part" of US policy toward Ukraine.⁷⁴⁴ Yovanovitch furthered this policy by helping Ukrainians who wanted to fight against corruption.⁷⁴⁵ She was the official spokesperson for that policy in Ukraine.⁷⁴⁶ The BBC's Paul Wood recalls meeting her in the summer of 2017. He described Yovanovitch as "a cautious State Department bureaucrat."⁷⁴⁷

If the potential election of Donald Trump was a matter of great importance in the US, it appeared that within Ukraine it was considered a life-or-death matter. The theme of the Yalta European Strategy Conference (YES) in 2016 was "The World, Europe and Ukraine: Storm of Change"⁷⁴⁸ The title of 2016's "American Lunch" panel at the conference encapsulated the view of many participants. "US Elections: Wild Campaign or System Crisis and What Does It Mean for Us?"⁷⁴⁹ The panel was full of such well known US political figures as Newt Gingrich, David Axelrod, Karl Rove, and Barney

Frank.[750] The moderator, *BBC HARDtalk* presenter Stephen Sakur, described the 2016 presidential election as "the most extraordinary, remarkable, unprecedented US presidential election in any of our lifetimes . . . we've never seen a candidate quite like Donald J. Trump."[751] "One could argue" Sakur said, "that his rise to the Republican nomination and now to a horse race in which he might end up in the White House is truly the most unbelievable political story that America has generated, perhaps in a century."[752] Former Democratic Congressman Barney Frank described the prospect of a Trump presidency: "the level of fright is . . . in two parts, one is the likelihood . . . I'm very frightened of the negative impact . . . I think a Trump election would be disastrous starting with here [Ukraine]."[753]

The US panelists, perhaps freed from domestic political restraint, painted a far darker picture than they might have on the cable news panels they often appeared on in the US. Gingrich said that the "entire Western world is drifting to a pivot. Donald Trump shows up as a part of a wave of distrust [of the] establishment."[754] Vis-à-vis Ukraine, Karl Rove wondered which Donald Trump was going to show up for Ukraine, "The guy who spoke to you last year or the guy who says Putin seems to be a nice guy and says nice things about him?"[755]

In the conference's closing panel, CNN's Fareed Zakaria discussed the risks to the world:

> The third great risk, I believe, is that the Western world is turning inward, between globalization, free trade, refugee flows,

you are seeing a distinct move inward and the most dramatic move inward of course would be if Donald Trump were elected President of the United States . . . so if you imagine a President Trump were to come into power and to think to himself I can deal with Putin, we can make a deal on Ukraine, Crimea's full of Russians anyway, what difference does it make? . . . all these things can be done unilaterally by the President of the United States . . . and the expectations that it would set off strike me as very dangerous I actually think that's the number one risk to the world. The greatest danger is in Washington, DC.[756]

Given these circumstances it is not surprising that Ukraine would make a an apparently disadvantageous peace. While it cannot be ruled out that Crimea was the price that Firtash and Lyovochkin asked of Poroshenko at the April 2014 meeting to push his opponent Klitschko out of the race for the Ukrainian presidency, the looming danger of a Trump election provided reason enough. In 2019, Jonathan Brunson wrote a little-noticed piece on the influential Washington, DC, blog *War on the Rocks* entitled "Implementing the Minsk Agreements Might Drive Ukraine to Civil War. That's Been Russia's Plan All Along."[757]

From the vantage point of 2019, Brunson described the prospective situation that faced Petro Poroshenko in late 2016: "European eagerness to make a deal with the continent's largest army, and US reluctance to ever fight that army, have left Kyiv with Minsk as its only option."[758] Should Trump win, Poroshenko would be out of options. Merkel's willingness to write a peace as disadvantageous as Minsk II made German, and thus European, support less likely.

For Poroshenko, perhaps the best time to make a deal would be *before* Trump's victory was assured. His leverage would be greater when a Trump win was only a possibility and if Clinton won, he could repudiate the secret deal altogether. A deal prior to a Trump win would prevent Russia from using a future President Trump in negotiations against him.

Poroshenko knew the Russians were helping the Trump campaign—Barack Obama had even announced it to the world. If the Opposition Bloc party demonstrated to Poroshenko that they had access to Trump's closely guarded internal polling, it would provide troubling proof of Russia's influence with Trump and that Trump's chances to win were a lot higher than most public polling indicated. [759] Such access implied that Trump was sympathetic to the Russian position on Ukraine. Paul Manafort's towering political reputation in Ukraine meant that Poroshenko could not ignore Trump's chances, no matter what US public opinion polling said.

Poroshenko would have accepted the internal polling as authentic—he had known Manafort and Gates for nearly a decade and they had pitched their firm's services to him during his 2014 run for the Ukrainian presidency. Perhaps Poroshenko even knew more than that—he controlled an intelligence and law enforcement apparatus of his own that doubtless monitored the Ukrainians who formed part of the back channel of the Russian operation to help Trump.   At any rate, nothing could have been more convincing to Poroshenko than the facts on the ground in Donbas. Russia had deployed an entire tank army to eastern Ukraine, including 700 main battle tanks, 1,000 armored personnel carriers, 1,250 tubed artillery pieces and 300 multi-launcher rocket systems.[760] In comparison, the entire nation of Germany had 408 main battle tanks.[761]

For both Putin and Trump, a peace with Ukraine initiated prior to a potential Trump presidency would be ideal. It would make it appear that Russia's good fortune in forging a deal with Ukraine was unrelated to its interference campaign in the US elections. It would also keep his chosen candidate, Donald Trump, out of a public role in the negotiations. If Trump changed the US position on Crimea and Donbas *after* Trump's election, it could constitute evidence of an illegal bargain between Putin and Trump—interference in the US election in exchange for recognition of Russia's annexation of Crimea.

Brunson's description of the options left for Ukraine in 2019 unintentionally illuminated Ukraine's circumstances two years earlier:

> If Ukraine cannot prevail militarily, there are really just two alternatives: Partition is the only way to resolve the conflict, but Ukraine and allies have opted for long-term non-recognition instead. No other humane solution aside from mass resettlement exists. "Frozen conflict is better than a hot one" has become vernacular. Drastic resolutions have disappeared from debate: Either surrender secessionist enclaves to focus on realigning the rest of the country West; or swap Crimea for Donbas, long the

fear of many as a surreptitious goal of any Trump-Russia channel.[762]

The surreptitious goal of the Trump-Russia channel was exactly that, a trade of Donbas for Crimea and a pro-Russian autonomous zone in the new, decentralized Ukraine. For Petro Poroshenko to go along with such a treaty, he would have to keep the negotiations secret from the Ukrainian public, which polling showed did not support a Crimea-Donbas swap. Before announcing such a peace, he would have to cripple Ukrainian opposition to it. Were evidence of such a peace being contemplated to appear, he would have to strongly deny it until it was finalized and politically expedient. All of these things, excluding the finalization of peace would come to pass.

Perhaps concerned about the very real risks a Trump presidency would pose for Ukraine, Poroshenko's government reached out. Just as the YES conference was beginning, Ambassador Valeriy Chaly again reached out to the State Department official that had introduced him to Manafort, Frank Mermoud.[763]

On September 14, Mermoud reached out to Gates, who was still on the Trump campaign with what he described as "something of extreme interest."[764] Mermoud told Gates that President Poroshenko was seeking a meeting with Trump on the sidelines of the United Nations General Assembly being held in New York.[765]

Mermoud texted Gates back, asking what Manafort's opinion on the meeting was.[766] When the dates did not work out a phone call was proposed between Trump and Poroshenko which Gates told Mermoud to put onl hold until he could speak with the campaign's scheduler and Manafort.[767] No evidence has emerged that a call took place.

THE DEATH OF THE WARLORD MOTOROLA

Blocking any deal were the separatists Russia had deployed in the east of Ukraine. The Ukrainians had long stated that they would never negotiate with those who had committed war crimes there. In mid-September 2016, as the US presidential campaign was reaching a frenzied pace post-Labor Day, Yevhen Zhylin, a separatist commander who tried to declare a "Kharkiv People's Republic" like those in Luhansk and Donetsk, arrived for a meal in an upscale restaurant in suburban Moscow.[768] When he sat down, a man, who had been sitting at a nearby table for twenty minutes, got up and shot Zhylin and his companion and fled to a waiting car outside.[769]

Around the same time as the hit in the restaurant, Gennadiy Tsypkalov, a political leader of the Luhansk separatists was arrested. Tsypkalov was reported dead in detention in mysterious circumstances the day after Zhylin was killed in Moscow.[770] In the past, diplomatic observers had widely speculated that such killings were linked to upcoming peace negotiations, either as a demonstration of good faith on the part of Putin, or perhaps a way to get rid of commanders who would not make peace at the Russian president's whim. Public eliminations of separatists might enhance the willingness of Ukrainian leaders to enter peace talks.

The summer of 2016 had been tense, with some observers expecting an all-out invasion of Ukraine by Russian forces.[771] One high-ranking advisor to the Ukrainian Interior Ministry thought otherwise, opining that "Putin's strategy relies on bargaining with Ukraine over the return of Donbas provided that we abandon all attempts to ever regain Crimea."[772] The increasing capabilities of Ukrainian forces made a hot war less appealing to Putin, who wished to avoid the effect of a war on his domestic situation.[773] Tensions decreased when the rebels suggested a cease-fire, which Putin indicated he would support.[774]

The sudden arrival of peace talks gave credence to those who believed killings of Donbas separatists were linked to the peace process. A few days after Ukraine floated a Trump-Poroshenko UN meeting to Gates and Manafort, things began to move on the peace front.

On September 21, days after the YES conference that Kuchma had attended, the Trilateral Contact Group announced a breakthrough, without describing it as one: the parties had agreed, after three months of negotiation, to a "Framework on Disengagement of Forces and Hardware."[775] All forces in the Donbas were to be pulled back to disengagement zones when the process was initiated.[776] The parties were now discussing implementation specifics for the Minsk peace.

A burst of diplomatic activity on Ukraine followed in October. Merkel, Hollande, and Putin spoke about Ukraine by phone on October 5.[777] On October 13, French president François Hollande spoke with Petro

Poroshenko by phone.[778] Hollande mentioned a Normandy Format principals' meeting in the very near future, calling it "urgent."[779] Poroshenko agreed.[780]

As if to underline that serious peace talks were at hand, on October 16, 2016, the Donbas separatist commander who went by the nom de guerre Motorola was also killed. His real name was Arsen Pavlov and he worked at a car wash in Russia before becoming an infamous warlord in the Donbas, credibly accused of war crimes. That evening, as he was riding the elevator up to his apartment, the elevator exploded.[781]

Reporters noted that the attack happened days before the scheduled Normandy Format meeting in Berlin.[782] First a man was shot in front of dozens of patrons at a restaurant. Another had disappeared and been killed, with the death then reported by his killers. A third was blown up by a bomb on an elevator. Whoever was killing the Russia-backed separatist leaders of the Donbas wanted to send a message by assassinating them in very conspicuous fashion.

The reason for the killings became clear days later. On October 18, Petro Poroshenko announced suddenly that a Normandy Format peace conference between Russia, France, Germany, and Ukraine had been scheduled for the next day, October 19, in Berlin.[783] Vladimir Putin attended the meeting himself.[784] It was to be the first principals meeting since Minsk II. According to Putin's spokesperson, Russia's position had changed, too: Putin saw "no alternative" but to implement Minsk.[785]

The next day, Poroshenko had a scheduled stop at NATO headquarters in Brussels, including a press briefing with Jens Stoltenberg, the NATO Secretary-General. Stoltenberg praised the new "plan to create a new road map for implementing the Minsk Agreement."[786] This road map, observers noted, included "tight sequencing of political and security moves and specific implementation dates."[787] Poroshenko posted about the new roadmap on his Facebook page.[788] Peace might be coming.

Sometime in October 2016, the new US ambassador, Marie Yovanovitch met with Prosecutor General Yuriy Lutsenko for the first time.[789] At some point in the meeting, Ambassador Yovanovitch stated that politically motivated prosecutions of Artem Sytnyk of NABU were something the United States was not happy about.[790] The seemingly uneventful meeting would have great significance three years later.

"AN INCREDIBLE PIECE OF SHIT"

But if Poroshenko was to win the best deal for Ukraine, he would need to counter Putin's back channel influence over Trump, whom the world now understood the Russian leader was helping.

Poroshenko needed a back channel. Reporting indicates that he next turned to a trusted former aide who spoke English well,[791] to solve the problem of reaching out to Donald Trump.[792][793] He followed the tried and true post-Soviet model of political intelligence operations—he tasked the job to an oligarch, Boris Lozhkin, who until August 29, 2016, was the chief of the

Presidential Administration of Ukraine.[794] Lozhkin owned a media empire in Ukraine.

When Lozhkin resigned that post, Poroshenko made him head of the National Investment Council and kept him as a "freelance advisor."[795] Lozhkin also remained as head of the National Reforms Council of Ukraine, a government board.[796]

From that post, Lozhkin opened the first part of the back channel by directing the National Reforms Council to obtain representation in Washington via a US lobbying firm.[797] At some point that fall, he directed the Council to select BGR International, a GOP-linked lobbying firm, to represent Ukraine in the United States.[798] Lobbying records show that the first day the firm began making contacts on behalf of Ukraine was December 9, 2016.[799] All of Washington understood that BGR was to represent the presidential administration of Ukraine.

A second, hidden backchannel was opened via the international Jewish religious organization called Chabad with whom Lozhkin was also associated.[800] Chabad originated in the Russian Empire in the late 1700s, eventually spreading to the entire Russian Empire, of which Ukraine was a part.[801] By 1950, the movement was headquartered in Crown Heights, Brooklyn.[802] Importantly for Lozhkin, the Chabad movement had connections with five Americans who would prove critical to opening and maintaining the back channel: Michael Cohen, Rudy Giuliani, Felix Sater, Lev Parnas, and Igor Fruman.

The key to opening the back channel would be sham campaign contributions originating from Ukraine, and a meeting between a Ukrainian government principal and Trump campaign officials that would not be covered by the media, demonstrating that the country was serious about trading for influence with Trump. The campaign contributions would also conveniently allow for contact at a closed event.

The method chosen to obtain these ends was ostensibly a real estate fundraising deal in South Florida involving Lev Parnas. Parnas, born in Odesa when Ukraine was the Ukrainian SSR of the Soviet Union, had moved to Brooklyn as a child. In 1995 he moved to Boca Raton, Florida.[803] Parnas was friends with Felix Sater.[804] A long line of business disputes, unpaid judgments, and even a fraud involving an unwitting Jack Nicholson as a prop followed him throughout Florida.[805] One person, when asked about Parnas, was blunt: "He's an incredible piece of shit," the man responded.[806]

Despite his past, Parnas was an ideal choice. First, he had long been connected to Trump. In the 1990s, Parnas got his start selling condos for Fred Trump.[807] Second, he was a US citizen and could legally donate money to US political campaigns in his own name. His criminal background provided assurance he would be willing to violate US law when necessary. Finally, he spoke Russian and Ukrainian.

Accordingly, in September 2016, Parnas and a partner, David Corriea, began working for a real estate developer in South Florida, Hudson Holdings, to engage in a deal with many features of the Russian Laundromat. The pair were to ostensibly raise funds for a building the developer had a contract to purchase—the St. Louis Railway Exchange Building, a landmark in Missouri.[808] Parnas and Corriea quickly raised $200,000 and were supposed to obtain funds for the deal from Russian Azerbaijani oligarch and Putin confidant Farhad Akhmedov.[809] They were to be provided cars, monthly salaries, and a reimbursement of costs as well as 50 percent of the value of the development.[810] Unusually for a deal of this size, the contract for the pair consisted of an unsigned letter addressed to Parnas that granted them millions of dollars.[811]

Parnas had met Akmedov in Florida.[812] He told Hudson Holdings about his access to Akhmedov and "dangled the prospect" of a $100 million dollar loan from the oligarch to capitalize the project.[813] That deal fell through, likely because Ahkmedov was deeply entangled in divorce litigation in London that went to trial in the first week of December 2016.[814]

The pair then provided a second, lesser loan opportunity. Via a connection with Roman Nasirov, the head of the State Revenue Service of Ukraine and a former member of the Petro Poroshenko Bloc in the Rada, the pair provided access to a $10 million loan from a Ukrainian oligarch and member of Poroshenko's party.[815] Nasirov himself was known to be quite close to the Ukrainian president.[816]

Although the papers for this deal would not be signed till later, it gave Parnas the ability to plausibly interact with a senior Ukrainian official. That official could then indicate who its messenger would be regarding the peace deal.

That messenger was Andrii Artemenko, a "patriotic lawmaker" according to one account, with "contacts" at the Chabad of Port Washington on Long Island in New York.[817] Andrii Artemenko indeed felt that presenting his peace plan was his "patriotic duty."[818] Artemenko's "personal contact" at the Chabad of Port Washington was none other than Felix Sater, the congregation's 2014 Man of the Year, according to Sater's own YouTube channel.[819] They had met earlier in 2016 to discuss the peace plan.[820]

Artemenko would be a perfect tool for Lozhkin to use on behalf of Poroshenko: he had already discussed a peace plan with Trump associates, making denial of his approach quite simple for Poroshenko. He had connections with Cohen and Sater. He could be disavowed if his approach was discovered and angered the Ukrainian public because it included the transfer of Crimea to Russia. He also spoke excellent English.

Parnas was also closely associated with the same Chabad organizations that Lozhkin was—he, along with his compatriot Igor Fruman, sat on the board of the American Friends of Anatevka, a Chabad-constructed village outside of Kyiv built ostensibly to house Jews displaced by the war in Ukraine's east.[821] Few such people actually lived there.[822] In 2019, *Bloomberg News* would report that prosecutors from the Southern District of New York were looking at fifty bank accounts associated with the group as part of their investigation of Parnas.[823] Some of the funding for Anatevka came from a powerful group for which Lozhkin served as vice president.[824] That group was the Euro-Asian Jewish Congress.[825] Boris Lozhkin was thus linked to Sater and Parnas through his associations with the Chabad movement. This was not unusual. Worldwide, Jews from the former Soviet Union were very involved in Chabad, and the organization led the way in reviving Jewish culture in the former Soviet Republics.[826] Also of note, in 2019, Rudy Giuliani was made honorary mayor of the village of Anatevka.[827]

Parnas now moved to make contact with the Trump campaign. On the evening of the October 19th Berlin meetings between Putin, Poroshenko, Merkel, and Hollande, the first photographs showing Lev Parnas amongst top Trump campaign backers were taken, showing Parnas standing next to Dr. Ben Carson at the presidential debate that evening.[828] Cryptically, an email regarding the debate received by Steve Bannon at 1:30 p.m. that day stated: "Steve, I am told [redacted] is in Vegas and willing to play any role in debate activities that is helpful. Our friend in FL is working hard on this."[829] This email was included as an exhibit in Steve Bannon's FBI 302 generated by the team of Special Counsel Robert Mueller, indicating his interest in this particular evening.[830]

Parnas now made large donations to Trump and Trump-associated campaign committees that were far beyond his personal means. On October 24, Parnas donated $50,000 to the Trump Victory super PAC.[831] He also donated $9,200 in hard money to several GOP state committees, $33,000 to the Republican National Committee and $2,700 to the Trump Campaign.[832]

Days later, he donated an additional $4,000 in hard money to GOP committees for a total just short of $100,000 in a four-day period.[833] All came within days of the Berlin peace meeting between Ukraine and Russia.

Days before the election, a GRU "persona influence operation" disguised as pro-Russian hacktivists "CyberBerkut" published the first counterstory to the Black Ledger, and Manafort's connections to it, on their blog.[834] The post was dated November 4. It foreshadowed the four years of disinformation that would ensue.

But the post started with a hidden message: the GRU wanted the FBI to know they knew all about the Steele dossier. The Simpson letter had no connection to the article other than it was a letter to Paul Manafort.[835] The GRU was trying to get ahead of the Steele dossier *before its existence had been disclosed, leave alone actually published.*

The GRU disinformation narrative then struck at Poroshenko's peace back channel. "As we have discovered," CyberBerkut explained, "the documents were handed over to Boris Lozhkin during his meeting with Evan Ryan, the US Assistant Secretary of State for Educational and Cultural Affairs, in Washington."[836] CyberBerkut continued with its disinformation story, claiming for the benefit of all that the Black Ledger was part of a US State Department operation:

> The whole operation was designed to leak this information to the media. Viktor Trepak, the former first deputy chairman of the Security Service of Ukraine, while leaving the intelligence

agency incidentally picked up a pack of documents and somehow miraculously escaped prosecution. Then he gave these documents for the analysis both to the National Anti-Corruption Bureau of Ukraine and Serhiy Leshchenko, the Ukrainian MP, who had long been known as an American agent of influence.[837]

CyberBerkut had a complete alternate explanation for the revelation of the Black Ledger. It was all a US State Department plot.

Immediately after the election Manafort began to make efforts to reach out to Poroshenko to try to create a relationship between Trump and the Ukrainian President. Manafort had taken to calling the plans to connect Poroshenko and Trump "the Frank project" after Frank Mermoud, the State Department official who had facilitated the attempts to widen contacts between Trump and Poroshenko.[838]

On November 10, Kilimnik updated Manafort via email on the special anti-corruption prosecutor's investigation into the Black Ledger.[839] The Russian intelligence operative had access to interviews conducted by investigators and emailed them to Manafort. Manafort then tried to arrange a call between President-Elect Trump and President Poroshenko.[840] The purpose of the call would be to discuss the ongoing Ukrainian investigation of the Black Ledger.[841]

On November 15, 2016, President Petro Poroshenko had his first telephone call with President-Elect Trump.[842] Four days later, on November 19, the Ukrainian government announced that despite its investigation of the Black Ledger, it saw no reason to charge Paul Manafort criminally. The special anti-corruption prosecutor, Nazar Kholodnytsky, argued to the press that there were no signatures in the book from Manafort, only his name next to disbursement amounts.[843]

As the thaw between Trump and Poroshenko continued, BGR Government Relations began its work to handle his formal lobbying in the US.[844] BGR, founded by Haley Barbour, the former head of the Republican National Committee and two-term governor of Mississippi, had extensive Republican connections.[845] Barbour was known as a "super-lobbyist" and had a large foreign agent representation practice.[846]

The contract between BGR and Ukraine provided for BGR Government Relations to be paid $50,000 per month.[847] One of BGR's key European team members was a former CIA employee and Foreign Service hand covering Europe in the State Department, Ambassador Kurt Volker.[848] Volker had previously served as US ambassador to NATO, an important asset for Ukraine as it dealt with issues related to Russia.[849]

Next, on November 28, the Ukrainian deputy minister for Temporarily Occupied Territories told Ukrainian outlet *Apostrophe* that the Russians were putting a slow squeeze on the Luhansk and Donetsk People's Republics, reducing the funds and utilities available to the rebels there.[850] In a second installment, the minister expected changes to come in the "spring or summer of next year and noted the issues with Donbas coal and the new focus that the Ukrainian state coal utility had on external sources of coal."[851] Most unusually, the minister also predicted the deaths of rebel leaders Givi (a nom de guerre), Igor Plotnitsky, and Alexander Zakharchenko.[852] The minister also boldly predicted the territories would be integrated back into Ukraine by the end of 2017.[853] The prediction was a quick peace between Russia and Ukraine.

The next day the promised November follow up to the Normandy Format occurred in Minsk. The four foreign ministers of the Normandy Group, not the Trilateral Group would lead the meeting.[854]

★ ★ ★

In mid-November, Sir Andrew Wood, former British ambassador to Russia, was at the Halifax International Security Conference in Atlantic Canada.[855] While there, he pulled aside David Kramer, the head of the McCain Institute for International Leadership.[856] Sir Andrew wanted to see if Kramer would listen to some disconcerting facts that were coming from a friend, the owner of Orbis Intelligence and former MI6 officer, a man named Christopher Steele.[857] In the course of an assignment, Steele had come across information indicating that Vladimir Putin had compromising information on the president-elect and that there was evidence that the Trump campaign had possibly colluded with the Russians.[858] The former ambassador wanted to know if Senator McCain would be interested in learning more.[859] Kramer said yes.

McCain sat down with the British official. The three met on the margins of the conference, along with a McCain staffer.[860] After hearing what Wood had to say, McCain turned to Kramer and asked him to fly to London and meet with Steele.[861] Kramer agreed.

On the Sunday after Thanksgiving, Kramer flew to London.[862] Sir Andrew had told him he would be met upon arrival.[863] Upon landing he received a text, "I'm in a blue jacket holding a *Financial Times*."[864] After finding a man in a blue coat with a *Financial Times*, Kramer introduced himself to Christopher Steele. Steele drove Kramer to his suburban home.[865]

Steele let him read the report and told him that he would arrange for Kramer to get a copy in the United States.[866] Steele explained that he was concerned that the FBI was not taking his dossier seriously because he had heard nothing from the FBI for months.[867]

Steele also discussed the level of confidence he had in the information. Steele had some concerns—for example he was concerned about the information regarding Michael Cohen being in Prague—the information could be interpreted that he had been in the Czech countryside or even Budapest in neighboring Hungary.[868] Steele also confided in Kramer that he believed there was a second compromising tape showing Trump with prostitutes in possession of the Russians.[869] Next to the dossier, Steele had a piece of paper with the names of his sources on it.[870] Kramer recognized two of them as "serious people."[871]

Steele instructed Kramer to meet with Glenn Simpson of Fusion GPS. On November 29, he met with Simpson in Washington.[872] Simpson gave him the Steele dossier, which Kramer gave to McCain.[873] McCain asked Kramer what he should do with it. Kramer told him give it to the director of the FBI and the director of the CIA.[874]

THE BIRTH OF THE BURISMA DISINFORMATION CAMPAIGN AGAINST JOE BIDEN

Unsurprisingly, when Trump won in 2016, his former business partner in Ukraine, Oleksandr Onyshchenko, was pleased. The fugitive oligarch told the Ukrainian web publication *Strana* that he had congratulated Trump and that they were discussing the future of Ukraine and that Trump would bring peace.[875] Onyshchenko also told *Strana* that the election would help his criminal case in Ukraine.[876] He was the first to advance theories that would later become a staple of Trump associates' disinformation narratives in the US: the Black Ledger was fake, created by the US State Department and that Ukraine, and Russia had not interfered in the US elections in 2016.[877] He insisted that Vice President Biden had personally cancelled his visa.[878]

On November 30, 2016, Onyshchenko tried a new gambit—he attempted to get the FBI to investigate President Poroshenko.[879] He claimed he had been secretly recording Poroshenko and his associates using his watch.[880] FBI agent Karen Greenaway flew to Spain to interview Onyshchenko.[881]

On December 1, 2016, Onyshchenko was indicted in absentia on the charges from the previous summer. The State Security Bureau told journalists that Onyshchenko held a Russian passport and worked for the

FSB, the Russian intelligence agency.[882] Onyshchenko responded to his arrest the very next day by launching a blizzard of claims in the Ukrainian press regarding corruption of many major political figures.[883] He primarily talked to *Strana*, a pro-Russian outlet in Ukraine and *Channel 24* a Russian TV channel known for its closeness to the Kremlin.[884]

The charges he leveled ranged from the claim that an agent of a government figure would come to his office and collect "pocket change" of $1 million in cash, to spending $3 million in bribes on behalf of Poroshenko to get Viktor Shokin approved as general prosecutor, to pressuring media firms to provide pro-Poroshenko content.[885]

But Onyshchenko's most critical claims were those about Burisma and its owner, Mykalo Zlochevsky.[886] According to Onyshchenko, Poroshenko sought to cancel the many licenses for natural gas that Zlochevsky had granted himself during his time as ecology minister, as well as gas licenses controlled by Rinat Akhmetov of the pro-Russian Opposition Bloc.[887] Onyshchenko claimed to be point man for Poroshenko's failed efforts to use bribes to control the appointment of the ecology minister and his deputy.[888] When this effort failed, the fugitive legislator claimed, Poroshenko extorted money from Burisma by freezing their assets and demanding a bribe to release them.[889]

Akhmetov, Burisma, and Poroshenko denied the charges.[890] Poroshenko accused the renegade lawmaker with links to Putin of being an agent of disinformation working for the Kremlin.[891]

Perhaps Poroshenko was right about the truthfulness of these charges. On December 15, a tape came out that showed that whoever was backing Onyshchenko was making a critical mistake. On November 23, Onyshchenko had prepared an interview to air on 112UA, a TV network owned by Opposition Bloc leader Akhmetov.[892] B-roll was included with the video, obtained by competing outlet *Obozrevatel*.[893] In it, Onyshenko was being coached by Viktor Zubritsky, an associate of former Ukrainian president Viktor Yanukovych. Zubritsky had fled Ukraine at the end of the EuroMaidan revolution and was indicted for arranging pro-government thugs to conduct attacks on civilians during the uprising.[894] "When I wave my hand" Zubritksy told Onyshchenko, you "talk."[895] Zubritsky told Onyshchenko to say, "I considered him a partner but then the situation changed."[896] Zubritsky gave further instructions to say:

> He is an aggressor, understand? And you had to follow his lead. And so now it turns out that you are his partner, who escaped from him. And then you need pressure. Then I will ask you . . . I just won't be right now . . . I will ask you a question when you tell me everything, I'll say, well, how do you feel when you make such statements, are you not afraid for your life, for the situation?[897]

On the tape, Onyshchenko denied being afraid for his life and Zubritsky had to "remind" the MP that he had told him earlier that he *was* afraid for his life.[898]

Zubritsky complained about the lack of specifics in the facts and figures Onyshchenko had provided him, to which the fugitive responded that a reporter named Svetlana Kryukova, from the pro-Russian outlet *Strana*, had the details.[899] Oleksandr Onyshchenko could not remember the details of the bribery schemes he claimed to be revealing. *Obozrevatel* argued there was little chance that the FSB was not involved in the case.[900] 112UA and other channels had been offered similar interviews and apparently had not run the tape.

There was more bad news for Onyshchenko. The US government swiftly announced that they wanted nothing to do with the fugitive who claimed to the world that he had provided the Trump administration with information.[901]

"A VERY MINOR WINK"

After the US election, the Russian government also acted as if a peace plan was about to be finalized. On December 8, Manafort got an email from Konstantin Kilimnik. The message was the same peace plan Kilimnik had broached at the August 2 meeting with Manafort and Gates at the Havana Room.[902] "All that is required to start the process is a very minor 'wink' (or slight push) from DT saying 'he wants peace in Ukraine and Donbas back in Ukraine' and a decision to be a 'special representative' and manage this process," argued Kilimnik.[903] He also suggested that if Manafort himself was designated as the envoy, Yanukovych could get him a reception in Russia "at the very top level."904 Kilimnik was extremely confident about Poroshenko's reaction to these moves and claimed that once Manafort started the process "it will go very fast and DT could have peace in Ukraine basically within a few months after inauguration."905

On December 9, 2016, the *Washington Post* ran a story that said that US intelligence officials had concluded that Russia had attempted to interfere in the 2016 presidential election in order to help Donald Trump win.906 Officials noted that both the DNC and RNC had been hacked, but that only materials from the DNC hack had been released.907 Trump went to the airwaves to claim that anyone could have done it including "some guy in his home in New Jersey."908

"I'M NOT COMING THROUGH THE GOLD-GILDED LOBBY OF THE TRUMP TOWER"

In December 2016, Rex Tillerson was getting calls from the Trump transition team and in his words: "I was not taking those calls, as was my practice generally."909 Tillerson was the chair and chief executive officer of the ExxonMobil Corporation. The chair's assistant came to him to tell him that Vice President-Elect Mike Pence was on the telephone. Tillerson thought: "Well, I'll take that call."910 Pence had a request:

> A number of people have told the President that he should spend a little time talking with you because of your position, your role in the world. You know all the heads—you know many of the

> heads of state of countries that are important. You have a perspective on the current state of our relationships and affairs, and would you be willing to come up and just talk to the President about that?[911]

Tillerson agreed, on one condition:

> And so I told him that I would. I had had conversations with previous Presidents. And so I said I will come up, but I'm not coming through the gold-gilded lobby of the Trump Tower because that was the revolving door of everybody that was interviewing for a job. I said, you know, I'll come up if you can get me in discreetly. So I went up through a residential entrance, and that was the first time I met President-elect Trump.[912]

Tillerson entered Trump's office in Trump Tower. Reince Priebus, Jared Kushner, and Steve Bannon were there. After an awkward introduction, Tillerson said:

> I just started to walk around the globe like I would do in briefing anyone that would ask me that. And we just went from one region to the next. And I described to the President my assessment of what the current US relationship was in the region, what I viewed to be the biggest challenges confronting the country, where I believed -- and where I believed we had certain strengths to address those and where we were going to have challenges. And, you know, I kind of summed it all up at the end by giving the President a general assessment of where I thought US foreign policy and relationships stood at that point. But I was fairly optimistic in my assessment that, while they were

in pretty bad condition in a number of locations, that those could all be turned around.⁹¹³

After about an hour or so, Tillerson wrapped up. "At that point," Tillerson recalled, Trump, "went into a bit of a sales pitch and asked me to be the Secretary of .State, and I was stunned. Bannon looked at me and he said: 'You're surprised.'"⁹¹⁴ When Tillerson protested that he already had a job, Trump replied "Yeah, but you're going to retire soon, aren't you?"⁹¹⁵ Tillerson took the job.

While Tillerson was becoming the designate secretary of state, the Ukrainians worked on opening the back channel with another "investment deal," this one for Michael Cohen. Cohen was already making plans to get paid in late October 2016. That month he set up bank accounts for a counsulting company he had started, Essential Consultants, LLC.⁹¹⁶ The next day, a wire came in to fund the new company. The purpose of the wire was listed as "retainer."⁹¹⁷

Like every other aspect of the back channel, it relied on connections between players in the Chabad movement. It began, like every other aspect of Poroshenko's back channel, in late 2016, when Michael Cohen was eating in a Midtown restaurant and a friend approached to say hello and introduced Cohen to his friend, Andrew Intrater.⁹¹⁸ Cohen placed the date of this encounter in December.⁹¹⁹

Intrater was director of a private equity firm called Columbus Nova, an investment vehicle for Intrater's cousin, Ukrainian Russian oligarch Viktor

Vekselberg.[920] At the time of this writing Viktor Vekselberg is the 119th richest person in the world. [921] As of this writing, Vekselberg suffered a 0.87 percent decline in his fortune, a loss of $103 million in one day.[922] *Forbes* described him as an "aluminum baron."[923] Vekselberg was the business partner of Oleg Deripaska, the Russian oligarch who originally hired Paul Manafort to work for Putin.[924]

As with so many others involved in the Ukrainian back channel, Viktor Vekselberg was also associated with the Chabad movement. The billionaire had made a "sizable contribution" to Chabad's Museum of the Holocaust, located in Russia.[925]

As the back channel began opening in New York, it also continued in Florida. The president-elect was staying at Mar-a-Lago, accompanied by National Security Advisor Designate Michael Flynn.[926]

That evening of December 16, 2016, Lev Parnas attended a party at Mar-a-Lago with the president-elect of the United States at the end of the celebration tour that Trump took across the US.[927] Parnas brought Roman Nasirov, the head of the State Revenue Service of Ukraine, to meet the newly elected American leader. Video of the party shows Parnas and Nasirov talking with Trump.[928] If Parnas needed to show that his back channel was from Ukraine, his introduction of Nasirov to Trump was more than adequate.

"CAN YOU CALL ME?"

From the beginning, Lieutenant General Michael Flynn was the front-runner for the position of national security advisor. In their one Oval Office meeting after the election, President Obama had warned Trump about Flynn.[929] Flynn himself told incoming White House Counsel Don McGahn that he was under federal investigation for lobbying issues.[930] What neither Flynn nor McGahn knew was that Flynn was a subject of Crossfire Hurricane, called by the code name Crossfire Razor in the documents.[931] His connections to Russia, including a paid appearance at a gala for Russian disinformation outlet *RT* gave counterintelligence agents fits—especially as photos of the event showed him sitting with President Vladimir Putin. Despite all of this, on November 18, 2016, Trump named him his national security advisor.[932]

In early December, Flynn, Kislyak, and Jared Kushner met at Trump Tower.[933] The three discussed setting up a back channel to facilitate easier communication between Trump and the Russian government.[934] The agents running Crossfire Hurricane did not know of this meeting and began to consider closing the investigation of Flynn in late December 2016.[935] Crossfire Razor had not had any contacts that they could definitively say indicated he was controlled by the Russians. A draft memorandum was prepared, pre-dated to January 4, 2017.[936]

On December 22, General Flynn called the Russian ambassador, Sergei Kislyak. The call record has been completely redacted.[937] Kislyak called Flynn back the next day. "Yeah, General . . . Thank you for picking up my call. I just wanted . . . as a follow up. To share with you several points. One. That your previous telephone call I reported to Moscow and it was considered at the highest level, in Russia."[938] Kislyak continued, "We are planning taking into account and rally your arguments to raise, ahem, a proposal of idea of continued consultations in NY."[939]

The purpose, the ambassador said was to "give time for working out something ahem, that would be, maybe less controversial."[940] Flynn wanted the Russians to abstain from a vote against Israel in regard to West Bank settlements.[941] The ambassador stated that he could only delay the vote, but that they had to vote for the measure.[942]

Flynn called back. When the general reached Kislyak, the ambassador asked him to set up an event in Kazakhstan, "to help the political process get started."[943] Kislyak asked for a secure video conference line with the Trump administration.[944] Flynn said he understood, and the Russian ambassador repeated that he wanted a "secure" line.[945]

The general then asked the ambassador to not allow the Obama administration's sanctions to "box us in!" Flynn feared the political impact of reciprocal sanctions from Russia on the chances for improved relations.[946] Kislyak told him they were working on doing something on that.[947]

At some point, Flynn called an official on the transition team for advice on what to tell the Russian ambassador.[948] That official was K. T. McFarland, soon to be named Flynn's deputy.[949]

In late December, Flynn was on vacation with his wife.[950] The Russian ambassador sent him a text message: "Can you call me?"[951] Flynn called back. Kislyak told him, "Your proposal that we need to act with cold heads uh, is exactly what is uh, invested in the decision."[952] The Russian ambassador told the general, "We found that these actions have targeted not only against Russia, but also against the president elect."[953] Flynn also told Kislyak that Trump was aware of the request for the secure video conferencing line suggested by the Russians.

After FBI leadership became aware of the telephonic contacts between Flynn and Kislyak and their discussions about sanctions, they decided on interviewing Flynn.[954] They would bypass Department of Justice (DOJ) and reach out directly to the White House Counsel's office.

During the transition, Christopher Steele continued to communicate with David Kramer by phone. Steele brought up some concerns he had regarding the information—some of the reliability of the information regarding Cohen's father was an example.[955] He also mentioned some information not included in the dossier—that General Flynn had had a sexual affair with a Russian woman in London.[956]

Around Christmas, Steele asked Kramer to let more people know about the dossier and asked him to get in touch with a reporter, Ken Bensinger of *Buzzfeed*.[957] Bensinger called Kramer and asked to meet with him in Washington. Kramer agreed.[958] On December 29, Bensinger met with Kramer in his office at the McCain Institute. Bensinger asked if he could take photos of the dossier with his phone. Kramer declined to let him.[959] Bensinger asked if he could read it, saying that he was a slow reader. Kramer agreed and left the room after a few minutes to take care of other things while Bensinger "read" the dossier.[960][961]

In late December, Viktor Pinchuk wrote an op-ed in the *Wall Street Journal*.[962] Pinchuk argued that Ukraine would have to endure "painful compromises" to get peace with Russia. It would have to give up on EU membership and an election would have to be held in the eastern territories before Ukraine could obtain full control of the rebel-held areas.[963] Crimea would be lost for some time, after which a revitalized Ukraine would be so attractive, the Crimeans would eagerly join it.[964]

Pinchuk's opinion within Ukraine was considered to be close to Poroshenko's opinion. The two were known to be close; in 2005, Poroshenko was accused of protecting Pinchuk from an investigation regarding Pinchuk's ownership of privatized nickel mines. As a result, Poroshenko had been forced to resign from his post as secretary of the National Security and Defense Council in Yushchenko's administration.[965]

Pinchuk was not the only one suggesting a Crimea-for-Donbas trade. A series of publications reported that Henry Kissinger was advising President-Elect Trump to "accept Crimea as a part of Russia."[966] Outlets as varied as *Politico* and Germany's *Der Bild* were reporting that Kissinger was "drawing up a master plan" for peace.[967] One expert stated that Kissinger was preparing a "diplomatic offensive."[968]

As the secret peace proceeded, the Obama administration released an unclassified version of a report on the Russian interference campaign on January 6, 2017.[969] It concluded that the campaign had been ordered personally by Vladimir Putin, and that the strategy had both covert and overt aspects and the intent was to elect Trump and discredit Clinton.[970] The very next day, January 7, *Buzzfeed* published the dossier as a series of photographs.[971] Ken Bensinger had photographed them without Kramer's consent.[972] The effect was electric. But it did not stop the peace plan mania that seemed to grip Kyiv and Washington.

The next day, January 8, Manafort flew to Madrid to meet with Georgiy Oganov, Oleg Deripaska's right-hand man. Manafort intended to get rid of the Deripaska lawsuit against him but the other issue on the agenda was "world politics." Manafort thought concealing the fact that "world politics" was discussed so important that he lied to the Senate Intelligence Committee and Robert Mueller, later recanting that lie as part of his plea deal.[973]

Manafort returned to Washington on January 12. On the 15th, he sent an email to K. T. McFarland, Flynn's deputy on the transition and the designated deputy national security advisor for Trump. Manafort asked if she was in DC and told her he wanted to meet informally, face-to-face. He wrote that he had "some important information I want to share that I picked up on my travels over the last month"[974]

McFarland forwarded the message on to Flynn, asking if they should meet. Not "until we're in the hot seats" he replied. The meeting would wait until after they had become government officials.975

"I HAVE NEVER MET VIKTOR VEKSELBERG"

In January 2017, world politics were moving very, very fast. First, on January 11, 2017, *Politico* ran an article it claimed was based on sources "with direct knowledge of the situation" regarding the revelation of the Black Ledger.976 Unsurprisingly, the article focused on Alexandra Chalupa, as her emails had been obtained in the DNC hack and indicated that she was the one within the DNC working on Manafort issues.977

The article claimed that Chalupa had met with Ukrainian officials at the Ukrainian Embassy in Washington in an effort to expose ties between Russia, Manafort, and Trump.978 It quoted a minor functionary at the Ukrainian Embassy, Andrii Telizhenko, as saying the effort involved asking him to pass on any information relating to Manafort and Ukraine.979 Telizhenko had a checkered past—the *Kyiv Post* reported that, as an assistant to the prosecutor general of Ukraine, he had solicited a $5,000 bribe for a meeting with his boss.980 After Viktor Shokin became prosecutor general, Telizhenko continued to work for the PGO and claimed that Shokin was not a political prosecutor and on the level.981 Telizhenko would return under the aegis of Rudy Giuliani two-and-a-half years later.982

As the inauguration came closer, the time had arrived to send the Ukrainian peace plan through the back channel that had been so elaborately constructed. It started with the money. Two separate deals appear to have financed the efforts. First, Intrater came to Trump Tower to visit Cohen and brought Vekselberg with him.[983]

When Vekselberg met with Cohen in Cohen's Trump Tower office, they discussed how to improve US-Russia relations.[984] They also discussed a peace plan that would involve Curt Weldon, who told an associate that Vekselberg was funding the plan.[985] Weldon was reportedly furious when the plan was revealed by the press.[986] The Russian oligarch was to pay Cohen $500,000 for promoting the plan.[987] Weldon denied knowing anything about it when questioned by the press, misspelling the oligarch's name and insisting in a message that: "I have never met Viktor Vekselburg [sic] and am not aware of any peace plan that he would have funded."[988]

Second, Nasirov had connected Parnas and Fruman with financing from Ukraine.[989] The vehicle was a Hungarian subsidiary of a Kyiv real estate development company named GEOS Development,[990] owned by Nikolay Negrich, a member of the Kyiv City Council and his father-in-law, billionaire construction oligarch Mykola Golytsin.[991] Like Nasirov, Negrich was a member of the Petro Poroshenko Bloc.[992]

On January 31, 2017—eleven days after Trump's inauguration as US president, GEOS Development Hungary lent $10 ten million to Hudson Holdings to fund its purchase of the St. Louis Railway Exchange Building.[993]

In fact, Negrich's father-in-law, Mykhaylo Golytsin owned GEOS Development Ukraine.⁹⁹⁴ With a partner also sitting on the Kyiv City Council, Negrich and his father-in-law controlled much of the construction and real estate development industry of Kyiv.⁹⁹⁵ Again, oligarchs provided "loans" to key participants in a political disinformation operation.

Now that the back channel was funded, it was time to deliver the peace proposals from Poroshenko. According to Artemenko's account, mutual friends had put him in touch with Cohen."⁹⁹⁶ Undoubtedly, that meant Parnas and Sater, as Cohen's lawyer told *Vanity Fair* in 2019, were involved in an early 2017 approach to Cohen involving illegality:

> Parnas . . . contacted Cohen in the first few weeks after Trump took office. He introduced himself through text message and asked if he would be willing to set up a meeting with Trump, the purpose being that he wanted to propose a method to save the federal government money on fraud, waste, and abuse. Those who know Cohen also said that there was another occasion during which Parnas came in contact with Cohen that they said may be of interest to investigators looking into whether Parnas violated federal election laws.⁹⁹⁷

After the "introduction," in late January, Artemenko met with Felix Sater and Michael Cohen at the Loews Regency at the corner of 61 and Park in Manhattan, where he passed "his" peace plan to the Trump lawyer.⁹⁹⁸ Vekselberg's Columbus Nova Fund later signed a 1 million-dollar contract with Cohen's Essential Consultants, LLC.[999] At least $500,000 was wired to Essential Consultants from Columbus Nova.[1000]

Artemenko also brought what he described as information that could lead to the removal of Poroshenko.[1001] Reporting indicated the disinformation was almost certainly from Onyshchenko. When Onyshchenko was asked about the Artemenko peace plan, the fugitive oligarch told reporters he knew Artemenko well and called him an independent man.[1002] When asked by a reporter if he had discussed the peace plan with Artemenko, Onyshchenko told him, "I can't say this for the press," but expressed support for the peace plan.[1003] When asked if Artemenko's information showing corruption by Poroshenko was true, Onyshchenko responded, "Yes, it is true."[1004] When pressed, Onyshchenko demurred, stating it was "confidant [sic] information."[1005]

Those close to the back channel made statements demonstrating their knowledge of the Biden *kompromat*. In a now-deleted response to a Joe Biden tweet on January 22, 2017, Lev Parnas's business associate from the Hudson Holdings deal, David Correia, linked himself cryptically to Onyshchenko's information: "i [sic] assume the day your son took his position in Ukraine was also a great moment? I have a feeling that chapter isn't closed."[1006] The seeds of the Zelenskyy Affair had been planted. It would be two years before they emerged into sunlight.

Although the Artemenko peace plan included a trade of Crimea for the Donbas, it tracked the Ukrainian positions in a key area and opposed those of Putin on the question of elections in Donbas. Artemenko's plan had a tight schedule of deadlines. Prior to Russian withdrawal, there would be seventy-two hours for those who wanted to, to be able to leave for Russia.[1007] After that, an amnesty would be declared and Ukraine would regain Donbas, while Russia would retain Crimea.[1008] Under the Artemenko plan, only after Donbas had reverted to Ukraine would Ukraine hold a referendum of all its voters to determine the autonomous status of the area.[1009] When later asked by a reporter over Facebook Messenger if he had anything to do with the Ukrainian peace plan, Artemenko responded with "hahaha" and added a smiley face.[1010]

PEACE PLANS BLOOM

Rex Tillerson began to prepare to take over the role as US secretary of state. Tillerson had a "sherpa," a person whose job it was to guide the nominee through the confirmation process, a lawyer named Margaret Peterlin.[1011] Mostly, Tillerson was briefed by experts on the details he would have to know as secretary of state.[1012]

In the area of Russia, there was an exception. Rex Tillerson received a list of things that Vladimir Putin wanted from the Trump administration. That list came from an old friend of Jared Kushner's, Rick Gerson.[1013] During the 2016 presidential race, Kushner and Gerson would bump into one another from time to time and Kushner would brief Gerson on what was going on in the Trump campaign.[1014] Gerson was a hedge fund manager in New York who had business with the United Arab Emirates.[1015]

Gerson inadvertently became a link between Russia and the Trump campaign. The day after the election, Kirill Dmitriev, the head of the Russian Domestic Wealth Fund, reached out to George Nader, an American advisor to the UAE.[1016] When this approach did not get immediate results, Dmitriev reached out to other UAE officials and made a connection with Gerson.[1017] For some time the two exchanged messages which evolved into a "reconciliation plan."[1018] Dmitriev told Gerson that he had been tasked by Vladimir Putin to develop a reconciliation plan for Russia and the United States, and that he reported directly to the Russian president.[1019] In that role, he provided Gerson with a two-page document of what Russia wanted in a reconciliation.[1020] A final version of the document from the Russian included "something about Ukraine. Something following the Minsk Agreement on Ukraine. I didn't know what the Minsk Agreement of Ukraine was" Gerson told the Senate Intelligence Committee.[1021]

Gerson gave the document to Jared Kushner and informed Dmitriev that Kushner had received it.[1022] At a later meeting with Rex Tillerson and Steve Bannon, Jared Kushner retrieved two copies of the proposals and handed one to Bannon and one to Tillerson.[1023]

On January 11, 2017, Rex Tillerson appeared before the Senate Foreign Relations Committee for his confirmation hearing. On most questions regarding the annexation of Crimea, Tillerson told the senators it was illegal, it upset the international order, and was wrong. However, his views on the status of a peace agreement that might leave the peninsula in Russian hands were slightly nuanced to American ears:

> Senator Portman: Okay. Do you pledge that the United States would never recognize that annexation of Crimea if you serve as Secretary of State, similar to the way the United States never recognized the Soviet occupation of the Baltic states?
>
> Mr. Tillerson: The only way that that could ever happen is *if there were some broader agreement that was satisfactory to the Ukrainian people.* So absent that, no, we would never recognize that.[1024]

Senator Rubio pressed him on the point:

> Embedded in that was the notion that potentially at some point there could be an arrangement in which the United States would recognize Russia's annexation of Crimea *if the government in Kiev* [sic] *signed off on it or accepted it as part of a broader deal to ensure peace and stability.*
>
> Is that an accurate assessment of the testimony as I heard it?
>
> Mr. Tillerson: I think what I was trying to recognize is that since that was territory that belongs to Ukraine, Ukraine will have something to say about it *in the context of a broader solution to some kind of a lasting agreement.* I am not saying that that—that that is on the table.[1025]

Rex Tillerson left the door open for a "broader" settlement in Ukraine that would see Russian retain Crimea. How Tillerson was prepared for his confirmation hearing has since been the subject of intense investigation by both Robert Mueller and Congress.

At the time, the significance of Tillerson's remarks in America was negligible. In Ukraine the remarks were a bullhorn announcing an imminent peace deal involving surrender of the Crimea in exchange for control of the Donbas. The day after Tillerson's testimony, the *Kyiv Post* ran a piece by columnist Oleg Sukhov, "Bracing For Uncertainty: Trade Crimea and Donbas for Peace?"[1026]

The *EuroMaidan Press* also waded in, citing a Facebook post by a Kyiv academic who analyzed Tillerson's statement and said that the "logical conclusions" that flowed from the statement were that Trump's foreign policy team was "considering a big agreement" and that such an agreement was no longer "in the realm of conspiracy thinking" but now was "a reality."[1027]

The evidence on the ground in Ukraine was that "world politics" were about to deliver a peace for Ukraine. On January 17, 2017, the Ukrainian minister of the interior, Arsen Avakov, gave a briefing to the Ukrainian Border Guards leadership. Avakov told them to be prepared to take over the Donbas-Russia border in 2017.[1028] Avakov indicated it was an operational matter: "I want each one of you to understand that this is not a propagandist statement, not some sort of fixation—this is an objective reality that we will face in the near future," he told his commanders.[1029]

World politics soon reached the Trump Inaugural Committee. Rick Gates handled the donations operation for the Inauguration.[1030] Unsurprisingly, at least a dozen prominent Ukrainians came to Washington to see Trump inaugurated.[1031] Some positioned themselves as peace brokers, some as supporters of Russia, others as Ukrainian representatives.[1032] Konstantin Kilimnik reached out to Sam Patten and asked him to obtain Inauguration tickets for Serhiy Lyovochkin, the oligarch and former Party of Regions official who now was a member of the Opposition Bloc.[1033] Sam Patten bought the tickets for Lyovochkin.[1034]

In mid-January Lyovochkin was in Washington to use the tickets Sam Patten had purchased for him. He met with Manafort and Kilimnik at the Westin Alexandria Old Town, across the Potomac River from Washington.[1035] Kilimnik told him that Cohen had put a Ukrainian peace plan on Trump's desk.[1036] Manafort assured Kilimnik that the Ukrainian peace plan would go nowhere.[1037] The Artemenko plan was considered a "Ukrainian" plan by the Russians.

The topic of discussion turned to the Yanukovych peace plan. Manafort went over the details, which Kilimnik had provided him in the December email message.[1038][1039] On January 23, after the Inauguration, Lyovochkin posted an update on the Opposition Bloc website: "Those meetings, which I have held here [in Washington], give grounds for cautious optimism that the new administration of Trump will bring a new energy to the solution of the conflict in Donbas and in the establishment of peace in Ukraine."[1040]

After Kilimnik met Manafort, he met with Sam Patten and several others. He told Patten he was "scared" that he would run into Paul Manafort. He did not tell Patten that Lyovochkin had just met with Manafort.[1041]

Around this time, Russian disinformation sources began creating the false legends that surrounded both the Russian interference campaign and the Black Ledger.[1042] Kilimnik wrote an op-ed piece for Lyovochkin claiming the Black Ledger was falsified evidence.[1043]

State Fiscal Service head Roman Nasirov attended the Inaugural parade and was photographed watching it from an official reviewing stand in a Ukraine-branded jacket. Next to him were Lev Parnas's sons.[1044]

On Friday, January 27, 2017, FBI agents arrived at the White House to interview General Michael Flynn. They included Peter Strzok, the deputy assistant director of the bureau.[1045] In the interview, Flynn denied having asked Ambassador Kislyak to not react to sanctions.[1046]

Two days later, on the 29th, Assistant Attorney General Sally Yates came to the White House and sat down with Don McGahn.[1047] She told him that Flynn had not been truthful regarding his telephone conversations with the Russian ambassador and that Flynn could therefore be a blackmail target.[1048]

That same day, George Papadopoulos was at home on Chicago's North Side.[1049] FBI agents knocked on his door and asked him to voluntarily accompany them back to the Chicago Field Office.[1050] Crossfire Hurricane had reached one of the Trump campaign's go-betweens with Russia. The following Wednesday, the FBI called Papadopoulos seeking a meeting.[1051] At Papadopoulos's suggestion, they met at George's Ice Cream and Sweets at 5306 N. Clark.[1052] After that interview, the FBI wanted to ask more questions the next day.[1053]

Papadopoulos balked on further questioning. In a series of texts he told them he had talked to a lawyer who had advised him not to discuss the matter with the FBI.[1054] In all, the FBI generated five Form 302ss for Papadopoulos in early 2017.[1055] Further interviews were briefly discussed and then not pursued.

On January 31, contemporaneous with Artemenko's meeting with Cohen, Dale Armstrong, a conservative US evangelical pastor, incorporated his lobbying firm, Armstrong and Associates, in Pennsylvania.[1056] Artemenko became a client of Armstrong's new lobbying firm, a relationship that would not be revealed until after the peace deal was disclosed in the *New York Times.*

On February 3, the next steps were taken to widen the back channel between the Ukrainian government and the Trump camp. Viktor Pinchuk's lobbyist Doug Schoen hired Fox's Monica Crowley to consult on the account in early 2017.[1057] On February 3, she sat down for lunch in London with

Pinchuk where they discussed the US-Ukraine relationship and the peace process specifically.[1058] On February 7, 2017, she texted Rudy Giuliani, asking him if he would give a speech at Mr. Pinchuk's foundation in March.[1059] The next day, according to Schoen's FARA filings, Giuliani spoke with her by telephone and told her he would consider it.[1060]

From the very first days of the Trump presidency, new officials in the State Department were tasked with creating the basis for a quick rapprochement between Russia and the US.[1061] Two officials sent a tasking order to the State Department's Bureau of European and Eurasian Affairs to prepare a set of options to improve relations with Russia in exchange for help with the war against the Islamic State in Syria.[1062] The purpose was to create a grand bargain with Moscow, drop the sanctions, and prepare the way for a summit between the two leaders.[1063]

State officials were concerned and reached out to a former Obama state appointee who then reached out to Democrats on Capitol Hill.[1064] In a show of bipartisanship that would be unheard of even a year later, Senators Lindsey Graham, John McCain, and Ben Cardin banded together to draft legislation that would require the president to submit a plan for review to Congress before acting.[1065] These acts were not overlooked by the Trump administration. U.S. Ambassador to the United Nations Nikki Haley backtracked publicly, telling the UN that the US would not drop sanctions against Russia until it returned Crimea to Ukraine.[1066] But behind the scenes, the efforts for a settlement moved forward.

Perhaps the leadership of the rebel forces did not share the hope for upcoming peace. On February 4, the defense minister of the Lugansk People's Republic was killed by a car bomb in the city.[1067] Two days later, one of the most well-known rebels, Mikhail Tolstykh, AKA [1068]Givi, was killed by a rocket-propelled grenade fired into his office, just as the deputy minister for the Temporarily Occupied Territories had predicted in his November interview.

The article that Konstantin Kilimnik wrote for Serhiy Lyovochkin appeared in *US News and World Report* on February 6.[1069] It advanced the disinformation themes that were soon to surround Trump associates' messaging about the Black Ledger—it was a manufactured case against Manafort.[1070] The article then turned to promoting a pro-Russian view of the next steps for Ukraine which "must end the conflict in the country's east." "Kyiv" the piece argued "must take its boot off the neck of . . . local communities." The Viktor Pinchuk op-ed published in the *Wall Street Journal* was cited approvingly.

Diplomatic efforts then continued. On February 7, the German ambassador to Ukraine gave an explosive interview to *RBC Ukraine* where he stated that Russia could hold elections over the future of the Donbas prior to Russian troops withdrawing.[1071] The result was a firestorm in the Ukrainian and German press the next day.[1072] But even amid controversy the parties prepared for a Normandy meeting between the foreign ministers of the

Germany, France, Russia, and Ukraine at the Munich Security Conference to be held in February.[1073]

In the midst of this diplomatic offensive, on February 9, Oleg Sukhov and a colleague at the *Kyiv Post* revealed the secret peace. According to the paper, "sources interviewed by the *Kyiv Post* and public statements by figures linked to the government show that Ukrainian authorities are, indeed, in talks with Russia and the West on reintegrating the occupied territories and urgently trying to reach a compromise with Russia."[1074] Two presidential aides declined to dispute the claim. Both said that there would be no concessions beyond the Minsk Protocol.[1075] The sources told the *Kyiv Post* that the negotiations intensified at the beginning of the year as Trump "took office."[1076] The piece quoted one of Ukraine's own negotiators as saying the talks were about to reach a "painful stage" for Ukraine, and the German ambassador as saying the elections could happen even before the Russian troops withdrew.[1077] The article noted that a key role in the negotiations was being played by a close friend of Putin's, Viktor Medvedchuk.[1078]

On February 15, Pinchuk held his annual Yalta European Strategy (YES) luncheon in Kyiv to prepare for the conference in September. Monica Crowley attended the luncheon, where they discussed US-Ukraine relations.[1079]

On February 10, Papadopoulos met with the FBI with a lawyer present. He told agents he had met Mifsud, who had told him the Russians had emails. When asked if he had ever told any diplomats about it, Papadopoulos lied and said no.[1080] When asked if he was sure, he stated that he was "sticking to that story."[1081] The day after a follow-up interview on February 16, Papadopoulos deleted his Facebook account that contained copies of his communications with Mifsud and Russian nationals and created a new, clean profile.[1082]

On the night of February 13, after it was revealed that he had lied to Vice President Pence about his telephone call with Kislyak in December, General Michael Flynn resigned as national security advisor.[1083] The next day, Chris Christie was visiting the White House when Trump told him that the firing of Flynn would mean the end of the Russia investigation. "No way," responded the former New Jersey governor, "we'll be talking about this on Valentine's Day 2018."[1084]

That same day President Trump asked James Comey for a private word after a briefing.[1085] The president asked Comey to go easy on Flynn: "I hope you can find your way clear to letting this go, to letting Flynn go."[1086] "He is a good guy," the president continued, "I hope you can let this go."[1087] Trump's anxiety regarding the Flynn investigation was palpable. The Artemenko peace plan and Flynn's role in it had not yet been revealed.

That was to happen presently. The 53rd Munich Security Conference was scheduled for February 17 to 19. But before any agreement regarding Ukraine could be obtained, a bombshell went off in Washington. On the 19th, the *New York Times* published a story stating that Michael Cohen had conveyed the Artemenko peace plan to Flynn during the brief period when he was national security advisor.[1088] Artemenko spoke with the newspaper. He referred to the *kompromat* on Petro Poroshenko that he had included.[1089] "A lot of people will call me a Russian agent, a US agent, a C.I.A. agent," he told the paper. He made no mention of a Ukrainian principal. He also said that he had received encouragement from some of Putin's top aides.[1090] Absolutely nothing Artemenko said could in any way link him to Petro Poroshenko. Unusually, however, Artemenko was also anxious for the paper's reporters to know that Petro Poroshenko and Paul Manafort had never met.[1091] The back channel had been exposed.

Everyone went on the offensive against Artemenko. The Ukrainian ambassador stated that the "Crimean lease provision is a gross violation of the Constitution."[1092] The ambassador wanted to make it clear that "such ideas can be pitched or pushed through only by those openly or covertly representing Russian interests."[1093] On February 20, he was expelled from Ukraine's Radical party.[1094]

No doubt angered by Artemenko's inclusion of materials in the peace plan that embarrassed him, Poroshenko went on the warpath. By February 21, Lutsenko was already opening a case for treason against Artemenko, despite the fact that his peace plan was no different than that of Pinchuk's.[1095] Even those associated with the Opposition Bloc denied that they had anything to do with the plan.[1096] Dimitry Peskov, Putin's spokesperson, denied responsibility, saying that Russia was not going to lease its own territory.[1097] Artemenko was a bit more forthcoming to

Ukrainian publications, claiming that Oleh Lyashko, the head of his party, was fully aware of his trip and the peace initiative.[1098]

Artemenko had dual citizenship in Canada. On March 18, Poroshenko submitted a new law that would make a person ineligible to hold office in Ukraine if they had dual citizenship.[1099] Artemenko's hiring of his unusual lobbyist—the pastor Dale Armstrong—was reported by the press.[1100] There has been no explanation for how Armstrong knew that Artemenko would need representation for a peace plan some nineteen days prior to the revelation that it existed. Artemenko sought to limit the damage from the "peace plan." Armstrong was allegedly called in to help rehabilitate Artemenko.[1101]

By April, the Poroshenko government was considering stripping Artemenko of his citizenship.[1102] By May, Artemenko was removed from the Rada.[1103] On May 5, 2017, Petro Poroshenko stripped Andrii Artemenko of his Ukrainian citizenship, , by presidential decree.[1104]

Artemenko was one of many with peace plans in the late winter of 2017. In Kyiv, new peace plans were so ubiquitous that one correspondent headlined a story with "Everyone Seems to Have a Peace Plan For Ukraine."[1105] "Each new plan—made by a mix of known politicians and shadowy operatives—has sparked fierce debate in Kyiv political circles and among the Ukrainian public" he added.[1106] The writer Christopher Miller summarized the pro-Russian version:

- Ukraine leasing the Russian-annexed Crimea to Moscow long-term, followed by a referendum to decide the Black Sea peninsula's fate once and for all;

- Temporarily setting aside the dispute over Crimea and Kyiv's continued integration with the European Union and flirtation with NATO membership to focus on stopping the conflict in the east;

- Reinstating elected officials from 2010—the last time nationwide elections included areas under the control of separatists—and bringing in UN peacekeepers;

- Allowing separatist leaders from the Donetsk and Luhansk regions to be included in Minsk negotiations with Ukrainian officials and reserving the option to hold a referendum on the status of the Donbas if Kyiv doesn't fulfill its part of the Minsk deal;

- Bringing back Viktor Yanukovych, Ukraine's ousted ex-president living in self-imposed exile in Russia since 2014, to head a pro-Russian eastern region with more autonomy.[1107]

The most recent of the plans, wrote Miller, came from Konstantin Kilimnik, who claimed from Kyiv that "many people want to start a dialogue" between the eastern regions and the rest of Ukraine.[1108] Kilimnik called his plan the Mariupol plan after the largest city in the Donbas still controlled by Kyiv.[1109] "[T]his should be the one of the roles of the Opposition Bloc and other opposition parties, which understand the necessity of bringing Donbas back into Ukraine."[1110] Kilimnik continued regarding the former president: "in theory, a figure representing Donbas, such as Yanukovych or someone else who has at least not killed people and can stop the war and fix the local economy, might be an option."[1111] In his article, Miller pointed out the very obvious problem with Yanukovych: "Many Ukrainians, though, believe the former president's hands are dripping with blood as they hold him responsible for the deaths of more than 100 protesters shot by riot police during the EuroMaidan protests in Kyiv in 2014."[1112]

Yanukovych had his own six-point plan, of which "four relate to the 'investigation into the crimes committed on the Maidan in February 2014,' for which he proposes a special commission to be established by the Council of Europe."[1113] Other plans existed. Artemenko told the Kyiv-based Miller that his plan included a referendum to decide if the eastern regions would have special status.[1114]

Another item appeared in the Kyiv press on February 23. The National Agency on Corruption Prevention, responsible for monitoring corruption amongst government officials, was investigating the Nasirov trip to Trump's Inauguration.[1115] It appeared that Ukrainian reformers had some idea that there were issues surrounding Nasirov and his trips to the US.

In mid-February Manafort met with Donald Trump Jr. and told him that Ukraine, not Russia, had interfered in the 2016 election.[1116] He followed up the meeting with an email linking to the January 11 *Politico* piece which accused Ukraine as interfering in the 2016 election.[1117]

A few days after Kilimnik's plan was detailed to Miller, Kilimnik once again met with Manafort, this time in Madrid, Spain. The pair met on the 26th, Manafort arriving from Washington and Kilimnik arriving from Moscow.[1118] Manafort first denied to Special Counsel Mueller that he even met Kilimnik.[1119] Later, he admitted that he had met with Kilimnik on that date, but denied that the peace plan had been discussed.[1120] Later a judge would find that Manafort lied about his contacts with Kilimnik and their discussions about the Yanukovych peace plan.[1121] Manafort claimed to Mueller that at the February 26 meeting in Madrid, the pair actually discussed the Black Ledger cases.[1122] Those cases blocked any chance of a Russian peace plan featuring Yanukovych.

The Russians moved to remedy the situation involving the evidence of Yanukovych's guilt in inviting Russian troops onto the soil of Ukraine after he was deposed in 2014. First, on February 20, Vitaly Churkin, Russia's UN Ambassador who had waived the letter from Yanukovych requesting Russian military assistance in 2014, died at work from what the Russian Foreign Ministry announced as a heart attack.[1123] He was sixty-four.[1124]

The NYPD found Churkin having a cardiac incident at 9:30 a.m. in front of the Russian mission on 67th Street in Manhattan.[1125] The New York City medical examiner ruled the cause of death inconclusive and ordered further tests.[1126] The Russians complained about the information regarding the autopsy being released, and the US State Department requested a gag order from New York City, which was granted.[1127] Churkin's official cause of death has never been revealed.

Within a few weeks of Churkin's sudden death, Russia began rewriting the history of its 2014 invasion of Ukraine. On March 15, 2017, the Russian news service TASS ran a story quoting Kremlin spokesman Dimitry Peskov saying that, in fact, the letter that Churkin had waved in front of the cameras at the UN Security Council three years prior did not exist.[1128] The prosecutor general of Russia agreed no such letter had been sent by Yanukovych, despite the fact that Vladimir Putin himself had spoken of the letter on television.[1129] Yanukovych publicly argued he had never sent the letter to Russia.[1130] Vitaly Churkin could not be reached for comment. The alternate explanation could be costly for some.

* * *

The alternate explanation would later be costly indeed for Sergei Skripal, who was living in Salisbury, England, at that time. His backstory was most unusual. He was a Russian military attaché in the Spanish Embassy in Madrid when he was introduced to a man named Antonio Alvarez de Hidalgo. De Hidalgo was actually the legendary M-6 spy recruiter Pablo Miller, a 2007 *Kommersant* article claimed.[1131] Eventually, Skripal was caught and sentenced to thirteen years in a Russian prison for spying for the UK. But after the FBI caught a group of deep-cover suburban spies in the US in 2010, the Russians arranged a swap: The "illegals" the US caught for Skripal, who was pardoned by Putin as part of the deal.[1132]

In late February and early March 2017, three Russian men bearing the passports of Sergei Pavlov, Alexander Petrov, and Sergei Fedotov arrived in London, the first of two trips in two years they would make to the UK. In point of fact, the three men were Lieutenant Colonel Alexander Mishkin, Major General Denis Sergeev, and Colonel Anatoliy Chepiga of Unit 29155 of the GRU, and one year later they would involve Skripal in the effort to create an alternate explanation for the Steele dossier.[1133] Little is known about their trip.

One thing is known, however. In 2017 the GRU created a false trail of clues leading to a mysterious LinkedIn entry for Pablo Miller falsely indicating that Skripal had worked as a senior intelligence analyst for Orbis Intelligence, Christopher Steele's firm.[1134] In fact, Skripal had never worked with Steele, nor was he a source for any of the information in the Steele dossier.[1135]

* * *

On March 1, 2017, the *Washington Post* ran a story saying that Attorney General Jeff Sessions had met twice with Russian officials and had not disclosed those meetings to the Senate during his confirmation hearing.[1136] Trump, worried about potential recusal by Sessions, told White House

Counsel Don McGahn that he wanted Sessions to run interference on the investigation to avoid the administration being "derailed."[1137]

The next day, the attorney general in a brief press conference recused himself from any investigation of the Trump campaign.[1138] In response to a question, Sessions described a September 2016 meeting in his Senate office with Kislyak. "We listened to the Ambassador and what his concerns might be . . . and somehow the subject of the Ukraine came up," Sessions recalled.[1139] Crossfire Hurricane would be now supervised by Deputy Attorney General Rod Rosenstein.

UKRAINE REFORMERS STRIKE AT THE NASIROV BACK CHANNEL

Poroshenko's opponents, the Ukrainian reformers, went straight for Poroshenko's hit point—the back channel to Trump In the midst of the peace frenzy, on February 8, the Special Anticorruption Prosecutor (SAP) received a notice of suspicion from NABU for Roman Nasirov.[1140] On the 14th, NABU officials met with Kholodnytsky, the head of the SAP. He required some changes, but on the 28th approved the arrest.[1141] But Nasirov was not immediately arrested. Instead, on March 1, he went to the Bankova to see President Poroshenko, where he discussed some matters with the president.[1142] Kholodnytsky suspected that Nasirov had been tipped off that NABU had a case against him.

On March 2, anti-corruption officials arrested Roman Nasirov for a $75 million embezzlement scheme.[1143] Sergii Leshchenko posted the news to Facebook as it was happening.[1144] Nasirov feigned sickness and went to the hospital as anti-corruption activists led protests at his home.[1145] They had directly targeted the one government official associated with the Poroshenko-Trump back channel just as the Ukrainian president was in negotiations to trade Crimea for the occupied east. Police had to present the notice of suspicion to him in his hospital room.[1146]

In coded language, Poroshenko's opponents then told the world that they were going after the Trump-Poroshenko backchannel. Pundits described the arrest described as the biggest anti-corruption case in Ukraine's history and according to one observer, it was "the most important development in Ukraine since the 2014 revolution."[1147] When those observations were published in the Washington Post on March 7, 2017, the Ukrainian reformers let Poroshenko and Washington, DC, insiders know that Mr. Nasirov could be motivated to reveal things.

While the Nasirov drama unfolded in Kyiv, Dale Armstrong reached out to journalists and others attempting to bring the peace plan to fruition. On March 7–10 he contacted five different journalists. Sources indicate he was pushing a peace plan for Ukraine.[1148]

It cannot be known for certain, but it appears that a combination of the pressure on Trump, the Russian insistence on a return to power in Donbas for Yanukovych, the revelation of the Artemenko peace plan caper, and the targeting of Nasirov by the Ukrainian reformers caused Poroshenko or Trump or both to back away from the peace plan. Regardless of the reason, Curt Weldon told others in March of 2017 that "[w]e were so close" on the peace plan.[1149] Ukraine began signaling no. First, on March 11, they took the issue of elections prior to Ukrainian control of the Donbas-Russia border off the table at the Trilateral Contact Group talks.[1150] Next, on March 14, Poroshenko seemingly put Yanukovych out contention to lead the east for good when Lutsenko charged former president Yanukovych with treason.[1151]

Having temporarily put the peace plan on hold, Poroshenko signaled he wanted to meet Trump before Putin did. In early March of 2017, a Poroshenko advisor, Konstiantyn Yeliseyev, told *Interfax Ukraine* that it was "fundamentally important" that Poroshenko obtain a bilateral meeting with Trump prior to the American president's first meeting with Vladimir Putin, scheduled for July 7–8.[1152] At the same time, on March 1, Monica Crowley followed up with Giuliani about a speaking engagement in Kyiv at the Victor Pinchuk Foundation.[1153] The speech was eventually given in June.

On March 31, Secretary of State Tillerson spoke at the NATO Foreign Ministerial in
Brussels. He gave the State Department's front channel message: "We do not, and will not, accept Russian efforts to change the borders of territory of Ukraine."[1154] Tillerson also spoke about the need for powerful anti-corruption efforts in Ukraine: "It serves no purpose for Ukraine to fight for

its body in Donbas if it loses its soul to corruption. Anti-corruption institutions must be supported, resourced, and defended."[1155]

On March 14, the SAP Nazar Kholodnytsky appeared on Ukrainian TV giving an interview to *Livyi Bereh*.[1156] He told the news site that he was ready to take the first case from the Black Ledger, that of Central Election Commission chair Okhendovsky, to court.[1157] He also told the site that the signature next to a bribe listed next to Okhendovsky's name was genuine.[1158] Sitting in the Special Anti-Corruption Prosecutor's office, on television, Kholodnytsky admitted the Black Ledger was real.

On March 20, 2017, FBI Director Comey testified in front of the House Permanent Select Committee on Intelligence.[1159] Comey revealed that the Trump campaign was under investigation to determine if it had engaged in a conspiracy to assist the Russians in their attempt to interfere in the presidential election.[1160] The information seemed to shock the committee's Republican chair, Devin Nunes of California.[1161] Late the next night, Nunes appeared at the National Security Council's offices in the Old Executive Office Building, where he met with NSC staffers Michael Ellis and Ezra Cohen-Watnick. The pair showed Nunes classified documents.[1162]

The next day, Nunes called a news conference where he told reporters that sources had provided evidence that US security services had monitored Trump's transition team.[1163] Within days, reporters had revealed that in fact, Nunes's "sources" were the two White House officials he had met with late on March 21.[1164] Nunes "recused" himself from the House Intelligence

Committee's Russian interference investigation, but curiously refused to delegate the subpoena power he held regarding the investigation, keeping him in the loop on the committee's subpoena issuances.[1165]

At some point, an FBI team began operating in Kyiv for Crossfire Hurricane, and eventually, Special Counsel Robert Mueller.[1166] Its leader was Supervisory Special Agent Karen Greenaway.[1167] Early in the year, Greenaway interviewed Sergii Leshchenko. The parliamentarian and investigative reporter gave her the contract involving alleged $750,000 in computer sales that he had found in Manafort's Kyiv office.[1168]

On April 10, two Associated Press reporters, seeking background information on an article they were going to publish regarding Manafort's finances, met with members of the FBI's Washington International Corruption Squad. They sought confirmation that the information they had about Manafort was accurate in preparation for an article to be published the next day.[1169] After the FBI confirmed the story about the financial information, the reporters asked them if they knew that Manafort had a storage unit in Alexandria.[1170] The agents had not known of it.

The Associated Press article ran on April 11 and confirmed the authenticity of the contract Leshchenko found for the $750,000 paid to Manafort for the computers.[1171] The reporters confirmed that the payment in the contract matched up with an entry in the Black Ledger.[1172] The story also detailed a second payment of $455,249, which they also confirmed was in the ledger.[1173]

In April, Tillerson met with Putin, whom he knew well.[1174] Tillerson explained to Putin that the election interference campaign and the taking of the Crimea and East Ukraine were obstacles to the better relationship between the US and Russia both wanted.[1175] Apparently, Putin was surprised and unhappy with Tillerson. By August, it would be reported that Putin said that Tillerson had "fallen in with bad company" and was a disappointment to Russia.[1176]

★ ★ ★

The Department of Defense call sign for the White House switchboard is ROYAL CROWN, and the switchboard is called that by many in the government.[1177] On the morning of May 3, 2017, FBI director James Comey received a telephone call from ROYAL CROWN at 8:13 a.m.[1178] That morning, Comey was scheduled to testify in front of the Senate Judiciary Committee regarding Crossfire Hurricane.[1179] In the conversation, Trump told the FBI director that he was under a "cloud" due to the Russia investigation and that could be in the way of him trying to "make deals for the country."[1180] The president did not explain what international deals were being thwarted by the investigation.

On May 9, CNN learned from sources that a grand jury in Alexandria in prior weeks had issued a series of subpoenas to associates of Michael Flynn.[1181] As they readied a story for air, President Trump sent an aide with a letter to FBI headquarters, firing James Comey, a project that had been in the works for some time.[1182]

"PREPARE A VISIT TO KHARKOV BY THE FORMER MAYOR OF NEW YORK, RUDY GIULIANI."

That same day, the back channel between Trump and Poroshenko opened wider. Rudy Giuliani, the former US attorney, mayor of New York City, and one-time GOP presidential candidate, provided security consulting worldwide through his firm Giuliani Safety and Security (GSS).[1183] His longtime associate, John Huvane was the CEO of GSS in 2017.[1184] On May 9 Huvane traveled to Kharkiv, Ukraine, to meet with Gennady Kernes, the mayor of Kharkiv and former member of the Party of Regions, known as a "mini-oligarch."[1185] Ostensibly, Huvane was there to negotiate a deal to provide a study on streamlining municipal emergency services.[1186] But the city of Kharkiv did not pay for the study. Instead, Pavel Fuks, a Ukrainian American oligarch footed GSS's bill for Kharkiv—another politically sensitive action paid for by an oligarch.[1187] The trip was a pathfinding one—Kharkiv's website stated that it was to "prepare a visit to Kharkov by the former Mayor of New York, Rudy Giuliani."[1188] But even before that visit to Kharkiv,[1189] Giuliani would arrive to give a speech in early June in Kyiv.

On May 10, in Washington Ukrainian foreign minister Klimkin and Russian foreign minister Lavrov met separately with Trump, who tweeted out the following day: "Yesterday, on the same day—I had meetings with

Russian Foreign Minister Sergei Lavrov and the Foreign Minister of Ukraine, Pavlo Klimkin. LET'S MAKE PEACE"[1190] The next day, Trump gave a disastrous interview with NBC's Lester Holt. In the interview, the president volunteered that the Comey firing was linked to the Russia investigation.[1191] The effect was a political firestorm. The president and his advisors tried to contain it.

Disinformation campaigns have casualties, and in the Trump administration's struggle of to get its footing after the firing of Comey, the family of Seth Rich became one of those casualties. In late 2016, a Fox News green room hanger-on named Ed Butowsky reached out to Seth Rich's family to offer help in getting justice for their son who was murdered on July 13, 2016, during what Washington, DC, police believed to be a botched robbery.[1192] Butowsky did not tell them of his Fox associations. In March 2017, Butowsky subtly upped the pressure and signed a contract with a private investigator in Washington, Rod Wheeler.[1193]

Butowsky wasted no time in calling in a Fox News reporter, Malia Zimmerman, who had a sensational story to file, if only it could be confirmed—that Seth Rich had given the DNC emails to WikiLeaks.[1194] The problem was the story was not true. That didn't deter Butowsky, who set out to make the story seem credible.

On May 10, Zimmerman claimed to have sources who would say Seth Rich may have been killed by a hit by Romanian hackers as revenge for selling the DNC emails to Wikileaks.[1195] Wheeler's job was to confirm this. On

May 14, Butowsky left a voice mail asking him to finish his investigation finding that Rich had given the DNC emails to WikiLeaks. "We have the full attention of the White House on this.... And tomorrow let's close this deal" he concluded.[1196] The next day, he texted Wheeler: "Not to add any more pressure but the president just read the article. He wants the article out immediately. It's now all up to you. But don't feel the pressure."[1197]

The pressure was ramping up on many people in Washington, DC, At 7:34 a.m. Deputy Attorney General Rosenstein called former FBI director Robert Mueller III at his law office and informed him he was thinking about appointing him special counsel in the Russia matter.[1198] On May 12, Deputy Attorney General Rosenstein pulled acting FBI director Andrew McCabe aside to discuss the Russia investigation.[1199] Rosenstein mentioned appointing a special counsel.[1200] That afternoon, McCabe advised Rosenstein to go ahead and appoint a special counsel pursuant to Department of Justice regulations.[1201] After discussions with others, McCabe opened investigations of Trump's relationship with Russia and whether or not the president was obstructing justice.[1202]

In the early hours of May 16, as Mueller's appointment was being finalized, Zimmerman told her bosses at Fox that she would publish her sensational story early the next morning.[1203] She was scooped by her own local affiliate and her source, Rod Wheeler.[1204] Within minutes of the story going live on the Fox News website, *Fox and Friends* announced the story. The Riches, devastated, denied it.[1205] The story fell apart as law enforcement sources denied it all to national outlets. For a week, Sean Hannity pounded the story as it collapsed around him, until, on the 23rd, Fox News retracted it.[1206]

But perhaps it had already served a purpose to distract from the appointment of a Special Counsel. On May 17, the investigation of President Trump became public knowledge. Rosenstein appointed FBI director Robert Mueller to be Special Counsel to the Justice Department to investigate the Russian campaign of interference in the 2016 election.[1207]

★ ★ ★

While Washington boiled with scandal, the first of two unusual videos appeared on Google's video service in mid-May on a channel named "Storozh."[1208] With all the trappings of an insinuation campaign devised by Russian media wizard Vladislav Surkov, an unnamed narrator with an unusual accent, in front of a projected background, played the role of a news announcer for "International News Live."[1209] The "announcer" then informed the viewer that:

> Authorities Sunday announced they've made progress in an investigation into AntAC, the Anticorruption Action Center, led by [Ukrainian activist] Daria Kaleniuk. The long-time activists have been under investigation for over a year regarding a two-million-dollar grant allocated for reforms in the Prosecutor General's Office, PGO, but that the office never received.[1210]

The news reader then went on to mention the fact that the funds came from the "United States Embassy."[1211] An alternate explanation floated was that it was the anticorruption groups who were corrupt, not the billionaire oligarchs.

Within days, a second video appeared, this time with an American "announcer" named "Michael-John Wolfe" alleging, "In our next story, authorities Sunday confirmed they've made progress into an investigation into the finances of anticorruption activist Vitaly Shabunin, whose organization received hundreds of thousands of dollars from the United States for government reforms."[1212] The video then insinuated that Shabunin's purchase of a house and a car for $150,000 were illegally obtained.[1213]

The origin of these videos would remain a mystery for two years. In 2019 an investigative journalist linked the videos to Psy-GROUP, an infamous Israeli firm run by a GOP-connected Australian Israeli man, Joel Zamel.[1214] The journalist, *Forensic News*'s Scott Steadman, reviewing court documents regarding Psy-GROUP's involvement in a Canadian business dispute, reported that Psy-GROUP ran the 2017 campaign to discredit Kaleniuk and Shabunin.[1215] A woman named Maja Bogovic in Zagreb, Croatia, had been contacted on May 9, 2017, via a gigging website and tasked by a Psy-GROUP associate to hire the actors, including the announcer of the Shabunin clip, John-Michael Steele.[1216] Petro Poroshenko had struck back against the Ukrainian reformers who derailed his peace plan.

On May 26, an FBI agent of one of the International Corruption Squads met with an employee of one of the many corporations that Manafort controlled about the storage locker the Associated Press had found.[1217] Unfortunately, for Manafort, his employee had used his own name on the storage unit, not Paul Manafort's or the corporation's. The employee agreed to let them look inside. The FBI found documents regarding Manafort's finances.[1218]

CHAPTER 5:

"SOMEBODY GAVE AN ORDER TO BURY THE BLACK LEDGER"

Petro Poroshenko faced a dilemma. The expanding Mueller investigation, and months of reporting, indicated that Putin had influence over Trump in ways that Poroshenko was quite familiar with. The Ukrainian president needed some influence of his own. Through Victor Pinchuk's lobbying efforts, Rudy Giuliani was coming to Kyiv for a speech. Poroshenko aimed to make the most of it.

"WHAT'S HOLDING YOU BACK IS CORRUPTION"

Giuliani was scheduled to speak in front of the Victor Pinchuk Foundation on June 7, 2017. In Kyiv, Giuliani gave remarks that would later seem more than a bit ironic, calling on Ukraine to "protect people and laws that are applied honestly and without corruption," adding, "I think what is holding you back is corruption. It has to be rooted out of your society" and that "to have a rule of law means to have honest police, honest prosecutors, honest judges, and honest political leaders."[1219] While there, Giuliani met with multiple Ukrainian officials: Poroshenko, Lutsenko, Klitschko, Foreign Minister Pavlo Klimkin, and the Prime Minister Volodymyr Groysman.[1220] After the speech was a dinner, attended by Ambassador Yovanovitch.[1221]

Two days after the speech, on June 9, 2017, the Specialized Anti-Corruption Prosecutor (SAP), Nazar Kholodnytsky, announced that he was suddenly dropping the Black Ledger cases.[1222] According to Viktor Trepak, the former deputy head of the Security Service of Ukraine who had turned the Black Ledger over to NABU in 2016, "[t]he fact that the black ledger case was passed to the Prosecutor General's Office means it will from now on be under political control."[1223] He added: "[i]t is clear for me that somebody gave an order to bury the Black Ledger, which I consider the most important high-profile corruption case in Ukraine."[1224]

Lutsenko handed the cases to Serhii Horbatiuk, head of Special Investigations at the General Prosecutor's Office. Events began to move rapidly. Five days after Kholodnytsky dropped the Black Ledger cases, Poroshenko got his Washington meeting. It was announced for only six days later, on June 20th.[1225] In eleven days, Poroshenko had turned the situation to his advantage.

In fact, Kholodnytsky kept one case open, the case against Central Election Commission head Mykhailo Okhendovsky.[1226] He suspended that case and left the remainder for NABU and Serhii Horbatiuk.[1227] Curiously, Poroshenko had left *all* of the members of the Central Election Commission from the Yanukovych era in place.[1228] With the charge hanging over the head of the commission's chair, Poroshenko had the commission in the palm of his hand. Okhendovsky sent his lawyers to court to remove this impediment. It would be almost a year until the case was decided.[1229]

"AIN'T BRAGGING IF YOU CAN DO IT"

During the Poroshenko visit on June 20, 2017, the Ukrainian president brought Trump political goods to trade. The trade was worked out in three bilateral meetings. In Washington, Poroshenko was first to meet with Secretary of Energy Perry and his closest aide, former Trump battleground states director Wells Griffith. Later, Poroshenko was to meet with Trump in the Oval Office. In Pittsburgh, Oleg Kozemko, CEO of the Ukraine state coal power Centrenergo, met with coal producers in Pittsburgh.

Perry and the Ukrainians specifically discussed a coal deal between Ukraine and the United States.[1230] Commerce Secretary Ross and Vice President Pence were also involved in the meetings with Ross credited with helping to negotiate a deal with Centrenergo—Pennsylvania coal would go to Ukraine.[1231]

From there, Poroshenko went to the White House.[1232] According to Trump's statements to press that day, the discussions went on all day and were very productive.[1233] A Russian account quoted a source close to the Poroshenko administration regarding the negotiations: "Since Trump is a businessman, we are taking a business approach. The essence of our proposals is that 90% of all contracts for the restoration of the destroyed Donbass [sic] infrastructure will go to American firms."[1234] Poroshenko's appearance in the Oval Office next to the president fulfilled his aim of letting his own electorate know that he was on the job.[1235] Vice President Pence also attended.[1236] Poroshenko's chief foreign policy aide told the *New York Times*, "It was a deal that pleased Trump . . . He had promised work for Pennsylvania coal miners. It was a win-win situation."[1237]

At its core, the coal deal offered something else—a cover story. If anyone ever accused Trump of using the Javelin missiles to control the outcome of the Black Ledger or obtain a Crimea-for-Donbas peace, the energy sales would provide an alternate explanation.

Trump aides gave a different account to the *Wall Street Journal*, stating that Trump told his advisors he wanted Ukraine to buy coal from the US. According to sources close to the White House, a Trump aide suggested that Poroshenko buy Pennsylvania coal.[1238]

While Poroshenko met Trump, Oleg Kozemko, the head of the Ukrainian state-owned coal company Centrenergo met with coal producers and representatives of elected GOP officials in the offices of Reed Smith, a

Pittsburgh law firm. The Reed Smith announcement stated that the "Centrenergo visit coincided with the Ukrainian president's meeting with President Trump and the Secretary of the US Department of Commerce, who also discussed coal exports."[1239] Attendees in Pittsburgh included coal company owners and coal pollution mitigation firms, as well as staffers for several GOP members of Congress including from the offices of Senator Pat Toomey, Congressman Glenn "GT" Thompson, and Congressman Keith Rothfus, all of Pennsylvania.[1240]

Kozemko left the meeting stating: "I want to thank Reed Smith for organizing the meeting and connecting us with the resources which would resolve our long-enduring coal supply issues. We can now import coal with confidence."[1241] A coal deal was in the works. The terms would emerge in July.

But coal and construction were not the only goodies on offer from Poroshenko. Days after returning from Washington, in an appearance on Ukrainian TV, Poroshenko announced that going forward, 55 percent of Ukraine's nuclear fuel would be bought from Westinghouse, a US company based in Butler County, Pennsylvania, that had begun selling nuclear fuel and equipment to Ukraine.[1242] Trump considered Pennsylvania critical to his 2020 prospects.

The same day, Trump told the "Unleashing American Energy" crowd regarding coal exports that "Ukraine already tells us they need millions and millions of metric tons right now."[1243] He singled out Energy Secretary Rick

Perry for his efforts: "I especially want to thank Secretary Perry for his tremendous leadership in this department. He has really done a terrific job . . . And if you don't say it, I don't know. You got to say it, right? And you're doing it right now with energy."[1244]

Perry responded: "Ain't bragging if you can do it."[1245]

"DECLARE A PUBLIC RELATIONS WAR ON THE FBI"

Beginning in spring 2017, Trump assembled his team to defend him politically and legally. The team was led by Don McGahn, the White House counsel, and starting in June it included John Dowd, an attorney known for his handling of the Pete Rose gambling report for Major League Baseball.[1246] There was one advisor that the president kept silent about: Paul Manafort Jr. Manafort entered into a joint defense agreement with Trump and the other potential defendants, allowing them to share information while keeping it from prosecutors.[1247]

From this perch, Paul Manafort began constructing the alternate explanation for the facts, linking himself and Trump to the Russian efforts by establishing the three overarching themes of Trump administration's messaging response to the Mueller investigation, and by extension the response of the Republican Party. These themes all relied on the politics of disinformation, which has dominated American politics since, up to this writing in August 2020.

Manafort maintained a steady backchannel to the White House throughout 2017 and 2018. Starting in Spring 2017, Manafort, via an intermediary, instructed the President and senior White House officials to discredit the investigation, the investigators and the witnesses.[1248] First, he advised the President to attack the FBI itself. The plan was to "declare a public relations war on the FBI," in order to delegitimize it.[1249] The president did exactly that. Starting on February 15, Trump continually attacked the FBI on Twitter. During his presidency, Trump has tweeted more than 300 attacks on the bureau.

Manafort also advised Trump to specifically discredit former FBI director James Comey.[1250] Since taking office, the president has attacked James Comey nearly 200 times on Twitter. Manafort also advised attacking Mueller. That would wait. Starting in December 2017, the president began attacking the Special Counsel in tweets. However, he soon made up for lost time, attacking Mueller over 280 times in the following three years.

Manafort also advised the White House and the president to attack the FBI's use of Foreign Intelligence Surveillance Court warrants to surveil Carter Page in the initial part of the investigation.[1251] In March 2017, Trump set off the FISA-theme of his defense by claiming his phone was "tapped" by Obama.[1252] Since the beginning of his presidency, Trump tweeted over 100 times regarding being supposedly surveilled by FISA. This attack was aimed at the counterintelligence investigation of the Trump administration.

Finally, Manafort advised the president and the White House to attack the DNC. This effort started even before Trump was inaugurated. The purpose was to create a false equivalence between the massive election interference campaign of the Russians and the confirmation of Manafort's name in the Black Ledger provided by NABU, Ukraine's National Anti-Corruption Bureau.

The White House followed the attack recommendation to the letter. On July 10, Trump's Press Secretary, Sarah Huckabee Sanders, told reporters:

> Frankly, I think something that may make sense is looking at the Democrat National Committee coordinated opposition research directly with the Ukrainian Embassy. This is not an accusation. That's an on-the-record action that they took. So if you're looking for an example of a campaign coordinating with a foreign country or a foreign source, look no further than the DNC, who actually coordinated opposition research with the Ukrainian Embassy. And no one in this room, to my knowledge, really had a big problem with that.[1253][1254]

The president's lawyers echoed Sanders's sentiments. Jay Sekulow, appearing on CNN to defuse the revelation of the Trump Tower meeting with the Russians, trotted out the claim that Ukraine did the same thing that Russia did:

> And campaigns involve opposition research, and the situation exchange that was released by Donald Trump Jr., and what was described there is—is—look at it and compare it to, for

instance, the situation with the Ukrainians and the DNC and the Clinton campaign, where information actually was shared.[1255]

As if on cue, Russian disinformation emerged about the election interference. Several pro-Russian blogs began claiming that Ukraine, not Russia had interfered in the 2016 election.[1256] An Internet Research Agency-controlled Twitter account, @usa_gunslinger, began advancing the theory in mid-July.[1257]

Republican lawmakers joined the chorus. On July 24, Senator Charles Grassley publicized a letter he had written to Rod Rosenstein, asking him to investigate Alexandra Chalupa and the theory that Ukraine had interfered in the US election.[1258]

In Ukraine, pro-Russian member of the Rada Andriy Derkach,[1259] a former founding member of the People's Will Party began pushing a similar line in Ukraine. On July 24, Derkach wrote to Prosecutor General Lutsenko, asking that he open an investigation into "illegal interference in the election of President of the United States organized by a criminal organization."[1260] That organization, he claimed, was NABU.[1261] The next day, President Trump, remarkably well-informed about Derkach, tweeted: "Ukrainian efforts to sabotage Trump campaign—'quietly working to boost Clinton.' So where is the investigation A.G." and tagged Fox News host Sean Hannity.[1262] On August 2, Poroshenko's prosecutor general opened an investigation against NABU for pretrial disclosure of information from the Black Ledger investigation.[1263] Since the Giuliani meeting in June, the Poroshenko administration had provided Donald Trump with specific political favors he wanted.

On July 25, 2017, as the attacks on the Mueller Investigation began, Paul Manafort met with investigators for the Senate Select Committee on Intelligence to provide evidence for their Russia investigation.[1264] Later the same day the FBI knocked at the door of Manafort's Alexandria, Virginia, home. They had a warrant to search the premises.[1265] The press would not learn until early August that the raid had taken place.

Two days later, George Papadopoulos landed around 7 p.m. at Dulles Airport in suburban Washington, DC, arriving on a flight from Munich.[1266] Two men approached him and identified themselves as FBI agents, and escorted him to the US Customs and Border Protection area in the International Terminal.[1267] FBI agents informed Papadopoulos that he was being arrested for making false statements in his January 27, 2017, interview in Chicago.[1268] The agents read him his rights and informed him that the Special Counsel's office was attempting to contact his lawyer about the arrest.[1269] Altogether, nine FBI agents went to arrest Papadopoulos.

Papadopoulos stated to the agents that he did not understand why *he* was in this situation and Flynn and Manafort were not.[1270] He said he wanted to cooperate with the FBI.[1271] After a brief phone call with his lawyer, Papadopoulos expressed concern that he was just a small fish but was going to look like the fall guy.[1272]

As the president's defense team sought additional lawyers to deal with the four investigations swirling around the president, Trump told McGahn that he liked a defender of his who often appeared on CNN to attack the Russia investigation, an Iowa lawyer named Matthew Whittaker who had served as the US attorney for the Southern District of Iowa during the George W. Bush administration and later was the sole employee of FACT, the Foundation for Accountability and Trust, a dark-money group that did not have to disclose its donors.[1273] FACT existed to bring ethics and other charges against liberals and Democrats.[1274]

On July 31, McGahn brought Whittaker in to see if he would be interested in joining the president's team. Whittaker did not get the job, but McGahn and another lawyer prompted him to bring an FEC complaint against Chalupa and the DNC to provide cover for Trump.[1275] At a second meeting, Whittaker inquired further about how to coordinate with Trump's team.[1276] By the fall, Whittaker would be the deputy attorney general.[1277] Trump began laying out the lines of attack that he would use all the way up to the election of 2020.

KURT VOLKER GETS BACK IN THE GAME

The Trump administration immediately set about securing the coal deal. First, Trump assigned someone with whom the Ukrainians already had a relationship to lead all negotiations regarding Ukraine: BGR's Kurt Volker.[1278] [1279] Ukraine announced on July 5 that negotiations were ongoing between

Centrenergo and the United States.[1280] On July 14, representatives of Centrenergo and XCoal, a coal export marketing company, signed a deal for coal at $113 per metric ton.[1281]

Less than two weeks later, the full contours of the deal began to emerge. On July 31, as Volker announced that the United States was considering sending Javelin missiles to Ukraine on Radio Free Europe's Russian channel *Current Time*,[1282] the coal deal was announced by US chargé d'affaires George Kent at the US Embassy in Kyiv with Ernie Thrasher, XCoal CEO, looking on.[1283] Also on July 31, citing "US officials," the *Wall Street Journal* reported that the US had devised a plan to send Javelin missiles to Ukraine.[1284] The timing transparently linked the coal deal with the missiles.

"THE MOTHER OF ALL FAKE NEWS"

While Poroshenko was trying to get support for his version of peace with Russia, he was also trying to cut the international funding of the Ukrainian reformers who opposed the deal. In February, the Trump administration had asked for $41.7 billion for the entire foreign aid budget.[1285] This constituted a 40 percent drop, according to some accounts.[1286] The administration's Ukraine aid request included a cut from $460 million to $203 million.[1287]

Poroshenko also reached out to K Street for help. He apparently sought a bill stripping the reformers of funding that would be signed if it crossed Trump's desk. He started in late in 2016. In December, an NGO, the International Agency for Regional Development (Globee), hired Mercury

Strategies, home of lobbyist Vin Weber.[1288] The Globee organization was associated with Ihor Ranin.[1289] Rainin was the new head of the presidential administration.[1290] The purpose of the Mercury registration was listed as "Services related to Deputy Minister visit" indicating that in fact, the International Agency for Regional Development was a proxy for the government of Ukraine.[1291] This was a typical arrangement for Weber's Ukrainian work, as in 2019 he would resign from Mercury for representing a front organization for the Yanukovych government.[1292]

The result of the K Street hires appeared in the summer of 2017. No later than June 4, 2017, a website representing a new NGO appeared.[1293] Named the National Interest of Ukraine, it made its purpose obvious—to advance the alternate explanation that the anticorruption activists were the corrupt ones:

> Welcome to "National interest of Ukraine" Public Organization's website! "National interest of Ukraine" Public Organization is a [sic] association of people which can see and understand that stormy activities to reform the country often are imitation. Corruption [sic] swallowed up our country completely but fight against corruption conducts only on paper and in pseudo-fighteres's [sic] stories. In actual fact.[1294]

In fact, the group was associated with a political party, the People's Front, which at the time was in a coalition with Petro Poroshenko's party.[1295] It was the same party that Oleksandr Onyshchenko had represented in the Rada prior to his flight abroad. The NGO's chairman, Vasyl Apasov, was a member of the People's Front, which was also often allied with the Opposition Bloc.[1296]

On May 23, 2017, People's Front MP Pavlo Pyzenyk presented a "study" issued by the "National Interest of Ukraine" in the Rada, alleging that AntAC was involved in corruption.[1297] The material was passed on to the State Fiscal Service and they duly opened an investigation.[1298]

The move appears to have been a predicate for Weber to move in the United States against AntAC funding. On July 15, Mercury Executive VP Adam Ereli also advanced the alternate explanation in an op-ed for Fox News: "Corrupt Ukraine is Ground Zero in Clash between East and West, US and Russia."[1299] Ereli's claims echoed the mysterious Psy-Group videos from earlier in May:

> The senior leadership of Ukraine's Anti-Corruption Action Center, which has received significant funding support from the US government, has profited from sweetheart deals and kickbacks. Its Director, Vitaly Shabunin, earns $34,000 according to his tax filing. In 2010, he bought an apartment for $60,000. In 2014, he acquired land near Kiev for $20,000. In 2016, he sold his apartment for $34,000 and built a house for $83,000. All properties are registered in his wife's name and there are no mortgages on the properties.[1300]

Ereli also claimed there was corruption surrounding Dragon Capital, an investment fund partially owned by anti-corruption funder George Soros.[1301]

A second lobbyist had more opaque clients. His name was Connie Mack IV, a former GOP congressman from Florida. In early 2017, Mack registered to lobby for an "Interconnections Commerce S.A." for the purposes of increasing awareness of "corruption within the National Bank of Ukraine."[1302]

Mack's first steps did not overtly involve anticorruption. Instead, he lobbied the vice president's National Security Advisor to get Fiona Hill removed as Trump's main Russia hand for alleged connections to George Soros.[1303] On May 31, 2017, Roger Stone went on InfoWars and named Hill an agent of George Soros.[1304] Soon thereafter, Hill began to receive death threats.[1305] Soros Open Society Foundation was a large funder of anticorruption initiatives in Ukraine.[1306]

On September 25, 2017, viewers of Ukraine's NewsOne channel were treated to a tease for an unusual program:

> The highest levels of corruption in the NBU are known by the US Congressional Committee on Financial Issues. Only thanks to the systematic work of the team that collected evidence of corruption of the most important officials of the National Bank, the strongest of the world will find out about it. Shocking details and resonant details—live streaming on NewsOne! Turn on at 21:00—live from Washington DC.[1307]

It was, as one reporter put it, "the mother of all fake news."[1308] Mack, wearing his Member's pin, conducted a fake hearing in front of the Ukrainian TV cameras to publicize a report attacking the former head of the Ukrainian

Central Bank who had allowed the Ukrainian currency to float freely in response to IMF demands.[1309] When asked to respond as to why Mack was doing the "hearing," Mack dodged the question and attacked anti-corruption funding in Ukraine.

> We have an obligation, to both US taxpayers and our international allies, to ensure that such corruption is rooted out at the source and the individuals are punished in accordance with the rule of law. I hope for this discussion to serve as the initial step in the process of eliminating such damaging corruption. Together, we will engage in an informed discourse to examine the perils of kleptocracy, reforming the International Monetary Fund, and how to best ensure that US foreign assistance is being used to help our allies, not fatten the wallets of corrupt government officials.[1310]

It was the opening shot in a battle to rob the Ukrainian reformers of their power to disrupt agreements between the Trump administration and Poroshenko.

ROBERT WALDECK

CHAPTER 6:

"A STORY THAT IS PRETTY UNTOLD"

The summer efforts for a missile deal were the prelude for a big decision by Petro Poroshenko. In "August or September 2017" he "decided to completely end cooperation with the US agencies investigating Manafort."[1311] From September 2017 to May 2018 Poroshenko, Trump, and Putin tried to lay the groundwork for a peace that would happen in the summer of 2018, once the plan's opponents, the Ukrainian reformers and the US State Department, could be neutralized. First, the Ukrainian reformers would need to be neutralized. Next, the fears of a complete Russian takeover of Ukraine would have to be quelled by lethal US military assistance.

As Poroshenko was due to arrive in New York for the September UN General Assembly meetings, it became clear that Robert Mueller was not going to go away. That day's *New York Times* ran a story indicating that

Mueller was playing hardball. The *Times* wrote that "team has used what some describe as shock-and-awe tactics to intimidate" witnesses.[1312] Manafort's lawyers were told that Mueller intended to indict him.[1313]

Prior to the UN meeting with Trump, Poroshenko realized he needed more help in Washington. Naftogaz, the gigantic state gas company majority owned by the Ukrainian government, signed a new lobbyist, Daniel Vajdich, Ted Cruz's former foreign policy advisor. He headed Yorktown Solutions, LLC, a firm providing representation to foreign entities in the United States.[1314] Vajdich's Foreign Agents Representation Act filings listed the scope of the representation as providing:

> government affairs services to the foreign principal for the purposes of supporting full integration of the Ukrainian gas market with the energy market of the European Union, implementation of gas market reform in Ukraine, and attracting foreign investments to the Ukrainian oil and gas market.[1315]

But Vajdich began making high-level political contacts on behalf of his client almost immediately, indicating he was acting on behalf of the Poroshenko administration. In the days leading up to and following the Poroshenko-Trump summit, he reached out to key White House and State Department personnel, including Fiona Hill and Rex Tillerson's senior policy advisor, Brian Hook. He also contacted key opinion leaders in the area, including Anders Aslund and David Koryani of the Atlantic Council.[1316]

Trump met with Poroshenko on the sidelines of the UN three days after a story alleging that Manafort might soon be arrested was published.[1317]

Manafort's name did not appear on any written agenda. At the meeting, held at the Lotte New York Palace Hotel, Trump gave a cryptic description of the US-Ukraine relationship: "We spent some time recently in the White House, and I know you've made good progress since then—a lot of progress, actually."[1318] Poroshenko then noted the progress the two countries had made since their last meeting and referred to the fact that more American companies were doing business in Ukraine.[1319] Trump responded that the cooperation was an "a story that is pretty untold, but I think you'll see it more and more."[1320] The story would remain untold for three years.

To defeat the Ukrainian reformers, Poroshenko would have to remove the weapon they deployed in March to stymie the peace—NABU. Ukraine was corrupt. Those who opposed Poroshenko's foreign policy could obtain leverage on anyone from whom Poroshenko got help to complete his peace deal. Politically unpopular foreign negotiations required money that must not be traced, and intermediaries were often used whose skill sets meant that they were targets of criminal investigators. Poroshenko moved in the fall of 2017 to gut the entire anti-corruption system that American taxpayers had spent millions to help construct at his request. Neither the reformers nor the US State Department would stand idly by as that happened.

Poroshenko now made a series of moves to destroy the prosecutorial weapons in the hands of the Ukrainian reformers. Over the next three months, Poroshenko introduced through allies a series of three legislative initiatives to limit the ability of the Ukrainian justice system to prosecute corruption. Each one of the three would not only put the Black Ledger cases beyond prosecution and presumably, officially end any pressure to share information with Robert Mueller, but also halt NABU's ability to interfere with his peace plans. Ambassador Yovanovitch would play a large role in the successful fight to stop them. But it was Robert Mueller who put the most powerful weapon in the hands of Ukrainian reformers.

First, Lutsenko took personal charge of matters involving Konstantin Kilimnik and quietly but formally investigated him for being a Russian agent, starting in August of 2017.[1321] The investigation was closed in December without charges being pressed.[1322] The closure would give the government more latitude if need be to do as it wished with Kilimnik.

The effort to take NABU's power to indict out of the hands of the Ukrainian reformers began with modifications to the Criminal Code. The Petro Poroshenko Bloc sought to change the criminal law to reduce the amount of time prosecutors had to bring cases. As the Black Ledger was discovered in early 2014, but had not produced cases brought to court yet, the changes to the law would make the Black Ledger cases impossible to prosecute.

The legislative vehicle to shorten the time limits was a large omnibus measure known as Bill 6232. It was designed to amend multiple sections of Ukraine's Economic, Civil, and Administrative Code and contained the provisions establishing a Ukraine's new Supreme Court.[1323] Bill 6232 was therefore a must-pass measure, tailor-made for controversial amendments.[1324]

The amendment was introduced by the second-in-command of the Radical Party, MP Andriy Lozovy. He proposed an amendment to Bill 6232 that would start the clock for prosecutors to complete investigations at the moment the case file was opened, rather than at the point in time where the suspect was warned they were under suspicion.[1325] Prosecutors would have only six months to charge suspects under this statutory scheme, meaning that the years-old charges against Nasirov in March would also be prohibited from ever being filed.[1326] The changes were slated to be retroactive, not only paralyzing the Black Ledger and Maidan cases, which had taken several years to reach NABU, but any older corruption case the agency could try. It would instantly prevent the Ukrainian reformers from using any criminal case older than six months to defeat a future peace plan.

The Lozovy edits especially threatened a new development—for the first time Horbatiuk was able to charge crimes in the Maidan cases to senior government officials still serving in government on September 29.[1327] Flashy graphics provided to the court and displayed on television showed dozens of calls between the conspirators the night before snipers fired into the crowd on the Maidan.[1328]

The reformers responded on October 3, successfully passing an amendment in committee stripping the Lozovy edits from the final version of Bill 6232.[1329] But on October 3, 2017, when Bill 6232 was passed by the whole Rada the Lozovy edits were reported out intact in the version sent to the president.[1330] AntAC activists revealed that two texts of the law existed, one which removed the Lozovy edits and one that did not.[1331] Activists waited to see what language the bill Poroshenko signed contained.

The next day, NABU issued a press release asking that President Poroshenko veto Bill 6232 because it threatened complex corruption cases.[1332] The bill remained on Poroshenko's desk leading into the week of November 13, 2017.

During the fall sessions, the law granting the rebel-held areas of Eastern Ukraine special status was due to expire. On October 6, 229 deputies voted and passed the renewal of the law, which would grant amnesty to many separatist fighters if Russia withdrew and Ukraine was to regain its eastern border with Russia.[1333] Poroshenko signed it the next day.[1334]

The second battle in the fall involved reform of Lutsenko's Prosecutor General's Office. Porohsenko's 2014 Anti-Corruption Package set up a transfer of all investigative functions from the Prosecutor General's Office to other organs, to end the use of criminal justice for political aims.[1335] Under the reform, on November 20, 2017, all cases were to be transferred to a new agency, the State Investigative Bureau.[1336]

However, by late September 2017, the Rada had, rather purposefully, not passed a law in the intervening two years to actually set up the State Investigative Bureau of Ukraine as called for in the 2014 Anti-Corruption Package.[1337] This meant that if the deadline to transfer the cases was not changed, NABU's 200 detectives would be saddled with 3,500 cases.[1338] It would be hard for Sytnyk and NABU to charge anyone in such a situation. All corruption cases would essentially end.[1339] It would prevent another situation where prosecutions could reveal the Poroshenko-Trump back channel. It would also protect Poroshenko's political interest in protecting his opponents' myriad business interests.

As these efforts to push back on the anti-corruption agencies continued, an unusual lawsuit was filed in the Kyiv District Administrative Court in late October. An MP, Boryslav Rozenblat, filed a complaint seeking a decision holding that Sergii Leshchenko and Artem Sytnyk had violated Ukrainian law by publicizing the Black Ledger in August 2016.[1340] The suit accused the pair of interfering in the US presidential election.

MOCKINGBIRD 10.30.17

Perhaps by luck, perhaps not, Robert Mueller handed the Ukrainian reformers a weapon in their hour of need. On October 27, Mueller indicted Manafort and his deputy, Richard W. Gates.[1341] The pair faced twelve felony counts based on their work in Ukraine: conspiracy to launder money, conspiracy against the United States, being an unregistered agent of a foreign principal, false and misleading FARA statements, among other charges.[1342]

One day after the indictment was filed, but before it was unsealed, an anonymous user on the imageboard 4chan made a cryptic post:

> HRC extradition already in motion effective yesterday with several countries in case of cross border run. Passport approved to be flagged effective 10/30 @ 12:01am. Expect massive riots organized in defiance and others fleeing the US to occur. US M's will conduct the operation while NG activated. Proof check: Locate a NG member and ask if activated for duty 10/30 across most major cities.[1343]

The claims were nonsense. 4chan had been so important to the Trump campaign in 2016 that it had its own people search out the site for meme images that could be used by the candidate.[1344] Later that day, the anonymous poster returned with a long post which was just a string of references. They opened with the word "Mockingbird." At the bottom of the string of references was written "Mockingbird 10.30.2017."[1345] These cryptic postings would continue and soon garner millions of views. It was the beginning of QAnon, a disinformation network of Americans who truly believed in the conspiracy theories they spread on behalf of Trump. It alleged a counternarrative that involved Special Counsel Mueller using the cover of the Russia investigation to arrest prominent Democrats.

Two days after the cryptic posts, on October 30, Mueller unsealed the Manafort and Gates indictment, as well as the indictment and guilty plea of George Papadopoulos.[1346] The Trump team had predicted an end to the investigation by summer. It was actually just getting started.

Reformers in Ukraine were ecstatic. "I'm happy that he has been caught, and I'm happy the profile of this case is so high," said Daria Kaleniuk of AntAC.[1347] Anticorruption activists hoped that the Manafort case could "shine light on this side, too"[1348] The Ukrainian reformers promptly moved on Poroshenko's jurisdictional hole. On Nov. 10, 2017, they introduced Bill 7278, giving jurisdiction back to prosecutors no later than January 1, 2018.[1349]

But it was Serhii Horbatiuk who used the weapon Mueller provided. The prosecutor began granting interviews regarding the Manafort indictment, raising the specter of US and Ukrainian pressure to investigate the Black Ledger. He started in late October, first giving an interview to a Ukrainian radio program stating that he had two Manafort-related matters under investigation.[1350] Two days later, he seemed to threaten the burgeoning thaw between Trump and Ukraine. Horbatiuk told another radio show that he was preparing two more information requests for US prosecutors and stated that the indictments fit within the scope of his investigation.[1351]

But Horbatiuk wasn't done. On November 7, in what was perhaps the most consequential act of the anti-corruption struggle in Ukraine, he spoke with *Politico* in the US. Horbatiuk gave a detailed description of the Black Ledger and linked the Skadden report to the Mueller investigation in a 1,500-word article.[1352] The prosecutor proceeded to tell all of Washington that he intended to contact the Justice Department and request information from them regarding Manafort's actions in Ukraine. The outside world scarcely noticed, but there can be no doubt that the White House and the president's criminal defense team did.

Trump could not contain himself. On November 11, 2017, Trump alluded to the now-endangered peace plan in a tweet: "When will all the haters and fools out there realize that having a good relationship with Russia is a good thing, not a bad thing. There always playing politics - bad for our country. I want to solve North Korea, Syria, Ukraine, terrorism, and Russia can greatly help!"[1353] The next day, the peace plan apparently remained on his mind when he tweeted: "Does the Fake News Media remember when Crooked Hillary Clinton, as Secretary of State, was begging Russia to be our friend with the misspelled reset button? Obama tried also, but he had zero chemistry with Putin."[1354]

At the same time, NABU struck back with the weapon it had—investigations. On November 17, NABU announced that it had opened a criminal investigation of Prosecutor General Yuriy Lutsenko on October 30, alleging unlawful enrichment.[1355] That same day, Lutsenko struck back, opening an investigation of Sytnyk, the head of NABU, alleging a wiretap disclosed that Sytnyk may have illegally disclosed the contents of another wiretap over the telephone to an unauthorized party.[1356]

"IT IS NOT THEIR BRIEF TO HAVE AN OPINION ON THE NATIONAL SECURITY OR FOREIGN POLICY"

Someone in the United States reacted to these events as Giuliani was sent into this conflagration. On November 19, 2017, he arrived in Kharkiv for "meetings' with Gennady Kernes, where news photographs showed him exiting the private jet of oligarch Alexander Rovt as he greeted the Kharkiv mayor.[1357] The next day, Giuliani met with former professional boxer, "Dr. Ironfist" himself, Kyiv mayor Klitschko.[1358] He then met with Poroshenko. Poroshenko's press release stated that Giuliani met with the Ukrainian president and Prime Minister Groysman.[1359] John Huvane reached out to Ambassador Yovanovitch and invited her to meet with Giuliani when he was in Ukraine.[1360] With Mr. Giuliani and Mr. Huvane was Pavel Fuks, the oligarch who paid for Giuliani's services to Kernes's government in Kharkiv.[1361]

The Ukrainian government noted that it considered Giuliani's visit to be "as a friend of Trump."[1362] The press release included staged photos of a diplomatic-style setting, with the parties sitting on opposite sides of a table with name cards for the participants.[1363] The president stated that the "parties discussed ways to overcome Russian aggression against Ukraine," a seeming reference to the Javelins.[1364] Giuliani was thanked for his "strong and reliable support of Ukraine's sovereignty, territorial integrity and independence" and in a small sop to the cover of his semi-official role as a cyber security advisor, Poroshenko also noted the "special importance of Ukraine-USA cooperation in cyber security sphere."[1365]

Giuliani would later claim the meeting was for him to obtain Poroshenko's approval for his consulting contact in Kharkiv. However, no mention was made of the consulting aspect of the visit on the Ukrainian president's website.[1366] What was discussed at the table has not been revealed by prosecutors, Giuliani, or Poroshenko. But events moved quickly from there.

As Giuliani visited Kyiv, the situation came to a head. First, Bill 7278 failed to make it on the agenda on November 16, 2017.[1367] The Rada, controlled by skittish Poroshenko allies, had temporarily prevented the jurisdictional hole from closing.[1368] As of November 20, 2017, no agency held jurisdiction over the cases.[1369] But the pressure put on Poroshenko was too great. On December 15, 2017, the jurisdictional hole would be closed and Horbatiuk would get the cases back.[1370] The version of Bill 6232 signed by Poroshenko did not contain the Lozovy edits.[1371] The Ukrainian reformers had won. On December 15, 2017, Horbatiuk's Special Investigations Department was slated to reacquire jurisdiction over the Black Ledger. The cases remained open.

It appeared that Petro Poroshenko needed convincing about the importance of controlling the Black Ledger. Mick Mulvaney, head of the Office of Management and Budget responded. According to the sworn testimony of the State Department's Catherine Croft, in "November or early December" 2017, Mulvaney put a hold on the provision of Javelin missiles to Ukraine, and unusually argued that OMB's concerns about Russian reaction were the reason. "It is not their brief to have an opinion on the national security or foreign policy," Croft testified.[1372] The hold, according to Croft lasted "about two weeks."[1373]

In the heat of this battle, Rex Tillerson stepped up to defend NABU. On December 4, Heather Nauert, his spokesperson, issued a statement:

> Recent events—including the disruption of a high-level corruption investigation, the arrest of officials from the National Anti-Corruption Bureau of Ukraine (NABU), and the seizure of sensitive NABU files—raise concerns about Ukraine's commitment to fighting corruption. These actions appear to be part of an effort to undermine independent anti-corruption institutions that the United States and others have helped support. They undermine public trust and risk eroding international support for Ukraine.
>
> As Secretary Tillerson has said: "It serves no purpose for Ukraine to fight for its body in Donbas if it loses its soul to corruption. Anti-corruption institutions must be supported, resourced, and defended."
>
> Reflecting the choice of the people of Ukraine, the United States calls on all branches of Ukraine's government to work together cooperatively to eliminate corruption from public life. Eliminating corruption is key to achieving stability, security, and prosperity for all Ukrainians.[1374][1375]

The direct quote seemed to indicate that Tillerson himself was behind the statement. Similar statements were released by all of Ukraine's Western partners.[1376] December 4, 2017, was also the first day on the job for Nauert's new boss, undersecretary of state for Public Diplomacy[1377], Steve Goldstein.[1378]

Poroshenko played a final legislative card to try and cripple Sytnyk and NABU. On December 6, 2017, faction leaders of Petro Poroshenko Bloc and the People's Front coalition introduced a bill to modify the tenure of the leaders of the anti-corruption agencies.[1379] The Reanimation Package of Reforms NGO pointed out the danger to anti-corruption authorities in the bill:

> Should this draft law be adopted, National Anti-Corruption Bureau of Ukraine (NABU) will completely lose any guarantees of independence from the political will of the highest government leadership. The draft law enables the dismissal of NABU director based on a protocol on an administrative offense related to corruption. In addition, the document regulates the dismissal of heads of NABU, Specialized Anti-Corruption Prosecutor's Office (SAPO), National Agency on Corruption Prevention (NACP) and the State Bureau of Investigations by passing a no-confidence motion against them by a simple parliamentary majority. Such a voting may be initiated by the President of Ukraine, the Cabinet of Ministers of Ukraine or 150 MPs.[1380]

A night of "frantic trans-Atlantic calls" ensued.[1381] The overnight campaign of NGOs, foreign diplomats, and others led the Poroshenko forces to swiftly withdraw Bill 7622.[1382] Ambassador Yovanovitch was doubtless a leading voice in that conversation. The failure of the legislative efforts to control the Black Ledger and Maidan cases left Poroshenko with no lawful ability to stop Horbatiuk from investigating the cases.

"NO ONE CAN CONTINUE INVESTIGATING THEM"

The Mueller investigation hit a brick wall in Ukraine in November and December of 2017. The liaison with the United States on the Manafort matters had been switched to a senior presidential aide in the Bankova.[1383] When that aide cancelled November and December meetings with the CIA director and Special Counsel Mueller, the US government became aware that Ukraine was no longer cooperating with the Mueller investigation.[1384]

In early December 2017, around the time of the secret hold, two key Ukrainian anti-corruption officials, NABU head Artem Sytnyk and SAPO head Nazar Kholodnytsky arrived in Washington, DC, along with Lutsenko's deputy.[1385] The men were to attend the First Global Forum on Asset Recovery taking place at the World Bank, sponsored by the US and UK.[1386]

Unusually, the Ukrainian law enforcement agencies had decided to patch up their messy feud of the preceding months at the Ukrainian Embassy in Washington.[1387] Sytnyk gave his remarks at the forum just as Bill 7622 was put on the agenda in Kyiv, and his remarks alluded to the fact that this might be the last time he addressed them as head of NABU.[1388] The removal of the bill from the agenda saved him.

As the deadline approached to return the cases to Horbatiuk, Lutsenko had one final move. On December 14, 2017, he ordered the Black Ledger cases transferred to the Special Anti-Corruption Prosecutor.[1389] Within days, Kholodnytsky sent them back, arguing he should not have the cases.[1390] A game of ping-pong between the two prosecutors ensued, where the cases would be kept away from Horbatiuk until May 4, 2018.[1391] At the same time, on December 13, 2017, Kholodnytsky did send a notice of suspicion to sitting Central Election Commission chair Okhendovsky in a Black Ledger case.[1392] Poroshenko held his ace over the Central Election Commission.

The fugitive MP Onyshchenko had ended up in rural Spain in August of 2017.[1393] Ukraine moved to extradite him from there in August 2017.[1394] In December 2017, Onyshchenko added a new dimension to his corruption claims when he sat down for an interview with *Ukrayinska Pravda*. He darkly began hinting about Joe Biden. Specifically, the fugitive lawmaker told his interviewer that he had given information to the FBI and that they were planning on taking him to the US until "Poroshenko defended Biden."[1395] At that point, Onyshchenko claimed, the offers to present evidence to the DOJ dried up.[1396]

"WE HAVE CROSSED THE RUBICON, THIS IS LETHAL WEAPONS"

As if by magic, on December 22, 2017, eight days after the Black Ledger cases had been put in limbo, the sale of Javelin missiles to Ukraine was approved.[1397] The hold was gone. Trump aides made certain the press knew that he had personally approved the decision to provide lethal aid to Ukraine, a fact no doubt not lost on the Ukrainian government, who most certainly read the clippings.[1398] "We have crossed the Rubicon, this is lethal weapons and I predict more coming," remarked a senior Congressional official.[1399]

While the lethal aid was being approved in Washington, additional deals between Pennsylvania companies and Ukrainian state companies developed behind the scenes. The first was a deal for locomotives from General Electric's Erie plant, the same one Trump alleged Hillary's donors might demand close a year earlier. By 2016, the plant was producing only two locomotives a week, down from a peak of twenty.[1400] In July 2017, GE Transportation indicated it was going to close the plant and move production of its new Evolution rail engine to Fort Worth Texas, resulting in a loss of over 500 union jobs.[1401]

Sometime in October 2017, however, GE Transportation began negotiating for the sale of rail engines with the Ukrainian state railways. GE's negotiators, known as "Oceans 11" inside the company, began working to negotiate a deal with authorities in Ukraine.[1402] On February 23, 2018, GE Transportation announced a $1 billion dollar framework deal for locomotives for Ukraine.[1403] The deal, between PJSC Ukrzaliznytsia and GE Transportation, also included a purchase-and-sale agreement for thirty locomotives with Ukreximbank for $140 million.[1404] The deal was important enough for Petro Poroshenko to make a personal appearance at the signing of the documents. "This is a very important day for us" he told the reporters covering the event.[1405]

The agreement was critical to GE as it raised the value of GE Transportation at a time when its parent company was looking to spin it off. At some point in summer 2017, GE entered negotiations to sell its transportation unit with Wabtec, a supplier of rail parts.[1406] Wabtec eventually bought the company for $11 billion.[1407] The jobs remain in Erie as of this writing.

Poroshenko's nuclear fuel promise from June was also fulfilled. On January 29, 2018, Westinghouse announced a deal with Energoatom, the state nuclear power monopoly.[1408] The deal expanded one to fuel a single reactor signed in 2014, due to expire in 2020.[1409] The large deal was a godsend for the company located in Butler County, Pennsylvania, which had filed for bankruptcy in March of 2017.[1410] Like the coal producers and General Electric in Erie, it was an old industrial business in Pennsylvania that had fallen on hard times—Westinghouse had been in the Pittsburgh area for almost 140 years.[1411]

CHAPTER 7: THE FATAL STAIN

From its very outset, the Trump administration was defined and limited by its desperate goal to not be exposed by the four separate major investigations of Russian interference in the 2016 election: a group of at least four related counterintelligence investigations, the twin investigations of the House and Senate intelligence committees, and their criminal counterpart, the Mueller investigation. Erasing the fatal stain of the Russian interference campaign consumed the Trump administration's energies throughout Trump's first term. By extension, the Republican Party was pulled into this fight.

The administration's meager record prior to the outbreak of COVID-19 included exactly one legislative achievement—a tax cut that was largely disliked by the electorate. Instead, all of of the political might of the Trump administration were focused almost entirely on avoiding political and criminal responsibility for the Russian influence campaign. This struggle has defined American politics for more than three years.

In his influential 1964 essay, "The Paranoid Style in American Politics," Richard Hofstadter revealed a longstanding thread of American political thinking that thrived on conspiracy theories.[1412] Decrying its adoption by the Goldwater conservatives of his era, he described their position:

> Important changes may also be traced to the effects of the mass media. The villains of the modern right are much more vivid than those of their paranoid predecessors, much better known to the public; the literature of the paranoid style is by the same token richer and more circumstantial in personal description and personal invective. For the vaguely delineated villains . . . for the shadowy international bankers of the monetary conspiracies, we may now substitute eminent public figures like Presidents Roosevelt, Truman, and Eisenhower, secretaries of State like Marshall, Acheson, and Dulles, Justices of the Supreme Court like Frankfurter and Warren.[1413]

Donald Trump and his associates were about to turn that model on its head. Like the Goldwater Republicans of 1964, they were going after pillars of the state, two former FBI directors, the entire US intelligence community, and the nominee of the other party. But unlike Goldwater supporters, they were trying to stop an investigation into their own contacts with foreign forces emanating from Russia. The year 2018 saw the surreality of a Republican Party that had worn the "law and order" mantle since Nixon's 1968 election accuse the major law enforcement organs of the state, the US Justice Department and the Federal Bureau of Investigation, of being part of a conspiracy against *them.*

This conspiracy's chief weapon, the plot went, was an illegal investigation of the connections between the Russian election interference effort and the Trump campaign that benefitted from it. In short, those involved in a conspiracy with a foreign power against the United States used the power of the presidency to call those investigating them a conspiracy.

By the end of 2018, the results of this effort became apparent. On November 6, 2018, the Democratic party swept to power in the House, winning district after district with near presidential election turnout levels. The Democrats' election success would set the stage for the Zelenskyy Affair.

Manafort's plan to focus the politics of the United States on to questions surrounding the Mueller investigation, Steele dossier, and FBI and its use of FISA warrants was about to move from politics to policy. Republican politicians, following the movement of their Trump-enthralled voters, began to move as a group towards the positions outlined to Trump by Manafort in early 2017. In early 2020, only one Republican would vote to remove the president, despite his obvious guilt.

But in early 2018 the Republican Party had many different positions on Russian election interference, many of them some form of hiding from it. 2018 would be a year of political battles over the Russia hacking scandal and almost nothing else. Trump's approval rating had been low ever since the beginning of his term and his polling average hit the lowest it would reach that year on December 16, 2017, when only 36.4 percent of voters approved of him.[1414]

"THIS PHONY CLOUD"

Trump was not happy with the way the Mueller investigation had been turning out for him. At a press conference with the Norwegian prime minister in early January, he complained loudly: "For 11 months, they've had this phony cloud over this administration, over our government, and it has hurt our government."[1415] His anger boiled over: "It's a Democrat hoax that was brought up as an excuse for losing an election."[1416] Trump acted as if the investigation showed that he was not involved in the Russian attack on the 2016 election: "It has been determined that there's been no collusion—and by virtually everybody."[1417]

Like many things the president said, that was not quite true. On January 10, the Senate Foreign Relations Committee's Democratic minority released a two-hundred page report entitled "Putin's Asymmetric Assault on Democracy in Russia and Europe: Implications for US National Security."[1418] It detailed Putin's use of information warfare, first against his own people, second against weak post-Soviet states, and third against the West.[1419] Trump's response on Twitter was quick: "The single greatest Witch Hunt in American history continues. There was no collusion, everybody including the Dems knows there was no collusion, & yet on and on it goes. Russia & the world is laughing at the stupidity they are witnessing. Republicans should finally take control!"[1420] Republicans were about to try just that. They had one goal. To equate the sprawling Mueller investigation with the FISA warrants and the Steele dossier and then destroy both of them. In the main, they succeeded.

"JUNIOR VARSITY GAMESMANSHIP"

The war inside HPSCI flared up in December with one witness, David Kramer, the senior director for Human Rights and Freedom at the McCain Institute, who had met with Steele in 2016. Kramer appeared before HPSCI for the first time on December 19, 2017.[1421] Kramer's lawyer was concerned about leaks, and when asked about the origins of the *Buzzfeed* dossier story, he asked the committee to be sure they wanted the material they were asking for.[1422] Assured they would strive to keep the matter confidential, Kramer answered all the questions posed except the names of Steele's sources, which he declined to say.[1423] Kramer feared that if he said any names at all they would leak and those persons would be targeted by the Russian secret services for assassination.

Kramer's fear was not unfounded. Kramer obliquely referenced the death of FSB general Oleg Erovinkin in the back of his car in December 2017 as a case of particular concern.[1424] Pressed by Republicans, it was noted that Kramer's appearance was voluntary.[1425] Representative Mike Conaway, now chairing the HPSCI's Russia investigation for the Republican majority agreed, but added that the committee could subpoena him.[1426] Kramer refused to provide answers regarding sourcing to the GOP majority.

Within an hour, the fact of Kramer's appearance leaked.[1427] Three days later, Kramer's lawyer Larry Robbins received an email from Michael Cohen's attorney.[1428] Cohen's attorney informed Robbins over the telephone that a "little birdie" in "the House" had told him that some of what was in the Steele dossier was inaccurate and requested that he write a letter to the committee along the lines that the Steele dossier was not entirely accurate, an offer a furious Robbins refused.[1429] Robbins wrote an indignant letter to the committee.[1430]

The GOP response to Robbins showed just how important the Steele dossier was to their plan. Rather than apologize, they served him with a subpoena for Kramer to testify.[1431] Ten minutes later, Byron York of the *Washington Examiner* published a story detailing the subpoena to Kramer.[1432] They wanted one thing: the names of Steele's sources. They were willing to withdraw their subpoena if Kramer would supply the names of the sources, their safety be damned.[1433]

There was more "junior-varsity gamesmanship" as Robbins put it.[1434] The Majority staff led Robbins to believe that he could select a date within a range as both lawyer and client had immovable personal issues on the original return date.[1435] Late on January 9, Robbins learned that Kramer was required to show for testimony the *next day*.[1436] Robbins and Kramer hurried back to Washington.[1437]

In the transcript, Robbins appears to have exploded:

> But I have to tell you, sir, in all candor, before we move to the substantive portion of today's events, this junior varsity gamesmanship about the return date of the subpoena, followed, as it is, closely on the heels of a pattern of leaks, the likes of which are wholly unfamiliar to me in 40 years of law practice, suggests to me that somebody doesn't actually really want to engage this issue.
>
> What they really want is an opportunity to tell some false narrative to the press about Mr. Kramer's unwillingness to cooperate with this committee, which everyone in this room knows to be false.[1438]

After Robbins's attempt to invoke a legislative privilege based on McCain's order to Kramer failed to convince Conaway, he instructed his client to take the Fifth Amendment because he could be subject to an illegal, lawless prosecution:

> Because even though what David did, in my view, is worthy of nothing but praise, the fact remains that the Nation's chief law enforcement official, the President of the United States, has repeatedly characterized the dossier and its dissemination as a hoax calculated to undermine the administration of his Presidency. He has said it on more than one occasion.
>
> He has said that the Justice Department is within his control. And, indeed, recent events disclose that the Justice Department is responsive to the suggestions of the President. And what's more, only recently did two Senators from the Judiciary

> Committee refer Christopher Steele and the dossier to the Justice Department as a criminal referral. [1439]

Representative Conaway retreated to meet with the majority's lawyers. He came back and challenged the legislative privilege point and then had Committee Counsel go through the motions.[1440] After being warned that the chair could later rule his invocation of his right to remain silent out of order, Kramer invoked his Fifth Amendment right to remain silent to every question. Kramer never had to return to answer the questions.

A week earlier, on January 3, with the help of Speaker of the House Paul Ryan, the DOJ was coerced into handing over the Steele dossier and other FBI documents that were at the heart of the ongoing Mueller investigation.[1441] A series of stories from December 2017 had reported that it was the report of the Australian diplomat Alexander Downer that had triggered the Crossfire Hurricane investigation.[1442] In mid-December it became obvious to observers that it "looks like the House leadership capitulating to pressure from the White House and Steve Bannon."[1443]

Republicans also concentrated their fire on the Carter Page FISA warrant at a time when the reauthorization bill for warrantless wiretaps was up for reauthorization.[1444] Trump's tweets muddied the waters in the reauthorization vote: "House votes on controversial FISA ACT today. This is the act that may have been used, with the help of the discredited and phony Dossier, to so badly surveil and abuse the Trump Campaign by the previous administration and others?"[1445] The bill passed 256–194.[1446] Trump signed it.

On January 16, news outlets reported that Stephen Bannon, Trump's third campaign manager had been subpoenaed by Robert Mueller.[1447] The former aide quickly agreed to a private interview rather than appear before the Grand Jury.[1448]

On January 19, House Intelligence Committee sources told the press that a secret memo had been drafted by the Republican Majority staff that claimed the FBI abused their power in seeking a FISA warrant on Carter Page.[1449] The Democrats were caught off-guard by this new report, which they had not seen in advance. Nunes scheduled a vote to release the report to the entire House of Representatives.[1450]

The issuance of the report followed Manafort's recommendations to the president on discrediting the investigations from the year prior, focusing on the alleged role of the Steele dossier in the FISA warrant application and renewals regarding the Page warrant.[1451] Nunes's plan was simple. He focused the secret memo entirely on parts of the Page FISA warrant that used portions of the Steele dossier, ignoring the vast amounts of additional information that supported the Page warrant.[1452]

The question of whether this memo could be released was in the hands of Donald Trump. On February 19 a new hashtag emerged on Twitter, #ReleaseTheMemo.[1453] It rapidly rose to become the most retweeted item by Twitter accounts linked to Russia, which increased in frequency by 233,000 percent over a forty-eight-hour period.[1454]

On February 2, Trump indicated that he would not object to its publication.[1455] The memo asserted that the FISA warrant was deficient because it failed to reveal that Steele had been doing work for a political party.[1456]

On February 8, Fox News reporter Ed Henry published text messages between Democratic senator Mark Warner of Virginia and Adam Waldman, a lobbyist who was known to have represented Russian oligarch Oleg Deripaska.[1457] The texts were part of an effort by the Senate Intelligence Committee to get Christopher Steele and Julian Assange to provide information and possible testimony to the committee.[1458] Senator Richard Burr supported Warner, stating that he was aware of the effort at the time but not all the specifics.[1459]

Within the hour, Donald Trump tweeted: "Wow! -Senator Mark Warner got caught having extensive contact with a lobbyist for a Russian oligarch. Warner did not want a 'paper trail' on a 'private' meeting (in London) he requested with Steele of fraudulent Dossier fame. All tied into Crooked Hillary."[1460]

Senators Burr and Warner were so concerned about the activities of Devin Nunes that they went to House Speaker Paul Ryan, telling him they knew that Representative Nunes had leaked Warner's text messages to Fox News and they wanted it to stop.[1461] Soon after, the Democrats were able to get a memorandum of their own released to counter Nunes's "secret memo."[1462] It had no discernible political impact.

"HE CALLED MY LATE MOTHER A BITCH"

Far away from the battles in Washington, Petro Poroshenko had his own set of problems. His approval rating was extremely low after the events of the fall of 2017. His acts against the Ukrainian reformers in the fall had apparently harmed his already dismal support inside Ukraine.

The new year had started out in a personally enjoyable way for the Ukrainian president. He took a vacation in the Maldives with his family for Eastern Orthodox Christmas.[1463] Unfortunately for Porshenko, the Ukrainian voters learned about his trip in an exposé on the TV show *Skhemy*, known in English as "Schemes: Corruption in Detail."[1464] In great detail, *Skhemy* revealed the Ukrainian president had flown seven people aboard a Dassault Falcon 7X back to Kyiv on January 8.[1465] It was unclear when his taped Christmas greetings for the nation had been recorded, but he clearly hadn't been at home over the holiday.[1466] In excruciating detail, the network showed the plane's route around Crimean airspace, as if to point out that it was no longer Ukrainian territory.[1467] *Skhemy* then capped off the exposé with video of Poroshenko's efforts to remain unseen as he got into a motorcade without escort and drove straight to the presidential residence.[1468] The intrepid journalists then got a quote from a Turkish airline that chartered the plane about the cost of eight days rental of the aircraft—$500,000.[1469]

It came as no surprise therefore, that a February opinion poll had Poroshenko coming in fourth in a hypothetical race for the 2019 election.[1470]

The president only received 9.8 percent of the hypothetical vote.[1471] Ukrainian pollster and analyst Vitaly Bala cited the news about Poroshenko's Maldives vacation, the war, and Lutsenko's attacks on NABU as the primary reasons why.[1472]

Joe Biden, the presumed Democratic front-runner for president also had a low opinion of Petro Poroshenko. His memoir *Promise Me, Dad*, published in late 2017, went into significant detail regarding his efforts as Obama's point man on Ukraine. His opinion of the fight between Poroshenko and the reformers was harsh: "The Poroshenko and Yatsenyuk factions were wasting energy bickering with one another when they should have been creating institutions and security forces capable of defending against Putin" argued the former vice president.[1473] Biden was blunt about Poroshenko:

> I had been hard on Poroshenko since his election nine months earlier. I'd made it clear to him that he could not afford to give the Europeans any excuse for walking away from the sanctions regime against Russia. He had to continue to fight the elements of corruption that were embedded in the political culture of Ukraine's Soviet and post-Soviet governance—both in Yatsenyuk's rival party and in Poroshenko's own.[1474]

Biden went deep into his bona fides on Ukrainian corruption in the book, perhaps anticipating his actions there would be relitigated in the 2020 US presidential race.[1475] If so, his instinct was right.

Poroshenko began to try and regain his now-dented reputation as a converted reformer. First, he got Lutsenko to hold a showy treason trial in absentia for former president Yanukovych.[1476] Second, new hearings in the Maidan cases were announced.[1477] A week later, Poroshenko announced that he would be "personally involved" in the Maidan cases.[1478]

Even after leaving the office of the vice president, Joe Biden had continued to be interested in Ukraine and in December 2017, coauthored an article with Michael Carpenter entitled "How to Stand Up to the Kremlin" in *Foreign Affairs*.[1479] Carpenter, a former Obama deputy secretary of defense and foreign policy advisor for the vice president, ran Biden's Penn Center, a foreign policy think-tank in Philadelphia.[1480] On January 23, 2018, Joe Biden spoke in front of the Council on Foreign Relations in Washington, DC.[1481] It was here that Biden described the firing of Viktor Shokin two years earlier.[1482] Video of the discussion was posted on the internet.

The speech was not well received by Viktor Shokin, whose daughter, Alina, is an American citizen.[1483] She tweeted: "I considered the situation with the speech of Ex-Vice President Biden, in which he publicly insulted my deceased grandmother and my father."[1484] In a follow-up she explained that: "Given that this applies to my entire family, I plan to go to court to protect the dignity of my family."[1485] Viktor Shokin confirmed it was true and said, "I know she is going to do it."[1486] Shokin told another paper, "The fact that he called my late mother a bitch means that nothing is sacred for this man."[1487]

Shokin was especially anxious to use the Biden comments in his own court case.[1488] Shokin had sued for a declaration that his dismissal was illegal in late March of 2017.[1489] The case was first dismissed in late April of that year.1490 But in July 2017, the Supreme Court of Ukraine heard Shokin's appeal.1491

"PEOPLE ARE NOT ALWAYS WHO THEY APPEAR TO BE ON THE INTERNET"

Things had gotten so bad inside the House Permanent Select Committee on Intelligence (HPSCI) that a wall was being built in the middle of the room between the majority staffers and those who worked for the Democratic minority.1492 The Democratic minority responded to Nunes by drafting their own report, which the committee voted unanimously to release if Trump would approve it.1493 It was released on February 24, a date by which much had changed.1494

In a one-week period, the Mueller investigation broke wide open. Two weeks earlier, on February 16, Deputy Attorney General Rod Rosenstein called a press conference. From the podium, he told Americans that "people are not always who they appear to be on the Internet."1495 Mueller charged the Internet Research Agency with hacking the DNC.1496 Russian interference was suddenly real for everyday Americans. The publication of estimates of the reach of Russian misinformation were staggering.

At the same time, Manafort's partner, Rick Gates, was out of options. In January, Gates added Tom Green, a white-collar defense attorney known for his plea deals to his legal team.1497 On February 1, Gates's prior attorneys resigned from the case.1498 Gates lied at the first proffer session.1499 Within three weeks, it would be over. On February 22, Manafort filed a superseding indictment of Manafort and Gates, focused on tax issues.[1500] On February 23, a plea agreement was signed.[1501] Rick Gates was now cooperating with the Special Counsel.

WAR AND PEACE: WASHINGTON, MUNICH, KYIV, MOSCOW

As the Javelin deal continued to wend its way towards completion, the parties continued to work towards peace. No later than February 2018, Manafort was working on a new plan, entitled "New Initiative for Peace."[1502] On February 20, a day after the Munich Security Conference, he emailed the three-page document to two persons.[1503] The efforts were ongoing, if under the radar.

The Munich Security Conference is the largest gathering of diplomats and government officials to discuss issues of security and war. The 2018 version appeared less than successful. The conference opened a few days after the Internet Research Agency had been indicted by Robert Mueller.[1504] The agenda was dominated by conflict between Russia and everyone else.[1505] One participant put the issue succinctly: "This was not a good meeting."[1506]

Amid the accusations being hurled between the US and Russia, US deputy energy secretary Dan Brouillette met with Ukrainian prime minister, Pavel Klimkin.[1507] Accompanying him was Wells Griffith, the Trump battleground states director who had been a part of the Xcoal deal from the beginning.[1508]

Around this time the process for the Javelin sale was reaching a key point. Ted Cruz's former aide Daniel Vajdich, still lobbying for Ukrainian state-owned companies, stepped in. Between February 20 and 23, he began sending emails to the key Defense and State staffers involved in the Javelin sale, including Catherine Croft and Laura Cooper.[1509] The contacts were substantial and included Gregory Pollack, the acting deputy assistant secretary of defense for security cooperation, the official directly responsible for the Javelin sale.[1510] Congressional Armed Services Committee staffers from both parties were included his call lists.[1511] Congress did not vote to disapprove the sale.

Days later, the Javelin missiles cleared the next hurdle. On March 1, 2018, the proposed sale of the Javelin missiles was formally announced pursuant to the Arms Export Control Act.[1512] Under the AECA, Congress would have thirty days to reverse the sale.[1513] It would not be the last time Vajdich stepped in at key points in Javelin missile sales to Ukraine.

Despite Manafort's hidden efforts, peace was not about to break out. Russia and Ukraine were far apart on a key issue—the timing of elections in the Donbas relative to Ukraine taking over control of the disputed areas. In early 2018, the Germans had suggested a UN peacekeeping mission for Donbas, but Putin opposed such a force controlling the Donbas border with Ukraine.[1514] Events in Salisbury, England, were about to shatter the secret peace of October 2016 for good.

SUBSTANCE-33

During the run-up to the release of the HPSCI's report on the Russian attempt to interfere with the US elections, the focus of the US political universe was on the Steele dossier. On February 28, 2018, Donald J. Trump told the world via tweet he wanted action on his claims that the FISA process had been used against him illegally, claims that centered around the use of the Steele dossier in the Carter Page warrant. At 9:34 a.m. he tweeted: "Why is A.G. Jeff Sessions asking the Inspector General to investigate potentially massive FISA abuse. Will take forever, has no prosecutorial power and already late with reports on Comey etc. Isn't the I.G. an Obama guy? Why not use Justice Department lawyers? DISGRACEFUL!"[1515] 9:34 a.m. was 4:34 p.m. February 28 in Moscow.

That same day, the *New York Times* prepared a story for print. Citing two officials of the Senate Intelligence Committee the story reported that Devin Nunes had leaked the Warner texts to Fox News and that they wanted Nunes reigned in.[1516]

A day later, at 10:51 a.m. Moscow time, March 1, Major General Denis Sergeev of Unit 29155 of the GRU, using a phone linked to his cover identity "Sergey Fedotov," made a telephone call to an unusual number, registered to a non-existent person, Timur Agafonov.[1517] At 6 p.m. Major General Sergeev apparently learned that he was going to London that weekend, because after that call, the general made a series of phone calls to book a flight under his alias.[1518] At 8:09 p.m. he got a call from a travel agent who had booked him seat on the morning Aeroflot flight to London.[1519]

During the time he was in London, Sergeev had telephone calls with only one number, which is not in any database in Russia that tracks locations or SIM cards.[1520] In fact, the only place a reference to this number exists is in one telephone sharing app's directory in Russia. In that directory, the number is listed as "Amir—Moscow."[1521] General Sergeev called this number prior to leaving Moscow on the morning of March 2.[1522]

That morning General Sergeev flew to London and checked into a hotel near Paddington Station.[1523] For the next two days he barely left his hotel room according to location pings from his phone.[1524] The only long trip he took out of the hotel for the entire three days happened after a telephone call from the "Amir" number around 9 a.m. on March 3.[1525] At that time, "Sergeev took at least one trip outside the hotel. Between 11:30 and noon, his phone registered at least once at a cell tower near Oxford Circus. Then, between noon to about 1:30 pm, his phone connected several times near the Embankment, on the Thames west bank," later reports noted.[1526]

Coincidentally, fifteen minutes earlier, the telephones of Lieutenant Colonel Mishkin and Colonel Cheigpa of Unit 29155 of the GRU had also pinged cell towers near Waterloo Station, a mere ten-minute walk over Waterloo Bridge from the Embankment.[1527] They had traveled together to the UK on March 2 as photographs show both walking through the jetway into

Heathrow airport that day at 4:22 in the afternoon.[1528] At 12:50 p.m., the pair boarded a train to Salisbury.[1529] They returned at 4:10 that same day.[1530]

The next morning, March 4, General Sergeev prepared to check out as Lieutenant Colonel Mishkin and Colonel Chiegpa boarded a train for Salisbury once again.[1531] Sergeev headed to the airport. The two GRU officers headed straight for a private home in Salisbury, where they placed a substance on the door handle there.[1532]

Several hours later, a man and his daughter were eating at a restaurant named Zizzi on Castle Street in Salisbury. At some point the man began shouting and acting incoherently.[1533] At 3:35 in the afternoon on March 4, a passerby near a parking lot in Salisbury, England, came across the man and woman on a park bench. They were foaming at the mouth and gesturing strangely.[1534] An off-duty nurse saw to it that an ambulance was summoned and that they were treated.[1535]

Doctors at Salisbury District Hospital at first assumed they had overdosed on opioids, but another doctor present had worked at the UK's chemical agent facility at nearby Porton Down and told colleagues the patients had been exposed to a nerve agent.[1536] The next day at the hospital, new information was released: the male patient was Sergei Skripal, the exchanged GRU double agent, and the woman was his daughter, Yulia.[1537] Police came to guard the pair.[1538] They had been poisoned by Novichok, made from a derivative of VX and VR nerve agents known as substance-33.[1539] The only place on Earth that Novichok had ever been synthesized in large amounts was the Soviet Union.[1540]

Some reporters fell for the fake LinkedIn message that falsely linked Skripal to Orbis and began running stories stating that the former Russian double agent was associated with Steele.[1541] Surprisingly, Russian bot networks did not jump in on this alleged link right away.

"PERHAPS SOME BAD JUDGMENT, INAPPROPRIATE MEETINGS"

The next day, March 13, the HPSCI announced the major conclusion in its investigation into the Russian election interference campaign of 2016. Representative Mike Conaway started with a concession then an argument: "The Russians did commit active measures against our election in '16, and we think they will do that in the future.[1542] We disagree with the narrative that they were trying to help Trump."[1543] The Democrats on the committee, led by Adam Schiff, disagreed.[1544]

On the critical question of whether the Trump campaign was involved in the criminal acts committed by Russian agents, Conaway said, "we found no evidence of collusion. We found perhaps some bad judgment, inappropriate meetings." He asserted that these inappropriate meetings did not support a claim that there was a conspiracy between the campaign and Russia: "only Tom Clancy or Vince Flynn or someone else like that could take this series of inadvertent contacts with each other, or meetings, whatever, and weave that into a some sort of fictional page-turner spy thriller."[1545]

Conaway had a lot to say regarding the Steele dossier as well. He said the report would describe "how anti-Trump research made its way from Russian sources to the Clinton campaign" and that "we will say that there was an attempt to use foreign sources with respect to the Clinton campaign."[1546] He darkly hinted at attacks on the basis for the dossier: "It was clear that there was—at least Steele and however much he talked and didn't talk to Russians—that's foreigners and that information was paid for by the [Democratic National Committee] and the Clinton campaign"[1547]

That same day, a story appeared on the website *Consortium News*, a publication that was later cited by the Canadian Communications Security Establishment as being involved with Russian disinformation campaigns against the Canadian government.[1548] The *Consortium News* piece, written by James O'Neil, suggested "that Skripal was likely involved in the production of the Steele dossier. He was therefore in a position to offer potentially very damaging information into the circumstances of the Steele dossier" argued the piece.[1549] Within days of the report's release, pro-Russian social media accounts such as that of Putin-friendly film director Oliver Stone were tweeting the *Consortium News* take on the poisoning.[1550]

The committee's final report, released on March 22, wrongly stated that Putin did not favor a Trump election by casting doubt upon the Intelligence Community's tradecraft in reaching the conclusion that the Russians wanted to help Donald Trump win the presidency.[1551] It also attacked the Steele dossier, spending nearly three pages on Steele himself.[1552]

The Salisbury attack destroyed any chance of a Western agreement to agree to a Crimea-Donbas swap. On March 14, British prime minister May expelled twenty-three Russian diplomats.[1553] At a fiery session of the UN Security Council, both the US and UK Ambassadors called out the Russian Federation for the attempted murders.[1554] The United States expelled sixty Russian diplomats and forced the closure of the Russian consulate in Seattle.[1555] Trump even subjected Russia to sanctions for their election interference in 2016.[1556] Secretary of State Tillerson, aboard a plane heading back to the United States from Africa, told reporters the poisoning was "a really egregious act" that appeared to "clearly" have come from Russia.[1557]

It was the last official statement Rex Tillerson would make as secretary of state.

On March 13, 2018, Donald Trump fired Tillerson by tweet and named Mike Pompeo, then CIA director, the new secretary of state.[1558] It was 8:44 in the morning.[1559] Earlier in the day, as he flew back to the US, he told reporters, "I've become extremely concerned about Russia."[1560] Tillerson went into detail about what had happened: "We spent most of last year investing a lot into attempts to work together, to solve problems, to address differences. And quite frankly, after a year, we didn't get very far. Instead what we've seen is a pivot on their part to be more aggressive."[1561] One critic reluctantly pointed out that Tillerson's tenure had a "complicated epitaph."[1562] His public affairs chief Steve Goldstein was also fired.[1563]

Tillerson gave a farewell speech on March 22. "Never lose sight of your most valuable asset, the most valuable asset you possess: your personal integrity," Tillerson said. "Only you can relinquish it or allow it to be compromised. Once you've done so, it is very very hard to regain it. So guard it as the most precious thing you possess."[1564]

That same day, National Security Advisor H. R. McMaster was fired by Trump as well.[1565] McMaster was replaced by John Bolton, the former US ambassador to the United Nations, a well-known hawk on Iran and Russia.[1566]

THE 195TH RICHEST MAN IN UKRAINE

On February 20, 2018, a man named Igor Fruman donated $2,700 to the Trump Victory Fund and Donald J. Trump for President Campaign Committee.[1567] On March 3, 2018, Donald Trump appeared at a meeting for the Trump Victory Fund with his top donors at his Florida golf resort, Mar-a-Lago. A $2,700 minimum donation was required to attend.[1568] The fundraiser had been postponed on January 20 because of a government shutdown that had occurred even though the Republicans controlled Congress and the White House.[1569] In attendance at the meeting were Igor Fruman and Lev Parnas.[1570]

In the days immediately following the Trump fundraiser, two very unusual planted articles indicated a new disinformation effort was underway. They appeared in the obscure US Russian-language publication *Forum Daily*, "the Voice of Russian-Speaking America." Normally a general interest magazine that provided advice on immigration matters for new arrivals, on March 5 and 6, *Forum Daily* ran two detailed articles previewing the impeachment drama that would erupt eighteen months later.

On the 5th, *Forum Daily* ran an "exclusive"[1571] on an infamous corruption case in Ukraine. The unsigned article, citing "American sources," stated that in December 2016 Oleksandr Onyshchenko had given the FBI information regarding his involvement with an alleged corrupt scheme involving President Petro Poroshenko.[1572] Although the allegations had appeared in other Ukrainian outlets more than a year prior, as of December 2016, they had not appeared in any US publication.[1573]

The *Forum Daily* article included previously unpublished details about the case, details that could only have come from someone close to Onyshchenko. The story praised Onyshchenko's new lawyer, former federal prosecutor, Martha Boersch, a veteran of anticorruption prosecutions involving the former Soviet Union.[1574] Onyshchenko had earlier told the *Kyiv Post* that Boersch was not his defense lawyer, "but a consultant on issues that he would not like to discuss publicly."[1575]

But the unusually high degree of detail provided about the FBI interview indicated extensive insider knowledge of the Onyshchenko case.

The *Forum Daily* piece named the FBI agent involved—Karen Greenaway and her superior—and claimed that Ms. Boersch was more interested "in where the American money goes, which is provided to the Ukrainian state, goes to the budget, how it is obtained and where it goes in the future" seemingly a reference to the Biden allegations Onyshchenko would soon trumpet.[1576] Only someone close to Onyshchenko, and someone present at the interview would have had such information.

Strangely, the *Forum Daily* piece described Onyshchenko in glowing terms—with shots of him next to American movie stars from his Instagram account. He was described as "a deputy of the Verkhovna Rada, the owner of a beauty contest, an equestrian lover, a boyfriend of supermodels and a host of parties with American stars."[1577] The article seemed to have come straight out of Onyshchenko's camp.

Most unusual however was the fact that the very next day, *Forum Daily* ran a second article with one of the two people who had brought Onyshchenko's story to the Trump campaign the year before—Igor Fruman. This scoop was also unusual for a publication like *Forum Daily*—an insider's look into the beginnings of President's Trump's 2020 campaign.[1578] In the interview, Fruman claimed, "In the 2016 elections, I made donations to the Trump election campaign fund," raising the question of whether or not he had paid for Parnas's October 2016 donation spree.[1579] According to Fruman, the purpose of the recent meeting had been to kick off the president's 2020 reelection campaign.[1580] Fruman also mentioned that at the request of the chief rabbi of Ukraine, he had set up an organization known as "the American Friends of Anatevka."[1581]

Fruman stated that he was a businessman and that on March 6, three school busses donated to Anatevka by the group were running in Kyiv for the first time.[1582] In the short space of two days, the unknown *Forum Daily* had two big stories with bearing on the looming impeachment of the president eighteen months later. No one noticed the stories. The Zelenskyy Affair had begun. The purpose of all this would become apparent a month later.

Igor Fruman was not the model businessman that *Forum Daily* claimed. Fruman had been born in the former Soviet Union—in the Belarussian SSR to the north of Ukraine.[1583] As a businessman he was associated with the most powerful mobster in Odesa, Volodymyr "The Lightbulb" Galanternik.[1584] Fruman owned a series of businesses in Ukraine, including a Kyiv bar.[1585] He was listed as the 195th richest man in Ukraine.[1586] In addition, Igor Fruman and Paul Manafort had been friends for over a decade.[1587] He also operated a branch of his Kyiv restaurant in the tony Knightsbridge section of London.

Fruman owned an export-import business in New York, FD Import and Export Corp., a business linked to his luxury import business in Ukraine, Otrada Luxury Group, whose motto was "Welcome to Ukraine, Welcome to Luxury."[1588] The F stood for Fruman and the D for Sergei Dyablo, his partner in Ukraine.[1589]

Starting in mid-March 2018, Igor Fruman began making a series of donations under the false name of a supposedly different GOP donor, "Igor Furman."[1590] The purpose, Federal prosecutors would later allege, was to hide his donations so that he could make them in excess of legal limits.[1591] He first started with a small $271 donation to a single Republican congressional candidate on March 14.[1592] Five days later, Fruman donated almost $42,000, sending $271 to ten different GOP congressional candidates, $5,000 to the Make America Great Again Committee, a super PAC supporting Trump, and a big $33,000 donation to the National Republican Campaign Committee.[1593]

"THEY WERE OPERATING OFF OF A PRE-SOCIAL-MEDIA– PRE-FRAGMENTATION-OF-ALL-MEDIA–STRATEGY"

In March 2018, the president's private lawyer, Jay Sekulow, told Rudy Giuliani that the relationship between Trump and John Dowd, the lawyer in charge of his defense of the Mueller investigation, was souring.[1594] In the months prior, the discussion between the Special Counsel's Office and Trump's lawyers revolved around three issues, whether the president would be subpoenaed, whether he would sit down for an interview and whether he could legally be indicted.[1595] Cobb and Dowd had played it straight, convincing the president that cooperating with the Special Counsel was to his advantage.[1596] The president was eager to reduce the Mueller investigation to a single face-to-face interview, a personal arena he felt comfortable in. Dowd was not so sure.

The parties had chosen a date and location for a sit-down interview: Sunday January 27, 2018, at Camp David.[1597]

In January 2018, the Trump defense team cancelled the interview.[1598] Every day they wondered if it would be the day that Robert Mueller would subpoena the president.[1599] Dowd was pushed out on March 22.[1600]

On April 18, Trump settled on a new lawyer, Rudy Giuliani, the former mayor of New York City and hero of September 11, 2001.[1601] It was a critical time in the Mueller investigation—Federal agents had raided the home and office of Michael Cohen, the president's personal lawyer.[1602]

The issue, as Giuliani saw it, was that the public defense of the president was not working very well.[1603] In terms of impeachment, he argued, "the thing that will decide that the most is public opinion."[1604] Anthony Scaramucci, the New York lawyer who spent a brief period as Trump's communications director in 2017 told a reporter that "They were operating off of a pre-social-media—pre-fragmentation-of-all-media—strategy."[1605]

Giuliani's first attempts at putting out the fire did not go well. In an appearance on Sean Hannity's Fox News Channel show, Giuliani gave what would later be a common performance for him, erratic, rambling, and providing admissions to matters that were best left unaddressed.[1606] He admitted that the president had paid adult film star Stormy Daniels for her silence regarding their alleged sexual affair right before the election.[1607] Giuliani would repeat these performances for the next two years.

"HE STARTS HIS GAME"

On April 11, 2018, a company named Global Energy Producers associated with Lev Parnas and Igor Fruman, was incorporated in Delaware.[1608] Its purpose was to further the agenda of Ukrainian government officials regarding the removal of the US ambassador to that country.

Only eight days later, Oleksandr Onyshchenko released what he claimed was a bombshell tape—a recording of a conversation he alleged was between him and then-current Ukrainian president Petro Poroshenko.[1609] The voice alleged to be that of Poroshenko was in a conversation with Onyshchenko about Burisma owner Zlochevsky.[1610] The conversation turned to a potential deal: "I met Zlochevskiy [sic] in Dubai, he has been settling with [MP] Ihor [Kononenko] for a year. I don't know if you're getting reports about their agreements. Zlochevskiy asked me to talk with you and put forward some offers."[1611] The voice alleged to be Onyshchenko's discusses a potential business deal with Zlochevsky.[1612] The voice Onyshchenko alleged to be that of Poroshenko responded: "Yes, Mykola is a good guy. I'll think of what can be done. It's just the Americans have been on him lately."[1613] The "Onyshchenko" voice then responded that because Hunter Biden is a significant person in the company and that because "Senator" Joe Biden is his father, the US will not have a problem with Poroshenko entering into business with Burisma's Zlochevsky.[1614]

The tape was dismissed by many across the political spectrum in Ukraine. Poroshenko dismissed it as faked.[1615] Artem Sytnyk the director of

NABU, no friend of Poroshenko, was similarly skeptical: "There have been statements about bribery of deputies, lobbying of laws and plenty of other things, but these statements were of a general nature, without specific names, locations where money was handed over, and without references to the equipment used."[1616] Sytnyk openly doubted that the fugitive lawmaker was going to provide any tapes at all. "When it comes to specifics," the NABU director said, "he starts his game. I don't know if he's aware of that but he is also part [of those recordings]. And we can't be sure that, if Onyshchenko comes, the recordings or the recording device will also be there on him."[1617]

Meanwhile Kholodnytsky's freeze of the Black Ledger case against the head of the Central Election Commission hit a snag. In April, Mykhailo Okhendovsky's lawyers convinced the trial court that the case must be unfrozen.[1618] Kholodnytsky soon refroze the cases.[1619] In Ukraine, all things were possible.

According to later reports, during May 2018, Lutsenko, his deputy, and former prosecutor General Viktor Shonkin reached out to their US counterparts in federal law enforcement.[1620] Their goal was to pass information to the Trump administration that Ukrainians had instead worked to interfere in the 2016 presidential elections.[1621] These prosecutors later asserted that Ambassador Yovanovitch had stymied their attempts to come to the United States to present the information to the FBI.[1622]

THE "LONG-AWAITED WEAPON"

Two days after Onyshchenko released his latest tapes, Igor Fruman and Lev Parnas met with President Trump and high-level Republican operatives at Mar-a-Lago as part of a Make America Great Again Super PAC donor event.[1623] Also attending were Ronna McDaniel, the chair of the Republican National Committee, and Texas congressman Pete Sessions.[1624] Participants in the event were mostly wealthy donors. According to Federal prosecutors, Parnas and Fruman met Sessions for the first time at the meeting.[1625]

In the last days of April 2018, the pair stepped up their donations to Republican causes. On April 27, Fruman, again using the name "Igor Furman," donated nearly $100,000 in three transactions to the Republican National Committee and the NRCC.[1626] Fruman's total donations up to late April 2018 were $143,788.[1627]

While these large donations were being made in the US, Poroshenko moved to decisively put the cases where Horbatiuk could not reach them. In early April, Horbatiuk wrote to Lutsenko requesting that the Black Ledger cases be returned to him, though Lutsenko refused, a decision attributed in news accounts to Poroshenko.

In late April 2018, the Javelin missiles were delivered, as the deadline for Congress to respond to the sale had expired on April 1, 2018. On Monday, April 30, 2018, Poroshenko announced on Facebook that the delivery of the "long-awaited weapon" had been completed.[1628] Poroshenko apparently had succeeded in procuring the missiles he'd promised to the Ukrainian people, but most of his actions to get them remained unknown.

That same day, Parnas and Fruman again met with President Donald Trump.[1629] According to a source close to the investigation, at an earlier meeting that day, Mr. Parnas heard both Donald Trump and his son, Donald Trump Jr., discuss the Javelin missiles that the US government had just announced it sold to Ukraine. Later, in an intimate meal setting, at the Trump International Hotel the pair sat for over an hour with the president and other luminaries.[1630]

The conversation turned to the subject Parnas wanted to discuss most urgently: US ambassador to Ukraine, Marie Yovanovitch. "The biggest problem there, I think where we need to start is we gotta get rid of the ambassador. She's still left over from the Clinton administration, she's basically walking around telling everybody 'Wait, he's gonna get impeached, just wait.'"[1631]

According to federal prosecutors, the funds donated by the pair were straw donations to advance the agenda of Ukrainian government officials with the Trump administration.[1632] The primary official in this case was Prosecutor General Yuriy Lutsenko.[1633] The agenda was to create enough of a political storm around US ambassador to Ukraine, Maria Yovanovitch that President Trump would remove her from her position.[1634]

At the end of the meeting, Fruman

handed over to the President of the United States a personal handwritten letter with blessings from the Chief Rabbi of Ukraine Moshe Reuven Azman. Despite some violation of the formal protocol, Donald Trump took and read this letter, and then hid the message from Kiev in his breast pocket of his jacket.[1635]

The president of the United States was receiving messages from Rabbi Azman in Ukraine. Reached by Shimon Briman, the piece's author, Azman "refused to disclose the contents of this letter to our portal, explaining this by the personal nature of the appeal to President Trump," but confirmed the fact of the transfer of letters and contacts with the first person of the United States through Igor Fruman."[1636]

Just two days later, one of the reasons for Yovanovitch's removal and Parnas's prescience came to light. Buried on page fourteen of Section A of May 2, 2018's morning edition of the *New York Times* was one of the most important articles of the decade. The headline read: "Ukraine, Seeking US Missiles, Halted Cooperation with Mueller Investigation."[1637]

BOOK II: THE ZELENSKYY AFFAIR

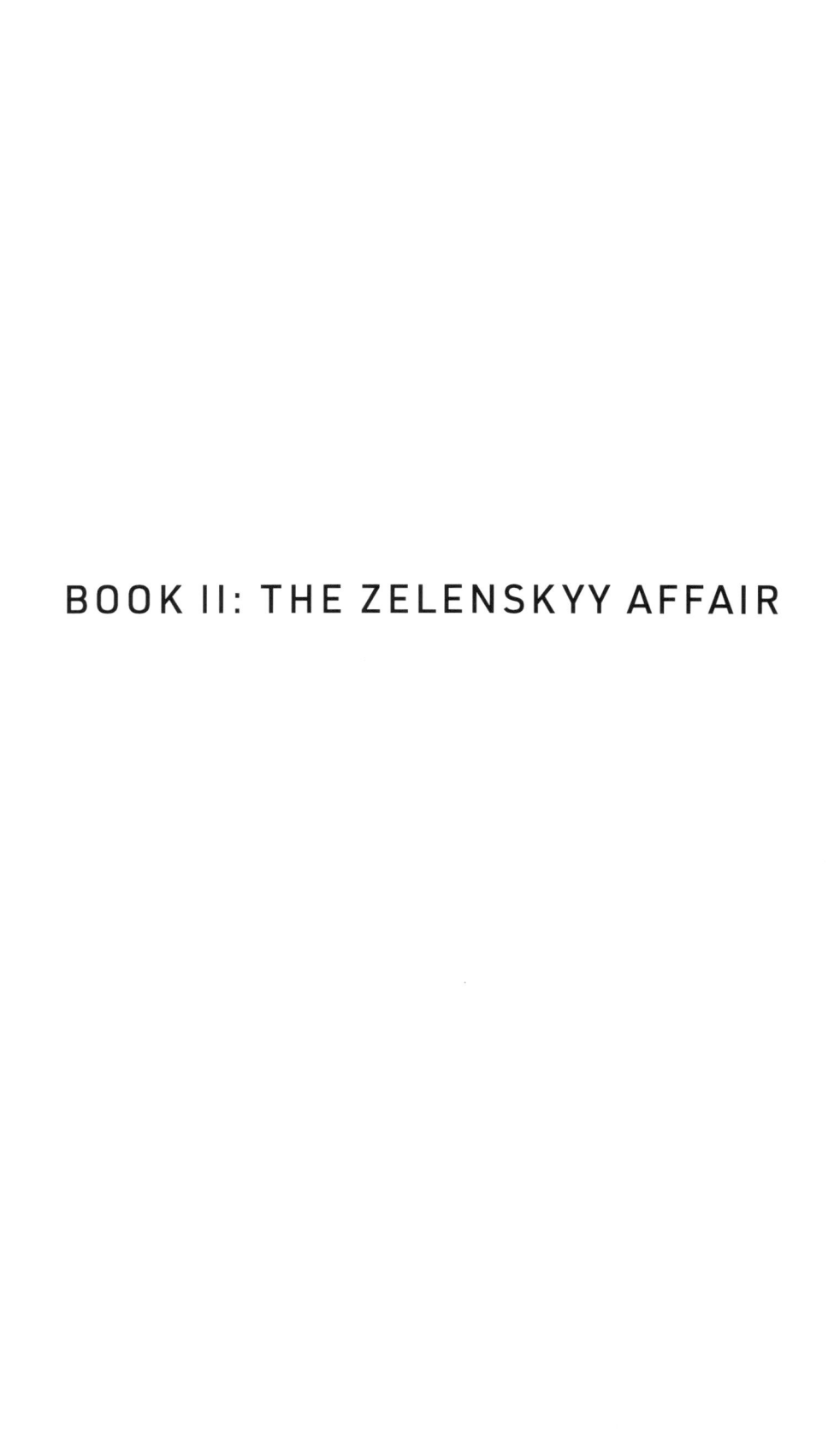

CHAPTER 8: A NAME TO A FACE

A CLASSIFIED STATE DEPARTMENT ASSESSMENT—THE SECRET MEMO

The *New York Times* story, written by Andrew Kramer, stated that "four meandering cases that involve Mr. Manafort, Mr. Trump's former campaign chairman, have been effectively frozen by Ukraine's chief prosecutor . . . the decision to halt the investigations," the piece continued, "was handed down at a delicate moment for Ukraine, as the Trump administration was finalizing plans to sell the country sophisticated anti-tank missiles, called Javelins."[1638] The article also asserted that by that date, a key witness in the Mueller probe, Manafort's right-hand man in Ukraine, Konstantin Kilimnik, had been allowed to escape from Ukraine.[1639]

The story's sourcing was murky, referring to "some lawmakers," but did not explain what country these lawmakers were in or to what legislative body they belonged.[1640] The next quote in the article came from a Ukrainian lawmaker, muddying the picture of the sourcing considerably.[1641]

On May 2, 2018, the president's lawyer, Ty Cobb, resigned.[1642]

Two days later, a detailed letter from three Democratic senators, Robert Menendez, Richard Durbin, and Patrick Leahy gave strong indication that the "some lawmakers" who sourced the *Times*' story were from the US Senate. Menendez sat on the Senate Foreign Affairs Committee.[1643] Durbin and Leahy both sat on a key Senate Appropriations subcommittee, State, Foreign Operations, and Related Programs. All would have access to key documents that were the basis of the *Times*' piece.

The letter showed more knowledge of the Javelin deal than the *Times*' article provided. The senators wrote directly to Yuriy Lutsenko, the prosecutor general of Ukraine, requesting that he reply to three questions.[1644] The first question tracked the *Times*' article, asking if his office had taken steps to restrict cooperation with the Special Counsel.[1645] But the second and third questions demonstrated that the three Senators were acting on information that went well beyond the *Times*' article—the senators wanted to know if Trump Administration officials had encouraged Ukraine not to pursue the cases and if the discussions regarding these choices were discussed at the United Nations General Assembly meeting between Trump and Poroshenko in September 2017.[1646] These allegations were not in the *Times*' story.

The source of those questions was a highly classified April 2018 State Department memorandum stating that Lutsenko had limited cooperation with Mueller and allowed Konstantin Kilimnik to escape from Ukraine to Russia.[1647] The memorandum also detailed the three Pennsylvania deals.

The memorandum was based on interviews of "Ukrainian office holders, prosecutors, and sources within the National Anti-Corruption Bureau of Ukraine."[1648] The sources in NABU told State Department officials that at the direction of senior officials in the Poroshenko administration, Lutsenko had blocked several investigations into Manafort.[1649] Classified State Department records showed Lutsenko was directed to do so by working with and "at the direction of several senior officials" in the Poroshenko administration according to US officials.[1650]

The classified report also noted that the Ukrainians were seeking military aid at the time.[1651] The report also indicated that the Kilimnik escape to Russia was authorized by senior officials of the Poroshenko administration.[1652] A *New York Times*' profile of Kilimnik written by Andrew Kramer had put Kilimnik in Kyiv as late as April 2018.[1653] State department analysts indicated in the report that it was highly unlikely these actions were taken without Poroshenko's personal approval.[1654]

Any report based on diplomatic cables and reports from Ukraine and interviews with Ukrainian government officials would most certainly involve the ambassador to Ukraine, Maria Yovanovitch. Not only did Yovanovitch champion NABU as part of her job, but she was also present at the June 7, 2017, Giuliani speech, the meeting between Poroshenko and Rick Perry at the Energy Department and the November 20, 2017, Giuliani visit to Kyiv. She would logically be the kind of witness that would be interviewed for the report.

It remains unclear as to why the report was produced. Although such reports touching on subjects involving the United States could be drafted, another possibility remains: that the State Department report was drafted in response to a request from Special Counsel Robert Mueller, or for the US counterintelligence operation that paralleled the Mueller investigation.

THE ORIGINS OF CONGRESSMAN-1

In early May 2018, Igor Fruman visited Anatevka for the opening of a children's school.[1655] A week later, Rabbi Azman offered up prayers for Trump in Kyiv, connecting them to positive developments for Israel, including "the historic decision of the US president to break the shameful nuclear deal with Iran," and the move of the US embassy in Israel from Tel Aviv to Jerusalem.[1656]

While the Javelin deal emerged into the open, Fruman and Parnas continued to work to pursue the dismissal of Yovanovitch. On May 3, Global Energy Producers made its first political donation, two weeks after its incorporation, a $15,000 donation to 35th Inc. a conservative Super PAC.[1657]

On May 9, Parnas and Fruman met with Texas congressman Pete Sessions to urge him to press for the removal of US ambassador to Ukraine, Marie Yovanovitch.[1658] They promised to raise at least $20,000 for Sessions's reelection campaign.[1659]

In response, Sessions wrote a letter to Mike Pompeo. The word "PRIVATE" in all caps was scribbled at the top.[1660] In it, he claimed he had "notice of concrete evidence from close companions that Ambassador Yovanovitch has spoken privately and repeatedly about her disdain for the current Administration in a way that might call for the expulsion of Ms. Yovanovitch as US Ambassador to Ukraine immediately."[1661] Sessions then made it clear what he wanted: "I kindly ask you to consider terminating her ambassadorship and find a replacement as soon as possible."[1662]

The pair soldiered on. On May 17, Parnas, using funds provided by Fruman from "a private lending transaction between Fruman and third parties," donated $325,000 to America First Action, the president's favored Super PAC.[1663] The donation was made in the name of Global Energy Producers.[1664]

"IT'S CLEAR THAT OUR SUPERIORS ARE TRYING TO CREATE OBSTACLES"

On May 23, 2018, an explosive story was published by the BBC's Paul Wood, a long-time foreign correspondent. The story went farther than the *New York Times* piece did. According to Wood, "Donald Trump's personal lawyer,

Michael Cohen, received a secret payment of at least $400,000 to fix talks between the Ukrainian president and President Trump[1665], according to sources in Kiev close to those involved."[1666] Wood went further: "Shortly after the Ukrainian president returned home, his country's anti-corruption agency stopped its investigation into Trump's former campaign manager, Paul Manafort."[1667]

Wood then said that a "high ranking Ukrainian intelligence officer" told him that Cohen was called in because Poroshenko could not get a meeting despite the efforts of the country's "high-priced lobbyists," no doubt a reference to BGR.[1668] According to the intelligence officer "the task was given to a former aide, who asked a loyal Ukrainian MP for help."[1669] That aide "used personal contacts in a Jewish charity in New York state, the Port of Washington Chabad."[1670] A second source in Kyiv confirmed the report, but gave the payment at $600,000.[1671] However, Cohen and "the two Ukrainians said to have opened the backchannel for their president" denied the report.[1672] The senior intelligence official that was one of the sources said that Cohen had been helped by Felix Sater.[1673]

There was more. The story pointed out the case had gone to the PGO and included a comment from Serhii Horbatiuk that "There was never a direct order to stop the Manafort inquiry but from the way our investigation has progressed, it's clear that our superiors are trying to create obstacles."[1674] Then it turned to the State report. Identifying it as "a report by a member of a Western country's intelligence community[1675] says Poroshenko's team believe they have established a "non-aggression pact" with Trump."[1676] This report, based on senior, "well-placed" intelligence sources in Kyiv, stated that "as soon as Trump was elected, the report says, Ukraine stopped "proactively" investigating Manafort."[1677]

Wood then extensively quoted the report, "Liaison with the US government was moved away from the National Anti-Corruption Bureau to a senior aide in the presidential administration."[1678] According to Wood, "The report states that Poroshenko returned from Washington and, in August or September, 2017, decided to completely end cooperation with the US agencies investigating Manafort.[1679] He did not give an order to implement this decision until November 2017."[1680] The report also said that "an "element of the understanding" between Poroshenko and Trump was that Ukraine agreed to import US coal and signed a $1 billion contract for American-made diesel trains.[1681] Wood also stated that the State Security Service of Ukraine had done their own secret report on Manafort.[1682] That report found that there were *three* documents that made up the "Black Ledger" and that Manafort had been paid "millions more" by Ukraine than had been disclosed.[1683]

The Ukrainian reaction was swift backpedaling. First, the day after the *New York Times* ran the article about the Javelin missiles, Lutsenko told Reuters "I am going to have negotiations with FBI officials and will talk about a joint investigation group with them" about Manafort.[1684] After the Wood BBC piece, Lutsenko also made an appearance on the Voice of America Ukrainian service and denied the *New York Times* story.[1685]

Josh Kovensky of the *Kyiv Post* asked a series of experts if they felt it was possible that the Wood story was true.[1686] All agreed it was possible. Kovensky also reached out to Andrii Artemenko and asked him if he was involved in the approach to Michael Cohen. "Artemenko replied 'hahaha,' before adding a smiley face emoji and declining to comment further."[1687] On June 1, 2018, Ukraine unfroze the cases again—apparently in response to the *Times* story.[1688]

"AT OUR QUIET DIRECTION"

On June 8, 2018, Paul Manafort was hit with a superseding indictment which also named Konstantin Kilimnik.[1689] The indictment accused him of being an unregistered foreign agent of the Party of Regions and the Opposition Bloc.[1690] The indictment detailed the creation of the Hapsburg Group to support Yanukovych, which it alleged Manafort, Gates, and Kilimnik set up to act "at our quiet direction"[1691] The government claimed that more than $75,000,000 flowed through the accounts set up by Manafort and that he had laundered more than $30,000,000 dollars of these funds.[1692] The superseding indictment went deep into the work performed by Manafort that was listed in the indictment, including his hiring of Skadden to defend the jailing of Tymoshenko.[1693]

Kilimnik was not charged as a coconspirator regarding the illegal foreign lobbying. Instead Counts 6 and 7 of the indictment alleged that Kilimnik and Manafort attempted to tamper with two witnesses in the case.[1694] On June 15, at the government's request, Manafort was taken into custody and his bail revoked.[1695] Trump tweeted that it was "very unfair" and that he "didn't know Manafort was the head of the Mob."[1696] Rudy Giuliani blithely told the *New York Daily News* that "when the whole thing is over, things might get cleaned up with some presidential pardons."[1697]

IT'S GOOD TO PUT A NAME WITH A FACE

In June 2018, Parnas and Fruman stepped up their donations to GOP groups. On June 6, Parnas, as CEO of Loan Crime Investigative Group, donated $3,300 to the National Republican Congressional Committee.[1698] The money was transferred to the Protect the House Joint Fundraising Committee.[1699] That same day Cherna Moskowitz, the wife of well-known GOP donor Dr. Irving I. Moskowitz, donated $1,000,000 to America First Action.[1700] Her son, Yechezekel, a politically active rabbi, was associated with a politically conservative group of Orthodox synagogues known as the Young Israel movement. Its president was Farley Weiss.[1701]

Rabbi Moskowitz and 150 other Trump supporters descended on the Trump International Hotel in Washington for an America First Action "summit meeting."[1702] Parnas and Fruman continued donating, with Parnas donating $2,700 to Pete Sessions on June 25,[1703] $5,000 to the Great America Committee on June 29,[1704] $11,000 to Protect the House,[1705] and $2,700 to Kevin McCarthy.[1706]

Fruman also made large donations. Prior to the Washington "summit" he made another set of illegal donations using the "Furman" alias. Thirteen Republican congressional candidates received over $2,700 from Fruman.[1707] He then dropped another $50,000 on Protect the House.[1708] After the America First Action meeting, he donated $2,700 each to an additional six GOP congressional candidates.[1709]

Parnas and Fruman also made friends. While there, they met a man named Dr. Joseph Frager, the first vice president of Young Israel.[1710] One of the main areas of interest for Dr. Frager was Israeli settlements in the West Bank.[1711]

Frager told the Jewish Telegraphic Agency that the men approached him because he was wearing a yarmulke.[1712] He also told reporters that he invited the pair to a summer trip to Efrat, a town in the Jordan Valley. The trip would include Fox News host Mike Huckabee, the former Republican governor of Arkansas, and Anthony Scaramucci, Trump's short-lived White House communications director.[1713] The pair agreed.

Parnas and Fruman also met two other men at the event: the president's new lawyer, Rudy Giuliani, and a Long Island personal injury lawyer named Charles Gucciardo.[1714] According to Parnas, Giuliani noticed him and said, "I've seen you around, it's good to put a name to a face."[1715] Parnas and Giuliani hit it off.

Testimony by Ambassador Yovanovitch indicates that Giuliani was already interested in Ukraine by June 2018. According to her account, a deputy of Lutsenko told the acting chargé d'affaires of the US Embassy Joseph Pennington, that Lutsenko and Giuliani met for the first time in June of 2018.[1716]

"GAY PARADE ON BLOOD"

While Parnas and Fruman were donating to GOP candidates to get rid of US ambassador Maria Yovanovitch, another American was also doing so—Pastor Dale Armstrong. On June 17, Kyiv Pride was held in the Ukrainian capital.[1717] Marie Yovanovitch and George Kent led more than sixty US Embassy staffers to support the marchers.[1718]

Groups of evangelical Ukrainians engaged in some American-style pressure group tactics when they alleged police brutality when they were not allowed to "join" the LGBTQ parade, which they labeled the "GAY PARADE ON BLOOD" on a webpage targeting the chief of the patrol police in Kyiv.[1719] The situation angered Pastor Armstrong, who tweeted his displeasure days later about Yovanovitch flying the rainbow flag, calling for her to resign.[1720]

Giuliani continued to defend the president with unusual and erratic performances. However, he understood his job was to provide a new version of truth. In May he suggested to the *Washington Post* that the Mueller investigation "may have a different version of the truth than we do."[1721] Giuliani crowed that Mueller's decision not to seek an exception to Justice Department policy that the president could not be indicted, but his appearances became bizarre demonstrations of the "alternate explanation" method common to Russian politics.[1722] His contradictions of the president didn't matter, he argued "those don't amount to anything—what is said to the press. That's political."[1723]

The politics went as follows: Trump's lawyers believed that if the GOP lost the midterms, the president would be impeached, and they sought to discredit the Mueller investigation as the election approached.[1724] The politics involved attacks on the FBI and the DOJ. Trump continuously called it a "witch hunt" on Twitter.[1725]

Representative Adam Schiff of California, then the ranking Democrat on the House Permanent Select Committee on Intelligence, was concerned about effect of these attacks on the Department of Justice. "This is an effort by the president to distract from his legal troubles and throw as much mud into the air as he can," Schiff told the *New York Times*, "but it's doing enormous damage to the Justice Department. If they think they can placate him, they'll probably find that doesn't work. That doesn't placate a bully."[1726]

"THE BLACK LEDGER WAS ALWAYS INVOLVED"

It appears that July 20, 2018, is the first date that Giuliani, Parnas, and Fruman began communicating over messaging apps. An extraction report of their conversations begins on that date.[1727] Parnas and Fruman were now in direct contact with the personal lawyer of the president of the United States.

These efforts did not go unnoticed, however. Lachlan Markay, reporter for the *Daily Beast*, had a newsletter focusing on money in US politics.[1728] He came across an unusual set of donations from a Delaware corporation to the president's favored SuperPAC, America First Action. That corporation was Global Energy Producers.[1729] In his newsletter, Markay wondered exactly who the people were associated with the company and asked for others to provide any information.[1730] Brendan Fischer worked for the Campaign Legal Center, a nonprofit devoted to monitoring the US election system.[1731] Fischer's colleague Margaret Christ found a request for a graphic designer to provide a logo for GEP.[1732] One of the donations led to a private address—that of Lev Parnas.[1733]

Using Google Translate, they found Shimon Briman's curious Russian-language articles based on his interviews with Fruman.[1734] They found discussions of a cryptic back channel between a Ukrainian national and the president of the United States—Azman.[1735] The accompanying photographs were even more interesting—they showed the two men with President Trump.[1736]

The Campaign Legal Center does more than just research violations of election law; they file complaints.[1737] And, with Margaret Christ as the named complainant, they did just that. On July 25, 2018, the center filed *Campaign Legal Center, et al. v. Parnas*.[1738]

> Based on published reports, there is reason to believe that GEP may have violated 52 USC. § 30122 by "[g]iving money . . . all or

part of which was provided to" GEP by Igor Fruman, Lev Parnas, or another person (i.e., the true contributor(s)) without disclosing the true source of money at the time of making the contribution to America First Action.[1739]

Bloomberg News picked up on the complaint, naming Parnas and Fruman in print.[1740] Lev Parnas and Igor Fruman now had their first appearance in the US media.

At some point, Rudy Giuliani decided that he needed to respond to whatever came out of the Mueller investigation. On July 30, Giuliani told reporters that he was working on a "counter report" to the Mueller report.[1741] The Special Counsel, Giuliani predicted, would have his report done by September 1. "I don't think he wants to be seen as interfering with the election" Rudy told *USA Today*.[1742]

According to Parnas, Giuliani was obsessed with rebutting the Black Ledger with a counter-report. "The Black Ledger was always involved," Parnas would later say.[1743] However, Giuliani needed help from Ukrainians in writing his report. According to Parnas, Giuliani chose to work with him and Fruman to get the information he needed involving Ukraine.[1744]

That required money. Coincidentally, Parnas and Fruman hired Giuliani to work with one of their many shell companies, Fraud Guarantee.[1745] Giuliani had learned dark political financing techniques from his post-Soviet teachers. Charles Gucciardo loaned the pair $500,000, labeled as a loan convertible into an interest in Parnas's Fraud Guarantee, a company that had no business and no customers. The funds allowed them to pay Giuliani his fee. The deal finalized in August and Giuliani was paid in two installments in September and October.

In late July, the pair went on the Israel trip with New York gastroenterologist Dr. Joseph Frager.[1746] While there, the group mingled with right-wing Israeli billionaire Simon Falic.[1747] Also in attendance was one of Benjamin Netanyahu's sons, and the US ambassador to Israel David Friedman, Trump's former bankruptcy lawyer.[1748] A tweet from Jacob Kornbluh identified the party as taking place at Falic's Jerusalem home, where a now-deleted video showed Mike Huckabee playing bass.[1749] The tweet also mentioned Parnas by name.[1750]

From Jerusalem, Parnas, Fruman, and Governor Huckabee apparently went to visit with Rabbi Moshe Azman outside Kyiv. Photos placed the three at Anatevka with Azman on August 2.[1751] Photos of Parnas with the president at a New York fundraiser on August 13 demonstrate that he had returned to the United States before the middle of the month.[1752]

On an August 2018 night, Rudy Giuliani treated a group of his closest friends to a private cruise around New York City.[1753] Parnas and Fruman were among the guests.[1754]

SERVANT OF THE PEOPLE

One of the most popular shows on Ukrainian television is the comedy *Servant of the People*, which first aired in 2015. Appearing on the network

1+1, it followed a schoolteacher whose students posted a YouTube video of him candidly cursing to a colleague about the state of Ukraine, its politics, and corruption.[1755] The video goes viral and the teacher is accidentally elected President of Ukraine, despite not campaigning.

The harried schoolteacher was played by comedian Volodymyr Zelenskyy.[1756] But some of the reality of corruption touched the show. The owner of 1+1 television and patron of *Servant of the People* was Ihor Kolomoisky, a banker who had fled Ukraine in 2017 after his Privatbank, the country's largest, had collapsed due to billions of dollars' worth of unsecured loans to associates of Kolomoisky in a large-scale fraud.[1757] On December 18, 2016, the Poroshenko government had nationalized the bank to prevent the loss of the savings of millions of Ukrainians.[1758] Eighty percent of the bank's capital had been disbursed in insider loans.[1759] The bank had a $4 billion hole on its balance sheet and controlled 73 percent of the deposits in the country.[1760] Kolomoisky fled to Israel. The total loss was $5.5 billion.[1761]

In late 2017, Zelenskyy's lawyer registered "Servant of the People" as a political party in Ukraine.[1762] By August 2018, Zelenskyy was running second in the upcoming presidential election to Yulia Tymoshenko, the country's most popular politician.[1763]

"SUCH RESPECT FOR A BRAVE MAN!"

Despite Rudy's rosy predictions, things were not going well for Donald Trump in the legal arena. Signs of a split between him and his former attorney, Michael Cohen, emerged. In late July, a tape of Trump and Cohen discussing hush payments regarding a Playboy model was released by the *New York Times*.[1764]

But the biggest political danger to the president was the upcoming trial of Paul Manafort in Alexandria. It began on July 31, with charges that involved tax fraud.[1765] From the witness stand, Rick Gates told jurors about shell companies, and Manafort's tax preparer described her efforts to shield his income from taxation.[1766] Ukrainians were surprised to learn from the trial of the $60 million that Yanukovych sent to a dizzying array of shell companies, and Manafort and Gates's brief work for Poroshenko in 2014.[1767]

On August 15, the case went to the jury.[1768] On the 21st, the jury came back. Guilty on eight of eighteen counts, with a lone juror preventing conviction on the other ten counts.[1769] A second trial, in the District of Columbia, remained.

There was more bad news for the Trump defense lawyers. On August 21, Cohen pleaded guilty to eight charges including campaign finance violations.[1770] The next day, Trump tweeted about the cases:

> I feel very badly for Paul Manafort[1771] and his wonderful family. "Justice" took a 12 year old tax case, among other things, applied tremendous pressure on him and, unlike Michael Cohen, he refused to "break" - make up stories in order to get a "deal." Such respect for a brave man![1772]

Fruman continued his travel. According to a story in *Livyi Bereh,* Igor Fruman appeared at the 120th anniversary of Azman's Brodsky Synagogue in Kyiv on August 26.[1773] The photos were taken by Shimon Briman, the same writer who had interviewed Fruman twice.[1774] Where went Fruman, so went Briman.

At the celebration, Fruman announced a fundraising drive for Anatevka. He told the Brodsky crowd that he wanted to raise a million dollars and would match donations up to that amount. The anniversary also included video greetings from Israeli prime minister Benjamin Netanyahu.[1775]

A week later, Azman flew to London to give a speech.[1776] While there, he received a video message from Giuliani, Fruman, and Parnas, apparently from the lobby of the Trump International in Washington.[1777]

On September 3, 2018, Petro Poroshenko sued the BBC, alleging defamation for its statement, published in an article by Paul Wood, that he had paid a bribe of $400,000 to open a back channel with Michael Cohen. The claim was that the BBC had stated "the Claimant had made or arranged for a secret payment of $400,000 to Michael Cohen, the personal lawyer of Donald Trump, in order to fix back-channel talks between him and the American president in June 2017, and were therefore guilty of serious corruption."[1778]

In British courts, the journalist or writer has the burden of proof and must show that the claim presented is true, unlike the rest of the world, where a defamation plaintiff must show that the statement was untrue.[1779] As a result, the UK is a destination for "libel tourism," where, according to a UK lawyer, "crooks and brigands from around the world come here to launder their reputations, where they couldn't get exculpation in either their home country or indeed in the United States of America."[1780] Although an amendment to UK law reduced libel tourism, in Poroshenko's case, the BBC's place of business was in the UK.[1781]

In a DC court on September 14, 2018, an assistant US attorney had a shocking statement to make. Paul Manafort was cooperating and would plead guilty.[1782] Within minutes, Paul Manafort told Judge Amy Berman Jackson: "I plead guilty."[1783] The parties had been negotiating since September 9.[1784] *Washington Post* writers pointed out that the plea deal would spare the administration weeks of negative stories during the thick of the 2018 midterm elections[1785],[1786]

Manafort confessed to a lengthy set of crimes and a criminal information indicated that he wanted to "plant some stink on Tymo" and then get "obama [sic] jews' [sic] to put pressure on the administration to disavow Tymoshenko and support Yanukovych."[1787] The "client shall cooperate fully, truthfully, completely, and forthrightly with the Government" the plea deal stipulated.[1788]

By September, Parnas and Giuliani often worked in the Trump International Hotel four or five times a week. Giuliani had his own table, roped off and with a plaque that reserved the place for "Mayor Giuliani," due to his near-constant presence in the hotel. But Parnas and Fruman were allowed to use the table when they pleased, even when Giuliani was not there, according to a source familiar with the meetings.

They would arrive in the morning nearly every day and eat breakfast and leave, sometimes returning later in the day. A source described Parnas and Fruman as looking like gangsters with T-shirts, sport coats, and gold chains. These meetings would continue for months.

"DON'T YOU THINK IT'S KIND OF STUPID FOR TWO STRAIGHT MEN TO BE CARRYING PERFUME FOR LADIES?"

On September 5, the British Crown Prosecution Service announced charges against two Russian men for the Skripal killing, Alexander Petrov and Ruslan Boshirov, which the UK government stated were aliases for two GRU officers whose names the government strongly hinted they already knew.[1789] Using a squad of "super recognizers," officers with an innate gift for memorizing faces, the Metropolitan Police went over 5,000 hours of footage and identified the two suspects.[1790]

Russia did not wait long to set up the alternate explanation with an interview. *Russia Today*'s editor-in-chief, Margarita Simonyan explained how she got the scoop: "You called my cell phone, saying that you were Ruslan Boshirov and Alexander Petrov."[1791] "You look like the people from the pictures and videos from the UK. So, who are you in reality?" Simonyan asked.[1792] The two insisted that they were indeed named Boshirov and Petrov and that they were in the fitness industry. They were visiting Salisbury because "our friends have been suggesting for quite a long time that we visit this wonderful city," though they admitted, "there's not that much to do there."[1793] The two displayed impressive details about the local tourist attractions, including the precise height of Salisbury Cathedral's 123-meter spire.[1794] When asked about the perfume bottle the police had identified as the murder weapon, Boshirov answered: "Don't you think that it's kind of stupid for two straight men to be carrying perfume for ladies?"[1795]

The independent open-source reporters Bellingcat went after "Petrov" and "Boshirov" with gusto. The next day, they had already associated the pair's passport numbers with a range linked to the Russian Security Service.[1796] Bellingcat's review of the men's travel records showed travel across Europe for the two years their passports existed.[1797]

By September 26, Bellingcat had identified Boshirov as Colonel Chepiga. From former Russian military officers the investigative news site learned that the best school for foreign language and covert operations training was the Far Eastern Military Command Academy, so they leafed through yearbook and reunion photos until they found Chepiga's picture.[1798] Using Russian databases leaked on the Internet, they soon had several addresses, his original passport number, and his military serial number.[1799] The comments on the article filled to the brim with commenters defending Russia in broken English.[1800]

Bellingcat's scoop drew a quick response. Dimitry Peskov, the spokesman for the Ministry of Foreign Affairs and close confidant of Putin, responded personally to the website, claiming to reporters that there was no evidence a Chepiga had ever been awarded the decorations Bellingcat claimed.[1801] The Bellingcat Investigation Team scoured the internet until it found the colonel's picture on a "wall of heroes" at the Far Eastern Military Command Academy.[1802]

Bellingcat turned to the second suspect. Working on the theory that some agents use most of their personal details in a cover story, the Bellingcat team used a reference to an older passport issued in St. Petersburg on the fake passport application of "Petrov," and reviewed leaked Russian databases for travel documents issued to persons with the same first name on the same day as "Petrov." They found Dr. Alexander Mishkin. They then reached out on social media to all graduates of the St. Petersburg military medical academy, who said that they knew Mishkin and that they recognized him as "Petrov" on the *Russia Today* broadcast.[1803] Mishkin's leaked passport application provided the ultimate proof—"Petrov" was Mishkin, also a Hero of Russia for his actions in Ukraine in 2014.[1804]

By early February 2019, Bellingcat had identified a *third* suspect, one who had not been charged by the Crown Prosecution Service. It was Major General Denis Sergeev.[1805]

By July 2019, Bellingcat had a near-complete record of the murder attempt, including tracking all the telephone calls the three made during their mission to kill Skripal.[1806]

"THEY WILL START A HUNDRED INVESTIGATIONS"

Bud Cummins was the foreign agent for Yulia Tymoshenko.[1807] Formerly the US attorney for the Eastern District of Arkansas, he was pushed out as part of George W. Bush's attempt to remake the US attorneys into more political operatives in 2007.[1808] In 2016, Cummins had served as Donald Trump's campaign director for Arkansas.[1809]

On October 18, 2018, he sent an email to the United States attorney for the Southern District of New York, Geoffrey Berman.[1810] The message contained information claiming to show that the Bidens were involved in corruption connected to Burisma. It also purported to show that the Black Ledger was false.[1811] The emails said that Yuriy Lutsenko had such information and wanted to meet with the FBI in order to provide it to prosecutors.[1812] Berman took no action.

Yulia Tymoshenko became the second major Ukrainian politician to fall into Trump's orbit. Once imprisoned with the help of Paul Manafort, she was now working on the same side as Manafort. She would not be the last.

As operatives like Cummins worked to bring forth information from Ukraine that allegedly implicated the Bidens, the midterm campaigns of 2018 were in full swing. The headwinds were against Trump from the start.

In 2017, the Trump revolution had its first test, the statewide elections in Virginia. The revolution hit stormy weather. The Democratic candidate for governor, Ralph Northam, won 53–44.[1813] Democrats came one race shy of tying the GOP lead in the House of Delegates, flipping fifteen out of 100 seats.[1814] In the formerly Republican suburbs of Chesterfield and Henrico counties, Democrats now ruled supreme.[1815]

Abigail Sparnberger lived in those suburbs. The former CIA agent and Arabic linguist, angered by Trump's attempt to repeal Obamacare, decided that she wanted to run against Dave Brat, a loyal Trump supporter whose surprise primary defeat of House Majority Whip Eric Cantor had been a herald of the Trump revolution.[1816]

In the general election, Brat went through the Republican playbook. At a debate Brat brought up "Nancy Pelosi" and her "liberal agenda" twenty-one times, prompting Spanberger to quip in response: "I question again whether Congressman Brat knows which Democrat in fact he's running against . . . My name is Abigail Spanberger."[1817] The playbook also included attacks on her job teaching English literature at a boarding school for Saudis in the DC suburbs that Brat ads dubbed "Terror High."[1818]

The Republicans acted scared for good reason. Despite riling up their base during the confirmation battle surrounding Supreme Court judge Brett Kavanaugh, polling showed that they were likely to lose the House.[1819]

Control of the speaker's gavel meant control of the largest investigative apparatus of an entire branch of government. This very much troubled Rudy.

Giuliani, who huddled with supporters in Queens at the home of the Young Israel vice president, Dr.Joseph Frager, five days before the elections. In addition to his work as a doctor, Frager was the first executive vice president of the National Council of Young Israel, a politically conservative Jewish organization.[1820] The topic was the midterm elections.

Lev Parnas stepped forward. He introduced Rabbi Moshe Azman to Giuliani, calling him "one of your biggest supporters."[1821] Giuliani warned: "the part of their winning is that the House will go crazy. They will start a hundred investigations."[1822] Parnas agreed: "Oh you're right."[1823] "They'll go overboard" Rudy predicted.[1824]

Election day arrived. Abigail Spanberger beat Dave Brat, winning a majority of the voters with a margin of 16,000 votes.[1825] The Democrats needed twenty-four votes to control the House. In a landslide, they won forty seats.[1826]

CHAPTER 9:

THE DESPERATE CIRCUS

One day after the 2018 midterm elections, Attorney General Jeff Sessions was forced out by Donald Trump.[1827] In September, Sessions had been compelled to take on Matt Whittaker as his deputy.[1828] The Departmental Ethics Office for the Department of Justice informed Whittaker that he should recuse himself from the Russia investigation due to his earlier defense of the President on television and filing of complaints against Democrats. He refused.[1829]

On December 7, Trump announced his replacement, former attorney general for George H. W. Bush, William Barr.[1830] His appointment began with an immediate controversy. His advocacy for pardoning scandal-plagued Bush officials gained him the nickname "Cover-up General Barr."[1831] Barr was one of the loudest voices supporting the theory of the "unitary executive" that held that the president had very broad powers to do almost whatever he wanted with the executive office.¹⁸³²

"I ACTUALLY KNOW THE GUY VAGUELY FROM YEARS AGO"

Although it is unclear how Giuliani became aware of Viktor Shokin as a possible witness in his drive to take down Joe Biden, the evidence points to Bud Cummins, the registered foreign agent for Yulia Tymoshenko. On October 24, 2018, Shokin lost his final appeal in his case to be restored as Ukraine's prosecutor general when the Court of Cassation in Kyiv ruled against him.¹⁸³³ His next move was to the European Court of Human Rights.¹⁸³⁴ A cluster of events in November and December of 2018 indicate that Giuliani's focus turned sharply toward Joe Biden, and Viktor Shokin in particular.

By mid-November, it appears that Giuliani and Parnas had become personally close. Texts from iMessage pulled from Parnas's phone show Giuliani asking Parnas, "Want to meet at Shelly's at 10 for a cigar???" in mid-November.¹⁸³⁵ Parnas messaged back that he was bringing Congressman Pete Sessions with him.¹⁸³⁶ Parnas and Fruman had moved very far, very fast. They were about to move even farther.

The first of the events that appear to have intensified the drive against the Bidens occurred late on the evening of November 26.¹⁸³⁷ The joint status report filed by the parties in *US v. Paul Manafort, Jr.* stated that the government asked that the case go immediately to a presentencing report because the defendant had breached his plea deal with the government.[1838] Manafort's lawyers predictably disagreed.[1839]

The next day, the *New York Times* revealed that Manafort's legal team had "repeatedly briefed" the president's legal team in the two and-a-half months since their client had signed a plea bargain.[1840] According to the report, the president's team knew what Manafort was telling Mueller's team.[1841] Giuliani confirmed the details to the *Times*.[1842]

Less than twenty-four hours later, Rudy Giuliani claims he was sitting in his office when he got a call from a former subordinate, Bart M. Schwartz,[1843] who had headed the Criminal Division of the US Attorney's Office when Giuliani led it. Now, Schwartz ran Guidepost Solutions, a corporate investigation firm headquartered in New York.[1844] Giuliani and Schwartz had also been in business together, running two investigation-related businesses in the early 2000s.[1845] Schwartz has an extensive donation history with the national Republican Party going back more than thirty years.[1846]

Schwartz had news for his old boss and business partner—he had a source that claimed that Ukraine had interfered in the 2016 election.[1847] The source, he said, wanted to let Giuliani know what he knew.[1848] That source was a man named Michael Guralnik. Giuliani claimed Schwartz had encountered Guralnik in an investigation he had been hired to complete.[1849]

Giuliani was cryptic about Guralnik. He told *Politico*, "I actually know the guy vaguely from years ago."[1850] He danced around the details surrounding Guralnik: "He had a bit of an investigatory background, which I can't—he had a bit of investigatory background, let me just say that."[1851]

Guralnik, according to Giuliani, was a Ukrainian who went back to Ukraine often and, while admitting that he did not have a first-hand knowledge, had "been told by many Ukrainians—and now it's so many I can't ignore it—a lot of things . . . solid evidence of Ukrainian involvement in the 2016 election with Democrats, specifically with Hillary Clinton's campaign."[1852] Giuliani claims he did a week of due diligence on Guralnik and then later Schwartz spent a significant amount of time with the source.[1853] Parnas also met Guralnik.[1854]

At almost the same exact time, Giuliani and outgoing HSPCI chair Devin Nunes turned their attention to Viktor Shokin. According to one of Lev Parnas's lawyers, Lev set up meetings between Viktor Shokin and Devin Nunes in Vienna in late November of 2018.[1855] Congressman Nunes has denied these meetings, but House travel records show that Nunes and two aides flew to Europe on HPSCI official business on November 30, returning on December 3.[1856] Although it is not clear if the meeting was associated with Dmytro Firtash, later events would demonstrate that Firtash was deeply involved in financing much of the anti-Biden operation.

According to Parnas, Nunes staffer Derek Harvey informed him that the congressman was conducting his own investigation of Biden and Burisma.[1857]

THE "SECRET MISSION"

On December 5, 2018, former President George H. W. Bush was eulogized in a funeral at Washington National Cathedral. Rudy Giuliani was invited. In a sign of their deepening personal and professional ties, Giuliani, Parnas, and Fruman came to the ceremony together.[1858]

The next day was Thursday, December 6, 2018. It was the day of the annual White House Hanukkah party. Rudy Giuliani took Lev Parnas, his son Aaron Parnas, and Igor Fruman to the event.[1859] Parnas and Fruman were photographed with the president, the vice president, and Giuliani, the president's lawyer.[1860] The gathering was raucous, as guests spontaneously drowned out the President with chants of "four more years."[1861]

At some point during the party, Giuliani went into a meeting with the president. Parnas and Fruman were told that they were needed in the Red Room with the president. The president told Parnas and Fruman that he was assigning them a mission—to go on a "secret mission" to pressure the Ukrainian government into investigating Joe and Hunter Biden.[1862] One of the friends told CNN that Parnas viewed the assignment as a "Great Crusade."[1863] Parnas posted a photograph of himself with Trump.[1864] It would be the last photo of himself and Trump that he would post to social media.

The next day, December 7, Rudy Giuliani remained in Washington. Parnas was thrilled to have been able to take his son to the White House and effusively thanked Giuliani for the opportunity, saying "you are the best and I truly mean that from my heart."[1865] That day, Giuliani had a meeting scheduled with Fatherland Party leader Yulia Tymoshenko.[1866] Tymoshenko was in Washington to meet with US leaders ahead of her 2019 run for the presidency of Ukraine. At the meeting, Giuliani asked Tymoshenko to invite Yuriy Lutsenko to meet with him and discuss Joe and Hunter Biden and Burisma.[1867] When she returned to Ukraine, she told Lutsenko that Giuliani had wanted to talk to her about Burisma and the Bidens, as well.[1868]

That day, Parnas sent Giuliani several articles, including one noting that Tymoshenko's new US lobbyist was GOP firm Livingston Partners.[1869] Parnas also got Giuliani up to speed on his and Fruman's earlier efforts. He messaged Rudy a copy of the letter Congressman Pete Sessions had sent to Pompeo in May.[1870]

That same day, the Special Counsel filed a submission stating that Manafort had lied about his contacts with Kilimnik; Kilimnik's role in the obstruction conspiracy; a payment in the indictment; information he provided regarding a case in another district; and his contacts with the Trump administration.[1871] That was not the worst outcome for the president in the courts that day. Prosecutors in New York filed a document in the Cohen matter which alleged that during the campaign, Trump had directed Cohen to make illegal hush-money payments to women Trump had had sexual encounters with that he wanted to conceal.[1872]

Giuliani caught a break in his quest to discredit the Black Ledger. On December 18, the Kyiv Administrative Court ruled that Sergii Leshchenko and Artem Sytnyk had acted illegally when the revealed that Manafort's name was found in the Black Ledger in August 2016.[1873] Giuliani would cite this decision as evidence the Black Ledger was fake long after it had been overturned on appeal the following summer.

Parnas and Giuliani were rapidly becoming quite close. Giuliani joked with Parnas: "On tarmac for one hour. I think Mueller knew I was on this plane and is delaying it so he gets me to say whatever he wants me to say," America's Mayor joked.[1874] "He wants me to say that 35 years ago DT didn't pay two parking tickets. You say what's so important? Well they may have been right in front of the Soviet Embassy. I WILL NOT BE BROKEN."[1875] Parnas responded "LOL."

Parnas then went to Ukraine, possibly with Fruman, returning, according to his messages, on December 23.[1876] They apparently met with a deputy of Lutsenko, a regional prosecutor who told Lutsenko that Giuliani wanted to meet with Lutsenko in New York.[1877]

Next, according to one of Lev Parnas's lawyers, Mr. Guralnik wrote two letters detailing his corruption accusations, one to Senator Lindsey Graham, the second to a Treasury official.[1878] The letter to the Treasury official mentioned that Guralnik was a ten-year veteran of the Soviet Army and a "former intelligence source." Both letters accused Ukrainian officials of arranging to purchase spare military parts from sanctioned Russian firms.[1879] These letters claimed Lutsenko attempted to investigate the case but was ordered by Poroshenko to stop because Poroshenko, Zlochevsky, former

Ukrainian Central Bank governor Valeriya Gontereva, and others were to profit from the alleged scheme.[1880]

Giuliani then engaged with both Yuriy Lutsenko, the current prosecutor general of Ukraine and his immediate predecessor, Viktor Shokin, regarding allegations about Biden. A first Skype call occurred with Shokin sometime in late 2018, likely December.[1881] The trio began to work toward a visa for Shokin and at least one other Ukrainian to come to the United States. The US Embassy in Kyiv informed Shokin on January 9 that his visa had been denied.[1882] Parnas, apparently in Ukraine, messaged Giuliani about the issue, and Giuliani told him, "I can revive it."[1883] Using his cell phone, Parnas sent along photos of both the denial and Shokin's passport.[1884]

The visa request for Shokin went awry. Shokin obtained tickets to fly to the United States on January 12 but the visa never came.[1885] iMessages between Parnas and Giuliani indicate that the three enlisted Jay Sekulow into the effort.[1886] Giuliani began making calls to the State Department.[1887]

Several days of intense discussions were undertaken. The State Department decided not to grant the visa, because according to Kent, "[k]nowing Mr. Shokin, I had full faith that it was a bunch of hooey, and he was looking to basically engage in a con game out of revenge because he'd lost his job."[1888] When the State Department refused to grant the visa, Giuliani called the manager by reaching out to Deputy White House Chief of Staff Rob Blair.[1889] Blair called State for a background on the situation and when Blair learned what was happening, he told Kent, Wess Mitchell, and a third official that he had heard enough.[1890] Shokin did not get the visa.

Accordingly, the group set a Skype call for January 23, 2019, with Giuliani, Parnas, Fruman, and Shokin.[1891] According to notes of the call, Mr. Shokin made allegations about Vice President Biden and Burisma.[1892] Mr. Shokin also claimed that Ambassador Yovanovitch had improperly denied him a US visa and that she was close to Vice President Biden.

According to a memorandum of the Skype call, Shokin claimed that then ambassador Pyatt told him in June or July of 2015 that Pyatt told him to handle the Burisma investigation with "white gloves," which Shokin claimed "implied do nothing."[1893] Shokin then stated that President Poroshenko had told him to stop investigating Burisma because, "it was not in the interest of "Joe and/or Hunter Biden."[1894] The claims were false, as Shokin had deliberately scuppered the Burisma investigation in 2015.

In regard to the Black Ledger, Shokin said there were leaks "by a person named Reshenko" of the "Ukrainian State Secret Service" and that there "is possible deceit" in the "Manafort Black Book."[1895]

On January 25 and 26, Prosecutor General Yuriy Lutsenko was in New York and met with Giuliani, Parnas, and Fruman, reportedly to discuss whether Ambassador Yovanovitch was "loyal to President Trump," as well as investigations into Burisma and the Bidens.[1896] For his part, Mr. Lutsenko later said he "understood very well" that Mr. Giuliani wanted Mr. Lutsenko to investigate former Vice President Biden and his son, Hunter. "I have 23 years in politics," Mr. Lutsenko said. "I knew. . . . I'm a political animal."[1897] He also provided documents to Giuliani. During the meeting, Giuliani called President Trump to excitedly tell him of Lutsenko's information.[1898] Rumors swept Kyiv that Trump spoke with Lutsenko and Giuliani.[1899]

During these sessions Lutsenko then made false claims about the Black Ledger. First, he described a large money laundering operation that began in 2010 for the purposes of political bribery, but stated that the funds for the bribery scheme were laundered via Franklin Templeton, a US investment firm, not in US real estate in New York City.[1900] The story was fake.

Lutsenko also falsely stated that the Black Ledger was ten to twelve pages, rather than 900 pages long, and was found near the home of "a former deputy of the Ukrainian Secret Service."[1901] No mention was made of its revelation in the Ukrainian press.

Lutsenko also claimed that the Black Ledger cases were opened "several weeks" after the discovery of the documents.[1902] Again, he repeated the claim that no signature existed next to Paul Manafort's name, but acknowledged that records existed of wire transfers from Kyrgyzstan.[1903]

When Lutsenko reached the accusations about the Bidens, his evidence got far thinner. While detailing the amounts he claimed were paid to board members of Burisma, Lutsenko conveniently told Giuliani that the amounts paid to Biden and his business partner, Devon Archer, were not revealed by Latvian authorities.[1904] However, Lutsenko told Giuliani, Parnas, and Fruman that the amounts disbursed by Burisma could reach the ridiculous amount of

$100 million.[1905] Lutsenko then claimed that in his first week in office, Yovanovitch asked him to drop three cases, including one against Serhii Leshchenko, despite the fact that the ambassador did not take office until months after his elevation to the position.[1906]

Rudy Giuliani reached out to Arsen Avakov, the long-serving interior minister of Ukraine, likely in late January, requesting assistance with efforts to find information on the Black Ledger.[1907] Avakov studiously avoided Giuliani's partisan efforts.[1908]

In mid-February, Giuliani sought to meet with Lutsenko again.[1909] Rudy was in Warsaw, attending a conference designed to drum up support amongst the Western Allies for more punitive measures against Iran. The Iranians called it a "desperate circus."[1910]

Giuliani messaged Parnas wanting to see if Lutsenko would join him. Parnas messaged back "The Attorney General of Ukraine will meet us for dinner tomorrow at 7 pm in Warsaw Poland."[1911]

At some point in February, Marie Yovanovitch learned that Rudy Giuliani was trying to get her fired. During a conversation with Interior Minister Arsen Avakov, the US ambassador was warned that Giuliani, Parnas, and Fruman were meeting with a series of Ukrainian officials seeking information on Joe Biden, Burisma, and the Black Ledger.[1912] It was the first Yovanovitch had heard of Parnas and Fruman.

Parnas and Fruman remained in Europe and headed to Ukraine. In late February they continued their campaign. This time, they met with the President Poroshenko, in the offices of the prosecutor general, Yuriy Lutsenko.[1913] In the meeting the pair pressed Poroshenko to launch investigations into the Bidens and Burisma in exchange for a new visit to the White House.[1914] Poroshenko thought that a White House visit would help him in his long-shot campaign to be reelected.[1915] Text messages indicate that Parnas told Giuliani that he just finished meeting with the "older gentleman" on February 16.[1916]

Immediately thereafter, Rudy Giuliani entered into a contract in Ukraine.[1917] Several agreements were circulated. The first contemplated Giuliani, and lawyers Victoria Toensing and Joseph diGenova representing Lutsenko to recover alleged funds stolen from the government of Ukraine for $200,000.[1918]

A series of text messages between Parnas and Giuliani next show Lev acting as middleman between the Ukrainian Ministry of Justice and the three lawyers involving a second proposed contract.[1919] Parnas arranged for a retainer agreement and payment on the 18th and 19th.[1920] The amount for this agreement was $300,000.[1921]

Months later, Giuliani would claim that he spent about a month considering a deal with the Ukrainian government, but that he decided not to move forward. "I thought it would be too complicated," he told the *New York Times*, "I never received a penny."[1922]

"A BIG, FAT, FISHING EXPEDITION DESPERATELY IN SEARCH OF A CRIME"

While Giuliani sought information to discredit the Mueller investigation, news of some of the subjects it concerned began to reach the public. Mueller was investigating Trump associates' attempts to broker peace between Russia and Ukraine. A failed redaction by Manafort's lawyers revealed that Manafort had directed polling information to Kilimnik, that he met with Kilimnik in New York and Madrid, and there were discussions surrounding the Russian peace plan.[1923]

Others were also nibbling away at the edges. In January 2019, one of the people whom Parnas had swindled in the past sued him and David Corriea in a Florida Court, seeking the funds that Parnas had used to make donations to Republicans, relying on the Campaign Legal Center's complaint to show that Parnas had access to funds they could recover.[1924]

At the same time, the *New York Times*, reported on criminal activities involving Ukrainians who came to the 2017 Inauguration, and brought their own peace plans. Investigations of these matters had been spun off from the Mueller probe, involving various US attorney generals' offices throughout the country.[1925] The story was sourced to "people with direct knowledge" and "others who were briefed" implying official sourcing.[1926]

Another group, perhaps related to those informing the *Times*, was also seeking information on exactly what Trump was doing—a set of top lawyers hired by the new Democratic House majority. The most prominent was Daniel Goldman, who had run into then ranking member of the House Intelligence Committee Adam Schiff in June 2018 in an MSNBC green room.[1927] For ten years, Goldman had been a federal prosecutor in New York, specializing in prosecuting Russian mobsters.[1928] On March 5, Schiff hired Goldman.[1929]

Goldman was one of two dozen top lawyers who joined House investigative committee staff. They included former Obama chief ethics officer Norm Eisen and Barry Burke, a white-collar defense attorney from New York.[1930] They were all led by Speaker Pelosi's new legal advisor, Doug Letter, a forty-year DOJ veteran.[1931]

Behind the scenes, other investigators were also working. Robert Mueller's Special Counsel's Office was writing its report. On March 5, Mueller had a meeting with Barr where they discussed the release of his report.[1932] Mueller had been spinning off cases to various US attorney's offices around the country, with a total of fourteen jettisoned to other prosecutors.[1933]

Trump was unhappy with the continued investigation. The same day that Barr met with Mueller, Trump tweeted: "The greatest overreach in the history of our Country. The Dems are obstructing justice and will not get anything done. A big, fat, fishing expedition desperately in search of a crime, when in fact the real crime is what the Dems are doing, and have done!"[1934]

A strange three-way synergy began to emerge—as Mueller signaled to Barr that he was about to complete the report, the dormant campaign to oust

Marie Yovanovitch reopened with sudden fury—all during the campaign for the Ukrainian presidential election was reaching a higher pitch. In early March, a group began meeting at the Trump International in Washington. It consisted of Lev Parnas, John Solomon, a right-wing editor and opinion writer for *The Hill*, married couple and Fox News contributors Joe DiGenova and Victoria Toensing, and occasionally, Nunes's aide Derek Harvey. Later news reports would deem this group the "BLT Team,"[1935] named after BLT Steak, the restaurant in the Trump International Hotel.

At the meetings, Parnas would facilitate connections between the political operatives and their chosen reporters with Ukrainians that could help the president obtain information that would be used to discredit the Black Ledger, Biden, and Yovanovitch.[1936] He also translated for the group. One source called the atmosphere surrounding Giuliani at the Trump International a "circus."

That week, there was a circus of another sort in Houston. Energy Secretary Perry was giving the keynote address at the CERAWeek energy conference on March 13. Perry was pushing "energy choice," which, amongst other things meant that "the United States supports competitive markets . . . the rule of law . . . and the sanctity of contracts."[1937] Part of this choice involved American investment in foreign fossil fuel production, including Ukraine.

As part of its anti-corruption drive, the West had insisted on changes in Ukraine's energy sector to include open bidding on gas and petroleum development blocks and a foreign advisory board for its state gas corporation Naftogaz.[1938] In November 2018, Secretary Perry had traveled to Kyiv to promote Ukrainian-American cooperation in the energy sector. He brought with him two of his political supporters, Michael Bleyzer and Alex Cranberg, whom he touted as experts in opening up Ukraine to foreign energy development.[1939]

Perry hit these same themes in his speech, arguing for more European deals through an international group designed to foster US-European energy cooperation.[1940] But at CERAWeek Perry was not the only person pushing transatlantic energy deals. Lev Parnas and Igor Fruman were teaming up with a big Trump donor, Harry Sergeant III, looking for an energy deal in Ukraine.[1941] At the conference, the three approached Andrew Favorov, a Naftogaz executive, to propose that he replace Andriy Kobolyev, Naftogaz's CEO.[1942] The plan was that they would team up with Favarov to import 100 tanker loads of US natural gas and help distribute it. Sergeant touted his connections to the President and told the executive that Trump supported the natural gas venture.[1943]

They told Favrov that Trump was going to get rid of US ambassador Marie Yovanovitch and replace her with someone more open to aiding their business efforts.[1944] Parnas and Fruman had a second scheme they proposed —a deal where Dmytro Firtash, still appealing extradition in Vienna, would be paid $200 million by Naftogaz.[1945] Like magic, Ukrainian officials of the

Poroshenko government began to put pressure on Kobolyev to leave Naftogaz when his contract ended.[1946]

As Parnas and Fruman sought paydays, Giuliani sought information to discredit the Black Ledger. He asked John Solomon over text on March 12 for a story about the Black Ledger, describing it as "the black book."[1947] An interview by Solomon of Nazar Kholodnytsky did not go well. Solomon then texted Giuliani, openly admitting that they sought damaging information on their rivals and that the information they had received so was not good enough:

> I've got nothing. The anti-corruption prosecutor made some very weak comments that are equivocal at best. And not consistent with the facts. Story would get blown up. Don't want to lead with my weakest hand.
>
> I need Porochenko [sic] and the AG on the record about the ambassador and Biden. Can u make that happen? Just starting to get cooperation from former AG Shokin. So we are moving in a good direction.[1948]

Solomon then began to get information from Shokin. Parnas texted to Giuliani a near-perfect English translation of an answer Shokin provided to Solomon regarding Biden, Burisma, and Yovanovitch.[1949] It seems likely that the translator was Parnas. Solomon and Parnas planned an interview with Lutsenko on March 14.[1950] Solomon sent a timeline of his version of the Burisma saga and asked "Lev, Victoria and Joe" to provide him with any information they could to advance the story.[1951]

Two days before Mueller was to provide the report to Attorney General Barr, Solomon published a story in *The Hill*. "As Russia collusion fades, Ukrainian plot to help Clinton emerges," featured a companion remote interview with Yuriy Lutsenko, who told Solomon that he was opening an investigation of whether NABU had released the pages of the Black Ledger in order to defeat Donald Trump.[1952] The article was riddled with falsehoods, claiming "the mystery of how the Manafort black ledger files got leaked to American media has never been solved," when in fact the Manafort pages were openly released to the press by NABU.[1953]

In the article, Solomon presented an entire fiction, casting the Black Ledger as having been secret until revealed by the *New York Times*. He failed to tell his audience that the Black Ledger was public knowledge in Ukraine, that it had been handed to NABU by a member of the Secret Service of Ukraine, that criminal cases were ongoing in Ukraine regarding the evidence in the Black Ledger, and that NABU had openly released the documents regarding Manafort's entries in the Black Ledger to the press.[1954]

Solomon linked the Mueller investigation directly with the US Embassy, stating "[w]e know the FBI set up shop in the US embassy in Kiev to assist its Ukraine–Manafort inquiry—a common practice on foreign-based probes—while using Steele as an informant at the start of its Russia probe."[1955] Yovanovitch would have been involved in such an effort. Solomon also reported that Lutsenko alleged that Yovanovitch had given him a "do-not prosecute list" and refused to allow him to investigate the same bogus charges regarding US aid at a 2016 meeting.[1956]

This was the reveal of the alternate explanation for the upcoming Mueller report—that there was no collusion between Russia and Trump, but that with the help of Yovanovitch, Ukraine had colluded with Clinton and the Democrats. Solomon relied on the US press not reviewing the record in Ukraine to show that the Black Ledger entries naming Manafort had been revealed to the US press prior to Yovanovitch arriving in Ukraine. His reliance was well-placed.

Seemingly out of nowhere, the GOP noise machine swung into high gear against an American Ambassador halfway across the world with absolutely no profile whatsoever in the United States. That evening, Solomon appeared on Sean Hannity's show on Fox News Channel. Hannity asked viewers during his opening, "Where's the Mueller investigation into this damning new story?"[1957]

After Hannity gave the opening monologue, he later turned to Solomon, who began referring indirectly to what would later be known to be the Onyshchenko tapes, and touting Lutsenko's alleged investigation.[1958] Joe diGenova and Victoria Toensing also appeared on the show.[1959] That evening, the president of the United States tweeted a link to the video on his own previously unknown ambassador to Ukraine.[1960] The next day, the State Department denied the accusations.[1961]

Trump was all ears. During a telephone call on March 21, he told John Bolton that Yovanovitch was "bad-mouthing us like crazy."[1962] "She's saying bad shit about me and about you," Trump assured Bolton.[1963] Trump told his National Security Advisor he wanted her fired "today."[1964]

Giuliani reached out to Kevin Downing, Paul Manafort's lawyer, to assist in the disinformation campaign by finding information about the Black Ledger.[1965] Giuliani's focus was determining whether or not the Black Ledger itself was real. Giuliani asked Downing if "there really was a black book."[1966] Downing acted as a go-between between Giuliani and Manafort.

The BLT Team sought any number of ways to get the allegations before the press. Parnas suggested over text to Victoria Toensing that he would falsely claim to have some sort of knowledge of the allegations to move the operation forward:

> You want me to go on Fox news and talk about it? I would not mention any names if I did that. I would just say a client approached me six months back with allegations that FBI and US Ambassador to Ukraine were playing favorites. And reference Burisma getting free pass and alleged ties to "high level Obama administration officials". Maybe mention allegations about setting up Manafort. The media could connect the dots from there.[1967]

The BLT Team would do or say just about anything to help secure the reelection of Donald J. Trump.

As the release of the Mueller report loomed, Parnas was apparently directing a second effort. Text messages show that a GOP operative, Robert Hyde, was in contact with a team of specialists keeping an eye on Ambassador Marie Yovanovitch. Parnas stated that Hyde was known for hanging around the bar at the Trump International in Washington.[1968]

Hyde was associated with a security monitoring company, Security Concepts, Inc., whose logo appeared on his office door.[1969] The company's website describes them as providing access control, video systems, and intrusion systems.[1970] Starting on the night of March 21, Parnas sent Hyde a series of articles from right-wing sources regarding their allegations against Ambassador Yovanovitch.[1971]

The next day, Friday, March 22, 2019, Robert Muller sent Attorney General William Barr what would become known as the Mueller report.[1972] Around noon, a security officer physically carried the report over to Main Justice.[1973] That same day, Barr wrote to the Chairmen and Ranking Members of the House and Senate Judiciary Committees, informing them that Mueller had submitted to him his Report and that "I may be in a position to advise you of the Special Counsel's principal conclusions as soon as this weekend."[1974]

Giuliani and his associates began to scramble as the report's release loomed. On the 22nd, Joe diGenova appeared on *Fox News* stating that Trump wanted to get rid of Ambassador Yovanovitch.[1975] Hyde, apparently after reading links sent to him by Parnas, responded to him over text the evening of the 22: "fuck that bitch."[1976] The next day, Hyde was all in: "Wow. Can't believe Trumo [sic] hasn't fired this bitch. "I'll get right in that."[1977] Hyde then forwarded a recording of a Slavic-accented man, stating "its confirmed she's in Ukraine."[1978]

On the 23rd, Speaker Pelosi rejected a GOP call for closed-door briefings of the Gang of Eight, the eight top congressional leaders.[1979] Schiff told CBS's *Face the Nation* that the GOP proposal for closed door briefings was "not going to fly. This report is going to have to be made public."[1980]

That same day, Barr wrote a letter to the chairs and ranking members of the judiciary committees of both houses, purporting to summarize the Mueller report without providing a copy, redacted or otherwise.[1981] Selectively quoting Mueller's findings, Barr told the lawmakers that the report stated, "the investigation did not establish that members of the Trump Campaign conspired or coordinated with the Russian government in its election interference activities."[1982] Barr also stated that the Special Counsel "did not draw a conclusion—one way or another—as to whether the examined conduct constituted obstruction."[1983]

Based on Barr's summary, headlines indicated that the president had been vindicated. "Mueller doesn't find Trump Campaign conspired with Russia," argued the *Wall Street Journal*.[1984] The Associated Press headlined their piece "Mueller Finds No Trump Collusion, Leaves Obstruction Open."[1985] CBS News said "Mueller Did Not Find Trump Campaign 'Conspired' with Russia."[1986] Robert Mueller was not happy with this result and he communicated this to the attorney general on the morning of March 25.[1987]

But if Barr had claimed that the Mueller report had exonerated the president, the group of people working to counter the report's conclusions did not act like it. Hyde continued to provide information to Parnas regarding surveillance of Yovanovitch. Hyde's contact with whoever was allegedly watching the ambassador in Ukraine went through an unusual Belgian man, Anthony de Caluwe.[1988] De Caluwe, who was dating a Ukrainian woman at the time, sent text messages to Hyde, informing him that Yovanovitch was under heavy guard in Kyiv, and Hyde forwarded the messages on to Parnas.[1989]

On the 25th, Hyde sent text messages to Parnas, asking him "[w]hat should I do with this" and "the guys over there asked me what I would like to do and what is in it for them."[1990] The focus appeared to be on where Yovanovitch was, who she was talking to, and where she might go, revealing a fear that she would leave Ukraine or communicate with someone that might be politically damaging to the president.[1991]

"They know she's a political puppet," Hyde messaged Parnas.[1992] "They will let me know when she is on the move," added Hyde.[1993] Yovanovitch's political value was of paramount concern to the pair, as if she may return to the US at any moment. It appeared her security detail was aware of the surveillance.[1994] Text messages seem to indicate that the effort petered out in late March.[1995]

On March 25, Bolton was called to meet the President. He found him in a White House dining room with Giuliani and Jay Sekulow. Giuliani, Bolton learned, was the source of the stories about Yovanovitch. According to Rudy, Yovanovitch was being protected by George Kent, deputy assistant secretary of state in the European bureau. Trump again asserted that he wanted Yovanovitch fired.[1996]

Inside the State Department, worry about Giuliani's campaign against Yovanovitch was spreading. David Hale asked Yovanovitch to send him a classified email regarding Giuliani's activities in Ukraine.[1997] Tweets from Trump and Donald Trump Jr. were eroding her position within Ukraine. Yovanovitch asked Hale to provide a statement of support from the State Department.[1998] Acting Assistant Secretary of State Phil Reeker explained that the secretary feared that any statement of support from the department could be undermined by a presidential tweet.[1999]

Solomon came out with another article on March 26, which strove mightily to argue some vague wrongdoing existed because George Soros helped fund the Anti-Corruption Action Centre, and that Karen Greenaway had collaborated with AntAC in working on cases involving Manafort and Firtash.[2000] The article also trotted out the old false accusations that AntAC had somehow misappropriated funds that were provided to the US Embassy in Kyiv.[2001] It appeared Solomon was circling slowly around the secret State Department report that linked the missile sales with obstruction of Robert Mueller.

Meanwhile, Robert Mueller was not happy with Attorney General Barr's summary letter. On March 27, Mueller, still displeased with the attorney general's tilted summary, sent a formal letter to Barr, providing redacted versions of the report's "Executive Summary" and asked, "that you provide these materials to Congress and authorize their public release at this time."[2002]

In the letter, Mueller reiterated his concerns that the "summary letter the Department sent to Congress and released to the public late in the afternoon of March 24 did not fully capture the context, nature, and substance of this Office's work and conclusions."[2003] "As a result," Mueller added, "There is now public confusion about critical aspects of the results of our investigation. This threatens to undermine a central purpose for which the Department appointed the Special Counsel: to assure full public confidence in the outcome of the investigations."[2004]

Accordingly, Barr began to walk back perceptions that his March 24 letter was a summary, telling lawmakers in a March 29 letter that his letter was not a summary.[2005] Barr stated that the report would be released soon and that he would be available to testify regarding the report in early May.[2006]

CHAPTER 10: "I WILL DO BIG PRACTICE IN ENGLISH"

The fury in Washington regarding the Mueller report happened while Petro Poroshenko's election prospects began dimming considerably in Ukraine. A March 14 poll had Zelenskyy leading, with 23 percent of the vote. Tymoshenko had 14 percent and the incumbent president, Petro Poroshenko had 12 percent.[2007] Zelenskyy bested those numbers in the first round, taking 30.24 percent of the vote to Poroshenko's 15.95 percent and Tymoshenko's 13.40 percent.[2008] A runoff between Poroshenko and Zelenskyy was set for April 21.

Zelenskyy's message followed that of the fictional president he played on *Servant of the People*—anti-corruption and change. In response, Poroshenko met with the very reformers he had made war upon for three years—in a two-hour meeting he agreed to finally appoint judges for the Anti-Corruption Court and fire a governor they believed to be corrupt.[2009]

Meanwhile, Giuliani's quest to get Yovanovitch fired continued. He met personally with Secretary of State Pompeo on March 26 about Yovanovitch.[2010] On March 28, he sent a large file of negative information regarding the ambassador to Pompeo.[2011] This included the Shokin and Lutsenko memoranda from January and several of Solomon's columns. Trump Organization folders were used to separate the information provided.

The same day, Solomon sent a draft of his March 26 story claiming that the US Embassy had asked the Prosecutor General's Office to stop an investigation of AntAC in early 2016.[2012] Solomon was working hand-in-glove with the president's paid defenders.

Giuliani also had a telephone call on March 29 with Pompeo, apparently to follow up with him in regard to what the press would eventually call the "dirt file" on Yovanovitch.[2013] A second call was set for the following Monday with Representative Devin Nunes.[2014]

This call came at the same time that Nunes's aides were attempting to meet with Ukrainian special anti-corruption Prosecutor Nazar Kholodnytsky. In late March, Derek Harvey had sought to fly to Ukraine to meet with Kholodnytsky and a regional prosecutor, Konstantin Kulyk.[2015] When the staffers realized that reporting requirements would mean the travel would be revealed to the chair of the Intelligence Committee, Adam

Schiff, they asked Parnas to set up a Skype call with SAP Kholodnytsky and Kulyk.[2016]

Kulyk had long been seen as a Poroshenko ally.[2017] However, as Poroshenko's polling declined, Kulyk drafted a "dossier" on Biden and indicted Poroshenko associates in the final days of the Ukrainian presidential election.[2018] The Kulyk dossier contained wild accusations—that Zlochevsky offered then US secretary of state John Kerry and Vice President Joe Biden a share of Burisma's profits in exchange for "lobbying and political support."[2019] According to the memo, NABU head Artem Sytnyk also stood to profit from the alleged scheme.[2020]

Kulyk was an interesting character—originally appointed by Yanukovych's prosecutor general, he somehow remained in his position during the Poroshenko administration.[2021] Kulyk had been indicted for corruption in 2016 and was linked to the Donbas separatists.[2022]

On April 1, Solomon published a third article in *The Hill*: "Joe Biden's 2020 Ukrainian Nightmare: A Closed Probe Is Revived," which advanced the theory that Hunter Biden had been involved in corruption. However, the article could only point to his actual pay as a director as money he accepted from Burisma.[2023]

Solomon continued supporting Giuliani's efforts to help the president. On April 7 he published an interview with Kulyk, who accused Yovanovitch of blocking his visa. The purpose of the meeting, he claimed, was to share information regarding Burisma and the Bidens.[2024] The headline screamed partisanship: "Ukrainian to US Prosecutors: Why Don't You Want Our Evidence on Democrats?" Kulyk seemed especially eager to link the Black Ledger with Democrats, claiming that a firm "tied to Democrats" was involved with Yovanovitch in $7 billion taken from Ukraine to be laundered in the US.[2025]

That same day, a leaker informed Betsy Swan of the *Daily Beast* that federal prosecutors in Cleveland were targeting Zelenskyy's patron Ihor Kolomoisky in a money laundering investigation just a week away from the final round of the Ukrainian presidential elections.[2026] Someone in the administration wanted to expose Zelenskyy's controversial patron prior to the election.

On April 18, Robert Mueller released his redacted version of the Mueller report to the public. It provided only an outline of the story, with significant parts entirely blacked out. The Mueller report weighed in at a considerable 635 single-spaced pages.

Barr had offered the "Gang of Eight" the right to review the unredacted report at the Department of Justice, but required that those reading it turn in all notes prior to leaving the Department.[2027] Instead, the House subpoenaed the entire report.[2028]

"DAD, THEY SAY ZELENSKYY IS THE PRESIDENT"

On April 21, 2019, Zelenskyy won the runoff election with 73 percent of the vote.[2029] Zelenskyy's six-year old son asked the president-elect, "Dad, they say on TV that Zelenskyy is the President.... So, it means that ... I am ... the President too?!"[2030] The election of Zelenskyy threw Giuliani's entire disinformation operation off the rails. Poroshenko could no longer provide any investigations going forward. Giuliani needed an "in" to Zelenskyy.

Trump called Zelenskyy that same evening. Zelenskyy must have been surprised that the president of the United States had called the winner of the presidential election in the thirtieth largest country in the world on the night of his election. Despite this, Zelenskyy wasted no time in requesting a major ask: he invited the president to attend his inauguration in a month's time.[2031]

After deflecting this request, Trump then veered into territory relating to Oleksandr Onyshchenko, perhaps inadvertently: "When I owned Ms. Universe, they always had great people."[2032] The President then invited Zelenskyy to the White House, which the President-Elect of Ukraine accepted.[2033] Zelenskyy promised Trump, "I will do big practice in English."[2034]

Shortly after Trump's April 21 call with Zelenskyy, the White House asked Pence to go to Zelenskyy's swearing-in ceremony.[2035]

As Zelenskyy was winning in Ukraine, Andrew Favorov met with an American, a former business partner in the Ukraine, Dale Perry.[2036][2037] He told Perry about his encounter with Parnas and Fruman and said that it felt like a shakedown.[2038]

Perry was so shocked that he decided it was his duty as an American to inform the US Embassy of what he had learned about Parnas and Fruman's activities in Houston.[2039] As Perry wrote to the US Embassy in Kyiv, he thought *"Am I crazy here? This can't really be happening."*[2040] He stated that Parnas and Fruman were targeting the ambassador, that they were seeking gas deals in Ukraine, and that they wanted to replace the head of Naftogaz.[2041] The letter was dated April 21.[2042]

In April, Parnas and Fruman continued their attempts to make changes to Naftogaz's board. At a meeting at DC's Capital Grille, the two, along with an employee of Harry Sergeant's company, met with Andrew Favorov and Naftogaz's CEO, Andriy Kobolyev.[2043]

The next day, Parnas, Fruman, and two Republican officials, Tommy Hicks Jr. and Jeff Miller met at the Trump International. There, they discussed shipping large amounts of US natural gas to Ukraine via Poland. Parnas and Fruman claimed to have connections that would reduce any bottlenecks in transshipment.[2044]

On April 23, Bolton was again called to meet with the president. He found Trump and Mulvaney in the Oval Office. The pair were on the telephone with Giuliani who again asked that the ambassador be removed.[2045] Giuliani "had spun Trump up" with news that she had spoken with Zelenskyy and told him that Trump wanted certain investigations stopped.[2046]

Bolton returned to his office and talked with Pompeo, who told him they were sending the "dirt file" Giuliani had brought to him over to justice. Pompeo said he would have her recalled that evening.[2047]

"REMEMBER THESE TWO NAMES: LEV PARNAS AND IGOR FRUMAN."

The same day, Giuliani directed Parnas and Fruman to meet with Zelenskyy's backer, Kolomoisky in Tel Aviv.[2048] The pair were tasked with inducing the president-elect to meet with Giuliani.[2049] They had a pretext—to discuss natural gas sales to Ukraine, but the meeting did not go well. Kolomoisky told the pair to get out of his office: "Did you see a sign on the door that says, 'Meetings with Zelenskyy arranged here?'" he admonished them.[2050]

That evening, Ambassador Yovanovitch received a telephone call from Carol Perez, the director general of the State Department, at 10 p.m.[2051] Perez told Yovanovitch, "things were going wrong, kind of off the track."[2052] The ambassador asked her if it was about the Giuliani and Parnas investigations—Perez surprisingly was unaware of them. Perez said she would call Yovanovitch back.[2053]

Perez called back at 1 a.m. Kyiv time and told Yovanovitch that she had to be on the next plane home. Perez told the ambassador that it was about her safety. Yovanovitch argued, but to no avail.[2054] As she packed to leave, she was given a copy of Dale Perry's letter warning her that Parnas and Fruman were targeting her. Yovanovitch left Kyiv with no announcement.

Parnas and Fruman had succeeded. Yovanovitch would not return to Kyiv. On May 9 it was announced that she was stepping down as US ambassador to Ukraine.

On April 25, a close Zelenskyy aide spoke with David Holmes, the US Embassy's political counselor.[2055] The Zelenskyy aide told Holmes that he had been speaking to Giuliani.[2056]

Also on April 25, Trump gave an interview to Fox News's Sean Hannity. In it he claimed that Attorney General Barr was about to undertake an investigation to prove that Ukraine had illegally helped Hillary Clinton by "leaking" the Black Ledger showing the payments to Manafort.[2057] The allegations, Trump assured Hannity, were "big, big stuff."[2058] The president of the United States was publicly casting doubt on Ukraine's Black Ledger on national TV.

On May 8, Bolton came to the Oval Office after a call from Trump. Giuliani was there with Pat Cipillone, the president's counsel, and Acting Chief of Staff Mick Mulvaney.[2059] Giuliani explained what he wanted—a meeting with Zelenskyy so that Giuliani could discuss investigations that Ukraine had interfered on behalf of Hillary Clinton in the 2016 election, and investigations involving Hunter Biden and Burisma.[2060] The theories were "intermingled and confused" Bolton remembers, and he could "barely separate the strands of the multiple conspiracies at work."[2061]

Trump turned to Bolton and ordered him to call Zelenskyy to ensure that Giuliani would have a meeting with the president-elect the next week.[2062] Bolton returned to his office, determined not to make a call to Zelenskyy. Two officials soon arrived, telling them that Trump wanted to go after the State Department's George Kent.[2063]

The *New York Times* ran a piece on Giuliani's efforts on May 9. The president's lawyer told the *Times* that he was going to Kyiv to sit with President Zelenskyy to urge him to press investigations that he thought would help Trump.[2064] Not for the first time, and certainly not for the last, Giuliani's bluster with reporters suggested that he was aware he was not acting legally: "We're not meddling in an election, we're meddling in an investigation, which we have a right to do," he told the *Times*' Ken Vogel.[2065] "There's nothing illegal about it," insisted the former mayor. "Somebody could say it's improper."[2066]

Giuliani claimed he was going to talk to a religious group about Middle East policy in Kyiv and implied the meeting with Zelenskyy was incidental to it.[2067] That group was the American Friends of Anatevka. For the first time, the *Times* connected the name Lev Parnas with Giuliani's efforts in Ukraine to find dirt on the Bidens.[2068] Parnas's name appeared seven times in Vogel's piece.

On May 10, Giuliani wrote a letter to President-Elect Zelenskyy, saying that he was writing as Trump's private attorney and requesting a meeting for May 13 or 14 and that he would be accompanied by Victoria Toensing.[2069] In a telephone call, Ambassador Volker told Giuliani not to go to Ukraine and that Lutsenko was "not credible."[2070] In rapid succession, Giuliani telephoned a National Security Council staffer, Kash Patel, an unknown number only listed as "–1" at the White House, and Parnas.[2071]

Parnas and Fruman met with Serhiy Shefir, a close aide to Zelenskyy at a Kyiv café and delivered a blunt message. If the Zelenskyy government did not commit to launching the investigations Giuliani wanted, Vice President Pence would not attend the inaugural.[2072] Shefir refused.

But Zelenskyy would not meet with him. Giuliani canceled his trip to Ukraine the next day.[2073] He claimed Zelenskyy was involved with enemies of President Trump, singling out reformist journalist and MP Serhii Leshchenko as a person who had helped Democrats in 2016—alluding to the revelation of Black Ledger.[2074] After that message, Parnas and Fruman's prediction came true: On May 13, Trump informed Pence that the vice president would not be attending Zelenskyy's inauguration.[2075] Rick Perry would lead the US delegation to the swearing-in on May 20. Lev Parnas would later allege that it was Perry's job to explain to Zelenskyy that aid to Ukraine was conditioned on investigations that Giuliani wanted.[2076]

On May 16, the news outlet *Skhemy* got word that Ihor Kolomoisky was returning to Ukraine for the first time in two years via private jet. Reporters watched it land in Kyiv and followed him to a bar, where they decided to ask for an interview. Their boldness paid off as the oligarch agreed on the spot to an interview. But after discussing Ukraine, Kolomoisky turned to a new subject, Giuliani. "Want details?" he asked the reporters. "But only if you publish it." Kolomoisky continued:

> There are two swindlers in Ukraine who are under investigation by the United States. One seems to be Lev Parnas, and the other, Igor, is either Fruman or Furman. And they go here to Ukraine, collect money from people, say that they are close to Mr. Giuliani —and that they will solve any issue with Mr. Lutsenko. Mr. Lutsenko does not even know about it. And I don't think Mr. Giuliani knows about it either. Two "Ostaps of Bender" who walk between the two countries and tell all sorts of things. . . . And in the near future, believe me, we will bring these two "subchiki" to the light of God. So that they don't think. . . . Remember these two names: Lev Parnas and Igor Fruman.[2077]

The name Ostap Bender was apt: Bender was the name of the prototypical Soviet swindler, the protagonist of *The Twelve Chairs*, the most popular Soviet novel by the writers Ilya Ilf and Yevgeny Petrov. Known as the "Great Combinator," the character had become a stand-in for hapless fraudsters around the world.

Other problems began to crop up for Giuliani. On May 16, Lutsenko gave an interview to Bloomberg News. He told the reporters that there was "no evidence" of wrongdoing and that neither the Bidens nor Burisma were under investigation.[2078]

According to police reports, on May 16, police in Doral, Florida, responded to the Trump National Doral regarding "a male in distress fearing for his life."[2079] That man was Robert F. Hyde, the person who had been texting Parnas in March regarding surveillance of Yovanovitch in Kyiv.

The police report was most unusual. Hyde stated to officers that he was "in fear for his life, was set up and that a hit man was out to get him. Mr. Hyde spoke about emails he sent that may have placed his life in jeopardy. Mr. Hyde explained several times that he was paranoid that someone was out to get him."[2080] Hyde, the report explained, cited "a variety of different names, contacts and provided information in reference to why he felt his life was in danger."[2081] Hyde told police "not to stop next to certain vehicles . . . [H]e explained that he was scared due to several painting workers and landscape workers trying to do harm to him because they weren't working."[2082] Hyde also complained "that his computer was being hacked by Secret Service. And then went on to further explain that the secret service [sic] was arrival [sic] on the premises watching him."[2083]

The Doral police, completely unaware that less than two months earlier, Hyde had been monitoring the US ambassador to Ukraine as part of an off-the-books political intelligence operation, had Hyde involuntarily committed.[2084] Hyde later posted a note on Instagram: "I'm not a traitor or a colluder or a conspiracy theorist."[2085] Hyde then had a message for whoever he believed was monitoring him: "eff you and your intelligence agencies or whatever or whoever was or is effing with me."[2086] In January 2020, his text messages were part of an impeachment inquiry. Someone *was* watching Mr. Hyde.

"GIVE ME NINETY DAYS"

A new plan was hatched to obtain more negative material on Joe Biden and to discredit the Black Ledger. Giuliani would meet with the Special Anticorruption Prosecutor Nazar Kholodnytsky and Shokin in Paris. Shokin had never been involved with the Black Ledger.

On May 17, Parnas met with Kholodnytsky and worked to set up a telephone call with Giuliani, while arranging a face-to-face meeting for Paris.[2087] Since a scandal where he had been caught coaching witnesses he was prosecuting on tape, the Ukrainian prosecutor's star had dimmed considerably. Inexplicably, he had remained in his position despite the scandal.[2088] Now his experience at the center of the Black Ledger investigation would be very useful to Giuliani.

On May 21, Giuliani was in Paris.[2089] At the cigar bar in the Hotel Raffles, he met with Dmitry Torner, an executive who worked for Dmytro Firtash.[2090] Giuliani sought information that could compromise the Bidens.[2091]

A second meeting was held with Kholodnytsky in Paris, lasting three hours.[2092] The pair were photographed next to a famous French corruption-fighting lawyer, which caused pro-Russian Ukrainian outlet *112 Ukraine* to speculate that the meeting "may indicate the preparation of a series of high-profile loud corruption exposures in Ukraine."[2093]

Later that day, Giuliani met with Rabbi Azman. The pair enjoyed cigars as the rabbi presented him with the key to Anatevka and named him honorary mayor of the village.[2094]

The day before, on May 20, Zelenskyy was inaugurated. At a meeting with the new president, Secretary Perry passed Zelenskyy a list of "people he trusts" to discuss regarding energy sector reform.[2095] Perry's talking points informed Ukraine it must make "the hard choices on corruption and good governance reforms."[2096] Perry also had a thinly veiled message regarding Pennsylvania company Westinghouse Nuclear and Ukraine. The US was interested in a world where "people are free to chart their own energy futures," the talking points insisted.[2097] The general was backed up with the specific: "Diversifying your nuclear fuel supply away from Russia is extremely important for Ukraine's energy security. Westinghouse fuel supplies reduce Russian leverage over Ukraine."[2098]

Upon the delegation's return to Washington, Charles Kupperman attended the debrief for the US delegation. There, Trump was adamant about Ukraine aid: "I don't want to have any fucking thing to do with Ukraine." Trump went on: "They fucking attacked me. I can't understand why. Ask Joe DiGenova."[2099] Trump then claimed that Hunter Biden had helped the Clinton campaign in Ukraine.[2100]

Rick Perry spoke up for Ukraine, saying a failed state there was not in the US interest. Trump replied, "Talk to Rudy and Joe." Perry asked for ninety days to make the relationship with Zelenskyy work. "I want the fucking DNC server," replied the president before granting his secretary of energy the requested three months.[2101] If the goal of Russian disinformation efforts was to affect the policy decisions of the United States government, they had succeeded. The president and his associates were actively pushing Russia's disinformation narrative in its war with Ukraine.

Also in May, Fiona Hill, the NSA staffer responsible for Ukraine and Russia, had an unusual request. Amos Hochstein, a former US Energy Department official asked to meet with her. Hochstein was serving on the board of Naftogaz.

Hochstein informed her that Rudy Giuliani and two business associates, Lev Parnas and Igor Fruman, were pushing for board changes at Naftogaz and that they were seeking an investigation of Burisma.[2102] Hill learned from colleagues that Fruman and Parnas were "notorious in Florida and bad news."[2103]

A new official began to be heard on Ukraine. His name was Gordon Sondland, a hotelier from Oregon who had donated $1 million to Trump's inaugural fund.[2104] In March 2018, Sondland had been appointed the US ambassador to the European Union. He had attended Zelenskyy's swearing-in and was at the debrief.[2105] During the following weeks, Sondland began pushing for an early Zelenskyy visit, despite the fact that Ukraine was not part of his duties as ambassador to the EU.[2106]

During the trip to the Zelenskyy swearing-in, Perry had pressured Ukrainian officials to make major changes to Naftogaz's board, hoping to replace Kobolyev, who had a reputation for cleaning up the gas company and making it profitable.[2107] Prior CEOs had allowed corrupt business owners to skim profits and treat the state company as a piggy bank instead of an operation designed to turn a profit.[2108] The attempt was withdrawn after Naftogaz lobbyist Daniel Vajdich fought back against the Ukrainian government's pressure campaign on Kobolyev in the US.[2109]

Throughout May, a rising sense of alarm spread among officials at the State Department and the National Security Council regarding Giuliani's interference with Ukraine.[2110] A possible successor to Marie Yovanovitch, William Taylor, was also concerned. George Kent had asked him to replace Yovanovitch, but he delayed accepting the position. Volker encouraged him, but Taylor told him over text that Kent had "described two snake pits, one in Kyiv and one in Washington."[2111] In late May he had still not made up his mind: "I am still struggling with the decision whether to go" Taylor texted to Volker.[2112] "Can anyone hope to succeed with the Giuliani-Biden issue swirling for the next 18 months?" he asked Volker.[2113] Taylor arrived in Kyiv on June 18, despite his worries.[2114] Within four months, he would be a household name and he would be played on television by actor Jon Hamm on *Saturday Night Live*.

John Bolton was one of the officials that was concerned about the Giuliani situation. At a June 13 meeting, he told Volker and an assistant that Giuliani was an obstacle to Ukraine assistance.[2115]

On May 29, Robert Mueller announced his departure from the Department of Justice. In an eight-minute statement read at the podium in the Department's briefing room, Mueller said that if his office "had had confidence that the president clearly did not commit a crime we would have said so."[2116] He informed reporters assembled in the Department of Justice press room that he could not, under Justice Department regulations, charge the president. "The Constitution requires a process other than the criminal justice system to formally accuse a sitting president of wrongdoing," he added.[2117] On June 25, the House Intelligence and Judiciary Committees announced that Robert Mueller would testify on July 17. The appearance was pursuant to a subpoena.[2118]

On June 18, 2019, the Pentagon announced that it would be releasing $250 million in military aid to Ukraine.[2119] The next day, the telephone rang in the office of Russell T. Vought, the acting head of the Office of Management and Budget. On the other end of the line was Robert Blair, an assistant to the president. Blair told Vought that $250 million in military needed to be halted: "We need to hold it up," he told Vought.[2120]

Donald Trump was also concerned about the military aid to Ukraine. In a video conference call with John Bolton from the Situation Room on June 25, he asked Bolton about the $250 million: "Did you approve it, John?"[2121] Trump was focused on the Ukrainian military aid and Bolton worried about why.

Two days later, Mick Mulvaney was on a flight to Japan when he emailed Rob Blair about the aid to Ukraine. Mulvaney wanted to tie up some "loose ends" and wanted to know, "Did we ever find out about the money for Ukraine and whether we can hold it back?"[2122] Blair emailed back telling Mulvaney to "expect Congress to become unhinged."[2123]

But first, career appropriations and defense officials became unhinged at this development. Push back from defense officials made it clear that the White House was hoping the president would cool down and change his mind.[2124]

Giuliani needed more evidence to go after Biden and discredit the Black Ledger. By late June, Yuriy Lutsenko was out of the picture—his future as prosecutor general in doubt as Zelenskyy took over. Giuliani now turned to another oligarch—Dmytro Firtash, still stuck in Vienna appealing his extradition order to the US.

In late June, Lev Parnas was in Vienna to help with that. During a telephone call with Giuliani, he sketched out the new plan on the stationery of the Ritz-Carlton hotel as Giuliani dictated the next steps to him over the telephone. "[G]et zalensky [sic] to Announce that the Biden Case will Be Investigated" the first bullet point read.[2125] The next bullet point was the task that had eluded them so far—start communications with Zelenskyy, but the notes indicated the task had to be done without the help of Ukrainians Viktor Pinchuk or Ihor Kolomoisky.[2126]

The notes detail an approach to Dmytro Firtash—whose lawyer at the time, Lanny Davis, was to be eased out and replaced by Victoria Toensing and Joe diGenova.[2127] Other tasks included getting all of the information on Firtash's case, getting information on Zlochevsky, the head of Burisma, and "Ukrain [sic] ledger," meaning information about the Black Ledger.[2128] The goal for Firtash was, according to the notes, to either cut a deal or get the charges dismissed.[2129]

And Lev Parnas proceeded to do just that. After an unnamed mutual acquaintance vouched for Parnas and Fruman, the pair obtained a meeting with Firtash in late June.[2130] Firtash agreed to the plan. Lanny Davis was eased out and diGenova and Toensing began to helm Firtash's legal team.[2131]

Originally, Firtash said that Parnas and Fruman pitched a natural gas deal that didn't make economic sense. But he paid their expenses, he claimed, because they offered him the chance to get a pair of lawyers close to the President who could pitch a deal for him.[2132] Parnas and Fruman offered a chance to get the Department of Justice to get "Exhibit A," the slide from McKinsey recommending bribery to get Indian titanium pulled from the evidence in his case.[2133]

Toensing and diGenova were to make $300,000 a month representing Firtash, with Parnas's $200,000 fee to be taken out of their payment.[2134] Parnas also told Firtash that diGenova and Toensing were seeking information on the Bidens.[2135]

The Firtash connection came just in time for Rudy. A second gambit by Rudy had failed in July when a Ukrainian appeals court reversed a finding that MP and journalist Serhii Leshchenko and Artem Sytnyk of NABU committed election interference in the 2016 US election by releasing the Black Ledger entries with Manafort's name on them.[2136] Giuliani was running out of people willing to feed him the disinformation he needed to move the Biden allegations forward.

On June 27, Sondland told Chargé Taylor that Zelenskyy needed to tell Trump that he was not standing in the way of investigations.[2137] David Holmes, Taylor's political counselor understood that to mean investigations into Burisma and the Bidens.[2138]

"GORDON, I THINK THIS IS ALL GOING TO BLOW UP"

As July arrived, the chaos in the White House increased. A July 10 meeting with top Zelenskyy aides at the White House loomed. The meeting was important and Daniel Vajdich, lobbyist for three state-owned Ukrainian companies, stepped in. On July 8, he sent emails to Tim Morrison, Fiona Hill, and Lieutenant Colonel Alexander Vindman, the three NSC principals involved in the upcoming meeting.[2139]

The meeting did not go well. Attending were Secretary Perry; Ambassadors Bolton, Sondland, and Volker; Lieutenant Colonel Alexander Vindman; and NSC staffers Wells Griffith and Hill.[2140]

The Ukrainians sought a White House meeting with President Trump for President Zelenskyy.[2141] Bolton studiously avoided to committing to a date prior to the upcoming Ukrainian parliamentary elections.[2142] Sondland suddenly blurted out that he had an agreement with Mulvaney to give a White House meeting to Zelenskyy if he committed to investigations in the energy sector.[2143]

Bolton stiffened.[2144] He suddenly said, "It was a pleasure meeting with you, looking forward to working with you" and made to leave.[2145] The parties took a photo and Hill and Bolton left for his office.[2146]

The US group then huddled to figure out tasks, but some of the Ukrainians remained in the room.[2147] Sondland tried to reconvene the meeting in the Ward Room.[2148] In his office, Bolton ordered Hill to go down to the Ward Room and find out what they are talking about and report back to him.[2149]

Sondland began speaking to the Ukrainian officials. Secretary Perry had another engagement and left the room.[2150]

Vindman, agitated, told Sondland that it was improper to condition meetings on these investigations.[2151] The Ukrainians noticed the discord between the US officials and left.[2152] At that moment, Hill returned from Bolton's office.[2153] Hill protested to Sondland that we cannot have these discussions in front of the Ukrainians. Sondland cut her off, as he contended that the Ukrainians had already reached an agreement for the meeting.[2154]

Volker remained silent.[2155] Hill insisted and Sondland backed down.[2156] After more discussion, Sondland left for other meetings.[2157]

Vindman and Hill talked in the hallway about briefly what they needed to do—report it up the chain.[2158] Lieutenant Colonel Vindman later went to NSC lawyer John Eisenberg's office and reported the conversation.[2159] Sondland, he told Eisenberg, had asked the Ukrainians for investigations of the Bidens and Burisma.[2160] Vindman gave Eisenberg the back story to the investigations and the NSC lawyer told him he would look into it.[2161] Eisenberg told Vindman to come directly to him with any concerns about the issue surrounding Giuliani and Sondland's request for investigations.[2162] It was Vindman's impression that meant any concerns were to only go to Eisenberg. At a later date, Eisenberg made his instruction more explicit and told Vindman not to talk to other people about the issue.[2163]

After the Sondland blow-up, Hill returned to Bolton's office and recounted what happened.[2164] Bolton exploded: "You go and tell Eisenberg that I am not part of whatever drug deal Sondland and Mulvaney are cooking up on this, and you go and tell him what you've heard and what I've said."[2165] Bolton later confirmed his words.[2166] Hill headed off to tell John Eisenberg what she had seen and what Bolton had told her.[2167]

The implications of Bolton's actions were not clear at the time, but in a few seconds he had dropped a hand grenade in to the middle of any future defense from the White House. The nation's premier foreign affairs lawyer had declared that what was going on involving Ukraine was illegal. This would complicate any attorney-client privilege claim which would not apply if any advice was given was to advance an illegal scheme. Hill's report would also complicate matters for the White House Counsel's Office—with an eyewitness account it would be hard to provide any alternate legal explanation and they would be required to make a criminal referral based on her statements.

On the 12th, Mulvaney informed the Office of Management and Budget that the Ukraine military aid was being held up.[2168] As the situation spun out of control, on July 19, Fiona Hill left her National Security Council position as planned. As Sondland gave her a good-bye hug, she calmly said, "Gordon, I think this is all going to blow up."[2169]

That same day, Kurt Volker connected a Zelenskyy aide with Rudy Giuliani.[2170] Yermak called Giuliani on the 22nd, a day after impressive parliamentary victories for Zelenskyy's Servant of the People Party. The two discussed the investigations Giuliani wanted and a prospective White House meeting for Zelenskyy.[2171] Volker learned the meeting went well and texted Sondland and Taylor that Giuliani was now "advocating" for a telephone call between the presidents.[2172]

In Ukraine, on July 16, an appeals court reversed the decision against Sergii Leshchenko and Artem Sytnyk regarding the release of the Manafort pages of the Black Ledger on August 19, 2016.[2173] Any claim that they had been found by a court to have interfered in the US presidential election would now be false. It would not stop Giuliani.

Just as Fiona Hill had predicted, things were about to blow up. On July 22, two articles emerged from a joint investigation involving the Organized Crime and Corruption Reporting Project (OCCRP) and *Buzzfeed*. "Meet the Florida Duo Helping Giuliani Investigate for Trump in Ukraine" was the title of the expose about Parnas and Fruman.[2174] The article took nearly 5,000 words to detail Parnas's history of unpaid debts and Fruman's ties to Odesa crime lord Volodymyr "the Lightbulb" Galanternik.

But the most devastating allegations linked the large donations made by Parnas and Fruman to Giuliani's efforts to find information on the Bidens.[2175] The reporters had carefully scraped the social media accounts of the pair to provide photos of White House visits and photos with Trump.

The two Ostap Benders had been brought to the Light of God. One man on the staff of the National Security Council made note of it.

CHAPTER 11:

STRAY VOLTAGE

On July 24, 2019, Robert Mueller appeared before the House Judiciary Committee and then the House Permanent Select Committee on Intelligence.[2176] Democratic members of both committees read from the report, which Mueller confirmed the accuracy of.[2177] Republicans pressed him on various conspiracy theories, which Mueller declined to respond to.[2178] Mueller introduced no new evidence and, according to the *New York Times*, "was a reluctant witness whose deflections sucked some of the punch out of his most damning findings, especially as Republicans sought repeatedly to undermine him and his investigation."[2179] For a prosecutor who had implied in his closing press conference that it was up to Congress to hold the president to account, he gave them no help at all.

The next day, fresh off the victory that was Mueller's underwhelming appearance, Donald Trump had a call scheduled with President Zelenskyy of Ukraine to congratulate him on the stunning win of the Servant of the People Party in the Ukrainian parliamentary elections on July 21, the successful sequel to his own election victory three months earlier. Trump was briefed that morning by Bolton.[2180] Members of the NSC staff were concerned about "stray voltage" on the call—information outside of the reasons planned for the call—this time specifically relating to Giuliani and his demands for investigations.[2181]

What the NSC staff did not know was that the so-called stray voltage was being discussed by those directly involved. Prior to the scheduled call that morning, Kurt Volker texted Yermak: "Good lunch—thanks. Heard from the White House—assuming President Z convinces trump [sic] he will investigate/ 'get to the bottom of what happened' in 2016, we will nail down date for visit to Washington."[2182]

THE FAVOR

The President took the call in the White House Residence at 9:03 a.m.[2183] Within a few minutes, stray voltage appeared—Trump turned to the Giuliani claims. "The United States has been very, very good to Ukraine," Trump said, adding "I wouldn't say that it's reciprocal necessarily because things are happening that are not good but the United States has been very, very good to Ukraine."[2184] Zelenskyy then asked for more Javelin anti-tank missiles. Trump responded:

> I would like you to do us a favor though because our country has been through a lot and Ukraine knows lot about it. I would like you to find out what happened with this whole situation with Ukraine, they say Crowdstrike . . . I guess you have one of your wealthy people . . . The server, they say Ukraine has it. There are a lot. of things that went on, the whole situation . . . I think you're surrounding yourself with some of the same people. I would like to have the Attorney General call you or your people and I would like you to get to the bottom of it. As you saw yesterday that whole nonsense ended with a very poor performance by a man named Robert Mueller, an incompetent performance, but they say a lot of it started with Ukraine. Whatever you can do, it's very important that you do it if that's possible. [Ellipses in original.][2185]

Zelenskyy responded:

> I will personally tell you that one of my assistants spoke with Mr. Giuliani just recently and we are hoping very much that Mr. Giuliani will be able to travel to Ukraine and we will meet once he comes to Ukraine. I just wanted to assure you once again that you have nobody but friends around us. I will make sure that I surround myself with the best and most experienced people. I also wanted to tell you that we are friends. We are great friends and you Mr. President have. Friends in our country so we can continue our strategic partnership. I also plan to surround myself

> with great people and in addition to that investigation, I guarantee as the President of Ukraine that all the investigations will be done openly and candidly. That I can assure you.[2186]

Trump responded positively: "Good, because I heard you had a prosecutor who was very good and he was shut down and that's really unfair. A lot of people are talking about that, the way they shut your very good prosecutor down and you had some very bad people involved."[2187] The US president then turned to specific instructions:

> Mr. Giuliani is a highly respected man. He was the mayor of New York City, a great mayor, and I would like him to call you. I will ask him to call you along with the Attorney General. Rudy very much knows what's happening and he is a very capable guy. If you could speak to him that would be great.[2188]

After a jab at Yovanovitch, Trump got down to what he wanted: "There's a lot of talk about Biden's son, that Biden stopped the prosecution and a lot of people want to find out about that so whatever you can do with the Attorney General would be great."[2189] Trump added, gratuitously, "Biden went around bragging that he stopped the prosecution so if you can look into it . . . It sounds horrible to me." (Ellipsis in original.)[2190]

Zelenskyy responded, indicating he would authorize investigations by his new prosecutor, who, he promised:

> [W]ill look into the situation, specifically to the company that you mentioned[2191] in his issue. The issue of the investigation of the case is actually the issue of making sure to restore the

honesty so we will take care of that and will work on the investigation of the case. On top of that, I would kindly ask you if you have any additional information that you can provide to us, it would be very helpful for the investigation to make sure that we administer justice in our country with regards to the Ambassador to the United States from Ukraine as far as I recall her name was Ivanovich [sic]. It was great that you were the first one. Who told me that she was a bad ambassador because I agree with you 100%. Her attitude towards me was far from the best as she admired the previous President and she was on his side. She would not accept me as a new President well enough.[2192]

Trump responded: "Well, she's going to go through some things. I will have Mr. Giuliani give you a call and I am also going to have Attorney General Barr call and we will get to the bottom of it."[2193] Zelenskyy then told President Trump that he wanted "to ensure [sic] you that we will be very serious about the case and will work on the investigation."[2194] Trump then told Zelenskyy that he would have Giuliani and Barr call him.[2195]

Inside the White House Situation Room, Tim Morrison, Fiona Hill's replacement, was listening to the call, along with Rob Blair. Lieutenant Colonel Alexander Vindman. Jennifer Williams and General Keith Kellogg from Vice President Pence's office were also listening, along with an NSC press aide.[2196] After hearing discussions during the call surrounding the false story regarding the DNC server being located in Ukraine, Morrison became concerned.[2197] He realized that the concerns shared with him regarding the Giuliani channel by Hill were in fact very real.[2198]

Lieutenant Colonel Vindman was concerned as well, and felt that Morrison was also having problems with the call when it strayed into Trump's requests for information.[2199] When the group began working to complete the press statement on the call, all of the "stray voltage" had been removed.[2200] A few days later, as the author of the memorandum of the conversation (MEMCON), Vindman had to do edits. But he found that it had been placed in the classified system, unlike standard MEMCONs with calls to foreign leaders.[2201]

At 3:00 in the afternoon on the 25th, Michael Duffey from OMB reached out to the secretary of defense's (SecDef) office to inform them that they were to "hold off on any additional DoD obligation of these funds."[2202] Duffey asked that the recipients of the email keep the information "closely held to those who need to know."[2203]

The president had now withheld security aid from Ukraine. There were two months before the failure to spend the aid would be fatal to the aid itself. If the obligated funds were not spent by the end of the fiscal year on September 30 they would be gone, resulting in a huge diplomatic loss for the US and Ukraine, vis-à-vis Russia. The situation could scarcely have been better for Putin. The American president's attempts to get dirt on his 2020 opponent were helping Russia in its war in Ukraine.

That same afternoon, the State Department emailed Laura Cooper, the DoD official shepherding aid to Ukraine—both the House Foreign Affairs Committee and the Ukrainian Embassy wanted to know what was going on.[2204] On July 26, Ukraine's foreign agent Daniel Vajdich again emailed five members of the NSC, including Croft, Vindman, Morrison, and Griffith.[2205] If the Ukrainians were not aware that something was wrong the day prior, it appeared they were fully informed the next day.

At least one NSC official went directly to NSC counsel John Eisenberg after the call to express concerns about what the president said.[2206] Lieutenant Colonel Vindman was one of the officials.[2207] By the end of the 26, two others had come to Eisenberg about their concerns.[2208] One of them was Tim Morrison who asked Eisenberg to place the call on the classified server.[2209]

The next day US officials were in Kyiv to meet with Ukrainian counterparts, including Zelenskyy.[2210] After Sondland met with Andriy Yermak, the ambassador took several US Embassy aides to lunch. In front of the aides, Sondland got on the phone with the president and informed him that Zelenskyy "loves your ass."[2211] Trump loudly and audibly asked Sondland if Zelenskyy was going to do the requested investigation. Sondland told the president "he's going to do it."[2212]

But it was too late.

Around the same time, a CIA analyst detailed to the White House sent an anonymous complaint to Courtney Simmons Elwood, the CIA's general counsel via a colleague. The analyst broadly reported that there were serious problems with the president's July 25 telephone call.[2213] Elwood, required by law to determine if there was a "reasonable basis" for the complaint, reached out to John Eisenberg, the deputy White House counsel for the NSC.[2214] Over the next few weeks, Eisenberg, who had received Fiona Hill and Alex Vindman's urgent complaints three weeks before, agreed with Elwood. There was a reasonable basis that the law had been violated.[2215]

The whistleblower, concerned that his report was not being taken seriously, then met with a majority staff member of the House Intelligence Committee.[2216] The staff member, following protocol, told the whistleblower that he needed to contact a lawyer and make a report to an inspector general.[2217] It was late July.[2218]

On August 1, John Bolton spoke personally to Attorney General Barr about his concerns regarding Trump. Bolton told Barr that he was concerned about the president's direct mention of Barr's name and the need to "rein in" Giuliani.[2219] But as Bolton, Defense Secretary Esper, and Pompeo discussed what was needed to turn Trump around on military aid to Ukraine they decided against direct confrontation of the president.[2220] Instead they would wait it out and hope to uncouple security aid to Ukraine from the package before it was too late.[2221] They were apparently unaware that this was the second time Trump had illegally held back aid for Ukraine, the first time having occurred in November 2017, when Poroshenko was still president of Ukraine.

On August 2, Andriy Yermak met with Giuliani and Parnas in Madrid.[2222] Parnas set up the meeting and told Rudy he would be met by a man with a sign that says "NUBA" at the door of the plane. That person,

Parnas told him, would take him through customs.[2223] From there, he proceeded to the estate of Venezuelan energy executive Alejandro Betancourt López, at that point listed as an unindicted coconspirator in a federal money laundering case in Miami.[2224] The next month, in early September, Giuliani would directly lobby top DOJ officials on López's behalf.[2225]

At the López estate, Giuliani explained to Yermak exactly what Trump needed—investigations into Hunter Biden and Burisma, and an investigation into allegations that Ukraine helped Hillary Clinton by releasing information on Paul Manafort contained in the Black Ledger.[2226] "Your country owes it to us and to your country to find out what really happened," Giuliani claims he told Yermak.[2227] They discussed the meeting that Zelenskyy wanted from Trump.[2228]

Apparently on this trip Giuliani also met with another resident of Spain, Oleksandr Onyshchenko. In July he had lost his extradition appeal in Spain and only a review by the Council of Ministers remained before he would be deported. The fugitive Ukrainian oligarch told British journalist Paul Wood that he wanted to "offer help and information" to Giuliani about the Bidens.[2229] Wood stated that two sources told him that Onyshchenko then hired Giuliani to be his lawyer.[2230]

At some point thereafter, Trump associates began to seek visas for Onyshchenko and others related to the impeachment effort. A new, entirely Trump-friendly media network, One America News, owned by a pro-Trump business magnate, financed the efforts, which included other Ukrainian officials.[2231]

After the Yermak-Giuliani meeting in Madrid, Rudy felt that Ukraine needed to make a statement regarding the requested investigations.[2232] Volker learned from Yermak that Ukraine was willing to make a statement.[2233] Sondland texted Volker: "To avoid misunderstandings, might be helpful to ask Andrey [Yermak] for a draft statement."[2234] Volker agreed.[2235]

Volker texted Giuliani requesting a conference call for the exact formulation Trump needed. Giuliani asked for the call now.[2236] Yermak provided a proposed text. On the 13th, the text of the statement was agreed upon by the US side. The US side added language that would state Zelenskyy was insisting on a "transparent and unbiased investigation" of "Burisma and the 2016 US elections."[2237]

Yermak wanted dates before he agreed that the Ukrainians would give a statement along the lines Trump was requesting. The Ukrainians also wanted an official request from the US Justice Department to investigate.[2238] Around August 18, the effort seemed to stall.[2239] Ukraine's stated concerns revolved around Lutsenko, who Zelenskyy was going to replace.[2240]

On August 12, the CIA whistleblower had obtained representation and forwarded on a complaint about the July 25 phone call and the preceding actions by Giuliani, Parnas, and Fruman.[2241] Addressed to the chairs of the Congressional intelligence committees, the letter was given to the inspector general of the Intelligence Community, Michael Atkinson.[2242] The complaint was blunt: "I have received information from multiple US government officials that the President of the United States is using the power of his office to solicit interference from a foreign country in the 2020 election."[2243] The complaint was detailed. Citing OCCRP's exposé on Parnas and Fruman's activity in Ukraine, it noted that the two Giuliani associates were involved and went back all the way to the start of the campaign to get Yovanovitch fired.[2244]

On August 14, Elwood had a conference call with her White House counterpart John Eisenberg and John Demers, the head of the National Security Division of the Justice Department.[2245] Elwood and Eisenberg told Demers that the substance of the July 25 phone call between the presidents of Ukraine and the US required the DOJ to look into the matter.[2246] None of the three lawyers knew about the formal whistleblower complaint submitted two days earlier regarding the call.[2247]

On the 26th, Atkinson wrote to Acting Director of National Intelligence McGuire.[2248] Following the statute, he had determined that the CIA whistleblower had reported "an urgent concern" that "appears credible."[2249] The letter explained how the whistleblower statute for the Intelligence Community worked. In essence, the CIA whistleblower was asking for permission to send his letter to the Chairs of the House and Senate intelligence committees. Atkinson was opening up his own investigation into whether or not there was a campaign finance violation and counterintelligence risk under security clearance statutes for those involved.[2250] The letter notified the DNI of his responsibility to forward the complaint letter and attached documents to the congressional intelligence committees.[2251]

Bolton had tried his luck again on the Ukrainian assistance on August 20, taking "Trump's temperature" on the matter.[2252] Trump told Bolton that he was not in favor of the aid being released until the Ukrainian government turned over the information on the Bidens, Burisma and the alleged 2016 plot by Ukraine to help Hillary Clinton.[2253] Bolton asked for a meeting for himself, Pompeo, and Esper for later in the week to discuss the matter. Trump agreed.[2254]

Bolton's deputy Charles Kupperman sat in for him when the matter came up again. But Esper, Pompeo, and Kupperman were only able to get Trump to say: "Let me think about it a couple of days."[2255]

"THE FINAL QUESTION COMES FROM JILL COLVIN WITH ASSOCIATED PRESS"

There were not a couple of days left. On the afternoon of August 28, *Politico* broke a story reporting that the White House was slow-walking US military aid to Ukraine despite the Department of Defense and both parties on Capitol Hill supporting the aid.[2256] Yermak texted Volker the link from Kyiv asking for a phone call.[2257]

On August 26, Bolton flew to Kyiv to meet with Zelenskyy and his team.[2258] Near the end of a meeting with them, Bolton pulled aside the new prosecutor general and briefly talked about the "investigations" issues and advised him to contact Attorney General Barr directly.[2259] Bill Taylor then discreetly asked National Security Advisor Bolton what to do about the swirling issue of Giuliani's requested investigations.[2260] Bolton advised Chargé Taylor to send a rare "first person" missive, a diplomatic cable directly to the Secretary of State detailing the problem, something reserved for only the most extraordinary of circumstances.[2261]

Bill Taylor did just that: on August 29 he sent the "first person" diplomatic cable to Pompeo from Kyiv, on "the folly I saw in withholding military aid to Ukraine," while Russia still was involved in active hostilities with the country.[2262] Taylor told Pompeo "that I could not and would not defend such a policy."[2263] Pompeo never responded to Taylor's letter.

On August 30, Trump, in response to the approach of Hurricane Dorian, canceled his trip to Poland to commemorate the anniversary of the beginning of World War II.[2264] This meant that he would miss the first bilateral opportunity for the presidents of the US and Ukraine to meet. Vice President Pence was sent in Trump's place. Volker texted Sondland and Taylor, hoping that Pence would keep the scheduled bilateral meeting.[2265] The same day Trump again said no to the Ukrainian aid in a staff teleconference in the Situation Room, suggesting that NATO pay for the Ukrainian aid, not realizing that US taxpayer dollars were the subject of the question.[2266]

The next day Taylor sought clarification on the requirements for a Zelenskyy White House visit, asking, "Are we now saying that security assistance and WH meeting are conditioned on investigations?"[2267] Declining to respond by text, Sondland asked the long-time State Department veteran to call him.[2268]

In the call, Sondland told Taylor there had been a mistake. The White House meeting and the security aid were indeed conditioned on the Burisma investigations.[2269] Taylor was horrified and asked Sondland to push back on Trump. Sondland said he would try.[2270]

Before the bilateral meeting between Pence and Zelenskyy, Gordon Sondland told Pence about his concerns that the security aid had been tied to investigations.[2271] At the meeting, Zelenskyy's first question to Pence was about the hold on the security aid.[2272] Pence dissembled, saying that he would provide Trump with the facts of Ukraine's "good progress on reforms" in order to get a decision on the security aid.[2273] He made it clear that the aid was tied to the Ukrainians doing more on corruption."[2274]

At the meeting, Sondland had a pull-aside with Yermak.[2275] Sondland told Yermak that Ukraine would likely not receive the military aid that had been allocated to it unless the Ukrainian government "provided the public anti-corruption statement that we had been discussing for many weeks."[2276]

Later at a photo op with Polish president Andrzej Duda, Pence took questions. At the end of the press conference, the moderator signaled a wrap: "the final question comes from Jill Colvin with Associated Press," he said. Colvin took the microphone: "Thank you very much, Mr. Vice President. I wanted to ask you about your meeting yesterday with the Ukrainian President and for an update on Ukrainian security aid money."[2277] Colvin then drew near to the truth: "Specifically, number one, did you discuss Joe Biden at all during that meeting yesterday with the Ukrainian President?[2278] And number two," Colvin added: "can you assure Ukraine that the hold-up of that money has absolutely nothing to do with efforts, including by Rudy Giuliani, to try to dig up dirt on the Biden family?"[2279] Pence dodged the question.

The Zelenskyy Affair was now under way.

In late August, Toensing and diGenova met with an old friend, AG Barr, and several of his subordinates regarding Firtash's case.[2280] They were hoping to get the case against Firtash closed.[2281] According to later reports, the effort failed.[2282]

On September 4, Viktor Shokin swore out a deposition in Kyiv "at the request of lawyers of Dmytro Firtash."[2283] "I do so entirely voluntarily and without any threat or inducement," the statement added.[2284] The deposition transcript stated that in 2015 the Ukrainian government, through Interior Minister Avakov, falsely claimed that there were three cases on which Firtash could be arrested under investigation.[2285] Shokin's statement said he received no evidence or materials "to support DF's [Dmytro Firtash's] involvement in criminality."[2286] Therefore, Shokin claimed, the Obama administration, "in particular the US Vice-President Joe Biden" manipulated the political

332

leadership of Ukraine on false pretexts to prevent Firtash from returning to Ukraine.[2287]

Shokin went further and falsely claimed to have been "leading a wide-ranging corruption probe in to Burisma"[2288] He claimed that Poroshenko had asked him to wind down the prosecution of Burisma and that when Shokin refused, "he said the US (via Biden) were refusing to release the USD$ 1 billion promised to Ukraine," and that "he had no choice, therefore, but to ask me to resign."[2289]

On September 5, the *Washington Post* Editorial Board pointed out what was now rapidly becoming obvious when it wrote a piece asking questions about what the president was doing: "Trump Tries to Force Ukraine to Meddle in the 2020 Election" was the headline.[2290] The article focused on Giuliani's open campaign to get the investigations done and questioned the hold-up on the aid when it had already been approved at every level.[2291]

Trump spoke with Sondland on September 7. Trump insisted that Zelenskyy had to go in front of a microphone and announce the 2016 election and Biden accusations.[2292] On September 8, Sondland reached out to Volker and Taylor to brief them. After some difficulties connecting, Sondland and Taylor spoke while Volker told them he could not hear them.[2293] Sondland told Taylor that there would be no White House meeting or military aid without the announcement of investigations.[2294] In a follow-up text, Taylor laid out the dangers: "The nightmare is they give the interview and don't get the security assistance. The Russians love it. (And I quit)."[2295]

That same day, the *New York Times* reported that the House Judiciary Committee had written a draft resolution to deal with cases of impeachment.[2296] The article stated that the committee had been involved in a full-scale impeachment inquiry against the president.[2297] Another article detailed the debates within the Democratic House Caucus, with Speaker Pelosi seemingly not on board.[2298]

September 9, 2019. was a Tuesday. Just after midnight in Washington, DC, Taylor and Sondland were sending text messages. "With the hold," Taylor argued with Sondland, "we have already shaken their faith in us. Thus my nightmare scenario."[2299] Taylor was in a prophetic mood: "Counting on you to be right on this interview, Gordon."[2300]

Sondland replied: "Bill, I never said I was 'right.' I said 'we are where we are,' and believe we have identified the best pathway forward. Let's hope it works."[2301]

Taylor brought his point home. "As I said earlier on the phone, I think it's crazy to withhold security assistance for help with a political campaign."[2302]

At 5:19 in the morning, Sondland replied. His demeanor had changed remarkably:

> Bill, I believe you are incorrect about President Trump. The President has been crystal clear no quid pro quo's [sic] of any kind. The President is trying to evaluate whether Ukraine is truly going to adopt the transparency and reforms that President Zelensky [sic] promised during the campaign I suggest we stop the back and forth by text If you still have concerns I recommend you give Lisa Kenna or S a call to discuss them directly. Thanks.[2303]

Something had changed the situation.

CHAPTER 12:

A SCANDAL OF MAJOR PROPORTION

The something that had changed the situation was soon to become apparent. But first, in separate calls that same morning, Bolton spoke with Esper and Pompeo about the Ukraine funding situation.[2304] They were confident that Trump would finally release the funds. For reasons they did not know about, they were right.

Sondland had been reacting to the Democrats. That morning, House Democrats opened up full bore. The chairs of the House Intelligence, Foreign Affairs, and Government Oversight committees sent a letter to the White House Counsel. "A growing public record" the letter said, "indicates that for nearly two years, the president and his personal attorney, Rudy Giuliani, appear to have acted outside legitimate law enforcement and diplomatic channels to coerce the Ukrainian government into pursuing two politically motivated investigations."[2305] The letter's citations reached all the way back to Giuliani's speech in Kyiv on June 7, 2017.[2306]

The letter then turned to the July 25, 2019, phone call, accurately stating that the president had focused on requesting investigations while discussing military aid to Ukraine.[2307] The chairs also demanded document preservation and set a deadline of September 16 for the White House to turn over records critical to the investigation.[2308] A second letter to Pompeo laid out the same argument and also demanded document retention and production.[2309] The letters showed careful preparation.

The same day, Inspector General Atkinson sent a letter to Adam Schiff, chair of the House Intelligence Committee, informing him that he had received a complaint and forwarded it on to the director of National Intelligence. But the Director had not forwarded the complaint on to the proper representatives in Congress, as required by law.[2310]

At 2:15 that same afternoon, National Security Advisor Bolton was called down to the Oval Office. The president began complaining about Bolton: "A lot of people don't like you. They say you're a leaker and not a team player."[2311] Trump complained about Bolton having his own airplane—which he did not.[2312] The president also complained that Bolton had too many of his own people on his staff.[2313]

Bolton stood up. "If you want me to leave, I'll leave," he replied to the president.[2314] Trump told him they would talk about it in the morning. Bolton says he returned to his office and pulled out his resignation letter, written months before, handed it to an assistant to put on White House stationery, intending to sleep on his resignation until the morning, then left for the day.[2315]

That evening, one of Mulvaney's deputies called Bolton's assistant Charles Kupperman and told him that Trump had said that Bolton was not to get the use of a military jet unless he personally approved it.[2316]

The next morning, Bolton claims, he signed his resignation letter and ordered it sent to the Outer Oval Office. Then Bolton left. At 11:50, Trump tweeted that he had informed Bolton his services were not needed the night before.[2317]

One day after opening the three investigations, House Democrats moved again. Schiff wrote to Acting DNI McGuire, informing him that his committee had learned of the whistleblower complaint and that the Administration was unlawfully withholding it.[2318] "Absent immediate compliance" the letter stated, "the Committee will resort to compulsory process."[2319]

On the morning of the 11th, the Trump administration caved in and began releasing the Ukrainian aid money.[2320] The night of the 11th, the hold on the $250 million in military aid was released.[2321] On the 12th, they announced that the hold had been lifted.

On September 13, Adam Schiff announced there was a whistleblower complaint and that the DNI had not responded to his letter demanding it.[2322]

Schiff came to a conclusion he had long sensed from months of prior investigation—"The Committee can only conclude, based on this remarkable confluence of factors, that the serious misconduct at issue involves the President of the United States and/or other senior White House or Administration officials."[2323] Schiff then accused the administration of a cover-up and attached a subpoena for the documents.[2324]

As the scandal rose in the news, Parnas, Fruman, and Giuliani began visiting the Trump International less and less. They no longer dined in the restaurant most mornings as they had in the past. One day, Giuliani held interviews for a spokesperson within the hotel's restaurant, with many young attractive women "in skirts" present, according to a source familiar with the interview process. The woman eventually selected was Christianné Allen, a twenty-year-old with connections to Trump-related groups.[2325] On September 10 an anxious Giuliani wanted Parnas back in DC. He wanted to bring Andrii Artemenko into the operation and wanted to know if Parnas knew him.[2326]

On September 19, the *Washington Post* was able to connect the dots. The whistleblower complaint "centers on Ukraine" the paper reported.[2327] The "complaint involved communications with a foreign leader and a "promise that Trump made" the *Post* informed its readers.[2328]

"WE HAPPEN TO HAVE THE MAN IN THE MIDDLE TONIGHT"

That evening, the pressure began to get to Rudy Giuliani. Sources familiar with meetings between Parnas and Giuliani in the final weeks of their partnership indicate that Giuliani would test out lines for television with Parnas during their meetings at the mayor's table some mornings. The results would be seen on television soon after.

The evening of the *Post* article about the CIA whistleblower, Rudy Giuliani was to appear on CNN's *Chris Cuomo Prime Time*. "All right, this whistleblower story is blowing up, and it's doing so on our watch," led Cuomo.[2329] "There is now breaking news on that urgent complaint about President Trump," he explained; "it involves Ukraine. This comes from the *Washington Post*."[2330] After a short run-down of what was known up until then, he turned to Giuliani: "So, that's where it stands. We happen to have the man in the middle tonight."[2331]

Cuomo thanked Giuliani for being on the show. "Oh, I'm glad I'm on tonight," Giuliani responded, taking off his glasses. "Because what you just said is totally erroneous."[2332] Giuliani haltingly explained that he had just spent the last two years investigating the Black Ledger:

> I was investigating, going back to last year, complaints that the Ukrainian people, several people in Ukraine, knew about a tremendous amount of collusion between Ukrainian officials, and Hillary Clinton, and the Democratic National Committee,

including a completely fraudulent document that was produced, in order to begin the investigation of Manafort.[2333]

Rudy then explained why Yovanovitch had been targeted: "they were being blocked by the Ambassador who was Obama-appointee, in Ukraine, who was holding back this information."[2334] "In the course of investigating that," Giuliani dissembled, "I found out this incredible story about Joe Biden that he bribed the President of Ukraine in order to fire a prosecutor who was investigating his son."[2335] Rudy had reversed the order of when Trump associates had got their information. Oynshchenko's Burisma information had been given to them in January 2017.

Cuomo could barely get in a word edgewise—"This scandal is a scandal," he went on, "of major proportion."[2336] After a Giuliani rant about the media, Cuomo got New York blunt: "Are you—are you done now?" he asked.[2337] The interview turned into a slugfest. The transcript consisted of the pair exchanging clauses to their sentences.

Giuliani complained: "You said I was I was investigating—" he stammered over Cuomo "—it for political purposes. I was not."[2338] Giuliani then went after the Anti-Corruption Action Centre in Ukraine, claiming that "they were going to lie about the conversation I was having with the President."[2339] It was unclear what president or conversation Giuliani was talking about. The story seemed remarkably similar to the June 7, 2017, meeting between President Poroshenko and Giuliani in Kyiv that led to the first Javelin missile sale to Ukraine.

Cuomo then asked him why he canceled his trip to Ukraine in May. Giuliani responded with "because I was told that the people at the meeting with the President were people who work for George Soros. And George Soros had been funding this whole thing from the very, very beginning."[2340] The responses were confusing and lacking in context. Giuliani began to aggressively flounder.

Giuliani began talking about AntAC. He claimed the organization "developed all the dirty information that ended up being a false document that was created in order to incriminate Manafort."[2341] Giuliani was claiming that AntAC had forged the Black Ledger.

Cuomo alluded to the fact that the Black Ledger was not a major part of the Mueller investigation: "Because, you know, the—the—" Cuomo responded over Giuliani's repeated interruptions "—the United States Attorney just found its—own stuff about Manafort."[2342] The president's lawyer and one of CNN's top hosts were arguing about the origins of the Black Ledger on national television and the president's lawyer was losing.

Rudy was bringing up the Trump Campaign's alternative explanation for how Manafort got caught and whether the Black Ledger was authentic to the public and it was a confused tangle. He turned next to a FBI Agent, supposedly named "Greenwood," who he said took an affidavit that "a court in the Ukraine that a man named—Telizhenko—Yushchenko, something like that that he produced a phony affidavit," said Giuliani, making errors with the names.[2343] It became clear Giuliani was confusedly referring to MP and investigative reporter Sergii Leshchenko's early 2017 meeting with the FBI. It was a comedy of errors. Giuliani had wrongly named Special Agent Karen Greenaway as "Greenwood," expressed anger that no one had reported that a lower court had found Leshchenko guilty of election interference while wrongly calling him by the name of a former Ukrainian President. Some mistakes were intentional, however—Giulinai had conveniently omitted the fact that the conviction had been overturned on appeal in July.[2344]

Rudy then trotted out the accusation that Shokin was fired to help Burisma. Cuomo called it a distraction from the main question. "Did you ask the Ukraine to investigate Joe Biden?"[2345]

"No, actually I didn't." responded Giuliani. But as his extended explanation seemed to indicate that Giuliani *had* asked Ukraine to investigate Biden.[2346]

Cuomo renewed his question: "So, you did ask Ukraine to look into Joe Biden?"

"Of course I did!" responded an exasperated Giuliani. Cuomo's face rippled into a look of confusion. Giuliani began walking back the admission, denying he had said that he asked Ukraine to look into the Bidens. "Its all recorded, Rudy," responded Cuomo.[2347] The host then asked Rudy to provide documents. Rudy said he would only give them to a court. The interview dissolved into a shout-fest and then Cuomo ended it.[2348]

In a little over twenty-eight minutes, Giuliani had grievously wounded himself and the president. The next morning, the full details were out. "Ukraine Pressured on US Political Investigations," read a *New York Times* headline.[2349] The article laid out the entire Giuliani effort from the beginning of the year.

At some time in September, money woes increased for Parnas. Dmytro Firtash came to the rescue, wiring a million-dollar loan to Parnas's wife, Svetlana.[2350]

On the 24th, Speaker Pelosi announced that the investigation was now an impeachment inquiry.[2351] The walls began to move in on Trump. On September 26, a redacted version of the CIA whistleblower's complaint was released. Parnas texted Giuliani to ask how he was doing. "Fighting" was the one-word response.[2352] The next day Parnas texted bad news. CNN was reporting Kurt Volker had resigned.[2353] Rudy responded a day later: "Hope you feel better. It's painful but we are on the right side."[2354]

The next day, the White House released a version of the July 25 call.[2355] The President claimed it was a "perfect call."

Leaks began to spring. On September 19, the staff of House Foreign Affairs Chair Eliot Engel reached out to John Bolton. They spoke on the 23rd. Bolton suggested, unprompted, that the Democrats ought to look into the firing of Ambassador Yovanovitch and implied there was something illegal about it.[2356]

The full extent of the damage from Giuliani's disastrous interview with Chris Cuomo became apparent on September 28. Over the preceding year, NBC's *Saturday Night Live* had been running Trump skits starring Alec Baldwin as the president. On that evening, the forty-fifth season of the comedy show cold-opened with Baldwin as Trump, fretting about impeachment. Trump called Giuliani, played by Kate McKinnon, who appeared on a split screen. McKinnon's Giuliani told Trump to relax because "nobody's gonna find out about our illegal side dealings with Ukraine. Or how we tried to cover up those side dealings. Or how we planned to cover up the cover up."[2357]

A relieved Trump asked McKinnon's Giuliani where he was: "I'm on CNN right now" as the camera pulled away to show him on the set of "Cuomo Prime Time."[2358] The big laugh the bit got showed just how bad things had gone for Trump since July. Giuliani had had a golden opportunity on national television to deploy the disinformation that had been carried over from Ukraine in early 2017. Yet he had failed, and much of the country saw the accusations as little more than a dumb joke.

"YOU'RE ONE LUCKY GUY"

The following Monday, the House issued subpoenas to Giuliani, Parnas, Fruman, and a fourth man.[2359] Notably, the subpoenas reached all the way back to January 2017 and touched on Giuliani's work in 2017 for Pavel Fuks and Kyiv mayor Vitaly Klitschko.[2360] Evidently, the House Democrats knew quite a lot of the backstory.

With subpoenas served to Parnas and Fruman, they needed lawyers. From Vienna, Parnas phoned Rudy, who suggested John Dowd.[2361] After a brief call, Dowd said he would look into it.[2362] Dowd called back in fifteen minutes indicating that there was a conflict with the president and that he did not think the president would waive it. Parnas told Dowd that he was certain the president would.[2363] Dowd called back in fifteen minutes, surprised. "You're one lucky guy," he said. The president had immediately waived the conflict.[2364]

Dowd's texts show how the intense media attention was fraying the Biden/Burisma story at its edges. A reporter texted him, pointing to Lev's story that he and Giuliani had met Guralnik while eating lunch together, but Giuliani said that Guralnik had approached him in November 2018, "two months before he began working with Lev."[2365] All could be proven to be lies. Giuliani had begun working with Parnas on the disinformation plot in the summer of 2018.

Parnas went to Dowd's house to discuss the subpoena. There they got on speakerphone with Jay Sekulow, Giuliani, and Toensing. The three explained to Lev that his work for Giuliani was covered by privilege and that they were advising him not to cooperate with the congressional investigation. Parnas agreed.[2366]

Another sign of the fraying of the disinformation story Giuliani sought to bring forth happened on October 1. That morning, Pompeo refused to allow testimony of State Department employees.[2367] Later, the inspector general for the State Department, Steve Linick, asked to meet with the impeachment committees to bring documents and discuss them with members and staff.[2368] The next day, he brought Giuliani's Yovanovitch "dirt file" to Congress, the "dirt file" Giuliani had originally given to Pompeo. By the end of the news cycle, Giuliani admitted he had brought the "dirt file" to Pompeo.[2369] Rudy's attempts to keep the scheme going were shredding the president's defense.

On October 3, Dowd responded to the congressional subpoena, claiming that Parnas and Fruman had been working for Giuliani, assisting him with Giuliani's work for Trump.[2370] The work with Firtash was covered by a claim of privilege too—Parnas and Fruman had also assisted Toensing and diGenova.[2371] Dowd carefully avoided mentioning Firtash's name. The same day, Kurt Volker testified in closed-door session for the impeachment committees.

Amazingly, the efforts of Giuliani and his helpers to push the Biden/Burisma story continued, despite the fact that the world was falling down all around them. The plan was to get Viktor Shokin a live interview on Fox News from Vienna, where Firtash remained a free prisoner. Text messages between Parnas and Hannity booker Alyssa Moni indicated that a studio in Vienna had been booked for a satellite interview.[2372] Delays had pushed the date of the interview back.[2373] Parnas and Fruman booked $8,000 one-way tickets to Vienna on the 8th for the evening of the 9th, Yom Kippur.[2374]

On the 8th, an explosive piece on the secret State Department report about the Javelin sale appeared in the *New York Review of Books*.[2375] The story[2376] garnered little notice—it revealed the secret State Department report that British journalist Paul Wood had to retract in January 2019 as part of a suit by Poroshenko. Citing State Department records and cables, it stated that the reformers in Ukraine had helped prepare the report. It firmly reported that Kilimnik had been allowed to escape and it stated that Poroshenko had made a decision in August or September to halt cooperation with the Mueller investigation.[2377]

On the 9th, Parnas and Fruman met with Giuliani at the Trump International for lunch at the "Mayor's Table" and afterwards headed for Dulles Airport for the overnight flight.[2378] The pair relaxed in the Lufthansa first-class lounge while they waited for their flight. As they walked down a glass-framed jetway, they were approached by two plainclothes officers and who asked them to hand over their passports.[2379] The pair were arrested and led back up the jetway to where a phalanx of police waited.[2380] Parnas and Fruman were booked by the Alexandria County Sheriff's Office and sent to the Alexandria County Jail where Manafort had been booked almost two years earlier.

"I WANT TO ADD THIS INVESTIGATION IS CONTINUING"

The next day, Geoffrey S. Berman, the US attorney for the Southern District of New York, held a press conference. He alleged that Parnas and Fruman had made contributions to two political action committees at the behest of a Ukrainian government official for the purposes of removing the US ambassador to Ukraine. David Correia was also indicted but not yet in custody. Berman ended his statement with "I want to add this investigation is continuing."[2381]

While he was in jail, Lev Parnas learned exactly who he was. He met with John Dowd and his new criminal attorney, Manafort's lawyer, Kevin Downing. Parnas asked Dowd why people weren't defending him and Fruman in the media.[2382] He was angry. The president's former lawyer asked Parnas who he thought he was, telling important people like Giuliani and the president what to do.[2383] In an interview with Rachel Maddow, Parnas said that he told Dowd: "If you don't get out of here right now, something bad is going to happen because I don't want to see the two of you."[2384] Downing hit the panic button in the prison meeting room.[2385] Security removed Parnas.

Parnas's new attorneys included Joseph A. Bondy, an unflappably polite defense attorney with a history of defending top mobsters and advancing the cannabis business. At a hearing on October 8, he hinted at a new defense: "We look forward to defending Mr. Parnas in court, based on the evidence, not a smear campaign, driven by self-serving, scheming leaks, apparently from the highest level of our government"[2386]

Andriy Derkach gave an interview to *Interfax-Ukraine* on October 11. He opened with a fact that he knew, but which America was only starting to realize: "Since 2016, Ukraine has been at the center of domestic politics and the political confrontation of its strategic partner, the United States," he said.[2387] It was true.

He had more truth to tell. He perfectly described what was happening: a "series of international scandals and corruption, in which some representatives of law enforcement and diplomatic bodies of the two countries are mired."[2388] The story of Russian interference in the 2016 election and the politics of disinformation that followed was really a story of a hybrid war for the future of Ukraine, whether the country would be dominated by Russia, or able set its own course. All the physical fighting occurred in Ukraine, but some of the disinformation war spilled into American politics.

Derkach turned these truths on their head. "We must show the United States and other countries that we are interested in punishing those responsible so that the situation does not happen again," he said.[2389] But the crimes and suspects were all false. The he insisted the bad guys were "NABU employees and officials of the US Embassy in Ukraine, the FBI."[2390] This was the ultimate alternate explanation. For supporters of Russia's interests in Ukraine and supporters of Donald Trump and the Republican Party, there was a whole different fact ecosystem to explain the political moment. It did not have to be true, but it had to have just enough internal consistency to be comfortable for them.

Derkach's set of alternate explanations revealed as much as they obscured. He admitted that Poroshenko's go-between with Trump, State Fiscal Service director Roman Nasirov, "was close to Trump's team" and he alleged it was "noteworthy" that NABU went after him around the time of Trump's Inauguration.[2391] Derkach was putting up a preemptive defense regarding Nasirov's participation in the peace plan.[2392] Up to that point the press had never associated Trump and Nasirov together. Now Derkach was telling everyone they were linked.

Derkach also included a blizzard of new claims with no evidence: that Hunter Biden and two others had been paid 16.5 million dollars, that Viktor Shokin "had a plan to investigate the activities of Hunter Biden," and that Joe Biden had pressured Ukraine to fire Shokin to stop this supposed investigation.[2393] Not included was any explanation how Shokin's secret plan to investigate Hunter Biden was learned of by his father.

Derkach laid it all on the line. The good relationship between Ukraine and the US was dependent on Ukraine undertaking the investigations requested of Zelenskyy by Trump. This must be done," he concluded, "because how Ukraine will be treated in the near future depends on it."[2394]

"HAVE YOU EVER HEARD OF THE BLACK LEDGER?"

The arrests supercharged the impeachment scandal. They came just as depositions in the matter began. Yovanovitch was deposed on the 11th, followed by Fiona Hill's testimony on the 14th. Hill's explosive testimony leaked that same day, as Bolton's "drug deal" comments were quickly confirmed by the former National Security Advisor.[2395] Kent, Sondland, and Taylor followed on the 15th, 17th, and 22nd respectively. For the first time in the Trump presidency, the Democrats had him on the defensive. Transcripts show the Republicans were focused on Biden and Burisma.

On the 22nd, Oleksandr Onyshchenko reappeared in the news. Onyshchenko, Trump's former business partner and friend, and the originator of the Biden-Burisma allegations, was always the closing witness in the alternate explanation for Biden's conduct fighting corruption in Ukraine. He had lost his extradition fight in Spain in July, and only the decision upholding the case by Spain's Council of Ministers remained to be decided.[2396] Suddenly, Onyshchenko was providing comment to Reuters on his version of what Hunter Biden did for Burisma.[2397]

Also on the 22nd, *Vanity Fair* ran a piece quoting Michael Cohen's lawyer Lanny Davis: "In my judgment, Michael Cohen is now even more valuable than before.[2398] *Vanity Fair* then apparently moved Davis into the "people familiar with the situation" position for the actual leak. These sources told the magazine in coded language about Parnas's approach on behalf of the Poroshenko peace plan—Parnas, the sources claimed "approached" Cohen.²³⁹⁹ A second approach, the sources told *Vanity Fair* "may be of interest to investigators looking into whether Parnas violated federal election laws"—likely a reference to the original Biden and Burisma allegations that Artemenko gave to the Trump camp in early 2017.²⁴⁰⁰

In late October, Charles Kupperman, Bolton's longtime aide, filed a suit for a declaratory judgment on whether or not to appear for a House deposition which the White House had told him to ignore.²⁴⁰¹ The suit was widely seen as a stalking horse for Bolton, who expected a subpoena of his own should a court rule in the House's favor.²⁴⁰² The House promptly withdrew the subpoena because it did not want to let the impeachment timetable be controlled by the courts.²⁴⁰³

On the 31st, the day that the House voted a formal impeachment inquiry, Catherine Croft, the DoD official in charge of foreign military aid, gave a deposition. Adam Schiff's questioning made it evident that the impeachment investigators knew much more than they were letting on about the original Javelin sale to Ukraine. In the midst of the deposition, Schiff jumped in and began drilling down on the first Javelin sale to Ukraine and its connection to the Mueller investigation:

> THE CHAIRMAN: And what was going on with respect to Ukraine during those 2 weeks, in terms of what you were following in press accounts? Do you remember?

MS. CROFT: I don't. I was very focused on the Javelin decision. I don't have a specific memory of what was happening in the press at the time.

THE CHAIRMAN: During the period, either before the hold, during the hold, on after the hold, were you aware of any discussions going on about Ukraine's participation or nonparticipation in assisting the Mueller investigation?

MS. CROFT: Nothing that I was doing in my work at the National Security Council in any way related to what was happening in the Mueller investigation.

THE CHAIRMAN: No, I understand that. But we're obviously looking at allegations concerning the hold-up of military assistance in 2019, we're looking at a call record in which the President of Ukraine asks—says he's almost ready to get more Javelins. And we know during this period there is a hold put on military assistance. And as I'm sure you're aware from public accounts, there are questions about why that hold was placed, and testimony that was related to political demands by the President. So what I'm asking you is, did it come to your attention in any way, shape, or form, through conversation, open reporting or otherwise, that there may have been factors behind the first hold on the Javelins, the 2017 hold on the Javelins, that were not related to policy, that may have been related to investigations that the President wanted the Ukraine to do, on work that the President wanted Ukraine to refrain from doing in connection with the Mueller investigation?[2404]

Although Croft would answer in the negative, Schiff's pointed questioning indicated that the HPSCI had information which allowed them to ask such pointed questions about the relationship between the first tranche of Javelin missiles and the Mueller investigation. Two sources familiar with the committee's investigation indicate that the impeachment committees were fully up to speed on the original Javelins-for-obstruction deal of 2017–2018 and their link to the three Pennsylvania deals. Representative Gerry Connolly told reporters as he left Croft's deposition, "If I were an enterprising reporter, I'd spend a little bit of time on the issue of Javelin missiles."[2405]

Enterprising reporters were doing just that. On November 4, the *New York Times* finally brought the 2017–2018 dealings between Trump and Ukraine into focus in the context of the impeachment hearings. "Inside Ukraine's Push to Cultivate Trump from the Start" chronicled the secret history of Ukraine's dealings with Trump.[2406] The *Times* detailed the three Pennsylvania deals that were part of Ukraine's trade for the Javelin missiles. It also married the first real analysis in American media of the anti-corruption fight in Ukrainian politics during the fall of 2017 to the story of the Javelin sale.[2407] A *Wall Street Journal* story detailed Ukraine's fall 2017 political battle over anticorruption, while a second detailed the White House version of the first Javelin sale.

Another problem loomed for Trump. Joe Bondy was crafting a new legal strategy for Parnas. The Southern District of New York had rejected his efforts to cooperate, citing truthfulness concerns. Bondy then found a different governmental body to cooperate, House investigators.[2408] His hope was to show the judge that Parnas was trying to do the right thing.

On November 5, Bondy announced that Parnas would be cooperating with House investigators.[2409] He later indicated Parnas would also testify if called. His goal was to set up a situation where Parnas would testify under a grant of congressional immunity. Anything Parnas said, Bondy would argue, the prosecutors got from his testimony throwing evidentiary issues in the way of a prosecution. Bondy also hoped the cooperation with House investigators would give him credit with a judge. By claiming prosecutors under Barr were deliberately keeping him from a deal in order to protect the President, Bondy could craft an argument that he deserved a cooperator's sentence under the Federal Sentencing Guidelines.

Formal hearings approached. The Republicans sought their own witnesses. They indicated that they were committed to reinforcing the Giuliani misinformation narrative.[2410] To discredit the Black Ledger and suggest Ukraine interfered in the 2016 election, they proposed Alexandra Chalupa, the DNC staffer who warned that Manafort would join Trump's campaign. Nellie Ohr of Fusion GPS was also on their list—the object of inviting her was to discredit the Steele dossier. To bring forward the Biden-Burisma disinformation narrative, they sought to depose Hunter Biden and Devon Archer.[2411] They also sought the testimony of the whistleblower.[2412] The investigation of a political cover up was being defended by continuing to prop up the long-discredited cover story used to cover up the facts. The witnesses were rejected by the majority.

The House GOP issued a strategy memo to its members. The memo relied on the fact that Trump had released the aid when he was caught and required a straight-up denial of the facts on whether Trump pressured Ukraine in the July 25 phone call.[2413] It also advanced disinformation narratives surrounding the Black Ledger—trying to make it appear that the release of the Black Ledger involved Trump and not the personal revenge of Viktor Trepak[2414] for his firing.[2415]

The hearings opened on November 13 with George Kent and William Taylor. After a Schiff opening statement, Devin Nunes's opening statement advanced the disinformation narrative pushed by Giuliani. Nunes claimed this was all part of a plot to paint the president as a Russian agent, part of what he called the Democrats' "Russia Hoax."[2416] It was all "a carefully orchestrated media smear campaign" Nunes insisted.[2417] Calling the effort "an impeachment sham," he wanted the hearings postponed so they could find "answers" to whether or not Ukraine interfered in the election of 2016 against Trump and what Hunter Biden was doing for Burisma.[2418] According to his opening statement, "elements of the FBI or the Department of Justice and now the State Department have lost the confidence of millions of Americans."[2419] The back channel continued to make war upon the front channel.

The witnesses appeared at the same time, making it easier for viewers to understand the lines of evidence. William Taylor, Marie Yovanovitch, and Lieutenant Colonel Vindman played the role of heroes. But it was one of the villains who drove home the Democrats' point. They gave Gordon Sondland an entire morning to himself, a wise choice. Sondland had gone back to amend his deposition transcript in ways that were damaging to the president. In his opening statement, he went further: "Secretary Perry, Ambassador Volker, and I worked with Mr. Rudy Giuliani on Ukraine matters at the express direction of the President of the United States."[2420] He added a catch phrase, "Everyone was in the loop. It was no secret. Everyone was informed via email on July 19, days before the Presidential call."[2421] The Republicans made the error of taking up his catch phrase, repeatedly questioning him about who "was in the loop."[2422]

Sondland thought he was charming and funny. The effect of his testimony was tectonic.

Again, *Saturday Night Live*'s cold open underlined the impact of his testimony. Alec Baldwin as Trump pretended to read a conversation between himself and Sondland: "no quid pro quo bro," it said.[2423] Then, Will Ferrell appeared as Sondland, to audience cheers. "Oh, right, right, right, keep the quid pro quo on the low low," Ferrell's Sondland responded.[2424]

Fiona Hill appeared on the final day. It was another excellent choice in timing. Her role appeared to be to thoroughly discount the disinformation narrative as an expert on Vladimir Putin. "Based on questions and statements I have heard," Hill testified, "some of you on this committee appear to believe that Russia and its security services did not conduct a campaign against our country."[2425] Hill went straight at the Giuliani narrative: "and that perhaps, somehow for some reason, Ukraine did. This is a fictional narrative that is being perpetrated and propagated by the Russian security services themselves."[2426] Hill's working-class British accent, a bane in the UK, gave her testimony the weight of authority to US listeners.

She continued: "President Putin and the Russian security services operate like a Super PAC. They deploy millions of dollars to weaponize our own political opposition research and false narratives."[2427] Nunes's cross examination was a confused mess, asking Hill and the other witness David Holmes, about the Steele dossier and the Ohrs, recycling talking points from the HPSCI battles of the previous spring, when Nunes's held the gavel.[2428] Nunes's questions appeared to originate on another planet.

But the most instructive testimony may have been that of David Holmes, the political counselor at the US Embassy in Kyiv. At some point, it appeared that Devin Nunes realized this would be the last moment in the hearings that he could return to the disinformation narrative the GOP had been pushing since the summer of 2016. His questions mapped out that narrative.

Nunes began asking about Ukrainians: "Now I want to talk a little bit about Ukrainians, Ukrainian government officials."[2429] "Are you familiar with Sergii Leshchenko?" asked Nunes, referring to the Ukrainian MP who had discussed the Black Ledger at a press conference in 2016.[2430] "Are you aware that when he was in the Parliament, that he had provided information to a Fusion GPS operative named Nellie Ohr?"[2431]

Holmes responded: "I'm not aware of Nellie Ohr. I'm not aware of who he [Leshchenko] provided information to. I'm aware that as a journalist he's provided information."[2432]

Nunes then got deep into the disinformation narrative: "Well, this is—he was in the Parliament at the time. This was in the 2016 campaign. He provided widely known as the black ledger. Have you ever heard of the black ledger?"[2433]

"I have," answered Holmes.

"And the Black Ledger, is that seen as credible information?" queried Nunes.

Holmes responded "Yes." He knew exactly what Nunes was trying to do.

Nunes pressed: "The Black Ledger is credible?"

"Yes," answered Holmes.

Nunes began to argue with the answers. "Bob Mueller did not find it credible," he claimed. "Do you dispute what Bob Mueller's findings were? They didn't use it in the prosecution or the report."

Holmes responded: "I'm not aware that Bob Mueller did not find it credible. I think it was evidence in other criminal proceedings, and its credibility was not questioned in those proceedings. But I'm not an expert on that matter."[2434]

Nunes then added another part of the disinformation claims: "So the motivation for Leshchenko was reported to—was to go after a Trump campaign official and undermine Trump's candidacy. Are you aware of that?"

"If you mean by the release of the Black Ledger, I think Leshchenko's motivation was the same motivation he's always expressed, which is to expose corruption in Ukraine," answered Holmes.

Nunes was anxious to get his next point across: "Right. But he's admitted motivation was to partly at least undermine the Trump candidacy that he did not support."

Holmes responded coolly: "He has not said that to me. If he said that to you, I'll take your word for it."[2435] The young political counselor had just highlighted Nunes's role in the perpetuation of the disinformation scheme around Ukraine as he deflected Nunes's reaching.

Nunes then went into the next piece of the disinformation scheme, the Steele dossier, which was not even a subject of the impeachment. "And you're aware that the—you heard Dr. Hill's testimony that the Steele dossier, that contained initially that initial information that was fed in the FBI. Were you aware that the Democrats had paid for that information?"[2436] More than six months after the Mueller report was released and Bob Mueller had again retired from government, the GOP was *still* on the subject of Russia and Steele. These two lines of questioning—the Black Ledger and the Steele Dossier might be doing the political spade work for a pardon of Paul Manafort.

Holmes told Nunes he was not involved in the Steele Dossier. Nunes struggled to make the witness relevant to the GOP's alternate explanation for the last four years: "I'm not accusing you of involvement. I'm just asking if you—and not even if you knew at the time, but you now know today that the Democrats had paid for that information?" Holmes vainly pointed out that he had nothing to do with the Steele dossier at all. Nunes bulldozed ahead: "But you're not disputing that the Democrats and the Clinton campaign were the source of funds that funded the Steele dossier?"[2437]

Holmes responded: "I wouldn't be in a position to dispute that, sir." He skillfully refused to confirm Nunes's line of questions.

Nunes kept pushing the disinformation narrative. "Do you think it's appropriate for political parties to run operatives in foreign countries to dig up dirt on their opponents?" Holmes said no. Nunes turned to Hill: "Dr. Hill, do you think it's appropriate for political parties to pay operatives to dig up dirt on their opponents?"

Hill responded, "I do not."[2438] With that, Nunes turned the questioning back over to minority counsel.

After a few minutes of background questions, a question about Rick Perry awkwardly brought Nunes back into the questioning. "Since we're on the topic of Ukraine energy, I think it's a good way for us to segue into Burisma, which I assume both of you are familiar with. You've heard about it for many, many years."[2439] He was now moving to the Biden-Burisma disinformation that Oleksandr Onyshchenko had created in 2016. Defending the president from impeachment was not the place the originators of this legend had expected to employ it.

"Did you know that the financial records show that this Ukrainian natural gas company, Burisma, routed more than $3 million to the American accounts of Hunter Biden?"[2440] asked Nunes, trying to turn Hunter Biden's salary into something nefarious because the money was "routed" to "American accounts of Hunter Biden."

Nunes followed with a series of questions involving various contacts of Burisma and officials, Ukrainian and American. Neither witness knew anything about his claims. Nunes pressed on, aware that the Republicans had paid dearly for this disinformation going to waste: "Dr. Hill, did you know about—I don't want to go through and ask all those questions over again—" Nunes was floundering.[2441]

"So just to—as far as you know, you did no briefings, no papers, answered no questions as it relates to the 2016 election or Burisma during your time there?"[2442] The answer was again no. Nunes then got it all out in one go:

Dr. Hill, I just want to drill down on this a little bit. The President of the United States, Commander in Chief, was concerned about the 2016 elections and Burisma. He had his personal attorney working these issues because he was under investigation by Robert Mueller, special counsel, partly beginning with an investigation that started with the Steele dossier, that we've already established that the Democrats had paid for and had been fed into the FBI. So at the end of the day, the Commander in Chief, concerned about 2016 election meddling by Ukraine, it sounds like you had just earlier testified that you weren't aware of that, but if that was the concern of the President, to try to get to the bottom of it, and it's the concern of Ambassador Sondland, who was trying to set up meetings on behalf of—to ensure, really, that meetings occurred and phone calls occurred to strengthen the relationship, I'm a little—I mean, I understand the people at the NSC, people at the State Department had issues with that, but at the end of the day, isn't it the Commander in Chief that makes those decisions?[2443]

After a long answer from Hill, Congressman Nunes was done. The entire narrative designed to scupper the Biden candidacy and provide an explanation for Trump's continued behavior towards Russia had been expended on defending the president from impeachment a full year prior to the election of 2020. Paul Manafort and Rudy Giuliani had failed.

The Democrats were having an effect. The announcement of the formal impeachment inquiry changed the game. From that point on, polling averages flipped. After months of a majority of the public not supporting impeachment, polling averages suddenly showed that a plurality now supported impeachment.[2444] From the beginning of the impeachment, a plurality of those polled supported removal of the president.[2445]

Joe Bondy went on the offensive on Twitter. He began to tweet appeals for Parnas to testify in late November under the hashtag #LetLevSpeak.[2446] He also began playing the political leak game like a pro, telling the *Washington Post* of Devin Nunes's direct role in the Giuliani disinformation campaign and revealing contacts between Parnas, Nunes and Nunes's top aide, Derek Harvey.[2447]

On November 14, NABU director Artem Sytnyk announced that Onyshchenko would be extradited to Ukraine, likely in December. When asked about the chance that the fugitive oligarch might flee to Germany where he had properties, Sytnyk said he was depending on the "efficiency of foreign colleagues."[2448] Onyshchenko told the Ukrainian press he was returning home. He texted a photo of a bargain basement plane ticket from Ryanair from Barcelona to Kyiv to prove his bona fides.[2449]

Instead, Onyshchenko did flee to Germany, where he was arrested in Aachen on December 4 at the request of Ukrainian authorities.[2450]

Despite the hammer blows that his disinformation case was taking in Washington, Giuliani went to Europe in early December 2019 to continue his fight for Trump.[2451] He met Lutsenko in Budapest on December 3, then flew to Kyiv to meet with former prosecutors Shokin and Kulyk.[2452] Rudy also squeezed in a meeting with Andriy Derkach.[2453] Giuliani was preparing the alternate explanation for three years of Trump's Ukraine policy on a new series he was hosting on One America News.[2454]

However, time was running out for Trump and Giuliani. On December 16, ahead of an impeachment vote, the House Judiciary Committee published a full report on "The Impeachment of Donald John Trump," as the proceedings were named.[2455]

On December 10, the House Democrats announced their impeachment resolution H.Res.755. It included two charges: Abuse of Power and Obstruction of Congress.[2456] On December 13, the Judiciary Committee voted to pass both articles of impeachment along party lines.

On December 18, 2019, the House took up Resolution 755. Around 8:30 p.m., the measure passed. Democrats Collin Peterson and Jeff Van Drew voted against.[2457] Van Drew promptly became a Republican. Justin Amash, a former Republican who had left the party, voted in favor, while pro-Russian Democratic presidential candidate Tulsi Gabbard of Hawaii voted present on both articles. Maine Democrat Jared Golden voted no on the obstruction count.[2458]

Pelosi and her committee chairs appeared for remarks soon after. Pelosi declined to say when the articles were going to go over to the Senate. She wanted to wait to see what the Senate's rules would be like before she appointed her impeachment managers.[2459] Trump tweeted a picture of himself with the words "In reality they're not after me, they're after you."[2460]

* * *

The drama of Putin's disinformation did not end with the Senate's vote to not remove Donald John Trump from the office of the presidency. Putin has made sure that one final act remains. Even after the senate vote, Giuliani continued harping on the Biden and Burisma allegations, hinting darkly that the part of the story was yet to come.

Trump had spent his first term making any investigative action against him a partisan act, drawing the powerful Republican base to him and neutralizing the possibility that Republicans might vote against him in any impeachment trial. Democrats knew that no allegations could cause the Senate to vote to remove.

Sensing this, the Democrats made a decision not to include any of the charges related to Trump's dealings with Ukraine between 2016 and 2018. That information would be held in reserve if Trump attempted to trot out the false Biden-Burisma allegations first hinted at by Oleksandr Onyshchenko in 2016. House Democrats have ensured that they will be prepared for the final part of the story, if and when the final act comes.

Oleksandr Onyshchenko would always be destined to play the most important role in any attempt to continue to weaponize Joe Biden's service as Vice President—the co-conspirator who would provide inside testimony. As the election of 2020 approaches, these things may yet come to pass.

Violating every rule of scandal politics, Giuliani continued to push the discredited Biden-Burisma allegations even after the Senate voted not to remove the President, largely on partisan lines. Rudy's "Common Sense" podcast continued to feature the claims. Giuliani claimed there would be more to come.

And there was. In the summer of 2020, as this book was going to print, Oleksandr Onyshchenko reappeared, again with "tapes." This time, they featured Joe Biden and a resurgent Petro Poroshenko, who was now the target of a classic corrupt prosecution pushed by President Volodymyr Zelenskyy. Zelenskyy had slowly shifted from reformer to pro-Putin stooge over the first year of his presidency.

These new tapes, advanced by Ukrainian lawmaker Andriy Derkach, showed signs of having been tampered with, and included Biden in a series of unusual nefarious fictious plots, to sabotage the Russians in Crimea and to "take care" of Onyshchenko's testimony to FBI Special Agent Karen Greenaway.[2461] Giuliani gave an interview to OAN claiming that other "far more damaging" tapes of Biden existed.[2462]

The pro-Russian outlet *Sputnik* broke the story in early July that Onyshchenko was behind the Derkach tape releases.[2463] The fugitive lawmaker explained that he had exchanged "hundreds of emails" with Giuliani about the allegations.[2464] Onyshchenko told the *Washington*

Post that he had provided the documents to the GOP-led Homeland Security Committee.[2465]

Onyshchenko explained that the curtain raising on the final act was only a matter of time: "Because of the coronavirus, they are waiting," Onyshchenko told *Sputnik*. "But in September, closer to the elections, they will begin to use them more," he promised.[2466] America waits.

ACKNOWLEDGMENTS

No book is written by one person, and this book is no exception. First, I must start by thanking my incomparable agent and editor, Philip Turner of Philip Turner Book Productions. His guidance, editing, and instincts made this book far better than it could have been. I'd also like to thank my book designers at ettio as well as my incomparable book engineer, Giullaume Bernardeau. I also want to thank Laura Rozen for her suggestions and support through the process of writing this book, as well as connecting me with Philip.

Everything I have ever done has been deeply influenced by my family: My late mother Kathleen, my father Dennis, and my brother Bart.

A big thank you to Casey Michel for a fantastic introduction. Thank you also to Linda Feldmann and Simona Weinglass. A special thank you to Meaghan O'Brien for copy editing the manuscript. A big thank you and a copy of the book for Phil Gaskell.

A special thanks to my close readers, Suanne Buggy and Kathlene Collins.

Thanks and love also to big helpers: Mike Beaver, Patricia Mumby, Ryan Mumby, Cliff Mumby, Maureen Hogan, Laura Armstrong, Lois Barton, Jackie Waldeck, Sarah Waldeck, Dalton Waldeck, my late Aunt Kathy Waldeck, Molly Shultz, Dave Lowenstein, Mary Mason, Bill Boyle, John Mason, Mark Mazzetti, Justin Volz, Murray Waas, Betsy Swann, Josh Kovensky, Dan Freidman, Matthew Kupfer, Sandy Fulton, Mark Ambinder, Nick Schwellenbach, Pete Modaff, Michelle Dorman, Max Linski, Juha Keskinin, Portalus Glam, Paul Kerr, Will Jordan, Steve Swanson, Garrett M. Graff, Brian Coffill, Natasha Bernhard, Scott Ellinger, Scott Steadman, and Tony Pierce.

Special thanks to Sergii Leshchenko for the cover photograph.

ROBERT WALDECK

Washington, D.C., September 2020

ABOUT THE AUTHOR

Robert Waldeck has been a lawyer, a librarian and a historian. He lives in Washington, DC. A graduate of the Catholic University School of Law, he also holds a master's degree in European history. In October and November 2019, he provided critical analysis of the role of Ukrainian politics in the impeachment scandal for articles in two national newspapers.

NOTES

PREFACE: THE SINGULARITY DISAPPEARED

[1] Bowie, David. Interview with Jeremy Paxman."David Bowie Speaks to Jeremy Paxman on BBC Newsnight (1999)." BBC Newsnight, 1999, https://www.youtube.com/watch?v=FiK7s_0tGsg.

[2] Synder, Timothy. *The Road to Unfreedom.* New York, Crown Publishing, 2018, p. 11.

[3] Friedersdorf, Conor. "Without Personal Honor There Is No Leadership." *The Atlantic*, 17 May, 2018, https://www.theatlantic.com/ideas/archive/2018/05/Rex-Tillerson/560612/.

[4] *Id.*

BOOK I

CHAPTER 1 "ALL DECIDED IN THE BACK ROOM"

[5] *Report of the US Senate Select Committee on Intelligence on Active Measures Campaigns and Interference in the 2016 US Election*, vol. 5, 2020, p. 35, https://www.intelligence.senate.gov/sites/default/files/documents/report_volume5.pdf

[6] *Id.* at p. 35.

[7] Quinn-Judge, Paul. "The Orange Revolution." *Time*, 28 Nov. 2004, http://content.time.com/time/magazine/article/0,9171,832225,00.html

[8] *Id.*

[9] Horwitz, Jeff, and Chad Day. "AP Exclusive: Before Trump Job, Manafort Worked to Aid Putin." *Associated Press*, 22 March, 2017, https://apnews.com/122ae0b5848345faa88108a03de40c5a/AP-Exclusive:-Before-Trump-job,-Manafort-worked-to-aid-Putin.

10 Higgins, Andrew, and Kenneth P. Vogel. "Two Capitals, One Russian Oligarch," *New York Times*, 4 Nov. 2018, https://www.nytimes.com/2018/11/04/world/europe/oleg-deripaska-russia-oligarch-sanctions.html.

11 *Report of the US Senate Select Committee on Intelligence on Active Measures Campaigns and Interference in the 2016 US Election*, vol. 5, 2020, p. 33, https://www.intelligence.senate.gov/sites/default/files/documents/report_volume5.pdf.

12 Richie, Martin. "Hongqiao Gets to Top of the World and Sinks Most Since IPO." *Bloomberg News*, 31 Aug. 2015, https://www.bloomberg.com/news/articles/2015-08-31/china-hongqiao-gets-to-top-of-the-world-and-sinks-most-since-ipo.

13 *Report of the US Senate Select Committee on Intelligence on Active Measures Campaigns and Interference in the 2016 US Election*, vol. 5, 2020, p. 33, https://www.intelligence.senate.gov/sites/default/files/documents/report_volume5.pdf.

14 *Id.*

15 "FBI Form 302 of Paul Manafort." *CNN*, 21 Sept. 2018, p. 3, https://www.cnn.com/2020/03/02/politics/read-fbi-mueller-documents/index.html.

16 *Report of the US Senate Select Committee on Intelligence on Active Measures Campaigns and Interference in the 2016 US Election*, vol. 5, 2020, p. 36, https://www.intelligence.senate.gov/sites/default/files/documents/report_volume5.pdf.

17 *Id.*

18 *Id.* at p. 37.

19 *Id.*

20 *Id.* at p. 38.

21 *Id.* at p. 154.

22 *Id.* at 38.

23 *Id.*

24 "FBI Form 302 of Richard Gates." *BuzzFeed* 2 Jul. 2014, p. 3. https://www.documentcloud.org/documents/7072561-Litigation-10th-Release-Leopold.html#document/p1.

25 *Report of the US Senate Select Committee on Intelligence on Active Measures Campaigns and Interference in the 2016 US Election*, vol. 5, 2020, p. 36, https://www.intelligence.senate.gov/sites/default/files/documents/report_volume5.pdf.

26 "Ukraine: Extreme Makeover for the Party of Regions?" *WikiLeaks*, Feb. 3, 2006, https://search.wikileaks.org/plusd/cables/06KIEV473_a.html.

27 Stone, Peter. "Konstantin Kilimnik: Elusive Russian with Ties to Manafort Faces Fresh Mueller Scrutiny." *Guardian*, 8 Nov. 2018, https://www.theguardian.com/us-news/2018/nov/09/konstantin-kilimnik-russia-trump-manafort-mueller.

28 *Report of the US Senate Select Committee on Intelligence on Active Measures Campaigns and Interference in the 2016 US Election*, vol. 5, 2020, p. 41, https://www.intelligence.senate.gov/sites/default/files/documents/report_volume5.pdf.

29 *Id.* at p. 20.

30 Miller, Christopher. "Person A in His Own Words," *Radio Free Europe/Radio Liberty,* 6 Apr. 2018, https://www.rferl.org/a/person-a-in-own-words-on-the-record-shadowy-operative-russia-probe/29150342.html

31 *Report of the US Senate Select Committee on Intelligence on Active Measures Campaigns and Interference in the 2016 US Election,* vol. 5, 2020, p. 49, https://www.intelligence.senate.gov/sites/default/files/documents/report_volume5.pdf.

32 Foer, Franklin. "Paul Manafort—American Hustler." *The Atlantic,* March 2018, https://www.theatlantic.com/magazine/archive/2018/03/paul-manafort-american-hustler/550925/.

33 Sturgis, Sue. "Paul Manafort's Role in the Republicans' Notorious 'Southern Strategy.'" *Facing South,* 3 Nov. 2017, https://www.facingsouth.org/2017/11/paul-manaforts-role-republicans-notorious-southern-strategy.

34 "Paul Manafort Joined the Trump Campaign in a State of 'Despair and Desperation.'" *Fresh Air,* 28 Jan. 2018, https://www.npr.org/2018/01/29/581478324/paul-manafort-joined-the-trump-campaign-in-a-state-of-despair-and-desperation.

35 Miller, "'Person A' in His Own Words."

36 *Id.*

37 Budryk, Zack. "Clip Surfaces of Paul Manafort and Wife on Nickelodeon Game Show." *The Hill,* 5 Sept. 2019, https://thehill.com/blogs/in-the-know/in-the-know/460061-clip-surfaces-of-paul-manafort-and-wife-on-nickelodeon-game.

38 "WWYD 2/2." *YouTube,* uploaded by UnknownNickelodeon, 29 Apr. 2011, https://www.youtube.com/watch?time_continue=173&v=-CsOyAzdURM&feature=emb_logo.

39 Foer, "American Hustler."

40 Swan, Betsy, and Tim Mak, "Top Trump Aide Led the 'Torturer's Lobby.'" *Daily Beast,* 6 Nov. 2017, https://www.thedailybeast.com/top-trump-aide-led-the-torturers-lobby.

41 Vogel, Kenneth P. "Paul Manafort's Wild and Lucrative Philippine Adventure." *Politico,* 10 June 2016, https://www.politico.com/magazine/story/2016/06/2016-donald-trump-paul-manafort-ferinand-marcos-philippines-1980s-213952.

42 Lightman, David. "Trump Criticizes Pequots, Casino." *Hartford Courant,* 6 Oct. 1993, https://www.courant.com/news/connecticut/hc-xpm-1993-10-06-0000003863-story.html.

43 Burns, Alexander, and Maggie Haberman. "Mystery Man: Ukraine's US Fixer." *Politico,* March 5, 2014, https://www.politico.com/story/2014/03/paul-manafort-ukraine-104263.

44 Kuzio, Taras. "Populism in Ukraine." *Problems of Post-Communism,* v. 57, 2010, p. 15, http://commonweb.unifr.ch/artsdean/pub/gestens/f/as/files/4760/25737_184750.pdf.

45 *Report of the US Senate Select Committee on Intelligence on Active Measures Campaigns and Interference in the 2016 US Election,* vol. 5, p. 44, https://www.intelligence.senate.gov/sites/default/files/documents/report_volume5.pdf.

46 *Id.* at p. 45.

47 "FBI Form 302 of Richard Gates III,"*CNN,* Jan. 29, 2018 p. 79–80, https://www.cnn.com/2020/02/03/politics/read-mueller-investigation-documents/index.html

48 "FBI Form 302 of Richard Gates III,"*Buzzfeed,* 2 Jul. 2014 p. 3,

⁴⁹ *Id.*

⁵⁰ *Report of the US Senate Select Committee on Intelligence on Active Measures Campaigns and Interference in the 2016 US Election*, vol. 5, p. 47, https://www.intelligence.senate.gov/sites/default/files/documents/report_volume5.pdf.

⁵¹ Tkach, Mikhail. "'Cashier' of the Party of Regions (Investigation)." *Radio Svboda*, 2 June 2016, https://www.radiosvoboda.org/a/27775258.html

⁵² *Id.*

⁵³ Neef, Christian. "The Underbelly of Ukrainian Gas Dealings." *Spiegel International*, 30 Dec. 2010, https://www.spiegel.de/international/europe/a-stockholm-conspiracy-the-underbelly-of-ukrainian-gas-dealings-a-736745.html.

⁵⁴ *Id.*

⁵⁵ "Ukraine: Firtash Makes His Case to the USG." *WikiLeaks*, 10 Dec. 2008, https://wikileaks.org/plusd/cables/08KYIV2414_a.html.

⁵⁶ *Id.*

⁵⁷ Myers, Steven Lee, and Andrew E. Kramer. "How Paul Manafort Wielded Power in Ukraine before Advising Donald Trump." *New York Times*, 31 July 2016, https://www.nytimes.com/2016/08/01/us/paul-manafort-ukraine-donald-trump.html.

⁵⁸ Neef, "The Underbelly of Ukrainian Gas Dealings."

⁵⁹ *Id.*

⁶⁰ *Id.*

⁶¹ *Id.*

⁶² *Id.*

⁶³ Motyl, Alexander J. "Containing the Con." *Kyiv Post*, 12 May 2010, https://www.kyivpost.com/article/opinion/op-ed/containing-the-on-66453.html.

⁶⁴ *Id.*

⁶⁵ Neef, "The Underbelly of Ukrainian Gas Dealings."

⁶⁶ *Id.*

⁶⁷ "Second Amended Complaint." *Tymoshenko, et al. v. Firtash, et al.* 11-CV-2794, 2011, p. 50, https://freebeacon.com/wp-content/uploads/2016/03/manafort-complaint-2.pdf.

⁶⁸ *Id.* at p. 32.

⁶⁹ Grey, Stephen, Tom Bergin, Sevgil Musaieva, and Roman Anin. "Putin's Allies Channeled Billions to Ukraine Oligarch." *Reuters*, 26 Nov. 2014, https://www.reuters.com/article/russia-capitalism-gas-special-report-pix/special-report-putins-allies-channelled-billions-to-ukraine-oligarch-idUSL3N0TF4QD20141126.

⁷⁰ *Id.*

⁷¹ *Id.*

⁷² *Id.*

73 *Id.*

74 "Factbox: Burisma, the Obscure Ukrainian Gas Company at the Heart of US Political Row." *Reuters*, 24 Sept. 2019, https://www.reuters.com/article/us-usa-trump-whistleblower-burisma-factb/factbox-burisma-the-obscure-ukrainian-gas-company-at-the-heart-of-us-political-row-idUSKBN1W91UG.

75 Kent, George. Interviewed by Permanent Select Committee on Intelligence, et al. *US House of Representatives Document Repository*, 2019, p. 80-84, https://docs.house.gov/meetings/IG/IG00/CPRT-116-IG00-D009.pdf

76 "Second Amended Complaint." *Tymoshenko, et al. v. Firtash, et al.* p. 24, 54.

77 James Greene, "Russian Responses to NATO and EU Enlargement and Outreach." *Chatham House: The Means and Ends of Russian Power Series*, 2012, https://www.chathamhouse.org/sites/default/files/public/Research/Russia%20and%20Eurasia/0612bp_greene.pdf.

78 "Class Action Complaint." *Tymshenko, et al. v. Firtash, et al.*, 11-CV-2794, 2011, https://www.courtlistener.com/recap/gov.uscourts.nysd.378317.1.0.pdf.

79 *Id.* at *passim.*

80 *Id.* at p. 14.

81 *Id.*

82 *Id.*

83 *Id.* at pp. 33-4.

84 *Id.*

85 Clarke, Katherine, and Will Parker. "Meet Paul Manafort's Real Estate Fixer." *The Real Deal*, 31 Aug. 2017, https://therealdeal.com/2017/08/31/meet-paul-manaforts-real-estate-fixer/.

86 "40 Under 40: Brad Zackson." *Crains New York Business*, 1995, https://www.crainsnewyork.com/awards/brad-zackson

87 *Id.*

88 "Second Amended Complaint," p.43.

89 *Id.* at pp. 43-4.

90 Clarke and Parker, "Meet Paul Manafort's Real Estate Fixer."

91 Second Amended Complaint, *Tymoshenko, et al. v. Firtash, et al.* 11-CV-2794, p. 34.

92 Berthelsen, Christian, and Greg Farrell, "With Bank Subpoenas, Mueller Turns Up the Heat on Manafort." *Bloomerg News*, 10 Aug. 2017, https://www.bloomberg.com/news/articles/2017-08-10/with-bank-subpoenas-mueller-is-said-to-turn-up-heat-on-manafort.

93 Manafort's campaign to align Ukraine's pro-Russian government with the Republican party mirrored Putin's to infiltrate the Republican party, via the National Rifle Association and others.

94 *Report of the US Senate Select Committee on Intelligence on Active Measures Campaigns and Interference in the 2016 US Election*, vol. 5, p. 45, https://freebeacon.com/wp-content/uploads/2016/03/manafort-complaint-2.pdf.

95 *Id.*

96 Harding, Luke. "Former Trump Aide approved 'Black Ops' to help Ukraine President." *Guardian*, 5 Apr. 2018, https://www.theguardian.com/us-news/2018/apr/05/ex-trump-aide-paul-manafort-approved-black-ops-to-help-ukraine-president.

97 Windelspecht, Devin. "Ukraine: Larry King Paid through 'Black Ledger.'" *OCCRP*, 22 Aug. 22, 2016). https://www.occrp.org/en/daily/5574-ukraine-larry-king-paid-through-black-ledger

98 Leshchenko, Sergii, and Anton Marchu. "Manuscripts Do Not Burn. Paul Manafort in Shadow Accounting of the
Party of Yanukovych." *Ukrayinska Pravda*, 19 Aug. 2019, https://www.pravda.com.ua/cdn/graphics/2016/08/manafort/.

99 Walters, Greg. "The Hapsburg Group: Paul Manafort's Shadowy European Network, Explained." *Vice News*, 15 June 2018, https://www.vice.com/en_us/article/kzkykm/the-hapsburg-group-paul-maforts-shadowy-european-network-explained.

100 Stack, Graham. "Exposed: The Ukrainian Poltician who funded Paul Manafort's Secret EU Lobbying Campaign." *OCCRP*, 4 Nov. 2019, https://www.occrp.org/en/investigations/exposed-the-ukrainian-politician-who-funded-paul-maforts-secret-eu-lobbying-campaign.

101 Vogel, Kenneth P., and Matthew Goldstein. "Law Firm to Pay $4.6 Million in Case Tied to Manafort and Ukraine." *New York Times*, 17 Jan. 2019, https://www.nytimes.com/2019/01/17/us/politics/skadden-arps-ukraine-lobbying-settlement.html.

102 "FBI Form 302 of [Redacted]." *Buzzfeed*, 19 Feb. 2018, p. 2, https://buzzfeed.egnyte.com/dl/jMwIzvDHrt/.

103 *Id.* at 5.

104 *Id.*

105 "FBI Form 302 of Greg Craig." *Politico*, 20 Oct. 2017, pp.2-3, https://www.politico.com/f/?id=0000016b-8be3-df00-a9fb-afe301890000.

106 *Id.* at pp. 13-14.

107 Yourgrau, Barry. "The Literary Intrigues of Putin's Puppet Master." *New York Review of Books*, 22 Jan. 2018, https://www.nybooks.com/daily/2018/01/22/the-literary-intrigues-of-putins-puppet-master/.

108 *Id.*

109 Sakwa, Richard. "Surkov: Dark Prince of the Kremlin." *Open Democracy*, 7 Apr. 2011, https://www.opendemocracy.net/en/odr/surkov-dark-prince-of-kremlin/.

110 Storey, Peter. "Vladislav Surkov: the (Gray) Cardinal of the Kremlin." *Cicero Magazine* (June 17, 2015). http://ciceromagazine.com/features/the-gray-cardinal-of-the-kremlin/

111 Pomerantsev, Peter. "The Hidden Author of Putinism." *The Atlantic*, 7 Nov. 2014, https://www.theatlantic.com/international/archive/2014/11/hidden-author-putinism-russia-vladislav-surkov/382489/.

112 *Id.*

113 *Id.*

114 *Id.*

115 *Id.*

116 Yourgrau, "The Literary Intrigues of Putin's Puppet Master."

117 Leshchenko and Marchuk, "Manuscripts Do Not Burn. Paul Manafort in Shadow Accounting of the
Party of Yanukovych."

118 Lipman, Masha. "Putin's Sovereign Democracy." *Washington Post*, 15 July 2006, https://www.washingtonpost.com/wp-dyn/content/article/2006/07/14/AR2006071401534.html.

119 Conley, Heather A. "Russian Malign Influence in Montenegro: The Weaponization and Exploitation of History, Religion, and Economics." *CSIS Briefs*, 14 May 2019, https://www.csis.org/analysis/russian-malign-influence-montenegro.

120 Arkhipov, Ilya. "Putin Approval Rating Falls to Lowest since 2000: Poll." *Bloomberg News*, https://www.bloomberg.com/news/articles/2013-01-24/putin-approval-rating-falls-to-lowest-since-2000-poll.

121 Chen, Adrian. "The Agency." *New York Times Magazine*, 2 June 2015, https://www.nytimes.com/2015/06/07/magazine/the-agency.html.

122 Soshnikov, Andrey. "The Capital of Political Trolling." *MR7*, 11 March 2015, https://mr-7.ru/articles/112478/.

123 Chen, "The Agency."

124 Mackey, Robert. "Reporters Should Stop Helping Donald Trump Spread Lies about Joe Biden and Ukraine." *The Intercept*, 22 Sept. 2019, https://theintercept.com/2019/09/22/reporters-stop-helping-donald-trump-spread-lies-joe-biden-ukraine/.

125 "The Russian Laundromat." *OCCRP*, 22 Aug. 2014, https://www.reportingproject.net/therussianlaundromat/russian-laundromat.php.

126 Mackey, Robert. "Is a Ukrainian Oligarch Helping Trump Smear Biden to Evade US Corruption Charges?" *The Intercept*, 17 Oct. 2019, https://theintercept.com/2019/10/17/ukrainian-oligarch-helping-trump-smear-biden-evade-u-s-corruption-charges/.

127 *Id.*

128 Bogdanich, Walt, and Michael Forsythe, "Exhibit A," *New York Times*, 18 Dec. 2018, https://www.nytimes.com/2018/12/30/world/mckinsey-bribes-boeing-firtash-extradition.html.

129 *Id.*

130 *Id.*

131 Gorchinskaya, Alexandra. "FBI Special Agent: I Don't Want People in Ukraine to Die for Money." *Novoye Vremya* 26 Dec. 2016, https://nv.ua/publications/spetsagent-fbr-ssha-ne-hochetsja-chtoby-ljudi-v-ukraine-umirali-za-dengi-364590.html.

132 "Schedule." *18th International Anti-Corruption Conference*, 22 Oct. 2018, https://18iacc.sched.com/speaker/karen_greenaway.1yoe5edj.

133 Daria Kaleniuk "Post." *Facebook*, 21 Feb. 2017, https://www.facebook.com/photo.php?fbid=10154983810254188&set=pb.709744187.-2207520000.1553617631.&type=3&theater.

134 Bogdanich and Forsythe, "Exhibit A."

135 *Id.*

136 "Government to Direct Most of International Monetary Fund's Loan to Currency Reserves." *Kyiv Post*, 10 May 2010, https://www.kyivpost.com/article/content/ukraine-politics/government-to-direct-most-of-international-monetar-66502.html.

137 "European Lawmakers: Association Agreement Should Not Be Signed with Opposition in Jail." *Kyiv Post*, 2 March 2012, https://www.kyivpost.com/article/content/ukraine-politics/european-lawmakers-association-agreement-should-no-123465.html.

138 Baker, Stephanie, and Daryna Krasnolutska. "Manafort Charges Renew Questions About Skadden's Work in Ukraine." *Bloomberg News*, 10 Nov. 2017, https://www.bloomberg.com/news/articles/2017-11-10/manafort-charges-renew-questions-about-skadden-s-work-in-ukraine.

139 Rettman, Andrew. "EU-Ukraine Summit 'Unlikely' This Year." *EU Observer*, 5 Nov. 2012, https://euobserver.com/foreign/118094.

140 "FBI Form 302 of Paul Manafort," *Buzzfeed*, 2 Sep. 2014 p. 4,

141 "EU to Ukraine: Reforms Necessary for Trade Pact." *Kyiv Post*, 25 Feb. 2013, https://www.kyivpost.com/article/content/eu-ukraine-relations/eu-to-ukraine-reforms-necessary-for-trade-pact-320910.html.

142 "Ukraine Suspends Preparations for EU Trade Agreement." *BBC News*, 21 Nov. 2013, https://www.bbc.com/news/world-europe-25032275.

143 "Huge Ukraine Rally over EU Agreement Delay." *BBC News*, 24 Nov. 2013, https://www.bbc.com/news/world-europe-25078952.

144 Miller, "'Person A' in His Own Words: On the Record with Shadowy Operative In Russia Probe."

145 "Ukraine Crisis: Timeline," *BBC News*, 13 Nov. 2014, https://www.bbc.com/news/world-middle-east-26248275.

146 Carpenter, Ted Galen. "America's Ukraine Hypocrisy." *Cato Institute*, 6 Aug. 2017, https://www.cato.org/publications/commentary/americas-ukraine-hypocrisy.

147 Butenko, Victoria, and Marie-Louise Gumuchian. "Lenin Statue Toppled in Ukraine Protest." *CNN*, 8 Dec. 2013, https://www.cnn.com/2013/12/08/world/europe/ukraine-protests/.

148 "EuroMaidan rallies in Ukraine—Dec.9" *Kyiv Post*, 10 Dec. 2013, https://www.kyivpost.com/article/content/euromaidan/euromaidan-rallies-in-ukraine-live-updates-332341.html.

149 Kauffmann, Sylvie. "Ukraine's Activists Are Taking No Chances." *New York Times*, 25 Apr. 2014, https://www.nytimes.com/2014/04/26/opinion/kauffmann-ukraines-activists-are-taking-no-chances.html?searchResultPosition=51.

150 *Id.*

151 *AntAC*, 2012–2020, https://antac.org.ua/en/.

152 Topol, Sarah A. "The Chocolate King Who Would Be President." *Politico*, 22 May 2014, https://www.politico.com/magazine/story/2014/05/the-chocolate-king-who-would-be-president-106998.

153 *Id.*

154 *Id.*

155 *Id.*

156 "Ukraine Crisis: Timeline."

157 *Id.*

158 "You Will Still Learn What Yanukovych Is!" *Argumentum*, 31 Jan. 2014, https://web.archive.org/web/20150512124627/http://argumentua.com/novosti/vy-eshche-uznaete-chto-takoe-yanukovich-zhirinovskii-zayavil-chto-posle-putinskoi-olimpiady-.

159 "War on the Streets of Kiev." *Ukrayinska Pravda*, 14 Feb. 2014, https://www.pravda.com.ua/articles/2014/02/18/7014151/.

160 "Yanukovych, Fugitive Ex-President Wanted for Mass Murder, Remains Missing (UPDATE)." *Kyiv Post*, 25 Feb. 2014, https://www.kyivpost.com/article/content/ukraine-politics/arrest-warrant-issued-for-yanukovych-and-other-former-officials-337482.html.

161 "Andrea Manafort Text Archives." p. 3976, https://ia903108.us.archive.org/5/items/ManafortTextMessages/Manafort%20text%20transcript.pdf.

162 *Id.*

163 "Yanukovych, Fugitive Ex-President Wanted for Mass Murder, Remains Missing (UPDATE)." *Kyiv Post*, 25 Feb. 2014, https://www.kyivpost.com/article/content/ukraine-politics/arrest-warrant-issued-for-yanukovych-and-other-former-officials-337482.html.

164 Sukhov, Oleg. "Prosecutor Says Interior Ministry Blocking EuroMaidan Cases." *Kyiv Post*, 3 Oct. 2017, https://www.kyivpost.com/ukraine-politics/prosecutor-says-interior-ministry-blocking-euromaidan-cases.html.

165 "Investigators: Hryniak and Other High-Ranking Interior Ministry Officials Led Berkut's Actions during the Assault on Maidan on February 18." *Texty*, 2 Oct. 2017, https://texty.org.ua/fragments/79981/Slidchi_Grynak_ta_inshi_vysoki_chyny_MVS-79981/.

166 *Id.*

167 "Readout of Vice President Biden's Call with Ukrainian President Viktor Yanukovych." *Office of the Vice President*, 18 Feb. 2014, https://obamawhitehouse.archives.gov/the-press-office/2014/02/18/readout-vice-president-bidens-call-ukrainian-president-viktor-yanukovych.

168 Biden, Joe. *Promise Me, Dad*. New York, Flatiron Books, 2017, p. 98.

169 "Investigators: Hryniak and Other High-Ranking Interior Ministry Officials Led Berkut's Actions during the Assault on Maidan on February 18."

170 Grytsenko, Oksana, and Oleg Sukhov, "Investigators deny stalling on Paul Manafort Cases," *Kyiv Post*, 8 Nov. 2019, https://www.kyivpost.com/ukraine-politics/investigators-deny-stalling-on-paul-manafort-cases.html.

171 Leshchenko, Sergii. "The True Story of Yanukovych's Black Ledger." *Kyiv Post* 24 Nov. 2019, https://www.kyivpost.com/article/opinion/op-ed/sergii-leshchenko-the-true-story-of-yanukovychs-black-ledger.html.

172 "Prize Catch for Ukrainians at Boat Harbor: A Soggy Trove of Government Secrets." *New York Times*, 26 Feb. 2014, https://www.nytimes.com/2014/02/27/world/europe/a-prize-catch-for-ukrainians-at-a-boat-harbor-an-ousted-presidents-secrets.html.

173 "YanukovychLeaks." OCCRP, https://yanukovychleaks.org/.

174 "Ukraine Crisis: Timeline."

175 *Id.*

176 Dan Peleschuk, "We Bow Our Heads in Memory of the Dead." *Public Radio International*, 22 Feb. 22, 2014). https://www.pri.org/stories/2014-02-22/ukraine-s-yanukovych-flees-capital-kyiv-opposition-hands

177 *Id.*

178 Losiev, Ihor. "The Chronicles of Alienation." *Ukrainian Week*, 16 March 2015, https://ukrainianweek.com/Politics/132098.

179 *Id.*

180 "Putin Describes Secret Operation to Seize Crimea." *Yahoo News*, 8 March 2015, https://news.yahoo.com/putin-describes-secret-operation-seize-crimea-212858356.html.

181 Weiss, Michael. "Putin Stages a Coup in Crimea." *Daily Beast*, 1 March 2014, https://www.thedailybeast.com/russia-stages-a-coup-in-crimea.

182 "Putin describes Secret Operation to seize Crimea."

183 Shrek, Carl. "From 'Not Us' To 'Why Hide It?': How Russia Denied Its Crimea Invasion, then Admitted It." *RFE/RL*, 26 Feb. 2019, https://www.rferl.org/a/from-not-us-to-why-hide-it-how-russia-denied-its-crimea-invasion-then-admitted-it/29791806.html.

184 Charbonneau, Louis. "Russia: Yanukovich Asked Putin to uUe Force to Save Ukraine." *Reuters*, 3 March 2014, https://www.reuters.com/article/us-ukraine-crisis-un/russia-yanukovich-asked-putin-to-use-force-to-save-ukraine-idUSBREA2224720140304.

185 *Id.*

186 Losiev, "The Chronicles of Alienation."

187 *Id.*

188 "Ukraine Crisis: Crimea Parliament Asks to Join Russia." *BBC News*, 6 March 2014, https://www.bbc.com/news/world-europe-26465962.

189 Losiev, "The Chronicles of Alienation."

190 "Ukraine 'Preparing Withdrawal of Troops from Crimea.'" *BBC News*, 19, March 2014, https://www.bbc.com/news/world-europe-26656617.

191 Ernst, Douglas. "Merkel on Putin: He Acts the Way He Does to 'Prove He's a Man.'" *Washington Times*, 9 Dec. 2014, https://www.washingtontimes.com/news/2014/dec/9/angela-merkel-vladimir-putin-he-acts-way-he-does-p/.

192 Coynash, Halya. "Glazyev Tapes Debunk Russia's Lies about Its Annexation of Crimea and Undeclared War against Ukraine." *Kharkiv Human Rights Group*, 26 Feb. 2019). http://khpg.org/en/index.php?id=1551054011

193 Chen, "The Agency."

194 *Id.*

195 "Ukraine Crisis: EU signs Association Deal." *BBC News*, 21 March 2014, https://www.bbc.com/news/world-europe-26680250.

196 *Id.*

197 *Id.*

198 "Ukraine: Pro-Russians Storm Offices in Donetsk, Luhansk, Kharkiv." *BBC News*, 7 April 2014, https://www.bbc.com/news/world-europe-26910210.

199 Roth, Andrew, and Sabrina Tavernise. "Russians Revealed among Ukraine Fighters." *New York Times*, 27 May 2014, https://www.nytimes.com/2014/05/28/world/europe/ukraine.html?_r=0.

200 "Ukraine Elections: Runners and Risks." *BBC News*, 25 May 2014, https://www.bbc.com/news/world-europe-27518989.

201 "The Chocolate King Rises." *Der Spiegel*, 22 May 2014, https://www.spiegel.de/international/europe/profile-of-petro-poroshenko-in-the-run-up-to-the-ukraine-elections-a-970325.html.

202 *Id.*

203 Weymouth, Lally. "Interview with Ukrainian Presidential Candidate Petro Poroshenko." *Washington Post*, 25 April 2014, https://www.washingtonpost.com/opinions/interview-with-ukrainian-presidential-candidate-petro-poroshenko/2014/04/25/74c73a48-cbbd-11e3-93eb-6c0037dde2ad_story.html.

204 Banks, Martin. "Klitschko Loses on Points." *EU Political Report*, https://www.eupoliticalreport.eu/klitschko-loses-on-points/.

205 *Id.*

206 Shields, Michael, and Angelika Gruber. "Ukrainian Gas Oligarch Firtash Arrested in Vienna on FBI Warrant." *Reuters*, 13 March 2018, https://www.reuters.com/article/us-ukraine-austria-firtash/ukrainian-gas-oligarch-firtash-arrested-in-vienna-on-fbi-warrant-idUSBREA2C14V20140313.

207 Stack, Graham. "Everything You Know about Paul Manafort is Wrong" *Kyiv Post*, 17 Sept. 2018, https://www.kyivpost.com/article/opinion/op-ed/graham-stack-everything-you-know-about-paul-manafort-is-wrong.html.

208 Walker, Shaun and Dan Roberts. "Ukraine Oligarch claims US Extradition Request is Political Interference." *Guardian*, 5 May 2015, https://www.theguardian.com/world/2015/may/05/ukraine-oligarch-brokered-deal-petro-poroshenko-president-dmytro-firtash.

209 Christopher Miller, "Poroshenko confirms 2014 Meeting with Manafort Team" *RFE/RL* (Aug. 8, 2018). Accessed at: https://www.rferl.org/a/poroshenko-administration-backtracks-confirms-2014-meeting-with-manafort-team/29420157.html

210 *Id.*

211 *Id.*

212 *Id.*

213 "FBI Form 302 of Paul Manafort, Jr." *Buzzfeed* 2 Jul. 2014 p. 6. https://www.documentcloud.org/documents/7072561-Litigation-10th-Release-Leopold.html#document/p1.

214 Weymouth, "Interview with Ukrainian Presidential Candidate Petro Poroshenko."

215 "2014 Presidential Election Results: CEC processed 51.99%." *Telegraf*, 26 May 2014, https://telegraf.com.ua/ukraina/politika/1300294-rezultatyi-vyiborov-prezidenta-ukrainyi-2014-tsik-obrabotala-51-99.html.

216 Topol, "The Chocolate King Who Would Be President."

217 *Report of the US Senate Select Committee on Intelligence on Active Measures Campaigns and Interference in the 2016 US Election*, vol. 5, p. 49, n. 213 [What does this stand for?] Note 213 on page 49. There are extensive factual notes.

218 Myers and Kramer, "How Paul Manafort Wielded Power in Ukraine before Advising Donald Trump."

219 *Id.*

220 *Id.*

221 Kuzio, Taras. "Taras Kuzio: US Law Firms, Political Consultants Helped Yanukovych and Allies Impose Censorship." *Kyiv Post*, 14 March 2018, https://www.kyivpost.com/article/opinion/op-ed/taras-kuzio-us-law-firms-political-consultants-helped-yanukovych-allies-impose-censorship.html.

222 "Ukrainian Businessman Dmitry Firtash arrested in Vienna." *BBC News*, 13 March 2014, https://www.bbc.com/russian/international/2014/03/140313_austria_firtash_arrest.shtml.

223 Modderkolk, Huib. "Dutch Agencies Provide Crucial Intel about Russia's Interference in US-Elections." *De Volkskrant*, 25 Jan. 2018, https://www.volkskrant.nl/wetenschap/dutch-agencies-provide-crucial-intel-about-russia-s-interference-in-us-elections~b4f8111b/?referer=https%3A%2F%2Fwww.google.com%2F.

224 Stone, Jeff. "Cozy Bear Kept Moving after 2016 Election, ESET Says." *Cyberscoop*, 17 Oct. 2019, https://www.cyberscoop.com/cozy-bear-return-espionage-russian-hacking/.

225 Modderkolk, "Dutch Agencies Provide Crucial Intel about Russia's Interference in US-Elections."

226 *Id.*

227 *Id.*

228 *Id.*

229 *Id.*

230 *Id.*

231 *Id.*

232 Roza, Matthew. "Who Are the 12 Russians Indicted by Robert Mueller?" *Salon*, 21 July 2018, https://www.salon.com/2018/07/21/a-look-at-the-12-russians-indicted-by-the-us-government/.

233 *Id.*

234 Faulconbridge, Guy. "What Is Russia's GRU Military Intelligence Agency?" *Reuters*, 5 Oct. 2018, https://www.reuters.com/article/us-britain-russia-gru-factbox/what-is-russias-gru-military-intelligence-agency-idUSKCN1MF1VK.

235 Poulsen, Kevin. "Mueller Finally Solves Mysteries about Russia's 'Fancy Bear' Hackers." *Daily Beast*, 20 July 2018, https://www.thedailybeast.com/mueller-finally-solves-mysteries-about-russias-fancy-bear-hackers.

236 *Id.*

237 *Id.*

238 Elder, Miriam. "Polishing Putin: Hacked Emails Suggest Dirty Tricks by Russian Youth Group." *Guardian*, Feb. 7, 2012, https://www.theguardian.com/world/2012/feb/07/putin-hacked-emails-russian-nashi.

239 Turovsky, Daniil. "Meet Anonymous International, the Hackers Taking on the Kremlin." *Guardian*, 7 April 2015, https://www.theguardian.com/world/2015/apr/07/anonymous-international-hackers-kremlin.

240 Shreck, Carl. "Germany Convicts Notorious Russian Hacker in Navalny Email Breach." *Radio Free Europe/Radio Liberty*, 15 Aug. 2015, https://www.rferl.org/a/hacker-hell-navalny-russia-germany-conviction/27172743.html.

241 "Russian Hackers Hunted Journalists in Years-Long Campaign." *Honolulu Star-Advertiser*, 11 Dec. 2017, https://www.staradvertiser.com/2017/12/22/breaking-news/russian-hackers-hunted-journalists-in-years-long-campaign/.

242 Modderkolk, "Dutch Agencies Provide Crucial Intel about Russia's Interference in US-Elections."

243 *Report of the US Senate Select Committee on Intelligence on Active Measures Campaigns and Interference in the 2016 US Election, v. 5, p.* 823.

244 *Id.* at 823-4, n. 5422.

245 *Id.* at 823-4.

246 Schwirtz, Michael. "Top Secret Russian Unit Seeks to Destabilize Europe, Security Officials Say." *New York Times*, 8 Oct. 2019, https://www.nytimes.com/2019/10/08/world/europe/unit-29155-russia-gru.html?smid=nytcore-ios-share.

247 "Skripal Poisoner Attended GRU Commander Family Wedding." *Bellingcat*, 14 Oct. 2019, https://www.bellingcat.com/news/uk-and-europe/2019/10/14/averyanov-chepiga/.

248 Schwirtz, "Top Secret Russian Unit Seeks to Destabilize Europe, Security Officials Say."

249 *Id.*

250 *Id.*

251 *Id.*

252 *Id.*

253 In June 2020, news reports were published alleging that Unit 29155 was paying bounties to the Taliban for killing US personnel in Afghanistan.

CHAPTER 2 "REVENGE RULES THE SOUL OF THE FOOL"

[254] "Decree No. 1507/99 of Ukrainian President Leonid Kuchma." *Verkovna Rada of Ukraine*, 29 Nov. 1999, https://zakon.*Rada*.gov.ua/laws/show/1507/99.

[255] Sonne, Paul. "Poroshenko Declares Victory in Ukraine Presidential Election." *Wall Street Journal*, 25 5May 25, 2014). https://www.wsj.com/articles/ukraine-seeks-to-regain-stability-as-voters-head-to-the-polls-1401007757?tesla=y

[256] Oleksiyenko, Oles. "A Heavy Mace for Mr. Poroshenko." *Ukrainian Week*, 30 June 2014, https://ukrainianweek.com/Politics/115440

[257] "Ukraine Crisis: Details of Poroshenko's Peace Plan Emerge." *BBC*, 20 June 2014, https://www.bbc.com/news/world-europe-27937596.

[258] *Id.*

[259] "EU Throws Its Weight behind Ukraine Peace Plan." *Euractiv*, 24 June 2014, https://www.euractiv.com/section/europe-s-east/news/eu-throws-its-weight-behind-ukraine-peace-plan/.

[260] "Origin of the Separatists' Buk: A Bellingcat Investigation." *Bellingcat*, 8 Nov. 2014, https://www.bellingcat.com/news/uk-and-europe/2014/11/08/origin-of-the-separatists-buk-a-bellingcat-investigation/.

[261] *Id.*

[262] Fitzpatrick, Catherine A. "Evidence of Separatists' Possession of the Buk System before Downing of MH 17." *The Interpreter*, 27 July 2014, http://www.interpretermag.com/evidence-of-separatists-possession-of-buk-system-before-downing-of-mh17/.

[263] Harding, Luke, and Shaun Walker. "Flight MH17 Downed by Russian-Built Missile, Dutch Investigators Say." *Guardian*, 13 Oct. 2015, https://www.theguardian.com/world/2015/oct/13/mh17-crash-report-plane-partially-reconstruced-blames-buk-missile-strike.

[264] Crosby, Alan. "Siren Call: The 'Distinctly High Voice' That Led MH17 Sleuths to a Russian Missile Suspect." *RFE/RL*, 25 May 2018, https://www.rferl.org/a/mh17-icannikov-suspect-bellingcat-distinctive-voice/29251023.html.

[265] Kramer, Andrew E., and Michael R. Gordon. "Ukraine Reports Russian Invasion on a New Front." *New York Times*, 27 Aug. 2014, https://www.nytimes.com/2014/08/28/world/europe/ukraine-russia-novoazovsk-crimea.html.

[266] *Id.*

[267] "EU, Ukraine to Sign Remaining Part of Association Agreement on June 27 – European Council." *Interfax-Ukraine*, 16 June 2014, https://en.interfax.com.ua/news/economic/209475.html.

[268] *Id.*

269 "Ukraine: Transactions with the Fund from May 01, 1984 to January 30, 2020." *International Monetary Fund*, https://www.imf.org/external/np/fin/tad/extrans1.aspx?memberKey1=993&endDate=2099%2D12%2D31&finposition_flag=YES.

270 "Press Release: IMF Executive Board approves US$15.15 Billion Stand-By Arrangement for Ukraine." *International Monetary Fund*, 28 July 2010, https://www.imf.org/en/News/Articles/2015/09/14/01/49/pr10305#P18_377.

271 "Ukraine Agrees to 50% Gas Price Hike Amid IMF Talks." *BBC News*, 26 March 2014, https://www.bbc.com/news/business-26758788.

272 *Id.*

273 Labott, Elise, and Tom Cohen. "US Strategy for Ukraine Crisis: Money Talks." *CNN*, 4 March 2014, https://www.cnn.com/2014/03/04/politics/ukraine-us-aid/index.html?iid=EL.

274 "Extended Fund Facility." *Ministry of Finance of Ukraine*, https://mof.gov.ua/en/mehanizm-rozshirenogo-finansuvannja.

275 "Medvedchuk Will Represent Ukraine in a Subgroup on Humanitarian Issues of the Tripartite Working Group." *Ukraine News*, 6 May 2015, https://ukranews.com/ua/news/329119-medvedchuk-predstavyt-ukrainu-v-pidgrupi-z-gumanitarnykh-pytan-trystoronnoi-robochoi-grupy.

276 "World: Europe Profile: Leonid Kuchma." *BBC*, 29 Oct. 1999, http://news.bbc.co.uk/2/hi/europe/486472.stm.

277 "#1605 Victor Pinchuk." *Forbes*, https://www.forbes.com/profile/victor-pinchuk/#328466a67935.

278 Marone, John. "Monopolies Thrive as Toothless State Bows to Moguls." *Kyiv Post*, 19 March 2010, https://www.kyivpost.com/article/content/business/monopolies-thrive-as-toothless-state-bows-to-mogul-62087.html.

279 Bar-Hillel, Mira. "£80m: Most Expensive House Sold in London." *Evening Standard*, 29 Feb. 2008, https://www.standard.co.uk/news/80m-most-expensive-house-sold-in-london-6660355.html

280 Tkach, Michael. "To Minsk for Negotiations: Who Pays for the Charter?" *Radio Svoboda*, 26 Jan. 2017, https://translate.google.com/translate?depth=1&hl=en&prev=search&rurl=translate.google.com&sl=uk&sp=nmt4&u=https://hromadske.ua/posts/ukrainski-delehaty-litaiut-na-minski-perehovory-na-pryvatnomu-litaku-pinchuka-skhemy.

281 *Id.*

282 *Id.*

283 De Galbert, Simond. "The Impact of the Normandy Format on the Conflict in Ukraine: Four Leaders, Three Cease-Fires, and Two Summits." *Center for Strategic and International Studies*, 23 Oct. 2015, https://www.csis.org/analysis/impact-normandy-format-conflict-ukraine-four-leaders-three-cease-fires-and-two-summits.

284 "Ukraine Crisis: Nato Top General Says Truce 'In Name Only.'" *BBC News*, 21 Sept. 2014, https://www.bbc.com/news/world-europe-29299092.

285 *Id.*

286 Beck, J. L., and Michael Johns. *Return of the Cold War: Ukraine, the West and Russia*, p. 235-6. London, Routledge (2014).

287 Goncharova, Olena. "Ukrainians Skeptical about Law Granting Special Status to Donbas Region." *Kyiv Post*, 24 Sept. 2014, https://www.kyivpost.com/article/content/war-against-ukraine/ukrainians-skeptical-about-law-granting-special-status-to-donbas-region-365853.html.

288 *Id.*

289 Herszenhorn, David M. "Judge Rebuffs US in Rejecting Extradition of Ukraine Billionaire." *New York Times*, 30 April 30, 2015, https://www.nytimes.com/2015/05/01/world/europe/dmitry-v-firtash-extradition.html.

290 "Firtash Takes Credit for Poroshenko's Election as President, Klitschko as Kyiv Mayor." *Kyiv Post*, 30 April 2015, https://www.kyivpost.com/article/content/oct-26-parliamentary-election/firtash-takes-credit-for-poroshenkos-election-as-president-klitschko-as-kyiv-mayor-387540.html.

291 Herszenhorn, "Judge Rebuffs US in Rejecting Extradition of Ukraine Billionaire."

292 "About YES." *Yalta European Strategy*, https://yes-ukraine.org/en/about.

293 Schmidt, Michael S., and Maggie Haberman. "Mueller Investigating Ukrainian's $150,000 Payment for a Trump Appearance." *New York Times* 9 Apr. 2018, https://www.nytimes.com/2018/04/09/us/politics/trump-mueller-ukraine-victor-pinchuk.html.

294 *Id.*

295 Amari, Sohrab. "An SOS From Battleground Ukraine." *Wall Street Journal*, 29 July 2015, https://www.wsj.com/articles/message-from-battlefield-ukraine-1438106297.

296 "Javelin." *MilitaryToday.com*, http://www.military-today.com/missiles/javelin.htm.

297 "Ukraine: Parliament Passes Important Laws to Tackle Corruption." *Kyiv Post*, 23 Oct. 2014, https://www.kyivpost.com/article/content/business-wire/ukraine-parliament-passes-important-laws-to-tackle-corruption-369122.html.

298 Marson, James, and Brett Forrest. "Ukrainian Corruption Showdown Sets Stage for Impeachment Inquiry." *Wall Street Journal*, 12 Nov. 2019, https://www.wsj.com/articles/ukrainian-corruption-showdown-sets-stage-for-impeachment-inquiry-11573605386.

299 Ceta, Blerta "Electronic Asset Declarations for Public Officials—Two Years after Its Launch. A Panacea against Corruption?" *United Nations Development Program*, 25 Aug. 2018, https://www.ua.undp.org/content/ukraine/en/home/blog/2018/the-expectations-and-reality-of-e-declarations.html.

300 "Foreign Aid Explorer," *USAID*, https://explorer.usaid.gov/.

301 Gorchinskaya, Alexandra. "Special Agent of the Federal Bureau of Investigation Karen Greenaway Talks about the High-Profile Details of the Yanukovych Case." *Novoye Vremya*, 26 Dec. 2016, https://nv.ua/publications/spetsagent-fbr-ssha-ne-hochetsja-chtoby-ljudi-v-ukraine-umirali-za-dengi-364590.html.

302 *Id.*

303 Kent, George, pp. 81–82.

304 Ivanova, Polina, Maria Tsvetkova, Ilya Zhegulev, and Luke Baker. "What Hunter Biden Did on the Board of Ukrainian Energy Company Burisma." *Reuters* 18 Oct. 2019, https://www.reuters.com/article/us-hunter-biden-ukraine/what-hunter-biden-did-on-the-board-of-ukrainian-energy-company-burisma-idUSKBN1WX1P7.

305 *Id.*

306 Walker, Shaun, and Oksana Grytsenko. "Ukraine Forces Admit Loss of Donetsk Airport to Rebels." *Guardian*, 21 Jan. 2015, https://www.theguardian.com/world/2015/jan/21/russia-ukraine-war-fighting-east.

307 Gonacherova, Olena. "At Least 6 Separatist Leaders Killed in Donbas before Motorola." *Kyiv Post*, 17 Oct. 2016, https://www.kyivpost.com/ukraine-politics/list-separatist-leaders-killed-donbas-motorola.html.

308 *Id.*

309 "Ukraine Crisis: Leaders Agree Peace Roadmap." *BBC*, 27 Feb. 2017, https://www.bbc.com/news/world-europe-31435812.

310 Pfifer, Steven, "Minsk II at Two Years." *Brookings Institution Blog*, 15 Feb. 2017, https://www.brookings.edu/blog/order-from-chaos/2017/02/15/minsk-ii-at-two-years/.

311 Gordon, Michael R., Alison Smale, and Steven Erlanger "Western Nations Split on Arming Kiev Forces." *New York Times*, 7 Feb. 2015, https://www.nytimes.com/2015/02/08/world/europe/divisions-on-display-over-western-response-to-ukraine-at-security-conference.html.

312 Pfifer, "Minsk II at Two Years."

313 "Minsk Agreement on Ukraine Crisis: Text in Full." *Telegraph*, 12 Feb. 2015, https://www.telegraph.co.uk/news/worldnews/europe/ukraine/11408266/Minsk-agreement-on-Ukraine-crisis-text-in-full.html.

314 Kent, George, p. 45.

315 *Id.* pp. 80–83.

316 *Id.*

317 *Id.* at 217.

318 *Id.* at 216.

319 "Remarks by US Ambassador Geoffrey Pyatt at the Odesa Financial Forum on September 24th, 2015." *Just Security*, https://www.justsecurity.org/wp-content/uploads/2019/09/Remarks-by-US-Ambassador-Geoffrey-Pyatt-at-the-Odesa-Financial-Forum-on-September-24-2015-ukraine.pdf.

320 Kent, George, p. 92.

321 "Letter from George Kent to Yuiry Stolyarchuk," Apr. 4, 2016, https://thehill.com/opinion/campaign/435029-as-russia-collusion-fades-ukrainian-plot-to-help-clinton-emerges?rnd=1582113932.

322 "Witness in 'Diamond Prosecutors' Case Discloses $200,000 Bribe Details." *Unian*, 13 June 2016, https://www.unian.info/society/1374130-witness-in-diamond-prosecutors-case-discloses-200000-bribe-details.html?utm_source=unian&utm_medium=related_news&utm_campaign=related_news_in_post.

323 Kent, George, p. 93.

324 *Id.*, pp. 93–94.

325 On March 5, 2019 the jeweler was shot dead in broad daylight on a Kyiv street, as Special Counsel Robert Mueller was finishing up the last parts of his report. "Man shot dead in Kyiv identified as Key Witness in 'Diamond Prosecutors' Case" Unian (March 5, 2019). Accessed at: https://www.unian.info/kyiv/10469457-man-shot-dead-in-kyiv-identified-as-key-witness-in-diamond-prosecutors-case.html Prosecutors would eventually charge a former police officer and a current police official in the crime.

326 *Id.*

327 Antonovych, Mariana, and Johannes Wamberg Andersen. "Reform Watch—Oct 1, 2015." *Kyiv Post*, 1 Oct. 2015, https://www.kyivpost.com/article/content/ukraine-politics/reform-watch-oct-1-2015-399175.html.

328 "On the National Anti-Corruption Bureau of Ukraine." *Bulletin of Verkhovna Rada of Ukraine*, no. 1698-18, no. 47, st. 2051, 2014. [What does this stand for?] some Ukrainian legal shit. I have no idea that is their cite.

329 Antonovych and Wamberg Andersen, "Reform Watch—Oct 1, 2015."

330 Sukhov, Oleg, Oksana Grytsenko, and Veronika Melkozerova. "Corrupt Empire Strikes Back." *Kyiv Post*, 8 Dec. 2017, https://www.kyivpost.com/ukraine-politics/corrupt-empire-strikes-back.html.

331 Olszański, Tadeusz A., Tadeusz Iwański, Wojciech Konończuk, and Piotr Żochowski. "The Bumpy Road. Difficult Reform Process in Ukraine." *Center for Eastern Studies*, 12 Dec. 2015, https://www.osw.waw.pl/en/publikacje/osw-commentary/2015-12-03/bumpy-road-difficult-reform-process-ukraine.

332 Sukhov, Oleg. "Oleg Sukhov: New Graft-Fighting bodies demonstrate Dependence on Poroshenko." *Kyiv Post*, 13 April 2017, https://www.kyivpost.com/article/opinion/op-ed/oleg-sukhov-new-graft-fighting-bodies-demonstrate-dependence-on-poroshenko-411906.html.

333 Cohen, Josh. "Why Poroshenko's Support for Shokin Is Dangerous." *Ukraine Alert, the Atlantic Council*, 4 Nov. 2015, https://www.atlanticcouncil.org/blogs/ukrainealert/why-poroshenko-s-support-for-shokin-is-dangerous/.

334 "The First Deputy Head of the SBU Trepak Confirmed that He Quit Because of Shokin." *Bulvar Gordon*, 21 Nov. 2015, https://gordonua.com/news/politics/pervyy-zamglavy-sbu-trepak-podtverdil-chto-uvolilsya-iz-za-shokina-107429.html.

335 Subramanian, Courtney. "Explainer: Biden, Allies Pushed Out Ukrainian Prosecutor because He Didn't Pursue Corruption Cases." *USA Today*, 3 Oct. 2019, https://www.usatoday.com/story/news/politics/2019/10/03/what-really-happened-when-biden-forced-out-ukraines-top-prosecutor/3785620002/.

336 "Foreign Affairs Issue Launch with Former Vice President Joe Biden." *Council on Foreign Relations*, 23 Jan. 2018, https://www.cfr.org/event/foreign-affairs-issue-launch-former-vice-president-joe-biden.

337 "Remarks by Vice President Joe Biden to the Ukrainian Rada." *Office of the President*, 9 Dec. 2015, https://obamawhitehouse.archives.gov/the-press-office/2015/12/09/remarks-vice-president-joe-biden-ukrainian-.

338 *Id.*

339 Kramer, Andrew E. "Ukraine Ousts Viktor Shokin, Top Prosecutor, and Political Stability Hangs in the Balance." *New York Times*, 29 March 2016, https://www.nytimes.com/2016/03/30/world/europe/political-stability-in-the-balance-as-ukraine-ousts-top-prosecutor.html.

340 "Letter from George Kent to Yuiry Stolyarchuk."

341 *Id.*

342 Kramer, "Ukraine Ousts Viktor Shokin, Top Prosecutor, and Political Stability Hangs in the Balance."

343 *Id.*

344 Entous, "The Ukrainian Prosecutor behind Trump's Impeachment."

345 *Id.*

346 *Id.*

347 *Id.*

348 *Id.*

349 "Former Ukrainian Minister Hospitalized in Clash with Police." *RFE/RL*, 11 Jan. 2014, https://www.rferl.org/a/ukraine-protests-lutsenko-injured/25226583.html.

350 Entous, "The Ukrainian Prosecutor Behind Trump's Impeachment."

351 "Ukrainian President's Ally Approved for Top Prosecutor's Post." *RFE/RL*, 12 May 2016, https://www.rferl.org/a/ukraine-prosecutor-general-lutsenko-no-legal-background/27731069.html.

352 Entous, "The Ukrainian Prosecutor behind Trump's Impeachment."

353 *Id.*

354 *Id.*

355 Zhartovska, Maria, and Roman Kravets, "Poroshenko's Orbits. Who influences the President and His Decisions?" *Ukrayinska Pravda*, 10 June 2016, https://www.pravda.com.ua/cdn/graphics/2016/06/two-years-of-poroshenko/eng.html.

356 Bonner, Brian. "Telychenko's Mission: Get Rid of 'Mafia' Prosecution.'" *Kyiv Post*, 18 June 2016, https://www.kyivpost.com/ukraine-politics/telychenkos-mission-get-rid-of-mafia-prosecution-416516.html.

357 Kent, George, p. 62.

358 *Id.* at p. 179.

359 Interfax-Ukraine, "Lutsenko Holds Staff Reshuffles in PGO." *Kyiv Post*, 1 June 2016, https://www.kyivpost.com/article/content/ukraine-politics/lutsenko-holds-staff-reshuffles-in-pgo-415147.html.

360 *Id.*

361 *Id.*

362 Sukhov, Oleg. "Oleg Sukhov: Reformer and Anti-Reformer of the Week." *Kyiv Post*, 16 June 2016, https://www.kyivpost.com/article/opinion/op-ed/oleg-sukhov-reformer-and-anti-reformer-of-the-week-13-416505.html.

363 Twohey, Megan, and Scott Shane. "A Back-Channel Plan for Ukraine and Russia, Courtesy of Trump Associates." *New York Times*, 19 Feb. 2017, https://www.nytimes.com/2017/02/19/us/politics/donald-trump-ukraine-russia.html.

364 Chervonenko, Vitaliy. "Radical Team Lyashko: Former Officials and Businessmen." *BBC Ukrainian Service*, 2 Oct. 2014, https://www.bbc.com/ukrainian/politics/2014/10/141001_lyashko_election_list.

365 Shakov, Alexander. "Andrey Artemenko: 'Trump Is the Only Person in the World whom Poroshenko Is Afraid Of.'" *Country*, 20 Feb. 2017, https://strana.ua/articles/interview/56592-sovetnik-trampa-poluchil-mirnyj-plan-po-ukraine-i-rossii-za-nedelyu-do-otstavki.html.

366 *Id.*

367 Steyer, Alex. "Manor College Hosts Forum on Ukraine's Stability." *Ukrainian Weekly*, 19 Feb. 2016, http://www.ukrweekly.com/uwwp/manor-college-hosts-forum-on-ukraines-stability/.

368 "Ukraine 2016: Stability Dialogue at Manor College Full Event Coverage." *YouTube*, uploaded by Manor College, 3 Feb. 2016, https://www.youtube.com/watch?v=NbLArcq_bV4.

369 Stone, Peter. "Inside the Ukraine Peace Plan in Mueller Probe: More Authors, Earlier Drafting than Believed." *McClatchy*, 22 June 2018, https://www.mcclatchydc.com/news/nation-world/article213655989.html.

370 *Id.*

371 *Id.*

372 Sergatskova, Ekaterina. "Who Is the Person that suggested to lease Crimea To Russia?" Translated by Fyodr Shulgin. *Hromadske International*, 21 Feb. 2017, https://en.hromadske.ua/posts/artemenko_peace_plan_trump_flynn_explained.

373 *Id.*

374 *Id.*

375 Stone, "Inside the Ukraine Peace Plan in Mueller Probe: More Authors, Earlier Drafting than Believed."

376 Shakov, "Andrey Artemenko: 'Trump Is the Only Person in the World whom Poroshenko Is Afraid Of.'"

CHAPTER 3 "A GENIUS KILLER"

377 "Federal Elections 2016." *United States Federal Elections Commission*, Dec. 2017, p. 6, https://transition.fec.gov/pubrec/fe2016/federalelections2016.pdf.

378 *Id.*

379 *Id.*

380 "Federal Elections 2016." p. 6.

381 Horowitz, Jason. "Donald Trump's Old Queens Neighborhood Contrasts with the Diverse Area around It." *New York Times*, 22 Sept. 2015, https://www.nytimes.com/2015/09/23/us/politics/donald-trumps-old-queens-neighborhood-now-a-melting-pot-was-seen-as-a-cloister.html.

382 Blair, Gwenda. "The Man Who Made Trump Who He Is." *Politico*, 25 Aug. 2015, https://www.politico.com/magazine/story/2015/08/the-man-who-made-trump-who-he-is-121647.

383 *Id.*

384 *Id.*

385 The question of the suffix on the end of the various Trump family members named Trump is confusing, as after the death of Donald J. Trump's father, the president's brother changed his suffix to be Junior, even though it could be Fred Trump, III. See Alan Feuer and Maggie Haberman, "Trump's Niece Presses Case Against Effort to Bar Publication of Her Book" New York Times (July 3, 2019). Accessed at: https://www.nytimes.com/2020/07/03/us/politics/mary-trump-book-publication.html

386 *Id.*

387 *Id.*

388 *Id.*

389 Brenner, Marie. "After the Gold Rush." *Vanity Fair*, Sept. 1990, https://www.vanityfair.com/magazine/2015/07/donald-ivana-trump-divorce-prenup-marie-brenner.

390 *Id.*

391 *Id.*

392 Squitieri, Tom. "A Look Back at Trump's First Run." *The Hill*, 7 Oct. 2015, https://thehill.com/blogs/pundits-blog/presidential-campaign/256159-a-look-back-at-trumps-first-run.

393 From the period 2015–17, prior to Stone's ban from Twitter, the author had intermittent contact with Stone via direct message. Stone was charming, funny, honest, and open, and occasionally shared tidbits from his sources.

394 Toobin, Jeffrey. "The Dirty Trickster." *New Yorker*, 23 May 2008, https://www.newyorker.com/magazine/2008/06/02/the-dirty-trickster.

395 *Id.*

396 Bagli, Charles V. "Real Estate Executive with Hand in Trump Projects Rose from Tangled Past." *New York Times*, 17 Dec. 17, 2007).

397 *Id.*

398 *Id.*

399 *Id.*

400 Kumar, Anita "Before His Claims of Corruption, Trump Tried to Build a Resort in Ukraine." *Politico*, 4 Nov. 2019, https://www.politico.com/news/2019/11/04/trump-ukraine-corrupt-resort-065075.

⁴⁰¹ *Id.*

⁴⁰² *Id.*

⁴⁰³ *Id.*

⁴⁰⁴ Plotnikov, Ilya. "Pro-Russia Oligarch Onyshchenko Could Help Destabilize Ukraine and Roil US Politics." *EUBlogAcitv*, 11 May 2018, https://guests.blogactiv.eu/2018/05/11/russia-ukraine-and-the-links-to-donald-trump/.

⁴⁰⁵ Sokolova, Vera. "We Will not Be Abandoned Immediately." *2000*, 11 Nov. 2016, p. 1, https://www.2000.ua/modules/pages/files/46796-18--24-nojabrja-2016-g__706433_1.pdf.

⁴⁰⁶ Laurenson, Jack, and Igor Kossov. "Eric Trump 'Was not Paid' for Miss Ukraine Universe Work, Pageant Claims." *Kyiv Post*, 9 Dec. 2019,: https://www.kyivpost.com/ukraine-politics/eric-trump-was-not-paid-for-miss-ukraine-universe-work-pageant-claims.html.

⁴⁰⁷ *Id.*

⁴⁰⁸ Plotnikov, "Pro-Russia Oligarch Onyshchenko Could Help Destabilize Ukraine and Roil US Politics."

⁴⁰⁹ "Onishchenko Alexander Romanovich." *Livyi Berech*, 11 July 2016, https://lb.ua/file/person/274_onishchenko_aleksandr_romanovich.html.

⁴¹⁰ Plotnikov, "Pro-Russia Oligarch Onyshchenko Could Help Destabilize Ukraine and Roil US Politics."

⁴¹¹ "MP Onishchenko's Company Will Supply Gas to Metinvest and ArcelorMittal Kryvyi Rih." *Interfax Ukraine*, 20 June 2013,https://web.archive.org/web/20161211143113/http://interfax.com.ua/news/economic/157916.html.

⁴¹² "Anti-Corruption Prosecutor Seeks Arrest of Opposition MP Onyshchenko." *Kyiv Post*, 16 June 2016, https://www.kyivpost.com/article/content/ukraine-politics/anti-corruption-prosecutor-seeks-arrest-of-opposition-mp-onyshchenko-416344.html.

⁴¹³ Plotinov "Pro-Russia Oligarch Onyshchenko Could Help Destabilize Ukraine."

⁴¹⁴ Kumar, Anita. "Buyers Tied to Russia, Former Soviet Republics paid $109 Million Cash for Trump Properties." *Reuters*, 19 June 2018, https://www.mcclatchydc.com/news/politics-government/white-house/article210477439.html.

⁴¹⁵ Orden, Erica, Kara Scannell, Pamela Brown, Stephen Collinson, and Gloria Borger. "Michael Cohen Pleads Guilty, Says He Lied about Trump's Knowledge of Moscow Project." *CNN*, 29 Nov. 2018, https://edition.cnn.com/2018/11/29/politics/michael-cohen-guilty-plea-misleading-congress/index.html.

⁴¹⁶ Savage, Charlie, and David Enrich. "Deutsche Bank Reported Its Own Russian Deal as Suspicious." *New York Times*, 31 Oct. 2019, https://www.nytimes.com/2019/10/31/business/deutsche-bank-russia-real-estate-deal.html.

⁴¹⁷ Apuzzo, Matt, and Maggie Haberman. "Trump Associate Boasted that Moscow Business Deal 'Will Get Donald Elected.'" *New York Times*, 28 Aug. 2017, https://www.nytimes.com/2017/08/28/us/politics/trump-tower-putin-felix-sater.html.

⁴¹⁸ *Id.*

⁴¹⁹ *Id.*

420 *Id.*

421 *Id.*

422 Schmidt, Michael S. "Hillary Clinton Asks State Department to Vet Emails for Release." *The New York Times* 15 Mar. 2015, https://www.nytimes.com/2015/03/06/us/politics/hillary-clinton-asks-state-dept-to-review-emails-for-public-release.html.

423 Schmidt, Michael S., and Matt Appuzo, "Hillary Clinton Emails Said to Contain Classified Data." *New York Times*, 24 Jul. 2015, https://www.nytimes.com/2015/07/25/us/politics/hillary-clinton-email-classified-information-inspector-general-intelligence-community.html

424 *Id.*

425 *Id.*

426 Vogel, Kenneth P., and David Stern. "Ukrainian Efforts to Sabotage Trump Backfire." *Politico*, 11 Jan. 2017, https://www.politico.com/story/2017/01/ukraine-sabotage-trump-backfire-233446.

427 *Id.*

428 *Id.*

429 *Id.*

430 Patten, Sam. "Kostya and Me: How Sam Patten Got Ensnared in Mueller's Probe." *Wired*, 14 Aug. 2018, https://www.wired.com/story/kostya-and-me-how-sam-patten-got-ensnared-in-muellers-probe/.

431 *Report of the US Senate Select Committee on Intelligence on Active Measures Campaigns and Interference in the 2016 US Election*, v. 5, p. 57.

432 *Id.* p. 53.

433 *Id.*

434 *Id.*

435 *Id.* p. 54.

436 *Report of the US Senate Select Committee on Intelligence on Active Measures Campaigns and Interference in the 2016 US Election*, v. 5, p. 54.

437 *Id.*

438 Satter, Raphael, Jeff Donn, and Chad Day. "Inside Story: How Russians Hacked the Democrats' Emails." *Fifth Domain*, 3 Nov. 2017, https://www.fifthdomain.com/international/2017/11/03/inside-story-how-russians-hacked-the-democrats-emails/.

439 *Report of the US Senate Select Committee on Intelligence on Active Measures Campaigns and Interference in the 2016 US Election, v. 5, p.* 176.

440 Vogel and David Stern, "Ukrainian Efforts to Sabotage Trump Backfire."

441 *Id.*

442 *Report of the US Senate Select Committee on Intelligence on Active Measures Campaigns and Interference in the 2016 US Election, v. 5, p.* 54.

443 "Andrea Manafort Text Archives," p. 6123.

444 *Report of the US Senate Select Committee on Intelligence on Active Measures Campaigns and Interference in the 2016 US Election*, v. 5, pp. 56–7.

445 Satter, Donn, and Day, "Inside Story: How Russians Hacked the Democrats' Emails."

446 *Id.*

447 *Id.*

448 *Id.*

449 "Indictment." *US v. Netyksho, et al.* 1:18-cr-00215-ABJ, 2018, pp. 6–9, https://int.nyt.com/data/documenthelper/80-netyksho-et-al-indictment/ba0521c1eef869deecbe/optimized/full.pdf?action=click&module=Intentional&pgtype=Article.

450 Satter, Donn, and Day, "Inside Story: How Russians Hacked the Democrats' Emails."

451 *Id.* at p. 57.

452 *Id.* at p. 58.

453 Vogel, Kenneth P., David Stern, and Josh Meyer. "Manafort's Ukrainian 'Blood Money' Caused Qualms, Hack Suggests." *Politico*, 28 Feb. 2017, https://www.politico.com/story/2017/02/manaforts-ukrainian-blood-money-caused-qualms-hack-suggests-235473.

454 *Report of the US Senate Select Committee on Intelligence on Active Measures Campaigns and Interference in the 2016 US Election, v. 5, p.* **62**.

455 The revelations of Vol. V of the SSCI Report point to Manafort being fully aware of the hacking campaign. The report has three redacted paragraphs that describe information linking him to prior knowledge of it. If so, the idea that the hacking campaign was Paul Manafort's idea in the first place cannot be dismissed.

456 *Id.*

457 *Id.* p. 67.

458 *Id.*

459 *Id.*

460 Vogel, Kenneth P., and Maggie Haberman, "Conservative Website First Funded Anti-Trump Research by Firm that Later Produced Dossier." *New York Times* 27 Oct. 2017, https://www.nytimes.com/2017/10/27/us/politics/trump-dossier-paul-singer.html?_r=0.

461 *Id.*

462 *Id.*

463 *Report of the US Senate Select Committee on Intelligence on Active Measures Campaigns and Interference in the 2016 US Election, v. 5, p.* **887**.

464 *Id.* at p. 916.

465 Bump, Philip. "Donald Trump has Officially Clinched the Republican Nomination, per AP. Here's How." *Washington Post*, 26 May 2016, https://www.washingtonpost.com/news/the-fix/wp/2016/05/25/donald-trump-is-now-just-a-handful-of-delegates-from-truly-clinching-the-gop-nomination/.

466 Oreskes, Benjamin. "Cruz-Team Targets Trump-Putin Lovefest." *Politico*, 20 March 2016, https://www.politico.com/story/2016/03/ted-cruz-trump-putin-221000.

467 Small, Prof. Melvin. "The Atlantic Council—The Early Years." *NATO*, 1 June 1998, p. 1, https://www.nato.int/acad/fellow/96-98/small.pdf .

468 Vajdich, Daniel. "What Putin's Embrace of Trump Tells Us about Trump." *National Review*, 22 March 2016, https://www.nationalreview.com/2016/03/donald-trump-why-putin-loves-him/.

469 Oreskes, "Cruz-Team Targets Trump-Putin Lovefest."

470 *Id.*

471 Zezima, Katie, and Sean Sullivan. "Inside Ted Cruz's Novel Strategy for Winning from Behind." *Washington Post*, 14 April 2016, https://www.washingtonpost.com/politics/inside-ted-cruzs-novel-strategy-for-winning-from-behind/2016/04/13/93a7fb7a-00ca-11e6-9d36-33d198ea26c5_story.html.

472 Jackson, David. "Ted Cruz's Long-Term Delegate Strategy Is Paying Off." *USA Today*, 13 April 2016, https://www.usatoday.com/story/news/politics/elections/2016/04/13/ted-cruz-donald-trump-delegates-republican-convention/82973810/.

473 Scott Detrow, "Cruz's Methodical Delegate Strategy narrows Trump's Path to GOP Nomination" *National Public Radio* (Apr. 9, 2016). https://www.npr.org/2016/04/09/473674198/cruz-puts-another-hurdle-on-trump-s-path-to-gop-nomination

474 Meghan Keneally, "Timeline of Paul Manafort's Role in the Trump Campaign" *ABC News* (Oct. 30, 2017). https://abcnews.go.com/Politics/timeline-paul-manaforts-role-trump-campaign/story?id=50808957

475 Bump, "Donald Trump has officially clinched the Republican Nomination, per AP. Here's how."

476 *Id.*

477 *Id.*

478 "Report on the Investigation into Russian Interference in the 2016 Presidential Election." p. 19, https://int.nyt.com/data/documenttools/mueller-report-june-2020-release/9d99a85a117e945a/full.pdf.

479 Bump, Phillip. "Timeline: How Russian Trolls Allegedly Tried to Throw the 2016 Election to Trump." *Washington Post*, 18 Feb. 2018, https://www.washingtonpost.com/news/politics/wp/2018/02/16/timeline-how-russian-trolls-allegedly-tried-to-throw-the-2016-election-to-trump/.

480 "Report on the Investigation into Russian Interference in the 2016 Presidential Election." p. 21.

481 *Id.* p. 14

482 *Id.* p. 23.

483 *Id.* p. 22.

484 *Id.* p. 25.

485 *Id.* p. 26.

486 *Id.*

487 Kirkpatrick, David D. "The Professor Behind the Trump Campaign Adviser Charges." *New York Times*, 31 Oct. 2017, https://www.nytimes.com/2017/10/31/world/europe/russia-us-election-joseph-mifsud.html.

488 *Id.*

489 *Id.*

490 *Id.*

491 *Report of the US Senate Select Committee on Intelligence on Active Measures Campaigns and Interference in the 2016 US Election, v. 5, p.* 181.

492 "Report on the Investigation into Russian Interference in the 2016 Presidential Election," pp. 80–81.

493 Trump, Donald J. "Transcript of Donald Trump's Foreign Policy Speech, April 27, 2016." *Fiscal Times*, 28 Apr. 2016, http://www.thefiscaltimes.com/2016/04/28/Transcript-Donald-Trump-s-Foreign-Policy-Speech-April-27-2016.

494 Raju, Manu, Evan Perez, and Jim Sciutto. "Comey Told Senators Sessions May Have Met Russia's Ambassador a Third Time." *CNN*, 8 June 2016, https://www.cnn.com/2017/06/08/politics/jeff-sessions-kislyak-meeting/.

495 "Report on the Investigation into Russian Interference in the 2016 Presidential Election," p. 41.

496 *Report of the US Senate Select Committee on Intelligence on Active Measures Campaigns and Interference in the 2016 US Election, v. 5, p.* 176.

497 *Id.*

498 *Id.* p. 42.

499 *Report of the US Senate Select Committee on Intelligence on Active Measures Campaigns and Interference in the 2016 US Election, v. 5, p.* 487.

500 "Report on the Investigation into Russian Interference in the 2016 Presidential Election," p. 42.

501 Campbell, Josh. *Crossfire Hurricane*. Chapel Hill, Algonquin Books, 2019, p. 75.

502 Viktor Trepak was made deputy proscutor general under President Zelenskyy and placed in charge of the cases involving Yanukovych's crimes against protestors during the EuroMaidan Revolution. In March 2020, as Zelenskyy began undoing his first steps towards fighting corruption, Trepak was forced out of the role. See "Ukraine's new Prosecutor General moves to reverse progress on solving Maidan crimes" *Kharkiv Human Rights Group* (March 30, 2020). Accessed at: http://khpg.org/en/index.php?id=1585490527

503 Denisov, Oksana. "Victor Trepak: 'I Handed over to NABU Evidence of the Total Corruption of the Authorities.'" *Dzerkalo Tyzhnia*, 28 May 2016, https://zn.ua/internal/viktor-trepak-ya-peredal-v-nabu-dokazatelstva-totalnoy-korrumpirovannosti-vlasti-_.html.

504 *Id.*

505 *Id.*

506 Chalupa, Alexandria. "FW: You Saw this, Right?" Received by Luis Miranda, 3 May 2016, https://wikileaks.org/dnc-emails/emailid/3962

507 *Id.*

508 *Id.*

509 *Id.*

510 Isikoff, Michael. "Exclusive: Suspected Russian Hack of DNC Widens—Includes Personal Email of Staffer Researching Manafort." *Yahoo News*, 25 July 2017, https://www.yahoo.com/news/exclusive-hacked-emails-of-dnc-oppo-researcher-point-to-russians-and-wider-penetration-154121061.html.

511 *Id.*

512 Chalupa, Alexandria. "FW: You Saw this, Right?"

513 Denisov, "Victor Trepak: "I Handed over to NABU Evidence of the Total Corruption of the Authorities."

514 "Court Cancels Kholodnytsky's Decision to Suspend Probe into Regions Party's 'Black Ledger.'" *Kyiv Post*, 20 April 2018, https://www.kyivpost.com/ukraine-politics/court-cancels-kholodnytskys-decision-suspend-probe-regions-partys-black-ledger.html.

515 Denisov, "Victor Trepak: "I Handed over to NABU Evidence of the Total Corruption of the Authorities."

516 *Id.*

517 *Id.*

518 *Id.*

519 *Id.*

520 Leshchenko, "The True Story of the Black Ledger."

521 "NABU Starts Identifying Persons in Party of Regions 'Shadow Costs' List." *Kyiv Post*, 2 June 2016, https://www.kyivpost.com/article/content/ukraine-politics/nabu-starts-identifying-persons-in-party-of-regions-shadow-costs-list-415247.html.

522 Tkach, Mikhail. "'Cashier' of the Party of Regions (investigation)."

523 *Id.*

524 "FD-302 of Steven Bannon." 14 Feb. 2018, https://assets.documentcloud.org/documents/6537542/LEOPOLD-BUZZFEED-NEWS-FBI-Mueller-302s-FOIA.pdf.

525 "Report on the Investigation into Russian Interference in the 2016 Presidential Election." p. 138.

526 *Id.*

527 *Id.*

528 *Id.*

529 *Report of the US Senate Select Committee on Intelligence on Active Measures Campaigns and Interference in the 2016 US Election, v. 5, p.* **70**.

530 *Id.*

531 *Id.*

532 "Report on the Investigation into Russian Interference in the 2016 Presidential Election." p. 134.

533 Synder, *The Road to Unfreedom*, p. 11.1

534 "Report on the Investigation into Russian Interference in the 2016 Presidential Election." p. 134.

535 *Id.*

536 *Id.*

537 *Id.*

538 *Report of the US Senate Select Committee on Intelligence on Active Measures Campaigns and Interference in the 2016 US Election, v. 5, p.* **829**.

539 *Id.*

540 *Id.*

541 *Id.*

542 *Id.* p. 830.

543 Shane and Mazzetti, "The Plot to Subvert an Election."

544 *Report of the US Senate Select Committee on Intelligence on Active Measures Campaigns and Interference in the 2016 US Election, v. 5, p.* **830**.

545 *Id.* p. 834.

546 Helderman, Rosalind S., and Tom Hamburger. "State Dept. Inspector General Report sharply criticizes Clinton's Email Practices." *Washington Post*, 25 May 2016, https://www.washingtonpost.com/politics/state-dept-inspector-general-report-sharply-criticizes-clintons-email-practices/2016/05/25/fc6f8ebc-2275-11e6-aa84-42391ba52c91_story.html.

547 "Statement by FBI Director James B. Comey on the Investigation of Secretary Hillary Clinton's Use of a Personal Email System." *Federal Bureau of Investigation*, 5 July 2016, https://www.fbi.gov/news/pressrel/press-releases/statement-by-fbi-director-james-b-comey-on-the-investigation-of-secretary-hillary-clinton2019s-use-of-a-personal-email-system.

548 Campbell, *Crossfire Hurricane*, p. 61.

549 *Report of the US Senate Select Committee on Intelligence on Active Measures Campaigns and Interference in the 2016 US Election, v. 5, p.* **835**.

550 Campbell, *Crossfire Hurricane*, p. 61.

551 *Id.*

552 "Report on the Investigation into Russian Interference in the 2016 Presidential Election," p. 110.

553 *Id.*

554 *Id.* p. 43.

555 *Id.*

556 *Id.* p. 44.

557 Vogel, Kenneth P. "The Trump Dossier: What We Know and Who Paid for It." *New York Times*, 25 Oct. 2017, https://www.nytimes.com/2017/10/25/us/politics/steele-dossier-trump-expained.html.

558 *Id.*

559 Steele, Christopher. "US Presidential Election: Republican Candidate Donald Trump's Activities in Russia and Compromised Relationship with the Kremlin." pp. 1–3, https://assets.documentcloud.org/documents/3259984/Trump-Intelligence-Allegations.pdf.

560 Bump, Philip. "What We Know about the Genesis of the Russia Investigation." *Washington Post*, 1 April 2019, https://www.washingtonpost.com/politics/2019/04/01/what-we-know-about-genesis-russia-investigation/.

561 *Id.*

562 *Id.*

563 "Report on the Investigation into Russian Interference in the 2016 Presidential Election," p. 52.

564 *Id.*

565 *Id.*

566 *Id.*

567 *Id.* p. 44.

568 *Id.* p. 45.

569 *Id.*

570 *Id.*

571 *Id.*

572 "Statement by FBI Director James B. Comey on the Investigation of Secretary Hillary Clinton's Use of a Personal Email System."

573 *Id.*

574 "Report on the Investigation into Russian Interference in the 2016 Presidential Election," p. 53.

575 *Id.*

576 "NABU: Onyshchenko Masterminded Corruption at Gas Company." *Ukrayniska Pravda*, 15 June 2016, https://www.pravda.com.ua/eng/news/2016/06/15/7111882/.

577 "'When I Wave my Hand . . . ' 'Political Emigrant' Onishchenko Instructed by the FSB." *Obazrevatel*, 12 Dec. 2016, https://www.obozrevatel.com/politics/34510-politemigrant-onischenko-instruktazh-fsb.htm.

578 Savchuk, Olena. "Ukrainian Lawmaker Suspected of $120 Million Fraud Flees to London." *Kyiv Post*, 30 July 2016, https://www.kyivpost.com/article/content/ukraine-politics/ukrainian-lawmaker-suspected-of-120-million-fraud-flees-to-london-419925.html.

579 "RNC 2016 Schedule of Events and Speakers." *Politico*, 18 July 2016, https://www.politico.com/story/2016/07/rnc-2016-schedule-of-events-and-speakers-225704.

580 Rogin, Josh. "Trump Campaign Guts GOP's Anti-Russia Stance on Ukraine." *Washington Post*, 18 July 2016, https://www.washingtonpost.com/opinions/global-opinions/trump-campaign-guts-gops-anti-russia-stance-on-ukraine/2016/07/18/98adb3b0-4cf3-11e6-a7d8-13d06b37f256_story.html.

581 *Id.*

582 Johnson, Carrie. "2016 RNC Delegate: Trump Directed Change to Party Platform on Ukraine Support." *National Public Radio*, 4 Dec. 2017, https://www.npr.org/2017/12/04/568310790/2016-rnc-delegate-trump-directed-change-to-party-platform-on-ukraine-support.

583 Vogel, Kenneth P., and David Stern. "Authorities Looked into Manafort Protégé." *Politico*, 8 March 2017, https://www.politico.com/story/2017/03/trump-russia-manafort-235850.

584 Bertrand, Natasha. "It Looks Like Another Trump Adviser has Significantly Changed His Story about the GOP's Dramatic Shift on Ukraine." *Business Insider*, 3 March 2017, https://www.businessinsider.com/jd-gordon-trump-adviser-ukraine-rnc-2017-3.

585 Rogin, "Trump Campaign Guts GOP's Anti-Russia Stance on Ukraine."

586 @Acosta. "Former Trump campaign nat sec adv JD Gordon tells me he and other nat sec adv's met with Russian Amb in Cleveland during GOP convention." *Twitter*, 2 March 2017, 6:16 p.m., https://twitter.com/Acosta/status/837441548501549056.

587 @Acosta. "Gordon says he discussed goal to forge better US relationship with Russia. But there was no conversation about Russians helping Trump camp." *Twitter*, 2 March 2017, 6:18 p.m., https://twitter.com/Acosta/status/837441989503242240.

588 Politico Staff, "Full Text: Donald Trump 2016 RNC Draft Speech Transcript." 21 July 2016, https://www.politico.com/story/2016/07/full-transcript-donald-trump-nomination-acceptance-speech-at-rnc-225974.

589 "Mike Pence VP Nomination Address." *American Rhetoric Online*, 20 July 2016, https://www.americanrhetoric.com/speeches/convention2016/mikepencernc2016.htm.

590 Shakov, "Andrey Artemenko: 'Trump Is the Only Person in the World whom Poroshenko Is Afraid Of.'"

591 *Report of the US Senate Select Committee on Intelligence on Active Measures Campaigns and Interference in the 2016 US Election*, v. 5, p. **95**.

592 *Id.*

593 *Id.*

594 Sanger, David E., and Maggie Haberman. "Donald Trump Sets Conditions for Defending NATO Allies against Attack." *New York Times*, 20 July 2016, https://www.nytimes.com/2016/07/21/us/politics/donald-trump-issues.html?_r=0.

595 Corn, David. "How Paul Manafort Tried to BS Me." *Mother Jones*, 21 July 2016, https://www.motherjones.com/politics/2016/07/paul-manafort-trump-nato-interview/.

596 *Id.*

597 "Transcript: Donald Trump on NATO, Turkey's Coup Attempt and the World." *New York Times*, 21 July 2016, https://www.nytimes.com/2016/07/22/us/politics/donald-trump-foreign-policy-interview.html.

598 *Id.* p. 46.

599 Layne, Nathan. "Corsi, 'Person 1' in Roger Stone Indictment, Says He's Done Nothing Wrong." *Reuters*, 25 Jan. 2019, https://www.reuters.com/article/us-usa-trump-russia-corsi/corsi-person-1-in-roger-stone-indictment-says-hes-done-nothing-wrong-idUSKCN1PJ28C.

600 Fossum, Sam, and Tal Yellin. "Roger Stone's Indictment, Unmasked and Decoded." *CNN*, 25 Jan. 2019, https://www.cnn.com/interactive/2019/01/politics/stone-indictment-unmasked/.

601 "Report on the Investigation into Russian Interference in the 2016 Presidential Election." p. 53.

602 *Id.*

603 *Id.*

604 *Id.*

605 "Report on the Investigation into Russian Interference in the 2016 Presidential Election." p. 46.

606 Messer, Olivia. "Trump Asks Russia to Hack Hillary's Missing Emails." *Daily Beast*, 27 July 2016, https://www.thedailybeast.com/cheats/2016/07/27/trump-to-russia-find-hil-s-other-emails.

607 *Id.*

608 "Indictment," *US v. Netyksho, et al.*, pp. 7–8.

609 Office of Inspector General. "Review of Four FISA Applications and other Aspects of the Crossfire Hurricane Investigation." *Department of Justice*, 2019, pp. 50–1, https://www.justice.gov/storage/120919-examination.pdf.

610 *Id.* pp. 51–52.

611 *Id.* p. 52.

612 *Id.*

613 *Id.*

614 *Id.*

615 Apuzzo, Matt, Adam Goldman, and Nicholas Fandos. "Code Name Crossfire Hurricane: The Secret Origins of the Trump Investigation." *New York Times*, 16 May 2018, https://www.nytimes.com/2018/05/16/us/politics/crossfire-hurricane-trump-russia-fbi-mueller-investigation.html.

616 *Id.*

617 "Indictment." *US v. Stone*, 1:19-cr-00018-ABJ

618 Layne, "Corsi, 'Person 1' in Roger Stone Indictment, Says He's Done Nothing Wrong."

619 Steele,."US Presidential Election: Republican Candidate Donald Trump's Activities in Russia and Compromised Relationship with the Kremlin."pp. 7-9.

620 *Id.*

621 *Id.* p. 9.

622 *Id.* pp. 4-6.

623 *Id.* p. 7.

624 *Id.*

625 *Id.*

626 *Id.* p. 13.

627 LaFraniere, Sharon, Kenneth P. Vogel, and Maggie Haberman. "Manafort Accused of Sharing Trump Polling Data with Russian Associate." *New York Times*, 9 Jan. 2019, https://www.nytimes.com/2019/01/08/us/politics/manafort-trump-campaign-data-kilimnik.html?searchResultPosition=1.

628 "Report on the Investigation into Russian Interference in the 2016 Presidential Election." pp. 136-7.

629 "FBI Form 302 of Paul Manafort." p. 408.

630 *Id.* pp. 408-9.

631 *Report of the US Senate Select Committee on Intelligence on Active Measures Campaigns and Interference in the 2016 US Election, v. 5, p.* 75.

632 "'This Week' Transcript: Donald Trump, Vice President Joe Biden, and Ret. Gen. John Allen." *The Week*, 31 July 2016, https://abcnews.go.com/Politics/week-transcript-donald-trump-vice-president-joe-biden/story?id=41020870.

633 *Id.*

634 *Id.*

635 "Report on the Investigation into Russian Interference in the 2016 Presidential Election." p. 139.

636 "FBI Form 302 of Paul Manafort." p. 407.

637 "Report on the Investigation into Russian Interference in the 2016 Presidential Election." p. 140.

638 *Id.* pp. 139-140, n. 922.

639 *Id.*

640 *Report of the US Senate Select Committee on Intelligence on Active Measures Campaigns and Interference in the 2016 US Election, v. 5, p.* **82**.

641 *Id.* **p. 83.**

642 *Id,* **p. 80.**

643 *Id.* **p. 81.**

644 *Id.* **pp. 77–78.**

645 *Id.* **p. 81.**

646 "Report on the Investigation into Russian Interference in the 2016 Presidential Election." p. 140.

647 Fossum and Yellin, "Roger Stone's Indictment, Unmasked and Decoded."

648 Bertrand, Natasha. "Roger Stone's Secret Messages with WikiLeaks." *The Atlantic*, 27 Feb. 2018, https://www.theatlantic.com/politics/archive/2018/02/roger-stones-secret-messages-with-wikileaks/554432/.

649 "Report on the Investigation into Russian Interference in the 2016 Presidential Election." p. 56.

650 *Id.*

651 Assange, Julian. "Julian Assange on Seth Rich." *YouTube*, uploaded by Nieuwsuur, 9 Aug. 2016, https://www.youtube.com/watch?v=Kp7FkLBRpKg.

652 *Id.*

653 *Id.*

654 @wikileaks. "WikiLeaks Offers $20K Reward for Information in Murder of DNC Staffer Seth Rich." *Twitter,* 9 Aug. 2016, 1:25 p.m., https://twitter.com/wikileaks/status/763063624579551232.

655 Steele, "US Presidential Election: Republican Candidate Donald Trump's Activities in Russia and Compromised Relationship with the Kremlin." p. 17.

656 *Id.*

657 "Report on the Investigation into Russian Interference in the 2016 Presidential Election." p. 54.

658 *Id.* **p. 56.**

659 *Report of the US Senate Select Committee on Intelligence on Active Measures Campaigns and Interference in the 2016 US Election, v. 5, p.* **195**.

660 *Id.* **p. 91.**

661 *Id.*

662 Kramer, Andrew E., Mike McIntire, and Barry Meier. "Secret Ledger in Ukraine Lists Cash for Donald Trump's Campaign Chief." *New York Times*, 15 Aug. 2016, https://www.nytimes.com/2016/08/15/us/politics/what-is-the-black-ledger.html.

663 *Id.*

664 Leshchenko and Marchuk, "Manuscripts Do Not Burn. Paul Manafort in Shadow Accounting of the Party of Yanukovych."

665 *Id.*

666 "FBI Form 302 of [Redacted]." *Buzzfeed* 28 Nov. 2017, p. 11, https://www.documentcloud.org/documents/6933386-Litigation-7th-Release-Leopold-OCR.html

667 *Id.*

668 *Report of the US Senate Select Committee on Intelligence on Active Measures Campaigns and Interference in the 2016 US Election, v. 5, p.* 108.

669 "Donald Trump Campaign Rally in Erie, Pennsylvania." *C-SPAN*, 12 Aug. 2016, https://www.c-span.org/video/?413909-1/donald-trump-campaigns-erie-pennsylvania.

670 *Id.*

671 *Id.*

672 *Id.*

673 *Id.*

674 *Id.*

675 Steele, "US Presidential Election: Republican Candidate Donald Trump's Activities in Russia and Compromised Relationship with the Kremlin" p. 20.

676 *Id.*

677 Indictment, *US v. Stone*, 1:19-cr-00018-ABJ ¶ 14. (Jan. 24, 2019).

678 Schwab, Nikki. "Now John Podesta Suggests that Members of 'Trump Inc.' May Have Colluded with the Russians." *Daily Mail*, 18 Dec. 2016, https://www.dailymail.co.uk/news/article-4046382/Now-John-Podesta-suggests-members-Trump-colluded-Russians.html.

679 Indictment, *US v. Stone*, 1:19-cr-00018-ABJ ¶¶ 15-16.

680 *Id.*

681 Steele, "US Presidential Election: Republican Candidate Donald Trump's Activities in Russia and Compromised Relationship with the Kremlin," p. 23.

682 *Id.*

683 "Report on the Investigation into Russian Interference in the 2016 Presidential Election." p. 54.

684 *Id.*

685 Parascandola, Rocco, and Thomas Tracy. "Cops Hunt Pair of Vladimir Putin Fans Who Hung 40-foot Banner on Manhattan Bridge." *New York Daily News*, 8 Oct. 2016, https://www.nydailynews.com/new-york/nyc-crime/cops-hunt-putin-fans-hung-40-foot-banner-manhattan-bridge-article-1.2822623.

686 *Id.*

687 *Id.*

688 *Id.*

689 Shane and Mazzetti, "The Plot to Subvert an Election."

690 "Joint Statement from the Department of Homeland Security and Office of the Director of National Intelligence on Election Security." *US Department of Homeland Security*, 7 Oct. 2016, https://www.dhs.gov/news/2016/10/07/joint-statement-department-homeland-security-and-office-director-national.

691 *Id.*

692 *Id.*

693 "Report on the Investigation into Russian Interference in the 2016 Presidential Election." p. 58.

694 *Id.*

695 Corsi's statements vary widely and show evidence of witness tampering. He claimed to have been the person who put the October 7 release into motion, but then later disavowed this claim.

696 Fahrenthold, David. "Trump Recorded having Extremely Lewd Conversation about Women in 2005." *Washington Post*, 8 Oct. 2016, https://www.washingtonpost.com/politics/trump-recorded-having-extremely-lewd-conversation-about-women-in-2005/2016/10/07/3b9ce776-8cb4-11e6-bf8a-3d26847eeed4_story.html.

697 Stelter, Brian. "How the Shocking Hot Mic Tape of Donald Trump Was Exposed." *CNN Business*, 7 Oct. 2016, https://money.cnn.com/2016/10/07/media/access-hollywood-donald-trump-tape/index.html.

698 *Id.*

699 *Id.*

700 Fahri, Paul. "A Caller Had a Lewd Tape of Donald Trump. Then the Race to Break the Story Was On." *Washington Post*, 7 Oct. 2016, https://www.washingtonpost.com/lifestyle/style/the-caller-had-a-lewd-tape-of-donald-trump-then-the-race-was-on/2016/10/07/31d74714-8ce5-11e6-875e-2c1bfe943b66_story.html.

701 *Id.*

702 "FBI Form 302 of Jason Miller." *Buzzfeed*, 4 Dec. 2018, p 5, https://buzzfeed.egnyte.com/dl/ReT115dgxw/.

703 *Id.*

704 Fahrenthold, David. "Trump Recorded having Extremely Lewd Conversation about Women in 2005."

705 The author has considered the possibility that the Trump campaign itself leaked the video after learning that NBC would be running it the following Monday. In Washington, defensive leaks often appear late on a Friday so that they are buried, making them less newsworthy when they come to the public's attention early the next work week. Observers call this a "Friday night news dump." Stone's foreknowledge of the release would support this theory. Telephone records document a call from Stone to the *Washington Post* the morning of October 7[t].

706 "Report on the Investigation into Russian Interference in the 2016 Presidential Election." p. 58.

707 Nakashima, Ryan, and Barbara Ortutay. "AP Exclusive: Russia Twitter Trolls Deflected Trump Bad News." *Associated Press*, 7 Nov. 2017, https://apnews.com/fc9ab2b0bbc34f11bc10714100318ae1/AP-Exclusive:-Russia-Twitter-trolls-deflected-Trump-bad-news.

708 *Id.*

709 Toobin, Jeffrey. "How Rudy Giuliani Turned into Trump's Clown." *New Yorker*, 3 Sept. 2018, https://www.newyorker.com/magazine/2018/09/10/how-rudy-giuliani-turned-into-trumps-clown.

710 *Id.*

711 Naylor, Bryan. "Trump Apparently Quotes Russian Propaganda to Slam Clinton on Benghazi." *National Public Radio*, 11 Oct. 2016, https://www.npr.org/2016/10/11/497520017/trump-apparently-quotes-russian-propaganda-to-slam-clinton-on-benghazi.

712 Melanie Mizenko, "Crowd roars at Donald Trump's Second Appearance in Wilkes-Barre Township" *Wilkes-Barre Times-Leader* (Oct. 10, 2017). https://www.timesleader.com/news/local/595662/crowd-roars-at-donald-trumps-second-appearance-in-wilkes-barre-township

713 Wayne Barrett, "Meet Donald Trump's Top FBI Fanboy" *The Daily Beast* (Apr. 13, 2017). https://www.thedailybeast.com/meet-donald-trumps-top-fbi-fanboy

714 *Id.*

715 *Id.*

716 Steele, "US Presidential Election: Republican Candidate Donald Trump's Activities in Russia and Compromised Relationship with the Kremlin," pp. 18–19.

717 Corn, David. "A Veteran Spy Has Given the FBI Information Alleging a Russian Operation to Cultivate Donald Trump." *Mother Jones*, 31 Oct. 2016, https://www.motherjones.com/politics/2016/10/veteran-spy-gave-fbi-info-alleging-russian-operation-cultivate-donald-trump/.

718 Apuzzo, Matt, Michael S. Schmidt, and Adam Goldman. "Emails Warrant No New Action against Hillary Clinton, FBI Director Says." *New York Times*, 6 Nov. 2016, https://www.nytimes.com/2016/11/07/us/politics/hilary-clinton-male-voters-donald-trump.html.

719 "A Review of Various Actions by the Federal Bureau of Investigation and Department of Justice in Advance of the 2016 Election." *United States Dep. of Justice, Office of Inspector General*, 2018, p. 345.

720 Marshall, Josh. "Nunes: FBI Agents Leaked Clinton Info to Me." *Talking Points Memo*, 15 June 2018, https://talkinpointsmemo.com/edblog/nunes-fbi-agents-leaked-clinton-info-to-me.

721 Gabriel, Trip. "How Erie Went Red." *New York Times*, 12 Nov. 2016, https://www.nytimes.com/2016/11/13/us/politics/pennsylvania-trump-votes.html.

722 *Id.*

723 *Id.*

724 *Id.* at *passim*.

725 Kraus, Scott. "How Donald Trump Managed to Turn Pennsylvania Red." *Morning Call*, 9 Nov. 2016, https://www.mcall.com/news/local/mc-how-trump-won-pennsylvania-20161109-story.html.

726 "2012 President of the United States General Election Official Returns." *Pennsylvania Department of State*, https://www.electionreturns.pa.gov/General/CountyBreakDownResults?officeId=1&districtId=1&ElectionID=27&ElectionType=G&IsActive=0 .

727 "2016 President of the United States General Election Official Returns Butler County." *Pennsylvania Department of State*, https://www.electionreturns.pa.gov/General/CountyBreakDownResults?officeId=1&districtId=1&ElectionID=27&ElectionType=G&IsActive=0.

728 Panaritis, Maria, Dylan Purcell, Chris Brennan, and Angela Couloumbis. "How Trump Took Pennsylvania: Wins Everywhere (Almost) but the Southeast." *Philadelphia Inquirer*, 9 Nov. 2016, https://www.inquirer.com/philly/news/politics/presidential/20161110_How_Trump_took_Pennsylvania__Wins__almost__everywhere_but_the_southeast.html.

729 Schreckinger, Ben. "Inside Donald Trump's Election Night War Room." *Gentleman's Quarterly*, 7 Nov. 2016, https://www.gq.com/story/inside-donald-trumps-election-night-war-room.

730 Bluestien, Greg. "Meet the Georgia Delegate Wrangler Who Helped Trump Win the Nomination." *Atlanta Journal-Constitution*, 20 July 2016, https://www.ajc.com/news/state--regional-govt--politics/meet-the-georgia-delegate-wrangler-who-helped-trump-win-the-nomination/BEMtHaUN7A5TMoyaLkng7K/.

731 Coleman, Zack. "Meet Trump's New Climate Guy." *Energy and Environment News*, 27 March 2017, https://www.eenews.net/stories/1060077493/print.

732 Faris, Rob, and Hal Roberts, Bruce Eitling, Nikki Bourassa, Ethan Zuckerman, Yochai Benkler. "Partisanship, Propaganda, and Disinformation: Online Media and the 2016 U.S. Presidential Election." *Berkman-Klein Center For Internet and Society*, 16 Aug. 2017, https://cyber.harvard.edu/publications/2017/08/mediacloud.

733 *Id.*

734 *Id.*

735 Schreckinger, "Inside Donald Trump's Election Night War Room."

736 *Id.*

737 *Id.*

738 *Id.*

739 Mandeville, Laure. "At the Hilton, the Feverish Wait of Donald Trump Fans." *Le Figaro*, 8 Nov. 2016, https://www.lefigaro.fr/elections-americaines/2016/11/09/01040-20161109ARTFIG00009-les-fans-de-trump-reunis-au-hilton.php.

CHAPTER 4 A SECRET PEACE

740 LaFraniere, Sharon, Kenneth P. Vogel, and Peter Baker. "Trump said Ukraine Envoy Would 'Go through Some Things.' She Has Already." *New York Times*, 26 Sept. 2019, https://www.nytimes.com/2019/09/26/us/politics/yovanovitch-trump-ukraine-ambassador.html.

741 "Marie L. Yovanovitch (1958-)." *United States Department of State, Office of the Historian*, https://history.state.gov/departmenthistory/people/yovanovitch-marie-l.

742 "Chiefs of Mission for Ukraine," *United States Department of State, Office of the Historian*, https://history.state.gov/departmenthistory/people/chiefsofmission/ukraine.

743 "Marie L. Yovanovitch (1958-)."

744 "Deposition of Amb. Marie L. Yovanovich." *House Permanent Select Committee on Intelligence*, 11 Oct. 2019, p. 17, https://assets.documentcloud.org/documents/6538715/Read-the-deposition-of-Marie-Yovanovitch-the.pdf.

745 *Id.* at p. 38.

746 *Id.* at p. 172.

747 Wood, Paul. "Where Did the Money Come from for Rudy Giuliani's Ukraine Operations?" *The Spectator*, 9 Dec. 2019, https://spectator.us/paid-rudy-giulian-trumps-ukraine-operations/.

748 "Yalta Annual Meeting 2016 Conference Report." *Yalta European Strategy*, p. 2, https://yes-ukraine.org/files/Documents/YES_2016_WEB.pdf.

749 *Id.* p. 14.

750 *Id.*

751 "American Lunch | US ELECTIONS: Wild Campaign—or System Crisis? And What It Means for Us." *Yalta European Strategy*, https://yes-ukraine.org/en/photo-and-video/video/13-a-shchorichna-zustrich-yes/amerikanskiy-obid-prezidentski-vibori-v-ssha-diki-peregoni-chi-sistemna-kriza-shcho-tse-oznachaye-dlya-nas.

752 *Id.*

753 *Id.*

754 *Id.*

755 *Id.*

756 "Summing Up: Major Risks for the World, Europe, and Ukraine." *YouTube*, uploaded by Victor Pinchuk Foundation, 17 Sept. 2017, https://www.youtube.com/watch?v=ynGVS3ZWQTA.

757 Brunson, Jonathan. "Implementing the Minsk Agreements Might Drive Ukraine to Civil War. That's Been Russia's Plan All Along." *War on the Rocks*, 1 Feb. 2019, https://warontherocks.com/2019/02/implementing-the-minsk-agreements-might-drive-ukraine-to-civil-war-thats-been-russias-plan-all-along/.

758 *Id.*

759 "Report on the Investigation into Russian Interference in the 2016 Presidential Election." p. 136.

760 Sharkov, Damien. "Ukraine Claims Rebels Boast More Artillery and Tanks than Germany." *Newsweek*, 24 Oct. 2016, https://www.newsweek.com/ukraine-claims-rebels-boast-artillery-tanks-germany-513138.

761 *Id.*

762 Brunson, "Implementing the Minsk Agreements Might Drive Ukraine to Civil War. That's Been Russia's Plan All Along."

763 *Report of the US Senate Select Committee on Intelligence on Active Measures Campaigns and Interference in the 2016 US Election, v. 5, p.* **95.**

764 *Id.*

765 *Id.*

766 *Id.*

767 *Id.*

768 Goncharova, "At Least 6 Separatist Leaders Killed in Donbas before Motorola."

769 "Ukrainian Pro-Russian Group Leader Killed in Moscow Suburbs." *Livyi Bereh*, 19 Sept. 2016, https://en.lb.ua/news/2016/09/19/1873_ukrainian_prorussian_group_leader.html.

770 *Id.*

771 Sengupta, Kim. "What Lies behind the New Russian Threat to Ukraine." *The Independent*, 12 Aug. 2016, https://www.independent.co.uk/voices/the-rio-olympics-are-a-distraction-russia-is-positioning-itself-for-further-action-against-ukraine-a7186736.html.

772 *Id.*

773 *Id.*

774 Sengupta, Kim. "Ukraine Ceasefire: European Leaders Gather for Talks, but Locals in Kramatorsk Are Sceptical They Can Achieve Peace." *The Independent*, 15 Sept. 2016, https://www.independent.co.uk/news/world/europe/ukraine-ceasefire-european-leaders-gather-kramatorsk-donbas-locals-sceptical-peace-talks-a7309741.html.

775 "Special Representative of the OSCE Chairperson-in-Office in Ukraine Sajdik Welcomes Framework Decision on Disengagement of Forces and Hardware." *Organization for Security and Cooperation in Europe*, 21 Sept. 2016, https://www.osce.org/cio/266331.

776 *Id.*

777 "Hollande Ready for a Summit the Next Few Days with Merkel-Putin-Poroshenko." *El Diaro*, 13 Oct. 2016, https://www.eldiario.es/politica/Hollande-listo-cumbre-proximos-Merkel-Putin-Poroshenko_0_569043479.html.

778 *Id.*

779 *Id.*

780 *Id.*

781 Kramer, Andrew E. "Bomb Kills Pro-Russian Rebel Commander in Eastern Ukraine." *New York Times*, 17 Oct. 2016, https://www.nytimes.com/2016/10/18/world/europe/ukraine-rebel-arsen-pavlov-motorola-killed.html.

782 *Id.*

783 "Ukraine Announces 'Normandy Format' Meeting in Berlin on October 19." *Reuters*, 18 Oct. 2016, https://uk.reuters.com/article/uk-ukraine-crisis-meeting/ukraine-announces-normandy-format-meeting-in-berlin-on-october-19-idUKKCN12I0OO.

784 "Merkel to host Putin for Berlin Summit on Ukraine." *Euractiv*, 18 Oct. 2016, https://www.euractiv.com/section/defence-and-security/news/merkel-to-host-putin-for-berlin-summit-on-ukraine/.

785 *Id.*

786 "Joint Press Point with NATO Secretary General Jens Stoltenberg and the President of Ukraine, Petro Poroshenko." *North Atlantic Treaty Organization*, 20 Oct. 2016, https://www.nato.int/cps/en/natohq/opinions_136166.htm.

787 Frolov, Vladimir. "No Miracle after Berlin Meeting: Ukraine Deadlocked, Putin Stands Ground on Syria." *Moscow Times*, 21 Oct. 2016, https://www.themoscowtimes.com/2016/10/21/no-miracle-after-berlin-meeting-a55825.

788 Poroshenko, Petro. "Post." *Facebook*, 19 Oct. 2016, https://www.facebook.com/petroporoshenko/photos/a.474415552692842.1073741828.474409562693441/868228149978245/?type=3.

789 "Deposition of Marie Yovanovitch." p. 85.

790 *Id.* p. 100.

792 Wood, Paul. "Trump Lawyer 'Paid by Ukraine' to Arrange White House Talks." *BBC*, 23 May 2018, https://web.archive.org/web/20180523161139/https://www.bbc.com/news/world-us-canada-44215656.

* Days before Paul Manafort's trial in Washington, DC, Petro Poroshenko disputed the bribery allegations in a suit in the defamation-plaintiff-friendly High Court in London, where publications are forced to expose confidential sources to meet the burden that the reporting is truthful. The BBC settled the matter and withdrew the reporting. Subsequent reporting during the impeachment proceedings has proved every claim in Mr. Wood's reporting to be true.

794 Ledbed, Natalia. "Resignation of Kurt Volker: What Does this Mean for Ukraine?" *112UA*, 1 Oct. 2019, https://112.international/ukraine-top-news/resignation-of-kurt-volker-what-does-this-mean-for-ukraine-44078.html.

795 Wood, "Trump Lawyer 'Paid by Ukraine' to Arrange White House Talks."

796 Ledbed, "Resignation of Kurt Volker: What Does this Mean for Ukraine?"

797 *Id.*

798 *Id.*

799 "Supplemental Statement to Foreign Agents Registration Act Registration of BGR Government Affairs." *Department of Justice*, 30 June 2017, p. 32, https://efile.fara.gov/docs/5430-Supplemental-Statement-20170630-35.pdf.

800 Wood, "Trump Lawyer 'Paid by Ukraine' to Arrange White House Talks."

801 "About Chabad-Lubavich." *Chabad-Lubavich Media Center*, https://www.chabad.org/library/article_cdo/aid/36226/jewish/About-Chabad-Lubavitch.htm.

802 Feldman, Noah. "Remembering a Force in Jewish History." *Bloomberg News*, 25 June 2014, https://www.bloomberg.com/opinion/articles/2014-06-25/remembering-a-force-in-jewish-history?sref=Z6DDy2rA.

803 *Id.*

804 Samuelsohn, Darren, and Ben Schreckinger. "Indicted Giuliani Associate Attended Private '16 Election Night Party for "Friend"' Trump." *Politico*, 10 Oct. 2019, https://www.politico.com/news/2019/10/11/lev-parnas-giuliani-trump-private-party-044698

805 Musgrave, Jane, and John Pacenti. "Lev Parnas' Life in Boca Raton: Suburban Dad got his Start in Penny Stocks on 'Maggot Mile.'" *Palm Beach Post*, 24 Jan. 2020, https://www.palmbeachpost.com/news/20200124/lev-parnasrsquo-life-in-boca-raton-suburban-dad-got-his-start-in-penny-stocks-on-lsquomaggot-milersquo.

806 *Id.*

807 Helderman, Rosalind S., Josh Dawsey, Paul Sonne, and Tom Hamburger, "How two Soviet-Born Emigres Made it into Elite Trump Circles—and the Center of the Impeachment Storm." *Washington Post*, 12 Oct. 2019, https://www.washingtonpost.com/politics/how-two-soviet-born-emigres-made-it-into-elite-trump-circles--and-the-center-of-the-impeachment-storm/2019/10/12/9a3c03be-ec53-11e9-85c0-85a098e47b37_story.html.

808 Ostrowsky, Jeff, and Wayne Washington. "Lev Parnas in Palm Beach County: Unpaid Bills, Failed Business Deals." *Palm Beach Post*, 24 Oct. 2019, https://www.palmbeachpost.com/news/20191024/lev-parnas-in-palm-beach-county-unpaid-bills-failed-business-deals.

809 Helderman, Rosalind S., and Tom Hamburger. "Giuliani Associates Claimed to Have Sway with Both Foreign Billionaires and Trump Administration Officials." *Washington Post*, 26 Oct. 2019, https://www.washingtonpost.com/politics/giuliani-associates-claimed-to-have-sway-with-both-foreign-billionaires-and-trump-administration-officials/2019/10/26/c564139e-f791-11e9-8cf0-4cc99f74d127_story.html .

810 Ostrowsky and Washington, "Lev Parnas in Palm Beach County: Unpaid Bills, Failed Business Deals."

811 "Complaint," *Parnas et al. v. Hudson Holdings et al.*, Case no. 17 CA 00734, 28 June 2017, p. 32, Ex. B, https://www.scribd.com/document/448483199/David-Correia-Lev-Parnas-Newco-Partners-vs-Hudson-Holdings-LLC-Andrew-Greenbaum-Steven-Michael.

812 Helderman and Hamburger, "Giuliani Associates Claimed to have Sway with Both Foreign Billionaires and Trump Administration Officials."

813 *Id.*

814 "Tatiana Akhmedov v. Farkhad Akhmedov, et al." *Coutrs and Tribunals Judiciary*, EWFC 23 (Fam), 2018, p. 2, https://www.judiciary.uk/wp-content/uploads/2018/04/Akhmedova-v-Akhmedova-full-judgment.pdf.

815 Ballhaus, Rebecca, Aruna Viswanatha, and Alex Leary. "Lev Parnas Paid His Way into Donald Trump's Orbit." *Wall Street Journal*, 20 Jan. 2020, https://www.wsj.com/articles/lev-parnas-paid-his-way-into-donald-trumps-orbit-11579469071.

816 Zawada, Zenon. "Rada Approves Arrest of Onyshchenko."*Ukrainian Weekly*, 8 July 2016, http://www.ukrweekly.com/uwwp/rada-approves-arrest-of-onyshchenko/.

817 Wood, "Trump Lawyer 'Paid by Ukraine' to Arrange White House Talks."

818 Bertrand, Natasha. "Trump's Personal Lawyer Emailed Putin's Spokesman for Help on a Business Deal during the Election." *New Haven Register*, 28 Aug. 2017, https://www.nhregister.com/technology/businessinsider/article/I-will-get-Putin-on-this-program-and-we-will-get-12073695.php.

819 "Felix Sater—Man of the Year: Chabad of Port Washington." *YouTube*, uploaded by Felix Sater, 8 Aug. 2014, https://www.youtube.com/watch?v=xSpFtCmoD5o.

820 Stone, "Inside the Ukraine Peace Plan in Mueller Probe: More Authors, Earlier Drafting than Believed."

821 Weinglass, Simona. "Inside Anatevka, the Curious Chabad Hamlet in Ukraine Where Giuliani is 'Mayor.'" *Times of Israel*, 31 Jan. 2020 https://www.timesofisrael.com/inside-anatevka-the-curious-chabad-hamlet-in-ukraine-where-giuliani-is-mayor/.

822 *Id.*

823 Baker, Stephanie, and Daryna Krasnolutska. "Rudy Giuliani Has Curious Links to a Jewish Village in Ukraine." *Bloomberg News*, 27 Nov. 2019, https://www.bloomberg.com/news/articles/2019-11-27/rudy-giuliani-has-curious-links-to-a-jewish-village-in-ukraine.

824 "New Community Center Opens in 'Fiddler's' Picturesque Anatevka." *Crown Heights.Info*, 9 May 2019, https://crownheights.info/chabad-news/640353/new-community-center-opens-in-fiddlers-picturesque-anatevka/.

825 Weinglass, Simona. "At Swanky Philanthropy Conference, Politics Is the Elephant in the Room." *Times of Israel*, 27 March 2019, https://www.timesofisrael.com/at-swanky-philanthropy-conference-politics-is-the-elephant-in-the-room/.

826 "Former Soviet Union." *Chabad.org*, https://www.chabad.org/library/article_cdo/aid/244380/jewish/Former-Soviet-Union.htm.

827 Weinglass, "Inside Anatevka, the Curious Chabad Hamlet in Ukraine where Giuliani is 'Mayor.'"

828 @josephabondy. "Congratulations to @B_B_W_W for correctly answering Question 3 of the Lev Parnas #DailyTriviaChallenge—October 19, 2016, LasVegas, NV, Trump-Clinton Debate. Nice job! Still waiting on correct answers to Qs 2 and 3. #PhotosWithLev #LevRemembers." *Twitter*, 20 March 2020, https://twitter.com/josephabondy/status/1241110023603998720.

829 "FBI Form 302 of Steve Bannon."

830 *Id.*

831 "Individual Contribution Report of Lev Parnas." *Federal Election Commission*, 24 Oct. 2016, https://www.fec.gov/data/receipts/individual-contributions/?contributor_name=lev+parnas&two_year_transaction_period=2016.

832 *Id.*

833 *Id.*

834 *Report of the US Senate Select Committee on Intelligence on Active Measures Campaigns and Interference in the 2016 US Election, v. 5, p.* **89**.

835 "Department of State Secret Operation in Ukraine." *Cyber Berkut*, 4 Nov. 2016, http://www.cyber-berkut.ru/en/.

836 *Id.*

837 *Id.*

838 *Report of the US Senate Select Committee on Intelligence on Active Measures Campaigns and Interference in the 2016 US Election, v. 5, p.* 110.

839 *Id.* p. 109.

840 *Id.*

841 *Id.*

842 *Id.*

843 Melkozerova, Veronika. "Kholodnytsky Says There's No Grounds to Press Charges against Manafort." *Kyiv Post*, 19 Nov. 2016, https://www.kyivpost.com/ukraine-politics/kholodnytsky-says-theres-no-actual-grounds-press-charges-manafort.html.

844 "Exhibit A to FARA Registration Statement of BGR Government Relations." *Department of Justice*, 11 Jan. 2017, https://efile.fara.gov/docs/5430-Exhibit-AB-20170111-59.pdf.

845 Carr, Andy. "Barbour: 'I'm a Lobbyist.'" *Politico*, 1 Feb. 2011, https://www.politico.com/blogs/politico-now/2011/02/barbour-im-a-lobbyist-033321.

846 *Id.*

847 "Exhibit AB to FARA Registration Statement of BGR Government Relations." *Department of Justice*, 27 March 2017, https://efile.fara.gov/docs/5430-Exhibit-AB-20170327-61.pdf.

848 DeYoung, Karen, and Anna Gearan. "Kurt Volker, Trump's Special Envoy to Ukraine, resigns" *Washington Post*, (Sept. 28, 2019). https://www.washingtonpost.com/national-security/kurt-volker-trumps-special-envoy-to-ukraine-resigns/2019/09/28/b663cd92-e17c-11e9-b199-f638bf2c340f_story.html

849 "BGR Group Team: Ambassador Paul Volker." *BGR Group*, https://bgrdc.com/b/bio/30/Ambassador-Kurt-Volker.

850 Popovich, Dennis. "Georgi Tuka: Russia Will Return the Donbass in 2017, No Later than 2018." *Apostrophe*, 28 Nov. 2016, https://apostrophe.ua/ua/article/society/2016-11-28/georgiy-tuka-rossiya-vernet-donbass-v-2017-maksimum-v-2018-godu/8547.

851 Popovich, Dennis. "Georgy Tuka: There Is an Opportunity to Raise an Uprising in the Donbas." *Apostrophe*, 2 Dec. 2016, https://apostrophe.ua/ua/article/society/2016-12-02/georgiy-tuka-est-vozmojnost-podnyat-na-donbasse-vosstanie/8633.

852 *Id.*

853 Grytsenko, Oksana, and Oleg Sukhov. "Rumor Mill goes into Overdrive over Prospect of Secret Peace Deal with Kremlin." *Kyiv Post*, 9 Feb. 2017, https://www.kyivpost.com/ukraine-politics/rumor-mill-goes-overdrive-prospect-secret-peace-deal-kremlin.html.

854 "Belarus to host Four-Nation Ukraine Peace Meeting Tuesday." *World Bulletin*, 27 Nov. 2016, https://www.worldbulletin.net/europe/belarus-to-host-four-nation-ukraine-peace-meeting-tuesday-h180745.html.

855 Kramer, David J. Interviewed by House Permanent Select Committee on Intelligence. "Interview of: David J. Kramer." *Permanent Select Committee on Intelligence*, 19 Dec. 2017, pp. 6–8, https://intelligence.house.gov/uploadedfiles/dk24a.pdf.

856 *Id.*

857 *Id.*

858 *Id.*

859 *Id.*

860 *Id.*

861 *Id.* p. 9.

862 *Id.* p. 11.

863 *Id.* p. 11.

864 *Id.*

865 *Id.*

866 *Id.*

867 *Id.*

868 *Id.* p. 50.

869 *Id.* p. 77.

870 *Id.* p. 64.

871 *Id.*

872 *Id.* pp. 15–16.

873 *Id.*

874 *Id.* p. 17.

875 "Donald Trump Won the US Presidential Election. Chronicle of Events." *Strana*, 9 Nov. 2016, https://strana.ua/news/39365-zavtra-v-ssha-projdut-vybory-prezidenta-hronika-sobytij.html.

876 *Id.*

877 Myroniuk, Anna, and Jack Laurenson. "After 3 Years in Exile, Scandalous Millionaire to Return to Ukraine, Face Charges." *Kyiv Post*, 27 Nov. 2019, https://www.kyivpost.com/ukraine-politics/after-3-years-in-exile-scandalous-millionaire-to-return-to-ukraine-face-charges.html.

878 *Id.*

879 Koshiw, Isobel. "Fugitive Lawmaker Gives FBI Recordings of Poroshenko." *Kyiv Post*, 1 Dec. 2016, https://www.kyivpost.com/ukraine-politics/fugitive-lawmaker-gives-fbi-recordings-poroshenko.html.

880 *Id.*

881 "Ukrainian Oligarch Gives Testimony to the US Justice Department against the President of Ukraine—ForumDaily Exclusive." *Forum Daily*, 5 Mar. 2018, https://web.archive.org/web/20190112034403/https://www.forumdaily.com/en/ukrainskij-oligarx-daet-minyustu-ssha-pokazaniya-protiv-prezidenta-ukrainy-eksklyuziv-forumdaily/.

882 Gonchar, Olena. "Onishchenko Obtained Russian Passport and Is Cooperating with the FSB, and SBU." *Ukrainian News*, 1 Dec. 2016, https://ukranews.com/ua/news/463264-onyshhenko-otrymav-rosiyskyy-pasport-i-spivpracyuye-z-fsb-sbu.

883 Koshiw, "Fugitive Lawmaker Gives FBI Recordings of Poroshenko."

884 Suhkov, Oleg. "Onyshchenko Makes Sweeping Claims about Poroshenko Graft." *Kyiv Post*, 9 Dec. 2016, https://www.kyivpost.com/ukraine-politics/onyshchenko-makes-sweeping-claims-poroshenko-graft.html.

885 *Id.*

886 Suhkov, Oleg. "Onyshchenko Accuses Poroshenko of Pressuring Burisma, Energy Firm Linked to Biden, Kwasniewski." *Kyiv Post*, 28 Dec. 2016, https://www.kyivpost.com/ukraine-politics/onyshchenko-accuses-poroshenko-pressuring-burisma-firm-linked-biden-kwasniewski.html.

887 *Id.*

888 *Id.*

889 *Id.*

890 *Id.*

891 *Id.*

892 "'When I Wave My Hand . . .' the FSB Instructs the 'Political Emigrant' Onyshchenko." *Obozrevatel*, 15 Dec. 2016, https://www.obozrevatel.com/politics/34510-politemigrant-onischenko-instruktazh-fsb.htm.

893 *Id.*

894 "Former Producer of 112 Ukraine Zubrytskyi Published his Interview with Ex-Deputy Onyshchenko." *Detector*, 16 Dec. 2016), https://detector.media/infospace/article/121497/2016-12-16-kolishnii-prodyuser-112-ukraina-zubritskii-oprilyudniv-svoe-intervyu-z-eks-deputatom-onishchenkom/.

895 "'When I Wave My Hand . . .' the FSB Instructs the 'Political Emigrant' Onyshchenko."

896 *Id.*

897 *Id.*

898 *Id.*

899 *Id.*

900 *Id.*

901 Suhkov, "Onyshchenko Accuses Poroshenko of Pressuring Burisma, Energy Firm Linked to Biden, Kwasniewski."

902 "FBI Form 302 of Paul Manafort." p. 409.

903 "Report on the Investigation into Russian Interference in the 2016 Presidential Election." p. 151.

904 *Id.* p. 138.

905 *Report of the US Senate Select Committee on Intelligence on Active Measures Campaigns and Interference in the 2016 US Election*, p. 99.

906 Entous, Adam, Ellen Nakashima, and Greg Miller, "Secret CIA Assessment Says Russia Was Trying to Help Trump Win White House." *Washington Post*, 9 Dec. 2016, https://www.washingtonpost.com/world/national-security/obama-orders-review-of-russian-hacking-during-presidential-campaign/2016/12/09/31d6b300-be2a-11e6-94ac-3d324840106c_story.html.

907 Sanger, David E., and Scott Shane. "Russian Hackers Acted to Aid Trump in Election, US Says." *New York Times*, 9 Dec. 2016, https://www.nytimes.com/2016/12/09/us/obama-russia-election-hack.html.

908 Entous, Nakashima, and Miller, "Secret CIA Assessment Says Russia Was Trying to Help Trump Win White House."

909 Tillerson, Rex. Interview by House Foreign Affairs Committee. "Interview of Rex Tillerson before the House Foreign Affairs Committee." *Committee on Foreign Affairs*, 21 May 2019, p. 13, https://foreignaffairs.house.gov/_cache/files/e/7/e7bd0ed2-cf98-4f6d-a473-0406b0c50cde/23A0BEE4DF2B55E9D91259F04A3B22FA.tillerson-transcript-interview-5-21-19.pdf.

910 *Id.*

911 *Id.*

912 *Id.*

913 *Id.* pp. 14–17.

914 *Id.* p. 17.

915 *Id.* p. 17.

916 "FBI Form 302 of [Redacted]." *Buzzfeed News*, p. 1, 11 Sept. 2018, https://buzzfeed.egnyte.com/dl/ReT115dgxw/.

917 *Id.* p. 2.

918 Baker, Stephanie, Yuliya Fedorinova, and Irina Resnick. "Putin's 'American' Oligarch Privately Boasted of Trump Ties. Then He Lost Billions." *Bloomberg News*, 7 Dec. 2018, https://www.bloomberg.com/news/features/2018-12-07/viktor-vekselberg-met-michael-cohen-then-he-lost-billions.

919 "FBI Form 302 of Michael Cohen." p. 128.

920 Baker, Stephanie, Yuliya Fedorinova, and Irina Resnick. "Putin's 'American' Oligarch Privately Boasted of Trump Ties. Then He Lost Billions."

921 "#119 Viktor Vekselberg" *Forbes*, 7 March 2020, https://www.forbes.com/profile/viktor-vekselberg/#5e68808f30b1.

922 *Id.*

923 *Id.*

924 *Id.*

925 "Chabad in Russia: At What Cost?" *e-Jewish Philanthropy*, 5 Aug. 2015, https://ejewishphilanthropy.com/chabad-in-russia-at-what-cost/.

926 Swoyer, Alex. "Donald Trump Heading to Mar-a-Lago, Spending Christmas with Family." *Breitbart News*, 16 Dec. 2016, https://www.breitbart.com/politics/2016/12/16/trump-spending-christmas-mar-lago/.

927 Ballhaus, Viswanatha, and Leary. "Lev Parnas paid His Way into Donald Trump's Orbit."

928 @josephabondy. "Here's the "I don't know him at all, don't know what he's about, don't know where he comes from, know nothing about him" guy, w Lev Parnas & Roman Nasirov, former head of Ukrainian Fiscal Service, at Mar-a-Lago 12/16. @POTUS @realDonaldTrump @Acosta #LevRemembers #LetLevSpeak."*Twitter*, 16 Jan. 2020, https://twitter.com/josephabondy/status/1217932038260625410?lang=en.

929 Sullivan, Eileen. "What Trump Got Wrong on the Investigations into Michael Flynn." *New York Times*, 17 May 2019, https://www.nytimes.com/2019/05/17/us/politics/trump-flynn-investigation.html.

930 *Id.*

931 Jurecic, Quinta, and Benjamin Wittes. "Flynn Redux: What Those FBI Documents Really Show." *Lawfare*, 1 May 2020, https://www.lawfareblog.com/flynn-redux-what-those-fbi-documents-really-show.

932 McCarthy, Tom. "Michael Flynn: Timeline of the Former National Security Adviser's Case." *Guardian*, 4 Dec. 2018, https://www.theguardian.com/us-news/2018/dec/04/michael-flynn-timeline-former-national-security-adviser-trump.

933 Osnos, Evan, David Remnick, and Joshua Yaffa. "Trump, Putin and the New Cold War." *New Yorker*, 24 Feb. 2017, https://www.newyorker.com/magazine/2017/03/06/trump-putin-and-the-new-cold-war.

934 *Id.*

935 Jurecic and Wittes."Flynn Redux: What Those FBI Documents Really Show."

936 *Id.*

937 "Letter from John Ratcliffe to Senator Charles Grassley." *Chuck Grassley*, 29 May 2020, pp. 3-4, https://www.grassley.senate.gov/sites/default/files/2020-05-29%20ODNI%20to%20CEG%20RHJ%20%28Flynn%20Transcripts%29.pdf.

938 *Id.* p. 4.

939 *Id.*

940 *Id.*

941 *Id.*

942 *Id.* p. 5.

943 *Id.* p. 7.

944 *Id.*

⁹⁴⁵ *Id.*

⁹⁴⁶ *Id.* p. 8.

⁹⁴⁷ *Id.* p. 9.

⁹⁴⁸ Campbell, *Crossfire Hurricane*, p. 85.

⁹⁴⁹ Higgins, Tucker. "Jared Kushner Is the 'Very Senior' Trump Official Who Directed Flynn to Contact Foreign Officials: NBC." *CNBC*, 1 Dec. 2017, https://www.cnbc.com/2017/12/01/jared-kushner-is-very-senior-trump-official-who-directed-flynn-nbc.html.

⁹⁵⁰ "Form 302 of Interview of Michael T. Flynn." *Department of Justice*, 24 Jan. 2017, p. 3, https://assets.documentcloud.org/documents/5633260/12-17-18-Redacted-Flynn-Interview-302.pdf.

⁹⁵¹ *Id.*

⁹⁵² "Letter from John Ratcliffe to Senator Charles Grassley." p. 19.

⁹⁵³ *Id.* at 20.

⁹⁵⁴ Jurecic and Wittes, "Flynn Redux: What Those FBI Documents Really Show."

⁹⁵⁵ Kramer, David J. p. 56.

⁹⁵⁶ *Id.* p. 57.

⁹⁵⁷ *Id.* p. 23.

⁹⁵⁸ *Id.*

⁹⁵⁹ *Id.*

⁹⁶⁰ *Id.* pp. 24-25.

⁹⁶¹ In fact, Steele, Simpson, and Kramer shared the dossier with at least six news organizations. Simpson and Steele also shared the document with the State Department. McCain also ordered Kramer to give the document to the NSC. McCain himself shared the dossier with Senator Richard Burr of the Senate Intelligence Committee.

⁹⁶² Pinchuk, Viktor. "Ukraine Must Make Painful Compromises for Peace with Russia." *Wall Street Journal*, 29 Dec. 2016, https://www.wsj.com/articles/ukraine-must-make-painful-compromises-for-peace-with-russia-1483053902.

⁹⁶³ *Id.*

⁹⁶⁴ *Id.*

⁹⁶⁵ Rodriguez, Alex. "In Ukraine, Old Whiff of Scandal in New Regime." *Chicago Tribune*, 27 Sept. 2005, https://www.chicagotribune.com/news/ct-xpm-2005-09-27-0509270090-story.html.

⁹⁶⁶ Buncome, Andrew. "Henry Kissinger Has 'Advised Donald Trump to Accept' Crimea as Part of Russia." *The Independent*, 27 Dec. 2016, https://www.independent.co.uk/news/people/henry-kissinger-russia-trump-crimea-advises-latest-ukraine-a7497646.html.

⁹⁶⁷ *Id.*

⁹⁶⁸ *Id.*

969 Shane, Scott. "What Intelligence Agencies Concluded about the Russian Attack on the US Election." *New York Times*, 6 Jan. 2017, https://www.nytimes.com/2017/01/06/us/politics/russian-hack-report.html.

970 "Assessing Russian Activities and Intentions in Recent US Elections." *Office of the Director of National Intelligence*, 6 Jan. 2017, https://www.dni.gov/files/documents/ICA_2017_01.pdf.

971 Bensinger, Ken, Mirmam Elder, and Mark Schoofs. "These Reports Allege Trump Has Deep Ties To Russia." *Buzzfeed*, 10 Jan. 2017, https://www.buzzfeednews.com/article/kenbensinger/these-reports-allege-trump-has-deep-ties-to-russia.

972 Kramer, David J. pp. 24–25.

973 *Report of the US Senate Select Committee on Intelligence on Active Measures Campaigns and Interference in the 2016 US Election, v. 5, p.* 101.

974 *Id.* pp. 102–3.

975 *Id.* p. 103.

976 Vogel, Kenneth, and David Stern. "Ukrainian Efforts to Sabotage Trump Backfire." *Politico*, 11 Jan. 2017, https://www.politico.com/story/2017/01/ukraine-sabotage-trump-backfire-233446.

977 Chalupa, Alexandria. "FW: You Saw this, Right?"

978 Vogel and Stern, "Ukrainian Efforts to Sabotage Trump Backfire."

979 *Id.*

980 Kupfer, Matthew, and Oksana Grytsenko. "The Strange and Meteoric Rise of Giuliani's Favorite Ukrainian 'Whistleblower.'" *Kyiv Post*, 5 Dec. 2019, https://www.kyivpost.com/ukraine-politics/the-strange-and-meteoric-rise-of-giulianis-favorite-ukrainian-whistleblower.html.

981 *Id.*

982 When the author of this book began researching Telizhenko, he reviewed the Ukrainian's Twitter account, and saw that Telizhenko, unbeknownst to him, had followed the author months earlier.

983 Baker, Fedorinova, and Resnick, "Putin's 'American' Oligarch Privately Boasted of Trump Ties. Then He Lost Billions."

984 *Id.*

985 Bertrand, Natasha. "Senate Investigators May Have Found a Missing Piece in the Russia Probe." *The Atlantic*, 2 June 2018, https://www.theatlantic.com/politics/archive/2018/06/former-gop-congressman-embroiled-in-the-russia-probe/562343/.

986 *Id.*

987 *Id.*

988 *Id.*

989 Ballhaus, Viswanatha, and Leary. "Lev Parnas paid His Way into Donald Trump's Orbit."

⁹⁹⁰ Public databases also list an Ihor Onyschuk as the contact person for GEOS Development Hungary, which was created on September 14, 2016, and located at 1053 Budapest, Ferenciek tere 7-8, 5 Ihaz 1, em 2. In his anti-corruption e-declaration, Nikolay Negrich indicated that he owned a Hungarian company, N1 Development. Hungarian corporate databases list N1 development's address as 1053 Budapest, Ferenciek tere 7-8, 5 Ihaz 1, em 2, the same as GEOS Hungary. According to Mr. Negrich's own declaration, Ihor Onyschuk is the point of contact for N1 development as well. The co-located businesses were both controlled by Negrich's representative in Ukraine. Onyschuk signed the Hudson Holdings loan.

⁹⁹¹ "Nikolay Negrich: New Faces—Old Schemes." *Antikor*, https://antikor.com.ua/articles/310514-nikolaj_negrich_novye_litsa_-_starye_shemy.

⁹⁹² "Negrich Nikolai Mikhailovich." *Livyi Bereh*, https://lb.ua/file/person/2054_negrich_nikolay_mihaylovich.html.

⁹⁹³ "Complaint." *Parnas et al. v. Hudson Holdings et al.* Case no. 17 CA 00734, p. 29, Ex. A.

⁹⁹⁴ "The Billions of Golytsn." *Nashi Groshi*, 17 Oct. 2014, http://nashigroshi.org/2014/10/17/milyardy-holytsiko/.

⁹⁹⁵ *Id.*

⁹⁹⁶ Shakov, "Andrey Artemenko: 'Trump Is the Only Person in the World Whom Poroshenko Is Afraid Of.'"

⁹⁹⁷ Fox, Emily Jane. "'Michael Cohen Is Now Even More Valuable than Before.'" *Vanity Fair*, 22 Oct. 2019, https://www.vanityfair.com/news/2019/10/michael-cohen-more-valuable-than-before-giuliani-associate-lev-parnas.

⁹⁹⁸ Twohey and Shane. "A Back-Channel Plan for Ukraine and Russia, Courtesy of Trump Associates."

⁹⁹⁹ McIntire, Mike, Ben Protess, and Jim Rutenberg. "Firm Tied to Russian Oligarch Made Payments to Michael Cohen." *The New York Times*, 6 May 2018, https://www.nytimes.com/2018/05/08/us/politics/michael-cohen-shell-company-payments.html?hp&action=click&pgtype=Homepage&clickSource=story-heading&module=first-column-region&region=top-news&WT.nav=top-news.

¹⁰⁰⁰ *Id.*

¹⁰⁰¹ Twohey and Shane, "A Back-Channel Plan for Ukraine and Russia, Courtesy of Trump Associates."

¹⁰⁰² Miller, Christopher. "Obscure Ukraine Lawmaker behind 'Peace Plan' Delivered to Trump's White House." *RFE/RL*, 20 Feb. 2017, https://www.rferl.org/a/obscure-ukraine-lawmaker-behind-peace-plane-trump-white-house/28321127.html.

¹⁰⁰³ *Id.*

¹⁰⁰⁴ *Id.*

¹⁰⁰⁵ *Id.*

¹⁰⁰⁶ Elder, Miriam, and Jane Lytvynenko. "One of Rudy Giuliani's Indicted Associates Was Tweeting about Joe Biden and Ukraine Days after Trump's Inauguration." *Buzzfeed*, 16 Oct. 2019, https://www.buzzfeednews.com/article/miriamelder/david-correia-arrested-giuliani-biden.

1007 Shakov. "Andrey Artemenko: 'Trump Is the Only Person in the World Whom Poroshenko Is Afraid Of.'"

1008 *Id.*

1009 *Id.*

1010 Kovensky, Josh. "Poroshenko Paying for Access to Trump Sounds Believable to Some." *Kyiv Post*, 24 May 2018, https://www.kyivpost.com/ukraine-politics/poroshenko-administration-paid-for-trump-access-bbc-report-alleges.html.

1011 Tillerson, Rex. p. 22.

1012 *Id.* pp. 20–21.

1013 "FBI Form 302 of Richard Gerson." *CNN*, 28 Aug. 2018, p. 1, https://www.cnn.com/2020/03/02/politics/mueller-investigation-memos/index.html.

1014 *Id.*

1015 Kwong, Jessica. "Who Is Rick Gerson? Jared Kushner's Friend under Mueller Scrutiny Report Says." *Newsweek*, 1 June 2018, https://www.newsweek.com/who-rick-gerson-jared-kushners-friend-under-muellers-scrutiny-report-says-953483.

1016 *Report of the US Senate Select Committee on Intelligence on Active Measures Campaigns and Interference in the 2016 US Election.* p. 720.

1017 *Id.*

1018 *Id.* p. 724.

1019 "FBI Form 302 of Richard Gerson." *CNN*, 14 Sept. 2018, p. 1, https://www.cnn.com/2020/03/02/politics/mueller-investigation-memos/index.html.

1020 *Id.* p. 2.

1021 *Report of the US Senate Select Committee on Intelligence on Active Measures Campaigns and Interference in the 2016 US Election.* p. 725.

1022 "FBI Form 302 of Richard Gerson." p. 2.

1023 "FBI Form 302 of Jared C. Kushner." *CNN*, 11 April 2018, p. 32, https://www.cnn.com/2020/03/02/politics/mueller-investigation-memos/index.html.

1024 "Testimony of Rex Tillerson." *US Government Publishing Office*, S. Hrg. 115-4, 11 Jan. 2017, https://www.congress.gov/115/chrg/shrg24573/CHRG-115shrg24573.htm.

1025 *Id.*

1026 Suhkov, Oleg. "Bracing for Uncertainty: Trade Crimea and Donbas for Peace?" *Kyiv Post*, 12 Jan. 2016, https://www.kyivpost.com/ukraine-politics/bracing-uncertainty-behind-calls-trade-crimea-donbas-peace.html.

1027 "Outline of Possible 'Big Deal' between Putin and Trump on Ukraine Emerging, Oleshchuk Says." *Euromaidan Press*, 14 Jan. 2017, http://euromaidanpress.com/2017/01/14/outline-of-possible-big-deal-between-putin-and-trump-on-ukraine-emerging-oleshchuk-says/.

1028 Grytsenko and Sukov, "Rumor Mill Goes into Overdrive over Prospect of Secret Peace Deal with Kremlin."

1029 *Id.*

1030 "FBI Form 302 of [Redacted]." *Department of Justice*, 28 Nov. 2017, p. 60, https://assets.documentcloud.org/documents/6933386/Litigation-7th-Release-Leopold-OCR.pdf.

1031 Vogel, Kenneth P., Scott Shane, Mark Mazzetti, and Iuliia Mendel. "Prosecutors Examining Ukrainians Who Flocked to Trump Inaugural." *New York Times*, 10 Jan. 2019, https://www.nytimes.com/2019/01/10/us/politics/ukraine-donald-trump-inauguration.html.

1032 *Id.*

1033 *Report of the US Senate Select Committee on Intelligence on Active Measures Campaigns and Interference in the 2016 US Election.* p. 103.

1034 Vogel, Kenneth P., Sharon LaFraniere, and Adam Goldman "Lobbyist Sam Patten Pleads Guilty to Steering Foreign Funds to Trump Inaugural." *New York Times*, 31 Aug. 2018, https://www.nytimes.com/2018/08/31/us/politics/patten-fara-manafort.html.

1035 "Report of the Investigation into Russian Interference in the 2016 Presidential Election." p. 150.

1036 "FBI Form 302 of Paul Manafort." p. 5.

1037 *Id.*

1038 "Report of the Investigation into Russian Interference in the 2016 Presidential Election." p. 138.

1039 A close reading of the Mueller report indicates that the emails between Manafort and Kilimnik were saved to a draft folder on an account which both parties had the password for. Parties would log in and review the message, avoiding the messages having to be sent via email protocol over the open internet. This was Manafort's "shady" email.

1040 "MP Lyovochkin Says Meetings in Washington Give Grounds for Optimism." *Kyiv Post*, 23 Jan. 2017, https://www.kyivpost.com/ukraine-politics/mp-lyovochkin-says-meetings-washington-give-grounds-optimism.html.

1041 *Report of the US Senate Select Committee on Intelligence on Active Measures Campaigns and Interference in the 2016 US Election, v. 5, p.* 104.

1042 *Id.* p. 111.

1043 *Id.* p. 109.

1044 @ChristopherJM. "Fun fact: When I found this photo of disgraced former Ukrainian tax chief Roman Nasirov months ago, I thought the two kids on either side of him looked familiar. Then I realized they're Lev Parnas's sons." *Twitter*, 16 Jan. 2020, https://twitter.com/ChristopherJM/status/1217950457131405313.

1045 "Government's Surreply to Defendant's Reply in Support of His Motion to Compel the Production of *Brady* Material and for an Order to Show Cause" *US v. Flynn*, Crim. No. 17-232, Ex. 3, FBI Form 302, 2019, p. 2, https://www.courtlistener.com/recap/gov.uscourts.dcd.191592/gov.uscourts.dcd.191592.132.0_1.pdf.

1046 *Id.* at pp. 6-7.

1047 Woodward, Bob. *Fear.* New York, Simon & Schuster, 2018, p. 80.

1048 *Id.*

1049 "FBI Form 302 of George Papadopoulos." *CNN*, 2 Feb. 2017, p. 77, http://cdn.cnn.com/cnn/2020/images/01/17/cnn_litigation_4th_release.pdf.

1050 *Id.*

1051 "FBI Form 302 of George Papadopoulos." p. 82.

1052 *Id.*

1053 "FBI Form 302 of George Papadopoulos." p. 83.

1054 *Id.*

1055 Polantz, Katlyn. "List of Who Mueller Investigators Interviewed Released to CNN." *CNN*, 3 Jan. 2020, https://www.cnn.com/2020/01/03/politics/mueller-investigation-witnesses-interviewed-list/index.html.

1056 "Exhibit C to FARA Registration Statement of Armstrong and Assoc." *Department of Justice*, 6 Apr. 2017, https://efile.fara.gov/docs/6416-Exhibit-C-20170406-1.pdf.

1057 Kirkland, Allegra. "Monica Crowley Files to Lobby on Behalf of Ukrainian Oligarch." *Talking Points Memo*, 14 March 2017, https://talkingpointsmemo.com/dc/monica-crowley-registers-foreign-agent-lobbying-for-victor-pinchuk.

1058 "Supplemental FARA Statement of Doug Schoen."*Department of Justice*, 30 May 2017, p. 10, https://efile.fara.gov/docs/6071-Supplemental-Statement-20170530-12.pdf.

1059 *Id.*

1060 *Id.*

1061 Isikoff, Michael. "How the Trump Administration's Secret Efforts to Ease Russia Sanctions Fell Short." *Yahoo News*, 1 June 2017, https://www.yahoo.com/news/trump-administrations-secret-efforts-ease-russia-sanctions-fell-short-231301145.html.

1062 *Id.*

1063 *Id.*

1064 *Id.*

1065 Steinhauer, Jennifer. "Trump Has Provocative Words for Allies. Congress Does Damage Control." *New York Times*, 3 Feb. 2017, https://www.nytimes.com/2017/02/03/us/politics/trump-has-provocative-words-for-allies-congress-does-damage-control.html?searchResultPosition=1.

1066 Landler, Mark, Peter Baker, and David E. Sanger. "Trump Embraces Pillars of Obama's Foreign Policy." *New York Times*, 2 Feb. 2017, https://www.nytimes.com/2017/02/02/world/middleeast/iran-missile-test-trump.html.

1067 "Ukraine Conflict: Rebel Commander killed in Bomb Blast." *BBC*, 4 Feb. 2017, https://www.bbc.com/news/world-europe-38868600.

1068 *Id.*

1069 Lvoyochkin, Serhii. "Ukraine Can Win in the Trump Age." *US News and World Report*, 6 Feb. 2017, https://www.usnews.com/opinion/world-report/articles/2017-02-06/ukraine-will-be-fine-in-the-donald-trump-age.

1070 *Id.*

1071 Kalnysh, Valery, and Maxim Kamenev. "Ernst Reichel: It Is Not Necessary that Elections in the Donbass Can Take Place Only When There Are No Russian Troops There." *RBC-Ukraine*, 7 Feb. 2017, https://daily.rbc.ua/rus/show/ernst-rayhel-neobyazatelno-vybory-donbasse-1486395503.html.

1072 "Diplomatischer Eklat in Kiew." *Der Tagesspiegel*, 8 Feb. 2017, https://www.tagesspiegel.de/politik/ukraine-und-deutschland-diplomatischer-eklat-in-kiew/19365674.html.

1073 "Poroshenko Says Kyiv to Participate at Ministerial Normandy Format Meeting." *Kyiv Post*, 10 Feb. 2017, https://www.kyivpost.com/ukraine-politics/poroshenko-says-kyiv-participate-ministerial-normandy-format-meeting.html.

1074 Grytsenko and Sukov, "Rumor Mill Goes into Overdrive over Prospect of Secret Peace Deal with Kremlin."

1075 *Id.*

1076 *Id.*

1077 *Id.*

1078 *Id.*

1079 "Supplemental FARA Statement of Doug Schoen." pp. 10–11.

1080 "FBI Form 302 of George Papadopoulos." p. 88.

1081 *Id.*

1082 Glaser, April. "The Trump Campaign Adviser Who Pleaded Guilty Was Very Bad at Facebook." *Slate*, 17 Oct. 2017, https://slate.com/technology/2017/10/george-papadopoulos-charged-by-robert-mueller-was-suspiciously-bad-at-facebook.html.

1083 Haberman, Maggie, Matthew Rosenberg, Matt Apuzzo, and Glenn Thrush. "Michael Flynn Resigns as National Security Adviser." *New York Times*, 13 Feb. 2017, https://www.nytimes.com/2017/02/13/us/politics/donald-trump-national-security-adviser-michael-flynn.html.

1084 "FBI Form 302 of Chris Christie." *CNN*, 13 Feb. 2019, https://www.cnn.com/2019/12/02/politics/mueller-fbi-investigation-documents/index.html.

1085 Comey, James. "James Comey's Memos on His Meetings with Trump." *Washington Post*, 14 Feb. 2017, p.1, https://apps.washingtonpost.com/g/documents/politics/james-comeys-memos-on-his-meetings-with-trump/2913/

1086 *Id.*

1087 *Id.*

1088 Twohey and Shane, "A Back-Channel Plan for Ukraine and Russia, Courtesy of Trump Associates."

1089 *Id.*

1090 *Id.*

1091 *Id.*

1092 *Id.*

1093 *Id.*

1094 Melkozerova, Veronika, and Oksana Grytsenko, "Artemenko Goes from Obscurity to Notoriety." *Kyiv Post*, 24 Feb. 2017, https://www.kyivpost.com/ukraine-politics/artemenko-goes-obscurity-notoriety.html.

1095 *Id.*

1096 *Id.*

1097 *Id.*

1098 Shakov, "Andrey Artemenko: 'Trump Is the Only Person in the World Whom Poroshenko Is Afraid Of.'"

1099 Gurhin, Marin. "Persons with Dual Citizenship Will Not Be Able to Hold Public Office in Ukraine—Legislative Proposal."*BucPress*, 13 March 2017, https://www.bucpress.eu/politica/persoanele-cu-dubla-cetatenie-nu-3792.

1100 Wilson, Megan R. "Controversial Ukrainian Politician Hires Pastor as Lobbyist." *The Hill*, 25 April 2017, https://thehill.com/business-a-lobbying/lobbying-hires/330553-controversial-ukrainian-politician-hires-pastor-as.

1101 Wilson, Megan R. "Controversial Ukrainian Politician hires Pastor as Lobbyist."

1102 "Lawmaker Artemenko, Who Proposed Peace Plan to Trump, Could Lose Ukrainian Citizenship." *Kyiv Post*, 22 April 2017, https://www.kyivpost.com/ukraine-politics/pgo-asks-interior-minister-initiate-expatriation-procedure-mp-artemenko.html.

1103 "Rada Terminates Parliament Deputy Artemenko's Mandate." *Kyiv Post*, 16 May 2017, https://www.kyivpost.com/ukraine-politics/rada-terminates-parliament-deputy-artemenkos-mandate.html.

1104 "Ukrainian MP Who Offered Leasing Crimea to Russia Stripped of Citizenship." *Unian*, 5 May 2017, https://www.unian.info/politics/1909636-ukrainian-mp-who-offered-leasing-crimea-to-russia-stripped-of-citizenship.html.

1105 Miller, Christopher. "Everyone Seems to Have a Peace Plan For Ukraine." *RFE/RL*, 23 Feb. 2017, https://www.rferl.org/a/ukraine-russia-peace-plans-fighting-yanukovych-artemenko-kilimnik/28327624.html.

1106 *Id.*

1107 *Id.*

1108 *Id.*

1109 *Id.*

1110 *Id.*

1111 *Id.*

1112 *Id.*

1113 *Id.*

1114 *Id.*

1115 "Anti-graft Agency May Probe Nasirov's Finances to See Trump Oath" *UNIAN*, 23 Feb. 2017, https://www.unian.info/politics/1791966-anti-graft-agency-may-probe-nasirovs-finances-to-see-trump-oath.html.

1116 *Report of the US Senate Select Committee on Intelligence on Active Measures Campaigns and Interference in the 2016 US Election, v. 5, p.* 112.

1117 *Id.*

1118 "Report on the Investigation into Russian Interference in the 2016 Presidential Election." p. 143-44.

1119 *Id.*

1120 *Id.*

1121 Hymes, Clare, and Rob Legare. "Judge Rules Paul Manafort Lied to Investigators, Violating Plea Deal." *CBS News*, 13 Feb. 2019, https://www.cbsnews.com/news/judge-finds-that-paul-manafort-lied-to-special-counsel/.

1122 "Report on the Investigation into Russian Interference in the 2016 Presidential Election." pp. 143–44.

1123 Roberts, Rachel, and Tom Embury-Dennis. "Russian Ambassador to UN Vitaly Churkin Dead: Diplomat Dies Suddenly in New York." *The Independent*, 20 Feb. 2017, https://www.independent.co.uk/news/world/americas/russian-ambassador-un-vitaly-churkin-dead-diplomat-dies-suddenly-new-york-puton-a7590366.html.

1124 *Id.*

1125 *Id.*

1126 Tracy, Thomas. "NYC Medical Examiner Won't Release Russian UN Ambassador Vitaly Churkin's Autopsy Results." *Daily News (New York)*, 10 March 2017, https://www.nydailynews.com/new-york/nyc-officials-won-release-russian-ambassador-autopsy-results-article-1.2994404.

1127 "Vitaly Churkin: US Will Not Release Cause of Russian's Death." *BBC News*, 10 March 2017, https://www.bbc.com/news/world-europe-39237748.

1128 "Kremlin Got No Letter from Yanukovich Requesting to Send Forces to Ukraine." *TASS*, 15 March 2017, https://tass.com/politics/935880.

1129 "Prosecutor General: Yanukovych Did Not Ask Putin to Send Troops to Ukraine." *Grani*, 10 March 2017, https://graniru.org/Politics/World/Europe/Ukraine/m.259356.html.

1130 *Id.*

1131 Trifonov, Vladislav. "Tax Policeman Recognized His Recruiter." *Kommersant*, 16 Aug. 2007, https://www.kommersant.ru/doc/795751.

1132 Lamont, Tom. "Inside the Poisoning of a Russian Double Agent." *Gentleman's Quarterly*, 13 Aug. 2018, https://www.gq.com/story/russia-spy-poisoning.

1133 Shwirtz, "Top Secret Russian Unit Seeks to Destabilize Europe, Security Officials Say."

1134 Mendick, Robert. "Kremlin Accused of Laying False Trail Linking Sergei Skripal to Ex-MI6 Officer behind Trump Dossier." *The Telegraph*, 20 Jan. 2019, https://www.telegraph.co.uk/news/2019/01/20/kremlin-accused-laying-false-trail-linking-sergei-skripal-ex/.

1135 *Id.*

1136 Entous, Adam, Ellen Nakashima, and Greg Miller. "Sessions Met with Russian Envoy Twice Last Year, Encounters He Later Did Not Disclose." *Washington Post*, 1 May 2017, https://www.washingtonpost.com/world/national-security/sessions-spoke-twice-with-russian-ambassador-during-trumps-presidential-campaign-justice-officials-say/2017/03/01/77205eda-feac-11e6-99b4-9e613afeb09f_story.html.

1137 "FBI Form 302 of Don McGahn."*Department of Justice*, 30 Nov. 2017, p. 201, https://assets.documentcloud.org/documents/6933386/Litigation-7th-Release-Leopold-OCR.pdf.

1138 Blake, Aaron. "Transcript of Jeff Sessions's Recusal News Conference, Annotated." *Washington Post*, 2 May 2017, https://www.washingtonpost.com/news/the-fix/wp/2017/03/02/transcript-of-jeff-sessionss-recusal-press-conference-annotated/.

1139 *Id.*

1140 Koshkina, Sonya. "Nazar Kholodnytsky: 'The Speed of Landings Does Not Depend on Me.'" *Livyi Bereh*, 16 March 2017, https://lb.ua/news/2017/03/16/361334_nazar_holodnitskiy_shvidkist.html.

1141 *Id.*

1142 *Id.*

1143 Polityuk, Pavel, and Natalia Zinets. "Ukraine Tax Chief Falls Ill as Police Close in Over $75 Million Graft." *Reuters*, 3 March 2017, https://www.reuters.com/article/us-ukraine-crisis-corruption/ukraine-tax-chief-falls-ill-as-police-close-in-over-75-million-graft-idUSKBN16A0NW.

1144 "NABU Confirmed Nasirov's Detention in Feofaniya." *UA112*, 2 March 2017, https://112.international/ukraine-top-news/nabu-confirmed-nasirovs-detention-in-feofaniya-14697.html.

1145 Eristavi, Maxim. "Ukraine Is in the Middle of a Counterrevolution Again. Is Anyone Paying Attention?" *The Atlantic Council*, 29 March 2017, https://www.atlanticcouncil.org/blogs/ukrainealert/ukraine-is-in-the-middle-of-counterrevolution-again-is-anyone-paying-attention/.

1146 Koshkina, "Nazar Kholodnytsky: 'The Speed of Landings Does not Depend on Me.'"

1147 Eristavi, Maxim. "Why Ukraine Is Facing its Biggest Test in the Fight against Corruption." *Washington Post* (March 7, 2017). https://www.washingtonpost.com/news/democracy-post/wp/2017/03/07/why-ukraine-is-facing-its-biggest-test-in-the-fight-against-corruption/

1148 "FARA Supplemental Statement for Armstrong and Associates." *Department of Justice*, 30 Nov. 2017, p. 10, http://www.fara.gov/docs/6416-Supplemental-Statement-20171130-1.pdf.

1149 Eristavi, "Why Ukraine Is facing Its Biggest Test in the Fight against Corruption."

1150 "Aivazovskaya: Due to the Position of the Ukrainian Side, the Issue of Elections in the ORDLO Has Been Removed from the Agenda of the Negotiations in Minsk." *Channel 5 (Ukraine)*, 11 March 2017, https://www.5.ua/polityka/aivazovska-zavdiaky-pozytsii-ukrainskoi-storony-pytannia-vyboriv-v-ordlo-zniate-z-poriadku-dennoho-perehovo%20riv-u-minsku-140440.html.

1151 "The Case against Yanukovych Was Brought to Court." *Ukrayinska Pravda*, 14 March 2017. https://www.pravda.com.ua/news/2017/03/14/7138115/

1152 "Ukraine's Diplomats Believe Trump Should Meet Poroshenko before Putin." *Kyiv Post*, 11 March 2017, https://www.kyivpost.com/ukraine-politics/ukraines-diplomats-believe-trumps-meeting-poroshenko-precede-meeting-putin.html.

1153 "Supplemental FARA Statement of Doug Schoen." p. 11.

1154 Tillerson, Rex. "Remarks to the NATO-Ukraine Commission during the Foreign Ministerial." *NATO*, 31 March 2017, https://nato.usmission.gov/march-31-secretary-state-tillersons-remarks-nato-ukraine-commission/.

1155 *Id.*

1156 Koshkina, Sonya. "Kholodnytsky: 'Be Patient, Everything Will Be Fine, We're Just Doing Our Job." *Livyi Bereh*, 20 Mar. 2017, https://lb.ua/news/2017/03/20/361720_holodnitskiy_terpit_bude.html.

1157 *Id.*

1158 *Id.*

1159 Zengerle, Jason. "How Devin Nunes Turned the House Intelligence Committee Inside Out." *New York Times Magazine*, 24 April 2018, https://www.nytimes.com/2018/04/24/magazine/how-devin-nunes-turned-the-house-intelligence-committee-inside-out.html?searchResultPosition=2.

1160 *Id.*

1161 *Id.*

1162 *Id.*

1163 *Id.*

1164 *Id.*

1165 *Id.*

1166 Solomon, John. "As Russia Collusion Fades, Ukrainian Plot to Help Clinton Emerges." *The Hill*, 20 March 2019, https://thehill.com/opinion/campaign/435029-as-russia-collusion-fades-ukrainian-plot-to-help-clinton-emerges.

1167 *Id.*

1168 Mackey, "Reporters Should Stop Helping Donald Trump Spread Lies about Joe Biden and Ukraine."

1169 Solomon, "As Russia Collusion Fades, Ukrainian Plot to Help Clinton emerges."

1170. Gerstien, "Associated Press may have led FBI to Manafort Storage Locker."

1171 Gillum, Jack, Chad Day, and Jeff Horwitz. "AP Exclusive: Manafort Firm Received Ukraine Ledger Payout." 10 Apr. 2017, https://apnews.com/20cfc75c82eb4a67b94e624e97207e23.

1172 *Id.*

1173 *Id.*

1174 Tillerson, Rex. Interview by the House Foreign Affairs Committee. p. 51.

1175 *Id.*

[1176] Meyer, Henry, and Ilya Arkhipov. "Putin Says Tillerson 'Fell in with Bad Company.'" *Bloomberg News*, 7 Sept. 2017, https://www.bloomberg.com/news/articles/2017-09-07/kremlin-honoree-tillerson-fell-in-with-bad-company-putin-says.

[1177] "Military Callsign List." 16 Jan. 2003, http://www.ominous-valve.com/callsign.txt.

[1178] Comey, James. "James Comey's Memos on His Meetings with Trump."

[1179] Eckel, Mike. "FBI Chief Says Russia Continuing to Meddle in US Politics." *RFE/RL* 3 May 2017, https://www.rferl.org/a/fbi-comey-questioned-senate-russia-interference-election/28466233.html

[1180] Comey, James. "James Comey's Memos on His Meetings with Trump." pp. 1-2.

[1181] Perez, Evan, Shimon Prokupecz, and Pamela Brown, "CNN Exclusive: Grand Jury Subpoenas Issued in FBI's Russia Investigation." *CNN*, 9 May 2017, https://www.cnn.com/2017/05/09/politics/grand-jury-fbi-russia/index.html.

[1182] Dawsey, Josh. "Behind Comey's Firing: An Enraged Trump, Fuming about Russia." *Politico*, 10 May 2017, https://www.politico.com/story/2017/05/10/comey-firing-trump-russia-238192.

[1183] "Giuliani Safety and Security" https://www.giulianisecurity.com (danger insecure link) Its his firm. The Russians are the ones making it not secure.

[1184] Bykowicz, Julie, and Joe Palazzolo, "Giuliani's Longtime Business Partner Resigns from Security Firm." *Wall Street Journal*, 11 Oct. 2019, https://www.wsj.com/articles/giulianis-longtime-business-partner-resigns-from-security-firm-11570829118.

[1185] Suhkov, Oleg. "Kernes, Kharkiv Mayor, Ascapes all Criminal Charges." *Kyiv Post*, 7 Sept. 2018, https://www.kyivpost.com/ukraine-politics/kernes-kharkiv-mayor-escapes-all-criminal-charges.html.

[1186] Viswanatha, Aruna, Rebecca Davis O'Brien, and Rebecca Ballhaus. "Federal Prosecutors Scrutinize Rudy Giuliani's Ukraine Business Dealings, Finances" *The Wall Street Journal*, 14 Oct. 2019, https://www.wsj.com/articles/federal-prosecutors-scrutinize-rudy-giuliani-s-ukraine-business-dealings-finances-11571092100?mod=hp_lead_pos6

[1187] *Id.*

[1188] "On May 3, the Mayor of Kharkov, Gennady Kernes, Met with the Head of the GSS Company (USA) John Huvane." *City of Kharkiv*, 3 May 2017, https://www.city.kharkov.ua/ru/news/gotuetsya-zustrich-gennadiya-kernesa-i-rudolfa-dzhuliani-35273.html.

[1189] Where quotes use an older transliteration for Ukrainian words, the older spelling will be used to preserve accuracy. In all other cases, the new transliteration will be used, for example, Kyiv rather than Kiev and Kharkiv rather than Kharkov.

[1190] "Trump Urges 'Peace' after Meeting Russian, Ukrainian Envoys." *RFE/RL*, 12 May 2017, https://www.rferl.org/a/ur-president-rump-tweets-lets-make-peace-after-meeting-russian-ukrainian-top-diplomats-lavrov-klimkin/28481599.html

[1191] Trump, Donald. Interview by Lester Holt. "Partial Transcript: NBC News Interview with Donald Trump." *NBC News*, 11 May 2017, https://www.cnn.com/2017/05/11/politics/transcript-donald-trump-nbc-news/index.html.

[1192] Kroll, Andy. "Killing the Truth.ggbb" *Rolling Stone*, 16 Aug. 2020), https://www.rollingstone.com/politics/politics-features/seth-rich-fox-news-sean-hannity-wikileaks-donald-trump-1040830/.

1193 *Id.*

1194 *Id.*

1195 *Id.*

1196 *Id.*

1197 *Id.*

1198 "FBI Form 302 of Rod Rosenstein." *Buzzfeed*, 23 May 2017, p. 11, https://buzzfeed.egnyte.com/dl/h7xo1fzzTM/

1199 "FBI Form 302 of Andrew McCabe." *CNN,* 26 Sept 2017, p. 11, https://www.cnn.com/2020/02/03/politics/mueller-documents-witnesses-cnn-buzzfeed/index.html.

1200 *Id.* p. 6.

1201 *Id.* p. 11.

1202 *Id.*

1203 Kroll, "Killing the Truth."

1204 *Id.*

1205 *Id.*

1206 *Id.*

1207 Ruiz, Rebecca R., and Mark Landler. "Robert Mueller, Former FBI Director, Is Named Special Counsel for Russia Investigation." *New York Times*, 17 May 2017, https://www.nytimes.com/2017/05/17/us/politics/robert-mueller-special-counsel-russia-investigation.html.

1208 "Daria Kaleniuk Corruption." *YouTube*, uploaded by Storozh Ukraina, 14 May 2017, https://www.youtube.com/watch?v=vks_H-as0z0.

1209 *Id.*

1210 *Id.*

1211 *Id.*

1212 "Vitaliy Shabunin Corruption Charges—24h News Channel." *YouTube*, uploaded by Storozh Ukraina, 28 May 2017, https://www.youtube.com/watch?v=b2v-GVBi2aw&t=2s.

1213 *Id.*

1214 Entous, Adam, and Ronan Farrow. "Private Mossad for Hire." *The New Yorker*, 11 Feb. 2019, https://www.newyorker.com/magazine/2019/02/18/private-mossad-for-hire.

1215 Steadman, Scott. "Psy Group Ran 2017 Operation against Anti-Corruption Activists in Ukraine." *Forensic News*, 19 May 2019, https://forensicnews.net/2019/05/19/psy-group-ran-2017-operation-against-anti-corruption-activists-in-ukraine/.

1216 *Id.*

1217 Gerstien, Josh. "Associated Press May Have Led FBI to Manafort Storage Locker." *Politico*, 29 June 2018, https://www.politico.com/story/2018/06/29/paul-manafort-storage-locker-associated-press-687776.

1218 Gerstien, "Associated Press May Have Led FBI to Manafort Storage Locker."

CHAPTER 5 "SOMEBODY GAVE AN ORDER TO BURY THE BLACK LEDGER"

1219 "107th Mayor of New York City Rudy Giuliani Gave Public Lecture at the Invitation of the Victor Pinchuk Foundation." *Victor Pinchuk Foundation*, 8 June 2017, https://www.pinchukfund.org/en/news/20207/

1220 *Id.*

1221 "Dep. of Marie Yovanovich." p. 53.

1222 Melkozerova, Veronika. "'Black Ledger' Investigation Appears to Come to a Halt." *Kyiv Post*, 15 June 2017, https://www.kyivpost.com/ukraine-politics/black-ledger-investigation-appears-come-halt.html.

1223 *Id.*

1224 *Id.*

1225 "Poroshenko Will Visit Washington, Meet with Trump on June 19–20." *Kyiv Post*, 14 June 2017, https://www.kyivpost.com/ukraine-politics/poroshenko-will-visit-washington-meet-trump-june-19-20.html.

1226 "Court Cancels Kholodnytsky's Decision to Suspend Probe into Regions Party's 'Black Ledger.'"

1227 "Register of Dumped Cases." *AntAC*, http://sapfails.antac.org.ua/engsap#Ohendovskiy.

1228 Grytsenko, Oksana. "After Four Years, Parliament Appoints New Members to Central Election Commission."*Kyiv Post*, 20 Sept. 2018, https://www.kyivpost.com/ukraine-politics/after-four-years-parliament-appoints-new-members-to-central-election-commission.html.

1229 "Register of Dumped Cases."

1230 "Reed Smith Hosts Ukraine Clean Coal Delegation." *Reed Smith LLP*, 27 June 2017, https://www.reedsmith.com/en/news/2017/06/reed-smith-hosts-ukraine-clean-coal-delegation.

1231 Mazzetti, Lipton, and Kramer. "Inside Ukraine's Push to Cultivate Trump from the Start."

1232 @realDonaldTrump. "It was a great honor to welcome President Petro Poroshenko of Ukraine to the @WhiteHouse today with @VP Pence." Twitter, 20 June 2017, https://twitter.com/realDonaldTrump/status/877341043171241984?s=19.

1233 *Id.*

1234 Bertrand, Natasha. "Ukraine's Successful Courtship of Trump." *The Atlantic*, 3 May 2018, https://www.theatlantic.com/politics/archive/2018/05/ukraines-successful-courtship-of-trump/559526/.

1235 *Id.*

1236 Salama, Vivian, and Rebecca Ballhaus, "Trump's View of Ukraine as Corrupt Took Shape Early." *Wall Street Journal*, 16 Nov. 2019, https://www.wsj.com/articles/trumps-view-of-ukraine-as-corrupt-took-shape-early-11573900201.

1237 Mazzetti, Lipton, and Kramer, "Inside Ukraine's Push to Cultivate Trump from the Start."

1238 Salama and Ballhaus, "Trump's View of Ukraine as Corrupt Took Shape Early."

1239 "Reed Smith Hosts Ukraine Clean Coal Delegation."

1240 *Id.*

1241 *Id.*

1242 "President Poroshenko: Ukraine Intends to by 55% of Nuclear Fuel from Westinghouse." *Ukrinform*, 26 June 2017, https://www.ukrinform.net/rubric-economy/2254240-president-poroshenko-ukraine-intends-to-purchase-55-of-nuclear-fuel-from-westinghouse.html.

1243 "Remarks by President Trump at the Unleashing American Energy Event." *The White House*, 27 June 2017, https://www.whitehouse.gov/briefings-statements/remarks-president-trump-unleashing-american-energy-event/.

1244 *Id.*

1245 *Id.*

1246 Green, Miranda, and Ariane de Vogue. "Trump Adds Lawyer John Dowd to Russia Team." *CNN*, 16 June 2017, https://www.cnn.com/2017/06/16/politics/john-dowd-lawyer-donald-trump/index.html.

1247 Schmidt, Michael S., Sharon LaFraniere, and Maggie Haberman. "Manafort's Lawyer Said to Brief Trump Attorneys on What He Told Mueller." *New York Times*, 27 Nov. 2018, https://www.nytimes.com/2018/11/27/us/politics/manafort-lawyer-trump-cooperation.html.

1248 Waas, Murray. "Exclusive: Paul Manafort Advised White House on How to Attack and Discredit Investigation of President Trump." *Vox*, 14 Dec. 2018, https://www.vox.com/2018/12/14/18140744/paul-manafort-trump-russia-mueller-investigation.

1249 *Id.*

1250 *Id.*

1251 *Id.*

1252 @realDonaldTrump. "Terrible! Just found out that Obama had my "wires tapped" in Trump Tower just before the victory. Nothing found. This is McCarthyism!" *Twitter*, 4 March 2017, 6:35 a.m., https://twitter.com/realdonaldtrump/status/837989835818287106.

1253 Ye Hee Lee, Michelle. "The White House's Facile Comparison of the Trump-Russia and Clinton-Ukraine Stories." *Washington Post*, 25 July 2017, https://www.washingtonpost.com/news/fact-checker/wp/2017/07/25/the-white-houses-facile-comparison-of-the-trump-russia-and-clinton-ukraine-stories/.

1254 This briefing has been scrubbed from the White House website. According to Archive.org it was scrubbed between December 30, 2017 and January 4, 2018. Accessed at: https://web.archive.org/web/20180501000000*/https://www.whitehouse.gov/the-press-office/2017/07/10/press-briefing-principal-deputy-press-secretary-sarah-sanders-and

1255 "State of the Union." *CNN,* 16 July 2017, http://transcripts.cnn.com/TRANSCRIPTS/1707/16/sotu.01.html.

1256 *Report of the US Senate Select Committee on Intelligence on Active Measures Campaigns and Interference in the 2016 US Election.* p. 114.

1257 *Id.*

1258 Grassley, Chuck. "Grassley Raises Further Concerns over Foreign Agent Registration." *Senator Charles Grassley* 24 Jul. 2017, https://www.grassley.senate.gov/news/news-releases/grassley-raises-further-concerns-over-foreign-agent-registration.

1259 On August 7, 2020, William Evanina, director of the National Counter Intelligence and Security Center named Andiry Derkach as a person helping Russia spread disinformation to help President Trump win reelection. In September 2020, the US Treasury Department called him a Russian Agent and imposed sanctions on him for election interference.

1260 Stern, David. "Ukrainian MP Seeks Probe of Ukraine-Clinton Ties." *Politico*, 16 Aug. 2017, https://www.politico.com/story/2017/08/16/ukraine-andrei-derkach-clinton-investigation-241704.

1261 *Id.*

1262 @realDonaldTrump. "Ukrainian efforts to sabotage Trump campaign – 'quietly working to boost Clinton.' So where is the investigation A.G. @seanhannity." *Twitter*, 25 July 2019, https://twitter.com/realDonaldTrump/status/889788202172780544.

1263 "PGO Launches Inquiry into Possible Meddling in US Presidential Election." *Kyiv Post*, 15 Aug. 2017,: https://www.kyivpost.com/ukraine-politics/pgo-launches-inquiry-possible-meddling-us-presidential-election.html.

1264 Schmidt, Michael S., and Adam Goldman. "Manafort's Home Searched as Part of Mueller Inquiry." *New York Times*, 9 Aug. 2017, https://www.nytimes.com/2017/08/09/us/politics/paul-manafort-home-search-mueller.html?searchResultPosition=1.

1265 *Id.*

1266 Gerstein, Josh. "George Papadopoulos' Late Night with the FBI." *Poltico*, 4 Dec. 2017, https://www.politico.com/story/2017/12/04/george-papadopoulos-arrest-fbi-277760.

1267 "FBI Form 302 of George Papadopoulos." p. 93.

1268 *Id.*

1269 *Id.* pp. 93-4.

1270 *Id.* p. 94.

1271 *Id.* p. 94.

1272 *Id.* pp. 94-5.

1273 Novak, Viveca, and Anna Massoglia. "New Nonprofit Tied to Stealthy Circle of Dark Money Groups." *OpenSecrets News*, 15 April 2016, https://www.opensecrets.org/news/2016/04/new-nonprofit-tied-to-stealthy-circle-of-dark-money-groups/.

1274 *Id.*

1275 Waas, Murray. "Matthew Whitaker: The Ethical Mire of Trump's Top Law Officer." *New York Review of Books*, 15 Jan. 2019, https://www.nybooks.com/daily/2019/01/15/matthew-whitaker-the-ethical-mire-of-trumps-top-law-officer/.

1276 *Id.*

1277 *Id.*

1278 Prokip, Andrian. "Ukraine Quarterly Digest: July–September 2017." *Focus Ukraine: A Blog of the Keenan Institute*, 25 Jan. 2018, https://www.wilsoncenter.org/blog-post/ukraine-quarterly-digest-july-september-2017.

1279 It is interesting to note that no later than July 22, 2019, the press release noting Volker's appointment was scrubbed from state.gov. Other press releases from that date remain available. All 2017 press statements regarding Ukraine have been scrubbed from state.gov.

1280 "Deputy Energy and Coal Industry Minister Natalia Boyko says that State-Owned PJSC Centrenergo Is Holding Negotiations with the United States Regarding Coal Supplies to Ukraine." *Ukriniform*, 5 July 2017, https://www.ukrinform.net/rubric-rss_ticker/2260091-deputy-energy-and-coal-industry-minister-natalia-boyko-says-that-stateowned-pjsc-centrenergo-is-holding-negotiations-with-the-united-states-regarding-coal-supplies-to-ukraine.html.

1281 "Centrenergo Agrees with US XCOAL on Supply of About 700,000 Tonnes of Anthracite in 2017." *Interfax-Ukraine*, 31 July 2017, https://en.interfax.com.ua/news/economic/439504.html.

1282 "New Envoy Volker Says US Considering Sending Arms to Ukraine." *Current Time:RFE/RL*, 31 July 2017, https://www.rferl.org/a/ukraine-volker-sending-arms-russia-conflict/28637079.html.

1283 "Chargé Kent's Remarks at Centrenergo-XCoal Press Conference." *US Embassy in Ukraine*, 31 July 2017, https://ua.usembassy.gov/charge-kents-remarks-centrenergo-xcoal-press-conference/?_ga=2.220184474.269433735.1572631877-954665611.1571722661.

1284 Barnes, Julian E., Laurence Norman, and Felicia Schwartz. "Pentagon Offers Plan to Arm Ukraine." *Wall Street Journal*, 31 July 2017, https://www.wsj.com/articles/pentagon-offers-plan-to-arm-ukraine-1501520728.

1285 Saldinger, Adva, and Michael Igoe. "Set of Congressional Budget Hearings Lay Out US Aid Funding." *DevEX*, 22 June 2017, https://www.devex.com/news/set-of-congressional-budget-hearings-lay-out-us-aid-funding-92986.

1286 Schwanke, Beth, Erin Collinson, and Jared Kalow. "Skinny Budget, Skinny on Details." *Center for Global Development*, 27 March 2017, https://www.cgdev.org/blog/skinny-budget-skinny-on-details.

1287 Committee on Foreign Affairs. "Hearing No. 115-61." *United States House of Representatives*, 14 June 2017, p. 159, https://www.govinfo.gov/content/pkg/CHRG-115hhrg25840/pdf/CHRG-115hhrg25840.pdf.

1288 "Ex. A Form NSD-3 Ex. A to Registration Statement of Mercury Strategies." *Department of Justice*, 13 Dec. 2016, https://efile.fara.gov/docs/6170-Exhibit-AB-20161213-20.pdf.

1289 "GloBee—Washington Office—Kharkiv Delegation Visit." *YourGlobalStrategy*, https://www.yourglobalstrategy.com/globee-dc-office.

1290 "Poroshenko Announces Lozhkin's Resignation, Appoints Rainin New Head of Presidential Administration." *Unian*, 29 Aug. 2016, https://www.unian.info/politics/1491994-poroshenko-announces-lozhkins-resignation-appoints-rainin-new-head-of-presidential-administration.html.

1291 "Ex. A Form NSD-3 Ex. A to Registration Statement of Mercury Strategies." p. 4.

1292 Meyer, Theordoric. "Vin Weber Resigns from Lobbying Firm after Scrutiny over Ukraine work with Manafort." *Politico*, 30 Aug. 2019, https://www.politico.com/story/2019/08/30/vin-weber-lobbying-ukraine-manafort-1479231.

1293 "National Interest of Ukraine. https://web.archive.org/web/20170604152424/http://nin.org.ua/en/main/our-mission/.

1294 "Welcome to National Interest's Website." *National Interest of Ukraine*, http://nin.org.ua/en/publications/page/2/.

1295 "'National Interest' of the 'Narodnyi Front' Yatsenyuk Party." *AntAC*, 25 May 2017, https://antac.org.ua/en/news/national-interest-of-the-narodnyi-front-yatsenyuk-party/?utm_source=Broad%20subscribers&utm_campaign=be0842f511-EMAIL_CAMPAIGN_2017_08_18&utm_medium=email&utm_term=0_2e2aa5132c-be0842f511-85523335.

1296 *Id.*

1297 "Mr. Pynzenyk Requested to Shut Down AntAC as a Non-Profit Organization." *AntAC*, 23 May 2017, https://antac.org.ua/en/news/mr-pynzenyk-requested-to-shut-down-antac-as-a-non-profit-organization/.

1298 "The Senior Leadership of Ukraine's Anti-Corruption Action Center has profited from Sweetheart Deals and Kickbacks – Adam Ereli." *National Interest of Ukraine*, http://nin.org.ua/en/main/foxnews-the-senior-leadership-of-ukraines-anti-corruption-action-center-has-profited-from-sweetheart-deals-and-kickbacks-adam-ereli/.

1299 "Corrupt Ukraine is Ground Zero in Clash between East and West, US and Russia." *Fox News*, 15 July 2017, https://www.foxnews.com/opinion/corrupt-ukraine-is-ground-zero-in-clash-between-east-and-west-us-and-russia.

1300 *Id.*

1301 *Id.*

1302 Meyer, Theodoric. "Cornerstone Adds Shimkus Aide." *Politico*, 10 May 2017, https://www.politico.com/tipsheets/politico-influence/2017/05/cornerstone-adds-shimkus-aide-220241.

1303 Lederman, Josh. "How a Conspiracy Theory about George Soros is fueling Allegations of Ukraine Collusion." *NBC News*, 9 Dec. 2019, https://www.nbcnews.com/politics/trump-impeachment-inquiry/how-anti-semitic-conspiracy-theory-about-george-soros-fueling-allegations-n1094886.

1304 Johnson, Timothy. "Former NSC Staffer Fiona Hill Testified about Receiving Death Threats after Being Labeled a 'Soros Mole.' It started with Roger Stone." *Media Matters for America* 8 Nov. 2019, https://www.mediamatters.org/roger-stone/former-nsc-staffer-fiona-hill-testified-about-receiving-death-threats-after-being.

1305 *Id.*

1306 Marson and Forrest, "Ukrainian Corruption Showdown sets Stage for Impeachment Inquiry."

1307 Carroll, J. P. "The Mother of All Fake News." *Washington* Examiner, 29 Sept. 2017, https://www.washingtonexaminer.com/weekly-standard/the-mother-of-all-fake-news.

1308 *Id.*

1309 *Id.*

1310 *Id.*

CHAPTER 6 "A STORY THAT IS PRETTY UNTOLD"

1311 Wood, "Trump Lawyer 'Paid by Ukraine' to arrange White House Talks."

1312 LaFraniere, Sharon, Matt Apuzzo, and Adam Goldman. "With a Search Warrant and a Threatened Indictment, Mueller's Inquiry Sets a Tone." *New York Times*, 18 Sept. 2017, https://www.nytimes.com/2017/09/18/us/politics/mueller-russia-investigation.html?mcubz=3&module=inline.

1313 *Id.*

1314 Meyer, Theodoric. "Ukrainian Energy Firm Hires former Scott Walker Aide." *Politico*, 21 Nov. 2017, https://www.politico.com/newsletters/politico-influence/2017/11/21/ukrainian-energy-firm-hires-former-scottwalker-aide-030101.

1315 "FARA Registration Statement Form NSD-6 of Yorktown Solutions." *Department of Justice*, 19 Nov. 2017, http://www.fara.gov/docs/6491-Registration-Statement-20171119-1.pdf.

1316 "FARA Amendment to Registration Statement of Yorktown Solutions." *Department of Justice*, 30 Oct. 2018, https://efile.fara.gov/docs/6491-Amendment-20181104-2.pdf.

1317 Zinets, Natalia, Steve Holland. "Ukraine President Says Trump Shares Vision on 'New Level' of Defense Cooperation." *Reuters*, 21 Sept. 2017, https://www.reuters.com/article/us-usa-ukraine-poroshenko/ukraine-president-says-trump-shares-vision-on-new-level-of-defense-cooperation-idUSKCN1BW2BW.

1318 "Remarks by President Trump and President Poroshenko of Ukraine Before Bilateral Meeting." *The White House*, 21 Sept. 2017, https://www.whitehouse.gov/briefings-statements/remarks-president-trump-president-poroshenko-ukraine-bilateral-meeting/.

1319 *Id.*

1320 *Id.*

1321 Shane, Scott, and Andrew E. Kramer. "Trump Team's Links to Russia Crisscross in Washington." *The New York Times*, 3 March 2018, https://www.nytimes.com/2017/03/03/us/politics/trump-russia-links-washington.html.

1322 *Id.*

1323 "Parliament of Ukraine Took a Step Back in Adopting Judicial Reform-MP." *Front News International* 26 Sept. 2017, http://frontnews.eu/news/en/14285/Parliament-of-Ukraine-took-a-step-back-in-adopting-judicial-reform-MP.

1324 Kozlyuk, Stanislav. "'Lozov's Editin.g' How MPs Can Destroy Pre-Trial Investigations." *Ukrainian Weekly*, 4 Oct. 2017, https://m.tyzhden.ua/Society/201247.

1325 *Id.*

1326 *Id.*

1327 "Investigators: Hryniak and Other High-Ranking Interior Ministry Officials led Berkut's Actions during the Assault on Maidan on February 18."

1328 *Id.*

1329 Shabunin, Vitaly. "Authorities Falsify Criminal Procedure Code—An Edit Hiding NABU Investigation." *Pravda Ukraine*, 9 Nov. 2017, https://blogs.pravda.com.ua/authors/shabunin/5a045869d9b85/.

1330 Kozlyuk, "'Lozov's Editing.' How MPs Can Destroy Pre-Trial Investigations."

1331 Shabuinin, Vitaly. "Evidence of Falsification of the Text of the Criminal Procedure Code." *Pravda Ukraine*, 20 Nov. 2017, https://blogs.pravda.com.ua/authors/shabunin/5a12b1035a8b2/.

1332 "NABU Urges President of Ukraine to Veto Amendments to CCP that Paralyze the Work of Pre-Trial Investigation Bodies." *National Anticorruption Bureau of Ukraine*, 4 Oct. 2017, https://nabu.gov.ua/novyny/nabu-zaklykaye-prezydenta-ukrayiny-vetuvaty-zminy-do-kpk-yaki-paralizuyut-robotu-organiv.

1333 Ponomarenko, Illia. "Poroshenko Signs Controversial Law on Extending Special Status for Donbas." *Kyiv Post*, 7 Oct. 2017, https://www.kyivpost.com/ukraine-politics/poroshenko-signs-controversial-law-extending-special-status-donbas.html.

1334 *Id.*

1335 Sukhov, Oleg. "High-Profile Criminal Investigations Face Total Collapse." *Kyiv Post*, 23 Nov. 2017, https://www.kyivpost.com/ukraine-politics/high-profile-criminal-investigations-face-total-collapse.html.

1336 *Id.*

1337 *Id.*

1338 *Id.*

1339 *Id.*

1340 "Kyiv Court Opens Case against NABU Chief, MP Leshchenko on Manafort Leaks." *Kyiv Post*, 24 Oct. 2017, https://www.kyivpost.com/ukraine-politics/kyiv-court-opens-case-nabu-chief-mp-leshchenko-manafort-leaks.html

1341 "Indictment." *US v. Paul Manafort and Richard Gates*, 1:17cr-0201, 27 Oct. 2017, https://www.justice.gov/file/1007271/download.

1342 Politico Staff ."FULL TEXT: Paul Manafort Indictment." *Politico*, 30 Oct. 2017, https://www.politico.com/story/2017/10/30/full-text-paul-manafort-indictment-244307.

1343 Coaston, Jane. "#QAnon, the Scarily Popular Pro-Trump Conspiracy Theory, Explained." *Vox*, 2 Aug. 2018, https://www.vox.com/policy-and-politics/2018/8/1/17253444/qanon-trump-conspiracy-theory-reddit.

1344 Collins, Ben. "Donald Trump's Online Trolls Turn on Their 'God Emperor.'" *Daily Beast*, 27 Sept. 2016, https://www.thedailybeast.com/donald-trumps-online-trolls-turn-on-their-god-emperor.

1345 Coaston, "#QAnon, the Scarily Popular Pro-Trump Conspiracy Theory, Explained."

1346 Miller, Zeke, and Johnathan Lemire. "Trump Fumes as Mueller Investigation Opens New Phase with Charges." *Chicago-Sun Times*, 30 Oct. 2017, https://chicago.suntimes.com/2017/10/30/18340840/trump-fumes-as-mueller-probe-enters-new-phase-with-charges.

1347 Kramer, Andrew E. "Charges against Paul Manafort Resonate in Ukraine." *New York Times*, 31 Oct. 2017, https://www.nytimes.com/2017/10/31/world/europe/ukraine-manafort-indictment-yanukovych.html?searchResultPosition=6.

1348 *Id.*

1349 *Verkhovna Rada of Ukraine*, http://w1.c1.rada.gov.ua/pls/zweb2/webproc4_1?pf3511=62858.

1350 "Manafort Involved in Two PGO Investigations." *Ukrinform*, 31 Oct. 2017, https://www.ukrinform.net/rubric-society/2334945-manafort-involved-in-two-pgo-investigations-prosecutor.html.

1351 "GPU prepares New US Requests for Manafort – Gorbatiuk." *Radio Svoboda*, 2 Nov. 2017, https://www.radiosvoboda.org/a/news/28831844.html.

1352 Stern, David. "Kiev Is Buzzing about the Manafort Indictment." *Politico*, 7 Nov. 2017, https://www.politico.com/magazine/story/2017/11/07/paul-manafort-indictment-kiev-russia-215798.

1353 @realDonaldTrump. "When will all the haters and fools out there realize that having a good relationship with Russia is a good thing, not a bad thing. There always playing politics - bad for our country. I want to solve North Korea, Syria, Ukraine, terrorism, and Russia can greatly help!" *Twitter*, 11 Nov. 2017, 7:18 p.m., https://twitter.com/realDonaldTrump/status/929503641014112256.

1354 @realDonaldTrump. "Does the Fake News Media remember when Crooked Hillary Clinton, as Secretary of State, was begging Russia to be our friend with the misspelled reset button? Obama tried also, but he had zero chemistry with Putin." *Twitter*, 12 Nov. 2017, https://twitter.com/realDonaldTrump/status/929509950811881472?ref_src=twsrc%5Etfw%7Ctwcamp%5Etweetembed%7Ctwterm%5E929509950811881472&ref_url=http%3A%2F%2Fdidtrumptweetit.com%2F2017%2F11%2F11.

1355 "Ukraine's Anticorruption Bureau investigating Prosecutor-General." *RFE/RL*, 17 Nov. 2017, https://www.rferl.org/a/ukraine-prosecutor-general-anticorruption-bureau-probe/28859662.html.

1356 Zinets, Natalia. "Ukraine Prosecutors Open Case as Inter-Agency Conflict Escalates." *Reuters*, 17 Nov. 2017, https://www.reuters.com/article/us-ukraine-corruption/ukraine-prosecutors-open-case-as-inter-agency-conflict-escalates-idUSKBN1DH1NE.

1357 "Trump's Adviser Giuliani Arrived in Kharkiv." *112UA*, 19 Nov. 2017, https://112.international/society/trumps-adviser-giuliani-arrived-in-kharkiv-22830.html.

1358 "Vitali Klitschko with Rudolf Giuliani Visited Kiev Data Center and Discussed Security Cooperation." *City of Kiev*, 21 Nov. 2017, https://kyivcity.gov.ua/news/vitaliy_klichko_z_rudolfom_dzhuliani_vidvidali_kivskiy_data-tsentr_ta_obgovorili_spivpratsyu_u_sferi_bezpeki.html.

1359 *Id.*

1360 "Dep. of Marie Yovanovich," p. 54, l. 5, p. 55, l. 7.

1361 *Id.*

1362 Mazzetti, Lipton, and Kramer. "Inside Ukraine's Push to Cultivate Trump from the Start."

1363 "President Met with Former Mayor of New York City Rudolph Giuliani." *President of Ukraine*, 22 Nov. 2017, https://web.archive.org/web/20180528094016/http://www.president.gov.ua/en/news/prezident-zustrivsya-iz-kolishnim-merom-nyu-jorka-rudolfom-d-44562.

1364 *Id.*

1365 *Id.*

1366 Mazzetti, Lipton, and Kramer, "Inside Ukraine's Push to Cultivate Trump from the Start."

1367 Holub, Andriy. "Shadow-Boxing: Kramer vs Lutsenko." *Ukrainian Week*, 17 May 2018, https://ukrainianweek.com/Politics/214025.

1368 *Id.*

1369 *Id*

1370 *Id.*

1371 "Semi-Annual Report ENGAGE." *USAID*, p. 25, https://pdf.usaid.gov/pdf_docs/PA00T3RB.pdf.

1372 "Dep. of Catherine Croft," pp. 38–39.

1373 *Id.*

1374 Nauert, Heather. "Committing to the Fight against Corruption in Ukraine." *US Department of State*, 4 Dec. 2017, https://web.archive.org/web/20171205023753/https://www.state.gov/r/pa/prs/ps/2017/12/276235.htm.

1375 The link to the atate press release goes to an Archive.org link. This is because at some time in 2019, all press releases relating to Ukraine from the beginning of the Trump dministration until February 2018 were completely deleted from the State Department's website, a potential violation of federal record-keeping laws. Preliminary review of the Archive.org website indicates it occurred during the period Giuliani was trying to obtain information to slander Joe Biden. Other 2018 press releases remain.

1376 Melkozerova, Veronika. "West Backs NABU in Conflict with Prosecutor General's Office." *Kyiv Post*, 6 Dec. 2017, https://www.kyivpost.com/ukraine-politics/west-backs-nabu-conflict-prosecutor-generals-office.html.

1377 Goldstein's bio was scrubbed from State's website as well.

1378 Calia, Mike, and Dan Mangan."White House Fires Top Tillerson Aide Who Contradicted Account of Secretary of State's Dismissal." *CNBC*, 13 March 2018,https://www.cnbc.com/2018/03/13/white-house-fires-top-tillerson-aide-who-contradicted-account-of-secretary-of-states-dismissal.html.

1379 "RPR Calls on the Authorities to Stop the Attack on NABU and Other Anti-Corruption Authorities." *Reanimation Package of Reforms*, 6 Dec. 2017, https://rpr.org.ua/en/news/rpr-calls-on-the-authorities-to-stop-the-attack-on-nabu-and-other-anti-corruption-authorities/.

1380 *Id.*

1381 "From Paul Manafort to Donald Trump's Fateful Phonecall." *The Ecomomist*, 9 Oct. 2019, https://www.economist.com/briefing/2019/10/12/from-paul-manafort-to-donald-trumps-fateful-phonecall.

1382 Sukhov, Oleg. "With No Progress to Show, Lutsenko Attacks Enemies." *Kyiv Post*, 7 Dec. 2017, https://www.kyivpost.com/ukraine-politics/no-progress-show-lutsenko-attacks-enemies.html.

1383 Wood, "Trump Lawyer 'Paid by Ukraine to Arrange White House Talks.'"

1384 *Id.*

1385 "Ambassador Chaly Hopes to Reconcile NABU and GPU in Washington." *UA112*, 4 Dec. 2017, https://112.ua/politika/posol-chalyy-nadeetsya-pomirit-nabu-i-gpu-v-vashingtone-423314.html.

1386 Media Note, "United States and United Kingdom Host Global Forum on Asset Recovery." *Office of the Spokesperson, US Department of State*, 4 Dec. 2017, https://www.state.gov/united-states-and-united-kingdom-host-global-forum-on-asset-recovery/.

1387 *Id.*

1388 @ANTAC_ua. "Artem Sytnyk at #GFAR2017 : It may be the last time you see me in the capacity of the Director of NABU, but I want to assure you that we stay committed to fighting corruption and subsequent asset recovery." *Twitter,* 6 Dec. 2017, https://twitter.com/ANTAC_ua/status/938518930077952921 7.

1389 Holub, "Shadow Boxing: Kramer v. Lutsenko."

1390 *Id.*

1391 *Id.*

1392 "Court Cancels Kholodnytsky's Decision to Suspend Probe into Regions Party's 'Black Ledger.'"

1393 Cheretsky, Victor. "Will Spain Extradite Fugitive People's Deputy Onyschenko to Ukraine?" *Deutsche Welle*, 24 July 2019, https://www.dw.com/uk/a-44786090

1394 *Id.*

1395 Musaeva, Sevgil. "Onishchenko's Films a Year Later. What Did the President and Businessman Talk about at Bankova?" *Ukrayinska Pravda*, 14 Dec. 2017, https://www.pravda.com.ua/rus/articles/2017/12/14/7165467/.

1396 *Id.*

1397 "US Says It Will Enhance Ukraine's Defensive Capabilities; Russia Derides Move." *RFE/RL,* 22 Dec. 2017, https://www.rferl.org/a/us-ukraine-enhanced-weapons-javelin-missiles-russia-separatists/28934551.html.

1398 Rogin, Josh. "Trump Administration Approves Lethal Arms Sales to Ukraine." *Washington Post*, 20 Dec. 2017, https://www.washingtonpost.com/news/josh-rogin/wp/2017/12/20/trump-administration-approves-lethal-arms-sales-to-ukraine/.

1399 *Id.*

1400 Martin, Jim. "GE Transportation Trying to Reinvent Erie Locomotive Works." *Washington Times*, 23 July 2016, https://www.washingtontimes.com/news/2016/jul/23/ge-transportation-trying-to-reinvent-erie-locomoti/?utm_source=GOOGLE&utm_medium=cpc&utm_id=newsroom&utm_campaign=TWT+-+DSA&gclid=CjwKCAiAy9jyBRA6EiwAeclQhIeKYqLAwLo8JP2vhkTeRo-MOFWMRj98XCMzDfmFcgIiiKq6_ESlchoCO-YQAvD_BwE.

1401 *Id.*

1402 Pomerantz, Dorothy. "Next Stop, Kyiv: Ukrainian Railways' $1 Billion Deal With GE Is Set To Dispatch Its Trains Into the Future." *GE Reports*, 23 Feb. 2018, https://www.ge.com/reports/next-stop-kyiv-ukraines-railways-1-billion-deal-ge-set-dispatch-trains-future/.

1403 *Id.*

1404 "Ukrzaliznytsia, GE sign 15-Year Contract Worth $1 bln on Delivery of Locomotives, Their Localization and Maintenance." *Interfax-Ukraine*, 23 Feb. 2018, https://en.interfax.com.ua/news/economic/487415.html.

1405 *Id.*

1406 Moore, Daniel. "Wabtec Earnings Rise as Investors Parse GE Deal." *Pittsburgh Post-Gazette*, 3 July 2018, https://www.post-gazette.com/business/tech-news/2018/07/24/Wabtec-earnings-rise-GE-Transportation-locomotive-rail-freight/stories/201807240085.

1407 *Id.*

1408 "Westinghouse Expands Ukraine Presence with New Nuclear Fuel Deal." *Retuers*, 23 Jan. 2018, https://www.reuters.com/article/uk-ukraine-power-westinghouse/westinghouse-expands-ukraine-presence-with-new-nuclear-fuel-deal-idUSKBN1FI0V5.

1409 "Ukraine Signs Westinghouse Nuclear Fuel Deal." *Nuclear Power Daily*, 30 Dec. 2014, https://www.nuclearpowerdaily.com/reports/Ukraine_signs_Westinghouse_nuclear_fuel_deal_999.html.

1410 "Timeline: Westinghouse Electric Co." *Pittsburgh Business Journal*, 17 March 2017, https://www.bizjournals.com/pittsburgh/news/2017/03/29/timeline-westinghouse-electric-co.html.

1411 *Id.*

CHAPTER 7 THE FATAL STAIN

1412 Hofsteader, Richard. "The Paranoid Style in American Politics." *Harper's Magazine*, Nov. 1964, https://harpers.org/archive/1964/11/the-paranoid-style-in-american-politics/?single=1.

1413 *Id.*

1414 "Trump Approval Ratings." *Five Thirty Eight*, https://projects.fivethirtyeight.com/trump-approval-ratings/.

1415 Davis, Julie Hirschfeld, and Nicholas Fandos. "Trump Sidesteps Question on Mueller Interview." *New York Times*, 10 Jan. 2018, https://www.nytimes.com/2018/01/10/us/politics/trump-russia-election-interference.html?searchResultPosition=53.

1416 *Id.*

1417 *Id.*

1418 "Putin's Asymmetric Assault on Democracy in Russia and Europe: Implications for US National Security." 10 Jan. 2018, https://www.foreign.senate.gov/imo/media/doc/Cardin%20Russia%20Report%20Embargoed%20Committee%20Print.pdf.

1419 *Id.* at *passim.*

1420 @realDonaldTrump. "The single greatest Witch Hunt in American history continues. There was no collusion, everybody including the Dems knows there was no collusion, & yet on and on it goes. Russia & the world is laughing at the stupidity they are witnessing. Republicans should finally take control!" *Twitter,* 10 Jan. 2018, https://twitter.com/realDonaldTrump/status/951109942685126656.

1421 Kramer, David J. at *passim.*

1422 *Id.*

1423 *Id.* pp. 31–2.

1424 *Id.*

1425 *Id.* pp. 33–4.

1426 *Id.*

1427 "Letter from Lawrence Robbins to Reps. K. Michael Conaway and Adam Schiff." *Permanent Select Committee on Intelligence*, 5 Jan. 2018, p. 2, https://intelligence.house.gov/uploadedfiles/dkletter2.pdf.

1428 "Letter from Lawrence Robbins to Reps. K. Michael Conaway and Adam Schiff." p. 1.

1429 *Id.*

1430 *Id.*

1431 "Letter from Lawrence Robbins to Reps. K. Michael Conaway and Adam Schiff."

1432 *Id.* p. 2.

1433 "Letter from Lawrence Robbins to Reps. K. Michael Conaway and Adam Schiff." p. 2.

1434 Kramer, David J. pp. 11-12.

1435 *Id.*

1436 *Id.*

1437 *Id.*

1438 *Id.*

1439 *Id.* pp. 21–22.

1440 *Id.* pp. 21–24.

1441 Demirjian, Karoun, and Matt Zapotosky. "Top FBI, DOJ Officials Huddle with Ryan to Talk Dossier." *Washington Post*, 4 Jan. 2018, https://www.washingtonpost.com/powerpost/top-fbi-doj-officials-huddle-with-ryan-to-talk-dossier/2018/01/03/20384336-f0e0-11e7-b3bf-ab90a706e175_story.html.

[1442] LaFraniere, Sharon, Mark Mazzetti, and Matt Apuzzo. "How the Russia Inquiry Began: A Campaign Aide, Drinks and Talk of Political Dirt." *New York Times*, 30 Dec. 2017, https://www.nytimes.com/2017/12/30/us/politics/how-fbi-russia-investigation-began-george-papadopoulos.html?searchResultPosition=29.

[1443] Fandos, Nicholas. "House Intelligence Panel Is Rushing to Complete Russia Probe." *New York Times*, 15 Dec. 2017, https://www.nytimes.com/2017/12/15/us/politics/house-intelligence-committee-russia-interference.html?searchResultPosition=32.

[1444] Savage, Charlie, Eileen Sullivan, and Nicholas Fandos. "House Extends Surveillance Law, Rejecting New Privacy Safeguards." *New York Times*, 11 Jan. 2018, https://www.nytimes.com/2018/01/11/us/politics/fisa-surveillance-congress-trump.html?searchResultPosition=6.

[1445] @realDonaldTrump. ""House votes on controversial FISA ACT today." This is the act that may have been used, with the help of the discredited and phony Dossier, to so badly surveil and abuse the Trump Campaign by the previous administration and others?" *Twitter*, 11 Jan. 2018, https://twitter.com/realDonaldTrump/status/951431836030459905?ref_src=twsrc%5Etfw%7Ctwcamp%5Etweetembed%7Ctwterm%5E951431836030459905&ref_url=https%3A%2F%2Fwww.nytimes.com%2F2018%2F01%2F11%2Fus%2Fpolitics%2Ffisa-surveillance-congress-trump.html.

[1446] Savage, Sullivan, and Fandos, "House extends Surveillance Law, Rejecting New Privacy Safeguards."

[1447] Schmit, Michael S. "Bannon Is Subpoenaed in Mueller's Investigation." *New York Times*, 16 Jan. 2018, https://www.nytimes.com/2018/01/16/us/politics/steve-bannon-mueller-russia-subpoena.html?searchResultPosition=140.

[1448] Freifeld, Karen, Patricia Zengerle, "Trump Ex-Aide Bannon agrees to Mueller Probe Interview, avoiding Grand Jury." *Reuters*, 17 Jan. 2018, https://www.reuters.com/article/us-usa-trump-russia/trump-ex-aide-bannon-agrees-to-mueller-probe-interview-avoiding-grand-jury-idUSKBN1F61Y7.

[1449] Savage, Charlie, and Sharon LaFraniere. "Republicans Claim Surveillance Power Abuses in Russia Inquiry." *New York Times*, 19 Jan. 2018, https://www.nytimes.com/2018/01/19/us/politics/republicans-s urveillance-trump-russia-inquiry.html?searchResultPosition=6.

[1450] *Id.*

[1451] *Id.*

[1452] Savage, Charlie, Nicholas Fandos, and Adam Goldman. "FBI Texts and Dueling Memos Escalate Fight over Russia Inquiry." *New York Times*, 24 Jan. 2018, https://www.nytimes.com/2018/01/24/us/politics/devin-nunes-fbi-russia.html?searchResultPosition=2.

[1453] Bertrand, Natasha. "Russia-Linked Twitter Accounts Are Working Overtime to Help Devin Nunes and WikiLeaks." *Business Insider*, 19 Jan. 2018, https://www.businessinsider.com/release-the-memo-campaign-russia-linked-twitter-accounts-2018-1.

[1454] *Id.*

[1455] Fandos, Nicholas, and Adam Goldman. "Trump Clears Way for Secret Memo's Release." *New York Times*, 1 Feb. 2018, https://www.nytimes.com/2018/02/01/us/politics/republicans-secret-memo-nunes.html?searchResultPosition=7.

[1456] Nunes, Devin. "Read the GOP Memo." 18 Jan. 2018, p 2, https://apps.washingtonpost.com/g/documents/national/read-the-gop-memo/2746/.

1457 Henry, Ed. "Democratic Sen. Mark Warner Texted with Russian Oligarch Lobbyist in Effort to Contact Dossier Author Christopher Steele." *Fox News*, 8 Feb. 2018, https://www.foxnews.com/politics/democratic-sen-mark-warner-texted-with-russian-oligarch-lobbyist-in-effort-to-contact-dossier-author-christopher-steele.

1458 *Id.*

1459 *Id.*

1460 @realDonaldTrump. "Wow! -Senator Mark Warner got caught having extensive contact with a lobbyist for a Russian oligarch. Warner did not want a "paper trail" on a "private" meeting (in London) he requested with Steele of fraudulent Dossier fame. All tied into Crooked Hillary." *Twitter*, 8 Feb. 2018, https://twitter.com/realDonaldTrump/status/961802557646569475.

1461 Fandos, Nicholas. "Senate Intelligence Leaders Say House GOP Leaked a Senator's Texts." *New York Times*, 1 March 2018, https://www.nytimes.com/2018/03/01/us/politics/senate-intelligence-nunes-leaks.html?searchResultPosition=5.

1462 House, Billy. "Democrats' Memo Released Countering GOP Russia Probe Account." *Time*, 24 Feb. 2018, https://time.com/5174387/democrats-memo-released/.

1463 Romanyshyn, Yuliana. "Investigation Unveils Poroshenko's Secret Vacation in Maldives." *Kyiv Post*, 19 Jan. 2018, https://www.kyivpost.com/ukraine-politics/investigation-unveils-poroshenkos-secret-vacation-maldives.html.

1464 Schemes is paid for and hosted on a US government website, *Radio Svboda* as part of US public diplomacy. It uses slick graphics and editing and uses US-style investigative techniques.

1465 Tkach, Mykhailo, Natalie Sedltska. "Petro Incognito." *Kyiv Post*, 19 Jan. 2018, https://www.kyivpost.com/ukraine-politics/petro-incognito-poroshenkos-secret-holidays.html.

1466 *Id.*

1467 *Id.*

1468 *Id.*

1469 *Id.*

1470 Melkozerova, Veronika. "Poroshenko Comes in 4th Place in Presidential Poll." *Kyiv Post*, 20 March 2018, https://www.kyivpost.com/ukraine-politics/poroshenko-comes-4th-place-presidential-poll.html.

1471 *Id.*

1472 *Id.*

1473 Bonner, Brian. "Biden Chronicles His Frustrations with Ukraine's Corruption in New Book." *Kyiv Post*, 22 Dec. 2017, https://www.kyivpost.com/ukraine-politics/biden-chronicles-frustrations-ukraines-corruption-new-book.html.

1474 *Id.*

1475 *Id.*

1476 "Ukrainian Prosecutor General: Yanukovych's 1st Trial Will be Immediately Followed by 2nd." *Kyiv Post*, 3 Feb. 2018, https://www.kyivpost.com/ukraine-politics/ukrainian-prosecutor-general-yanukovychs-1st-trial-will-be-immediately-followed-2nd.html.

1477 "Open Court Hearings over Organizers of Euromaidan Killings to be held Soon,—Ukraine's Prosecutor General." *112 Ukraine*, 12 Feb. 2018, https://112.international/ukraine-top-news/open-court-hearings-over-organizers-of-euromaidan-killings-to-be-held-soon-ukraines-prosecutor-general-25755.html.

1478 Krasnikov, Denys. "Poroshenko Promises Personal Involvement in EuroMaidan Investigation." *Kyiv Post*, https://www.kyivpost.com/ukraine-politics/poroshenko-promises-personal-involvement-euromaidan-investigation.html.

1479 Biden, Jr., Joseph R., and Michael Carpenter. "How to Stand up to the Kremlin." *Foreign Affairs*, 5 Dec. 2017, https://www.foreignaffairs.com/articles/2017-12-05/how-stand-kremlin.

1480 *Id.*

1481 "Foreign Affairs Issue Launch with Former Vice President Joe Biden." *Council on Foreign Affairs*, 23 Jan. 2018, https://www.cfr.org/event/foreign-affairs-issue-launch-former-vice-president-joe-biden.

1482 *Id.*

1483 "Shokin's Daughter Sues Joe Biden." *Ukrayinska Pravda*, 5 Feb. 2018, https://www.pravda.com.ua/news/2018/02/5/7170643/.

1484 Tweet of Alina Shokin (Feb. 4, 2018). https://twitter.com/alina_oneworld/status/960191024269176832

1485 Tweet of Alina Shokin (Feb. 4, 2018). https://twitter.com/alina_oneworld/status/960193088026066945 [both of these links are dead and it looks like she may have left Twitter]

1486 "Shokin's Daughter Sues Joe Biden."

1487 Rudenko, Olga. "Shokin's Daughter to Sue Biden for 'Insulting Her Family.'" *Kyiv Post*, 6 Feb. 2018, https://www.kyivpost.com/ukraine-politics/shokins-daughter-sue-biden-insulting-family.html.

1488 "Former Prosecutor General Viktor Shokin responds to Joe Biden's Insult." *Front News International*, 5 Feb. 2018, http://frontnews.eu/news/en/22961.

1489 "Ukraine's Ex-Prosecutor General Viktor Shokin Applies to be Reinstated in his Office." *112 Ukraine*, 28 March 2017, https://112.international/politics/ukraines-ex-prosecutor-general-viktor-shokin-applies-to-be-reinstated-in-his-office-15491.html.

1490 "Higher Administrative Court Dismisses Shokin's Lawsuit against Poroshenko, Rada." *Kyiv Post*, 20 April 2017, https://www.kyivpost.com/ukraine-politics/higher-administrative-court-dismisses-shokins-lawsuit-poroshenko-rada.html.

1491 "Shokin Can Regain Chair of the Attorney General through the Court." *Front News*, 8 July 2017, http://www.frontnews.eu/news/en/6699/Shokin-can-regain-chair-of-the-Attorney-General-through-the-court.

1492 LaFraniere, Sharon, and Nicholas Fandos. "How Partisan Has House Intelligence Panel become? It's Building a Wall." *New York Times*, 8 Feb. 2018, https://www.nytimes.com/2018/02/08/us/politics/house-intelligence-committee-russia-nunes.html.

1493 Fandos, Nicholas. "Committee Votes to Release Democratic Rebuttal to GOP Russia Memo." *New York Times*, 5 Feb. 2018, https://www.nytimes.com/2018/02/05/us/politics/democratic-memo-adam-schiff-trump.html.

1494 House, Billy. "Democrats' Memo Released Countering GOP Russia Probe Account." *Time*, 24 Feb. 2018, https://time.com/5174387/democrats-memo-released/.

1495 "Grand Jury indicts Thirteen Russian Individuals and Three Russian Companies for Scheme to interfere in the United States Political System." *United States Department of Justice*, 16 Feb. 2018, https://www.justice.gov/opa/pr/grand-jury-indicts-thirteen-russian-individuals-and-three-russian-companies-scheme-interfere.

1496 *Id.*

1497 Polantz, Katlyn. "Exclusive: New signs Gates may be negotiating with Mueller's Team" *CNN* (Jan. 23, 2018). https://www.cnn.com/2018/01/23/politics/rick-gates-new-attorney-mueller-russia-investigation/index.html

1498 Kevin Breuninger, "Former Trump Campaign Official Rick Gates pleads Guilty to Lying and Conspiracy against the United States" *CNBC* (Feb. 23, 2018). https://www.cnbc.com/2018/02/23/former-trump-campaign-official-rick-gates-pleads-guilty-on-two-counts.html

1499 *Id.*

1500 Dan Mangan, "Mueller Hits Former Trump Campaign Officials Manafort, Gates with New Indictment." *CNBC*, 22 Feb. 2018, https://www.cnbc.com/2018/02/22/mueller-hits-manafort-gates-with-20-more-charges-than-initial-indictment.html.

1501 Breuninger, "Former Trump Campaign Official Rick Gates pleads Guilty to Lying and Conspiracy against the United States."

1502 Helderman, Rosalind S. "Clue in Mueller Filing Suggests Manafort Kept Working on Topic of Interest to Russia After Indictment." *Washington Post*, 17 Jan. 2019, https://www.washingtonpost.com/politics/clue-in-mueller-filing-suggests-manafort-kept-working-on-topic-of-interest-to-russia-after-indictment/2019/01/17/cae37626-19e7-11e9-88fe-f9f77a3bcb6c_story.html.

1503 *Id.*

1504 Shrek, Carl. "'We're In Trouble': Rancor Rules at Munich Security Conference." *RFE/RL*, 18 Feb. 2018, https://www.rferl.org/a/munich-security-conference-rancor-ukraine-iran-russia-ischinger-lavrov-gabriel/29046944.html.

1505 *Id.*

1506 *Id.*

1507 Office of International Affairs, US Dept. of Energy, "US Department of Energy Deputy Secretary Dan Brouillette Visits with Key Officials in Europe." *Office of International Affairs, US Dept. of Energy*, 20 Feb. 2018, https://www.energy.gov/ia/articles/us-department-energy-deputy-secretary-dan-brouillette-visits-key-officials-europe.

1508 *Id.*

1509 "Amendment to Registration Statement of Yorktown Solutions" pp. 30–95.

1510 *Id.* p. 46.

1511 *Id.* pp. 30–95.

1512 "Press Release 18-02." *Defense Security Cooperation Agency*, 1 March 2018, https://dsca.mil/major-arms-sales/ukraine-javelin-missiles-and-command-launch-units.

1513 Kerr, Paul. "Arms Sales: Congressional Review Process." *Congressional Research Service,* 3 March 2020, https://fas.org/sgp/crs/weapons/RL31675.pdf .

1514 "Germany Calls for Setting Up UN Peacekeeping Mission in Ukraine before Russian Election." *RFE/RL,* 4 Jan. 2018, https://www.rferl.org/a/germany-gabriel-calls-setting-up-un-peacekeeping-mission-ukraine-before-russian-presidential-election/28954057.html.

1515 @realDonaldTrump. "Why is A.G. Jeff Sessions asking the Inspector General to investigate potentially massive FISA abuse. Will take forever, has no prosecutorial power and already late with reports on Comey etc. Isn't the I.G. an Obama guy? Why not use Justice Department lawyers? DISGRACEFUL!" *Twitter*, 28 Feb. 2018, https://twitter.com/realDonaldTrump/status/968856971075051521.

1516 Fandos, "Senate Intelligence Leaders say House G.O.P. Leaked a Senator's Texts."

1517 "The GRU Globetrotters: Mission London." *Bellingcat,* 28 June 2019, https://www.bellingcat.com/news/uk-and-europe/2019/06/28/the-gru-globetrotters-mission-london/.

1518 *Id.*

1519 *Id.*

1520 *Id.*

1521 *Id.*

1522 *Id.*

1523 *Id.*

1524 *Id.*

1525 *Id.*

1526 *Id.*

1527 *Id.*

1528 Higgins, Eliot. "God-Level Trolling—Russian Ministry of Foreign Affairs Spokesperson Maria Zakharova Promotes Debunked Internet Conspiracy Theories on the Skripal Nerve Attack." *Bellingcat*, 6 Sept. 2018, https://www.bellingcat.com/news/uk-and-europe/2018/09/06/god-level-trolling-russian-ministry-foreign-affairs-spokesperson-maria-zakharova-promotes-debunked-internet-conspiracy-theories-skripal-nerve-agent-attack/.

1529 The GRU Globetrotters: Mission London."

1530 *Id.*

1531 *Id.*

1532 *Id.*

1533 Moran, Terry, Chris Vlasto, and James Gordon Meek. "Russian Ex-Spy's Poisoning in UK Believed from Nerve Agent in Car Vents; At Least 38 Others Sickened: Sources." *ABC News,* 18 March 2018, https://abcnews.go.com/International/russian-spys-poisoning-uk-believed-nerve-agent-car/story?id=53832515.

1534 Lamont, "Inside the poisoning of a Russian Double Agent."

1535 *Id.*

1536 *Id.*

1537 *Id.*

1538 *Id.*

1539 Peplow, Mark. "Nerve Agent Attack on Spy used 'Novichok' Poison." *Chemical & Engineering News,* 13 March, 2018, https://cen.acs.org/articles/96/i12/Nerve-agent-attack-on-spy-used-Novichok-poison.htmll.

1540 *Id.*

1541 Price, Greg. "Poisoned Russian Spy Linked to Trump-Russia Dossier Author Christopher Steele through Security Consultant." *Newsweek*, 8 Mar. 2018, https://www.newsweek.com/russia-poison-spy-steele-dossier-836768.

1542 Fandos, Nicholas. "Despite Mueller's Push, House Republicans Declare No Evidence of Collusion." *New York Times*, 13 March 2017, https://www.nytimes.com/2018/03/12/us/politics/house-intelligence-trump-russia.html?searchResultPosition=20.

1543 *Id.*

1544 *Id.*

1545 *Id.*

1546 Beavers, Olivia, and Katie Bo Williams. "House GOP Ending Russia Probe, Says No Collusion Found." *The Hill,* 12 March 2018, https://thehill.com/policy/national-security/378017-house-gop-ending-russia-probe-says-no-collusion-found.

1547 *Id.*

1548 Cooper, Sam. "'Canadian Eyes Only' Intelligence Reports Say Canadian Leaders Attacked in Cyber Campaigns." *Global News*, 10 Dec. 2019, https://globalnews.ca/news/6258755/intelligence-reports-canadian-leaders-attacked-cyber-campaigns/.

1549 O'Neil, James. "The Strange Case of the Russian Spy Poisoning." *Consortium News*, 13 March 2018, https://consortiumnews.com/2018/03/13/the-strange-case-of-the-russian-spy-poisoning/.

1550 @TheOliverStone. "James O'Neill's take on #Skripal poisoning makes most sense and connects it to today's horror show." *Twitter*, 19 March 2018, 1:51 p.m., https://twitter.com/search?q=https%3A%2F%2Fconsortiumnews.com%2F2018%2F03%2F13%2Fthe-strange-case-of-the-russian-spy-poisoning%2F&src=typeahead_click

1551 "Report on Russian Active Measures." *House Permanent Select Committee on Intelligence*, 22 March 2018, pp. 46-47, https://docs.house.gov/meetings/IG/IG00/20180322/108023/HRPT-115-1_1-p1-U3.pdf.

1552 *Id.* pp. 77-79.

1553 Pérez-Peña, Richard. "Britain Expels 23 Russian Diplomats over Ex-Spy's Poisoning." *New York Times*, 14 March 2018, https://www.nytimes.com/2018/03/14/world/europe/uk-russia-spy-punitive-measures.html.

1554 Schwirtz, Michael. "Diplomatic Fireworks at UN Over Britain-Russia Feud." *New York Times*, 14 March 2018, https://www.nytimes.com/2018/03/14/world/europe/russia-britain-poisoning-security-council.html.

1555 Rogers, Katie, and Eileen Sullivan. "Trump and Western Allies Expel Scores of Russians in Sweeping Rebuke over UK Poisoning." *New York Times*, 26 March 2018, https://www.nytimes.com/2018/03/26/world/europe/trump-russia-diplomats-expulsion.html.

1556 Baker, Peter. "White House Penalizes Russians over Election Meddling and Cyberattacks." *New York Times*, 15 March 2018, https://www.nytimes.com/2018/03/15/us/politics/trump-russia-sanctions.html.

1557 Williams, Abigail, and Rachel Elbaum. "Tillerson says UK Spy Poisoning 'Clearly' Came from Russia." *NBC News* 13 March 2018, https://www.nbcnews.com/news/world/tillerson-says-u-k-spy-poisoning-clearly-came-russia-n856056 .

1558 @realDonaldTrump. "Mike Pompeo, Director of the CIA, will become our new Secretary of State. He will do a fantastic job! Thank you to Rex Tillerson for his service! Gina Haspel will become the new Director of the CIA, and the first woman so chosen. Congratulations to all!" *Twitter*, 13 March 2018, https://twitter.com/realDonaldTrump/status/973540316656623616?ref_src=twsrc%5Etfw%7Ctwcamp%5Etweetembed%7Ctwterm%5E973540316656623616&ref_url=https%3A%2F%2Fwww.nytimes.com%2F2018%2F03%2F13%2Fus%2Fpolitics%2Ftrump-tillerson-pompeo.html.

1559 *Id.*

1560 Gladstone, Rick. "Tillerson's Firing Had Been Expected, But It Still Stunned Observers." *New York Times,* 22 March 2018, https://www.nytimes.com/2018/03/13/world/americas/tillerson-trump-reaction-world.html?searchResultPosition=12.

1561 *Id.*

1562 Gardiner Harris, "Tillerson Says Goodbye to 'a Very Mean-Spirited Town.'" *New York Times*, 22 March 2018, https://www.nytimes.com/2018/03/22/us/politics/tillerson-farewell-state-department-tweet.html?searchResultPosition=9.

1563 Calia and Mangan, "White House Fires Top Tillerson Aide Who Contradicted Account of Secretary of State's Dismissal."

1564 *Id.*

1565 Lander, Mar,k and Maggie Haberman "Trump Chooses Bolton for 3rd Security Adviser as Shake-Up Continues." *New York Times*, 22 March 2018, https://www.nytimes.com/2018/03/22/us/politics/hr-mcmaster-trump-bolton.html?searchResultPosition=18.

1566 *Id.*

1567 Belford, Aubrey, and Veronika Melkozerova. "Meet the Florida Duo Helping Giuliani Investigate for Trump in Ukraine." *Organized Crime and Corruption Reporting Project*, 22 July 2019, https://www.occrp.org/en/investigations/meet-the-florida-duo-helping-giuliani-dig-dirt-for-trump-in-ukraine.

1568 Briman, Shimon. "A Russian-Speaking Businessman Took Part in a Meeting of Trump with Potential Donors of his 2020 Campaign." *Forum Daily*, 6 March 2018, http://www.forumdaily.com/russkoyazychnyj-biznesmen-prinyal-uchastie-vo-vstreche-trampa-s-potencialnymi-donorami-ego-kampanii-2020-goda/.

1569 Bennett, George. "Mar-a-Lago Make up: Trump to Headline March 3 Fundraiser." *Palm Beach Post*, 3 Feb. 2018, https://www.palmbeachpost.com/2018/02/03/mar-a-lago-make-up-trump-to-headline-march-3-fundraiser/.

1570 Belford, Aubrey, and Veronika Melkozerova. "Meet the Florida Duo Helping Giuliani Investigate for Trump in Ukraine." *OCCRP*, 22 July 2019, https://www.occrp.org/en/investigations/meet-the-florida-duo-helping-giuliani-dig-dirt-for-trump-in-ukraine

1571 Most unusually, after the writer discovered this first article and began researching its connections to the Fruman interview that followed the next day, *Forum Daily* pulled the article completely in the Spring of 2020. However, a single scrape of the article was captured by the Internet Archive. It is that copy that is linked to here.

1572 "Ukrainian Oligarch Gives Testimony to the US Justice Department against the President of Ukraine—ForumDaily Exclusive." *Forum Daily* 5 March 2018, https://web.archive.org/web/20190112034403/https://www.forumdaily.com/en/ukrainskij-oligarx-daet-minyustu-ssha-pokazaniya-protiv-prezidenta-ukrainy-eksklyuziv-forumdaily/.

1573 "Fugitive MP Onyshchenko Claims He Secretly Recorded Talks with Poroshenko: Administration Calls out Report as Fake." *UNIAN*, 19 April 2018, https://www.unian.info/politics/10087469-fugitive-mp-onyshchenko-claims-he-secretly-recorded-talks-with-poroshenko-administration-calls-out-report-as-fake.html.

1574 Sukhov, Oleg. "Boersch Withdraws Candidacy for NABU Auditor, becomes Onyshchenko's Lawyer." *Kyiv Post,* 8 Feb. 2018, https://www.kyivpost.com/ukraine-politics/boersch-withdraws-candidacy-nabu-auditor-becomes-onyshchenkos-lawyer.html.

1575 *Id.*

1576 "Ukrainian Oligarch Gives Testimony to the US Justice Department against the President of Ukraine—ForumDaily Exclusive."

1577 *Id.*

1578 Briman, "A Russian-Speaking Businessman Took Part in a Meeting of Trump with Potential Donors of His 2020 Campaign."

1579 *Id.*

1580 *Id.*

1581 *Id.*

1582 *Id.*

1583 Nehamas, Nicholas, Kevin G. Hall, Tess Riski, and Ben Weider. "Meet the Soviet-Born Businessmen Tangled in Trump's Impeachment Inquiry. They Live in Florida." *Miami Herald*, 26 Sept. 2019, https://www.miamiherald.com/news/politics-government/article235501772.html.

1584 Belford and Melkozerova, "Meet the Florida Duo Helping Giuliani Investigate for Trump in Ukraine."

1585 Swan, Betsy. "Paul Manafort and Rudy's Indicted Associate Igor Fruman Go Way, Way Back." *Daily Beast*, 30 Jan. 2020, https://www.thedailybeast.com/paul-manafort-and-rudys-indicted-associate-igor-fruman-go-way-way-back.

1586 Kantchev, Georgi, Rebecca Davis O'Brien, and Joe Palazzolo. "A Businessman's Second Act Upends Giuliani's Ukraine Work for Trump." *Wall Street Journal*, 21 Nov. 2019, https://www.wsj.com/articles/a-businessmans-second-act-upends-giulianis-ukraine-work-for-trump-11574356632.

1587 *Id*.

1588 Hall, Kevin G., and Alexandra Marquez. "Giuliani Associate Made Millions in Ukraine before His US Fortunes Turned." *McClatchy*, 18 Oct. 2019, https://www.mcclatchydc.com/news/politics-government/article236340113.html.

1589 Plotnikov, "Pro-Russia Oligarch Onyshchenko Could Help Destabilize Ukraine and Roil US Politics."

1590 Markay, Lachlan, and Sam Stein. "Did Rudy Pal Igor Fruman Steal another Man's Identity to Make a $100K Campaign Donation?" *Daily Beast*, 17 Oct. 2019, https://www.thedailybeast.com/did-rudy-giuliani-pal-igor-fruman-steal-another-mans-identity-to-make-a-dollar100000-campaign-donation.

1591 *Id*.

1592 "Individual Donor Lookup, Igor Furman." *Open Secrets*, https://www.opensecrets.org/donor-lookup/results?name=Igor+Furman&order=desc&sort=D.

1593 *Id*.

1594 Toobin, Jeffrey. "How Rudy Giuliani Turned into Trump's Clown." *The New Yorker*, 3 Sept. 2018, https://www.newyorker.com/magazine/2018/09/10/how-rudy-giuliani-turned-into-trumps-clown.

1595 Freifield, Karen. "The Mueller Interview that Wasn't: How Trump's Legal Strategy Paid Off." *Reuters*, 26 March 2019, https://www.reuters.com/article/us-usa-trump-russia-interview-insight/the-mueller-interview-that-wasnt-how-trumps-legal-strategy-paid-off-idUSKCN1R72Y9.

1596 *Id*.

1597 Toobin, "How Rudy Giuliani Turned into Trump's Clown."

1598 Freifield, "The Mueller Interview that Wasn't: How Trump's Legal Strategy Paid Off."

1599 *Id*.

1600 Leonnig, Carol D., Josh Dawsey, and Ashley Parker. "Trump Has Trouble Finding Attorneys as Top Russia Lawyer Leaves Legal Team." *Washington Post*, 22 March 2018, https://www.washingtonpost.com/politics/trump-attorney-john-dowd-resigns-amid-shake-up-in-presidents-legal-team/2018/03/22/0472ce74-2de3-11e8-8688-e053ba58f1e4_story.html.

1601 Haberman, Maggie, and Michael S. Schmidt. "Giuliani to Join Trump's Legal Team." *New York Times*, 18 April 2018, https://www.nytimes.com/2018/04/19/us/politics/giuliani-trump.html.

1602 *Id*.

1603 Toobin, "How Giuliani became Trump's Clown."

1604 *Id*.

1605 *Id*.

1606 *Id.*

1607 *Id.*

1608 "FEC Complaint No.7442." *Campaign Legal Center, et al. v. Global Energy Producers, LLC*, 25 July 2018, https://campaignlegal.org/sites/default/files/2018-07/SIGNED%2007-25-18%20GEP%20LLC%20Straw%20Donor%20Complaint.pdf.

1609 "Fugitive MP Onyshchenko Claims He Secretly Recorded Talks with Poroshenko: Administration Calls Out Report as Fake." *Unian*, 19 April 2018, https://www.unian.info/politics/10087469-fugitive-mp-onyshchenko-claims-he-secretly-recorded-talks-with-poroshenko-administration-calls-out-report-as-fake.html.

1610 *Id.*

1611 *Id.*

1612 *Id.*

1613 *Id.*

1614 *Id.*

1615 *Id.*

1616 "Loud Statements, No Specifics: NABU Chief Skeptical about 'Onyshchenko Tapes.'" *Unian*, 25 April 2018, https://www.unian.info/society/10094807-loud-statements-no-specifics-nabu-chief-skeptical-about-onyshchenko-tapes.html.

1617 *Id.*

1618 "Court Cancels Kholodnytsky's Decision to Suspend Probe into Regions Party's 'Black Ledger.'"

1619 *Id.*

1620 Schreckinger, Ben. "'I'm the Real Whistleblower': Giuliani's Quixotic Mission to Help Trump in Ukraine." *Politico*, 27 Sept. 2019, https://www.politico.com/news/2019/09/27/giuliani-trump-ukraine-005098.

1621 *Id.*

1622 *Id.*

1623 Levine, Mike, John Santucci, and Soo Rin Kim. "2nd Tape Shows Trump Meeting with Congressman and Giuliani Sssociates Lev Parnas and Igor Fruman." *ABC News*, 30 Jan. 2020, https://abcnews.go.com/Politics/tape-shows-trump-meeting-congressman-giuliani-associates-lev/story?id=68645435.

1624 Alcindor, Yamiche. "Second Video Demonstrates Lev Parnas' Access to Trump." *PBS News Hour*, 30 Jan. 2020, https://www.pbs.org/newshour/politics/parnas-released-second-video-showing-his-access-to-trump.

1625 *US v. Parnas, et al*. 19 Crim. 725, p. 8, https://www.justice.gov/usao-sdny/pr/lev-parnas-and-igor-fruman-charged-conspiring-violate-straw-and-foreign-donor-bansd.

1626 "Individual Donor Lookup, Igor Furman."

1627 *Id.*

1628 "Ukraine Receives US Javelin Systems: Poroshenko." *Reuters*, 30 April 2018, https://www.reuters.com/article/us-ukraine-jevelin/ukraine-receives-us-javelin-systems-poroshenko-idUSKBN1I11ZY.

1629 Faulders, Katherine, John Santucci, Allison Pecorin, and Olivia Rubin 'Take Her Out': Recording Appears to Capture Trump at Private Dinner Saying He Wants Ukraine Ambassador Fired." *ABC News*, 24 Jan. 2020, https://abcnews.go.com/Politics/recording-appears-capture-trump-private-dinner-ukraine-ambassador/story?id=68506437.

1630 *Id.*

1631 *Id.*

1632 *US v. Parnas, et al.* p. 5.

1633 Winter, Tom, Dan De Luce, and Anna Schecter. "Lutsenko Is Unnamed Ukrainian Who Led Plot to Oust Yovanovitch, Says Official." *NBC News*, 11 Oct. 2019, https://www.nbcnews.com/politics/justice-department/lutsenko-unnamed-ukrainian-who-led-plot-oust-yovanovitch-says-official-n1065246.

1634 Upon Yovanovitch's removal from the position, Lutsenko telephoned reformer Daria Kaleniuk and told her that she had "ти позбулася даху" meaning she had lost her "roof," or protection. See: Andrew E. Kramer, Andrew Higgins and Michael Schwirtz, "The Ukrainian Ex-Prosecutor behind the Impeachment Furor" *New York Times* (Oct. 8, 2019). Accessed at: https://www.nytimes.com/2019/10/05/world/europe/ukraine-prosecutor-trump.html

1635 Briman, Shimon. "Jews of Ukraine Pray for the Success of Donald Trump." *Jewish World*, 10 June 2018, http://evreimir.com/146156/evrei-ukrainy-molyatsya-za-uspeh-donalda-trampa/.

1636 *Id.*

1637 Kramer, "Ukraine, Seeking US Missiles, Halted Cooperation with Manafort Investigation."

BOOK II: THE ZELENSKYY AFFAIR

CHAPTER 8 "A NAME TO A FACE"

1638 *Id.*

1639 *Id.*

1640 *Id.*

1641 *Id.*

¹⁶⁴² Apuzzo, Matt, and Michael S. Schmidt. "Trump Adds Clinton Impeachment Lawyer, Bracing for a Fight on Multiple Fronts." *New York Times,* 2 May 2018, https://www.nytimes.com/2018/05/02/us/politics/emmet-flood-ty-cobb-white-house-lawyer-special-counsel.html?smid=pl-share.

¹⁶⁴³ "Committee Assignments." *Office of Senator Robert Menendez*, https://www.menendez.senate.gov/about/committees.

¹⁶⁴⁴ "Letter from Sens. Robert Menendez, Richard Durbin and Patrick Leahy to Prosecutor General Yuriy Lutsenko." 4 May 2018, https://www.foreign.senate.gov/imo/media/doc/5-4-18%20Menendez%20joint%20letter%20to%20General%20Prosecutor%20of%20Ukraine%20on%20Mueller%20investigation.pdf.

¹⁶⁴⁵ *Id.* p. 1.

¹⁶⁴⁶ *Id.*

¹⁶⁴⁷ Waas, "Ukraine Continued: How a Crucial Witness Escaped."

¹⁶⁴⁸ *Id.*

¹⁶⁴⁹ *Id.*

¹⁶⁵⁰ *Id.*

¹⁶⁵¹ *Id.*

¹⁶⁵² *Id.*

¹⁶⁵³ Kramer, Andrew E. "He Says He's an Innocent Victim. Robert Mueller Says He's a Spy." *New York Times,* 6 April 2018, https://www.nytimes.com/2018/04/06/world/europe/robert-mueller-kilimnik-ukraine-russia-manafort.html?searchResultPosition=33.

¹⁶⁵⁴ Waas. "Ukraine Continued: How a Crucial Witness Escaped."

¹⁶⁵⁵ Briman. "Jews of Ukraine Pray for the Success of Donald Trump."

¹⁶⁵⁶ "Prominent Ukrainian Rabbi Inaugurates Prayer for Trump's Success." *Times of Israel,* 12 May 2018, https://www.timesofisrael.com/prominent-ukrainian-rabbi-inaugurates-prayer-for-trumps-success/.

¹⁶⁵⁷ Schedule A, FEC Form 3X of 35th, Inc. 3 May 2018, https://docquery.fec.gov/cgi-bin/fecimg/?201807139115430792.

¹⁶⁵⁸ Cobler, Paul. "A Timeline of Former Dallas Rep. Pete Sessions' Involvement in the Ukraine Scandal." *Dallas Morning News,* 15 Nov. 2019, https://www.dallasnews.com/news/politics/2019/11/15/a-timeline-of-pete-sessions-involvement-in-the-ukraine-scandal/.

¹⁶⁵⁹ *Id.*

¹⁶⁶⁰ "Letter from Rep. Pete Sessions to Sec. of State Mike Pompeo." 9 May 2018, https://upload.wikimedia.org/wikipedia/commons/8/87/HMKP-116-JU00-20191211-SD9015-imessages.pdf

¹⁶⁶¹ *Id.*

¹⁶⁶² *Id.*

1663 Barrett, Devlin, John Wagner and Rosalind S. Helderman. "Two Business Associates of Trump's Personal Attorney Giuliani Have Been Arrested on Campaign Finance Charges." *Washington Post*, 10 Oct. 2019, https://www.washingtonpost.com/politics/two-business-associates-of-trumps-personal-lawyer-giuliani-have-been-arrested-and-are-in-custody/2019/10/10/9f9c101a-eb63-11e9-9306-47cb0324fd44_story.html.

1664 *US v. Parnas, et al.* 19 Crim. 725 p. 6.

1665 As indicated in Book I, Poroshenko sued on the basis that he had bribed Cohen and the BBC settled the case and withdrew the story. Subsequent reporting has confirmed Wood's reporting. The two persons who opened the back channel who denied doing so would likely be Lev Parnas and Igor Fruman.

1666 Wood, "Trump Lawyer 'Paid by Ukraine' to Arrange White House Talks."

1667 *Id.*

1668 *Id.*

1669 *Id.*

1670 *Id.*

1671 *Id.*

1672 *Id.*

1673 *Id.*

1674 *Id.*

1675 The State Department's Bureau of Intelligence and Research is legally a member of the US Intelligence Community. See: https://www.state.gov/bureaus-offices/bureaus-and-offices-reporting-directly-to-the-secretary/bureau-of-intelligence-and-research/

1676 *Id.*

1677 *Id.*

1678 *Id.*

1679 Trump's meeting with Poroshenko on the sidelines of the U.N. occurred in September 2017.

1680 *Id.*

1681 *Id.*

1682 *Id.*

1683 *Id.*

1684 Strohecker, Karin. "Ukraine Anti-Corruption Court Can Start Work Early 2019: Prosecutor." *Reuters*, 3 May 2018, https://www.reuters.com/article/us-ukraine-corruption-court/ukraine-anti-corruption-court-can-start-work-early-2019-prosecutor-idUSKBN1I40VF.

1685 Leonova, Maria. "GPU Did Not 'Freeze' Manafort's Case and Offered the United States a Joint Investigation—Lutsenko." *Hromadske*, 23 May 2018, https://hromadske.ua/posts/hpu-ne-zamorozhuvala-spravu-manaforta-ta-zaproponuvala-ssha-spilne-rozsliduvannia-lutsenko.

1686 Kovensky, Josh. "Poroshenko Paying for Access to Trump Sounds Believable to Some." *Kyiv Post*, 24 May 2018, https://www.kyivpost.com/ukraine-politics/poroshenko-administration-paid-for-trump-access-bbc-report-alleges.html.

1687 *Id.*

1688 CASE No. 757/22213/18-K *Kyiv Court of Appeal*, http://www.apcourtkiev.gov.ua/CourtPortal.WebSite/Home/Sprava/38121698526.

1689 *United States v. Paul Manafort, Jr. et al.* Crim. 17-201, 8 June 2018, https://www.justice.gov/file/1070326/download.

1690 *Id.* p. 1.

1691 *Id.* p. 23.

1692 *Id.* p. 3.

1693 *Id.* pp. 21–22.

1694 *Id.* pp. 29–30.

1695 Voreacos, David, Steven T. Dennis, David McLaughlin, and Andrew M Harris. "Manafort Heads to Jail after Judge Faults Witness Tampering." *Bloomberg News*, 15 June 2018, https://www.bloomberg.com/news/articles/2018-06-15/manafort-sent-to-jail-after-judge-cancels-house-arrest-jig5977k?utm_campaign=socialflow-organic&utm_content=politics&cmpid%3D=socialflow-twitter-politics&utm_source=twitter&utm_medium=social&sref=Z6DDy2rA.

1696 @realDonaldTrump. "Wow, what a tough sentence for Paul Manafort, who has represented Ronald Reagan, Bob Dole and many other top political people and campaigns. Didn't know Manafort was the head of the Mob. What about Comey and Crooked Hillary and all of the others? Very unfair!" *Twitter*, 15 June 2018, https://twitter.com/realdonaldtrump/status/1007679422865006593.

1697 Sommerfeldt, Chris. "Rudy Giuliani Says Mueller Probe 'Might Get Cleaned Up' with 'Presidential Pardons' in Light of Paul Manafort Going to Jail." *New York Daily News*, 15 June 2018, https://www.nydailynews.com/news/politics/ny-news-rudy-muller-pardons-trump-manafort-20180615-story.html.

1698 "Schedule A of Form 3X of NRCC at 3339." https://docquery.fec.gov/cgi-bin/fecimg/?201907019150441609.

1699 *Id.*

1700 "Moskowitz, Cherna: Donor Detail." *OpenSecrets*, 10 June 2019, https://www.opensecrets.org/outsidespending/donor_detail.php?cycle=2018&id=U0000004063&type=I&super=N&name=Moskowitz%2C+Cherna.

1701 Sales, Ben. "How Partisan Politics Are Dividing an Orthodox Synagogue Movement." *Jewish Telegraph Agency*, 5 March 2019, https://www.jta.org/2019/03/05/united-states/how-partisan-politics-are-dividing-an-orthodox-synagogue-movement.

1702 Rogers, Katie, and Kenneth P. Vogel. "Outside Trump Hotel, an Uproar. Inside, a Calm Sea of Conservative Cash." *New York Times*, 20 June 2018, https://www.nytimes.com/2018/06/20/us/politics/trump-donors-america-first.html.

1703 "Schedule A, FEC Form 3 of Pete Sessions for Congress." 25 June 2018, https://docquery.fec.gov/cgi-bin/fecimg/?201807149115467756.

1704 "Schedule A, FEC Form 3X of America Great Committee." 29 June 2018, https://docquery.fec.gov/cgi-bin/fecimg/https://docquery.fec.gov/cgi-bin/fecimg/?201810209125894313https://docquery.fec.gov/cgi-bin/fecimg/?201807139115443055.

1705 "Schedule A, FEC Form 3 of Protect the House." 29 June 2018, https://docquery.fec.gov/cgi-bin/fecimg/?201807139115443055.

1706 "Schedule A, FEC Form 3 of Kevin McCarthy for Congress." 29 June 2018, https://docquery.fec.gov/cgi-bin/fecimg/?201810159125458467.

1707 "Individual Donations, Igor Furman." *Federal Election Commission*, https://www.fec.gov/data/receipts/individual-contributions/?contributor_name=Igor%20Furman.

1708 *Id.*

1709 *Id.*

1710 Sales, Ben. "Orthodox Synagogue Association Honored 2 Giuliani Associates Months before They Were Arrested." *Jewish Telegraph Agency*, 11 Oct. 2019, https://www.jta.org/2019/10/11/united-states/orthodox-synagogue-association-honored-2-giuliani-associates-months-before-they-were-arrested.

1711 *Id.*

1712 Sales, "Orthodox Synagogue Association honored 2 Giuliani Associates Months before They Were Arrested."

1713 *Id.*

1714 Vogel, Kenneth P., Ben Protess, and Sarah Maslin Nir. "Behind the Deal That put Giuliani Together With a Dirt-Hunting Partner." *New York Times*, 6 Nov. 2019, https://www.nytimes.com/2019/11/06/us/politics/ukraine-giuliani-charles-gucciardo.html.

1715 Hettena, Seth. "What Happened to America's Mayor?" *Rolling Stone*, 17 May 2020, https://www.rollingstone.com/politics/politics-features/rudy-giuliani-new-york-trump-997712/.

1716 "Dep. of Marie Yovanovich." p. 261.

1717 Miller, Christopher. "Evangelical Christians Also Wanted to Get Rid of the US Ambassador to Ukraine." *Buzzfeed*, 5 Feb. 2020, https://www.buzzfeednews.com/article/christopherm51/marie-yovanovitch-ukraine-mike-pompeo-dale-armstrong.

1718 *Id.*

1719 "Gay Parade on Blood." *June 20 Movement "All Together."* https://love-contra.org/bp/?fbclid=IwAR3utJsbrt1-4Alab4z7FlitR67ni9ofkp6kF0yPtm2ev75nFnxc7xAycpY.

1720 Miller, "Evangelical Christians also Wanted to Get Rid of the US Ambassador to Ukraine."

1721 Morin, Rebecca, and David Cohen. "Giuliani: 'Truth isn't Truth.'" *Politico*, 19 Aug. 2018, https://www.politico.com/story/2018/08/19/giuliani-truth-todd-trump-788161

1722 Schmidt, Michael S., Maggie Haberman, and Charlie Savage. "Mueller Won't Indict Trump if He Finds Wrongdoing, Giuliani Says." *New York Times*, 16 May 2018, https://www.nytimes.com/2018/05/16/us/politics/mueller-trump-indictment.html?searchResultPosition=43.

1723 Landler, Mark, and Noah Weiland. "Giuliani Says Trump Would Not Have to Comply With Mueller Subpoena." *New York Times,* 6 May 2018, https://www.nytimes.com/2018/05/06/us/politics/giuliani-says-trump-would-not-have-to-comply-with-mueller-subpoena.html?searchResultPosition=49.

1724 Schmidt, Michael S., and Maggie Haberman. "Shifting Strategy, Trump's Lawyers Set New Conditions for Mueller Interview." *New York Times,* 6 July 2018, https://www.nytimes.com/2018/07/06/us/politics/trump-special-counsel-interview.html?searchResultPosition=28.

1725 *Id.*

1726 Baker, Peter. "Trump Team's Mueller Strategy: Limit the Investigation and Attack the Investigators." *New York Times,* 21 May 2018, https://www.nytimes.com/2018/05/21/us/politics/trump-mueller-strategy-russia-inquiry.html?searchResultPosition=45.

1727 "Extraction Report, [Redacted]." 9 Oct. 2019, p. 1, https://upload.wikimedia.org/wikipedia/commons/8/87/HMKP-116-JU00-20191211-SD9015-imessages.pdf.

1728 Markay, Lachlan. "How the *Beast* Uncovered the Campaign Finance Scheme that Just got Giuliani Cronies Indicted." *Daily Beast,* Oct. 2019, https://www.thedailybeast.com/how-pay-dirt-uncovered-the-campaign-finance-scheme-that-just-got-giuliani-cronies-indicted.

1729 Marritz, Ilya. "How Parnas and Fruman's Dodgy Donation Was Uncovered by Two People Using Google Translate." *ProPublica,* 5 Feb. 2020, https://www.propublica.org/article/trump-inc-2020-how-parnas-and-frumans-dodgy-donation-was-uncovered-by-two-people-using-google-translate.

1730 *Id.*

1731 Ross, Jamie. "*Daily Beast's* Question Led to Breakthough that Began Parnas/Fruman Investigation, Says Report."

1732 Marritz, "How Parnas and Fruman's Dodgy Donation Was Uncovered by Two People Using Google Translate."

1733 Marritz, Ilya. "An Intimate Dinner with President Trump." *Trump Inc.*, 5 Feb. 2020, https://www.wnycstudios.org/podcasts/trumpinc/episodes/trump-inc-parnas-money.

1734 *Id.*

1735 *Id.*

1736 *Id.*

1737 "About." *Campaign Legal Center.* https://campaignlegal.org/about.

1738 "Complaint." *Campaign Legal Center, et al. v. Parnas, et al.* 25 July 2018, https://campaignlegal.org/sites/default/files/2018-07/SIGNED%2007-25-18%20GEP%20LLC%20Straw%20Donor%20Complaint.pdf.

1739 *Id.*

1740 Allison, Bill, Max Abelson, and Shahien Nasiripour,."Trump's Mysterious Super-PAC Donor Accused of Breaking Law." *Bloomberg News,* 25 July 2018, https://www.bloomberg.com/news/articles/2018-07-26/pro-trump-super-pac-got-illegal-contributions-complaint-alleges?sref=Z6DDy2rA.

1741 Jackson, David. "Rudy Giuliani Says Donald Trump Team Preparing Report to Counter Robert Mueller." *USA Today,* 30 July 2018, https://www.usatoday.com/story/news/politics/2018/07/30/rudy-giuliani-trump-team-preparing-counter-report-robert-mueller/858771002/.

1742 *Id.*

1743 Hettena, "What Happened to America's Mayor?"

1744 *Id.*

1745 Heldermann, Rosalind S., and Tom Hamburger. "As Impeachment Trial Ended, Federal Prosecutors Took New Steps in Probe Related to Giuliani According to People Familiar with Case." *Washington Post*, 14 Feb. 2020, https://www.washingtonpost.com/politics/as-impeachment-trial-ended-federal-prosecutors-took-new-steps-in-probe-related-to-giuliani-according-to-people-familiar-with-case/2020/02/14/7893bfb0-4e8a-11ea-bf44-f5043eb3918a_story.html.

1746 Kadisnky, Sergey. "Jamaica Estates' Dr. Joseph Frager Leads Delegation to Israel to Celebrate Efrat Expansion." *Queens Jewish Link*, vol. VII, no. 31, 2018, p. 26.

1747 *Id.*

1748 *Id.*

1749 @jacobkornbluh. "Spotted in Jerusalem: @USAmbIsrael David Friedman filming @GovMikeHuckabee playing Sweet Home Alabama at BBQ hosted by Simon Falic in Jerusalem. Also there @Scaramucci, @netanyahuyair, @ChaninaSperlin, @YLefkowitz, Lev Parnas, Dr. Joe Frager." *Twitter*, 29 July 2018, https://twitter.com/jacobkornbluh/status/1023651466119131137.

1750 *Id.*

1751 Zilber, Ariel. "PICTURED: Estranged Wife of Giuliani Associate Arrested in Campaign Finance Scandal Who Lives a very Luxurious Life in Miami and Counts Victoria's Secret Model Adriana Lima among Her Friends." *Daily Mail*, 15 Oct. 2019, https://www.dailymail.co.uk/news/article-7573657/Estranged-wife-Giuliani-associate-arrested-campaign-finance-scandal-luxury-boutique-owner.html.

1752 Ward, Vicky. "Exclusive: After Private White House Meeting, Giuliani Associate Lev Parnas Said He Was on a 'Secret Mission' for Trump, Sources Say." *CNN,* 16 Nov. 2019, https://www.cnn.com/2019/11/15/politics/parnas-trump-special-mission-ukraine/index.html.

1753 Rothfeld, Michael, Ben Protess, William K. Rashbaum, Kenneth P. Vogel, and Andrew E. Kramer. "How 2 Soviet Émigrés Fueled the Trump Impeachment Flames." *New York Times*, 19 Dec. 2019, https://www.nytimes.com/2019/12/19/nyregion/lev-parnas-igor-fruman.html.

1754 *Id.*

1755 Kao, Anthony. "Ukraine's 'Servant of the People' is a Hidden Gem of Political Comedy." *Cinema Escapist,* 6 June 2017, https://www.cinemaescapist.com/2017/06/ukraines-servant-people-hidden-gem-political-comedy/.

1756 *Id.*

1757 Troianovski, Anton. "A Ukrainian Billionaire Fought Russia. Now He's Ready to Embrace It." *New York Times*, 19 Nov. 2019, https://www.nytimes.com/2019/11/13/world/europe/ukraine-ihor-kolomoisky-russia.html.

1758 Kovensky, Josh. "Update: Government Nationalizes PrivatBank, Guarantees Deposits." *Kyiv Post.* 18 Dec. 2016, https://www.kyivpost.com/ukraine-politics/ukraine-government-nationalizes-privatbank.html.

1759 *Id.*

1760 *Id.*

1761 Zinets, Natalia. "Ukraine Central Bank Says PrivatBank Was used for Shady Deals, Money-Laundering." *Reuters,* 16 Jan. 2018, https://www.reuters.com/article/ukraine-privatbank/update-1-ukraines-cenbank-says-privatbank-was-used-for-shady-deals-money-laundering-idUSL8N1PB35E.

1762 Korinovska, Nastya. "Servant of the People Party Registered in Ukraine." https://hromadske.ua/posts/v-ukraini-zareiestruvaly-partiiu-sluha-narodu.

1763 "The Dark Operetta." *The Economist,* 3 Aug. 2018, https://www.economist.com/europe/2018/08/04/politics-surpasses-satire-in-ukraine.

1764 Apuzzo, Matt, Maggie Haberman, and Michael S. Schmidt. "Michael Cohen Secretly Taped Trump Discussing Payment to Playboy Model." *New York Times,* 20 July, 2018, https://www.nytimes.com/2018/07/20/us/politics/michael-cohen-trump-tape.html.

1765 Polantz, Katlyn, and Sara Murray. "Manafort Trial Begins in Biggest Test Yet for Special Counsel Robert Mueller." *CNN,* 31 July 2018, https://www.cnn.com/2018/07/31/politics/paul-manafort-trial-begins/index.html.

1766 Day, Chad, and Matthew Barakat. "Gates Admits Crimes with and Embezzlement from Manafort." *Associated Press,* 6 Aug. 2018, https://apnews.com/b851252ece1d4783a3534fe748265f9c.

1767 Stern, David. "Manafort Trial Has Ukraine Freshly Nervous about Trump." *Politico,* 19 Aug. 2018, https://www.politico.com/story/2018/08/19/trump-ukraine-manafort-trial-788028.

1768 Polantz, Katelyn, Eric Bradner, Marshall Cohen, Liz Stark, and Kara Scannell. "Jury Set to Begin Deliberations in Paul Manafort Trial." *CNN,* 15 Aug. 2018, https://www.cnn.com/2018/08/15/politics/paul-manafort-trial-closing-arguments/index.html.

1769 Zapotosky, Matt. "Lone Holdout on Manafort Jury Blocked Conviction on All Counts, Juror Says." *Washington Post,* 23 Aug. 2018, https://www.washingtonpost.com/world/national-security/lone-holdout-on-manafort-jury-blocked-conviction-on-all-counts-juror-says/2018/08/23/72fcf926-a685-11e8-8fac-12e98c13528d_story.html.

1770 Hong, Nicole, Rebecca Ballhaus, Rebecca Davis O'Brien, and Joe Palazzolo. "Michael Cohen Pleads Guilty, Says Trump Told Him to Pay off Women." *Wall Street Journal,* 21 Aug. 2018, https://www.wsj.com/articles/michael-cohen-to-plead-guilty-to-criminal-charges-1534875978.

1771 Manafort was released from prison on leave due to the COVID-19 pandemic. He is on home confinement in Alexandria, Virginia.

1772 @realDonaldTrump. "I feel very badly for Paul Manafort and his wonderful family. "Justice" took a 12 year old tax case, among other things, applied tremendous pressure on him and, unlike Michael Cohen, he refused to "break" - make up stories in order to get a "deal." Such respect for a brave man!" *Twitter,* 22 Aug. 22, 2018, https://twitter.com/realdonaldtrump/status/1032256443985084417.

1773 "An American Businessman Will Help Raise $1 Million to Build a Town for Jewish Refugees from Eastern Ukraine." *Livyi Bereh*, 27 Aug. 2018, https://ukr.lb.ua/world/2018/08/27/406045_amerikanskiy_biznesmen_dopomozhe.html.

1774 *Id.*

1775 *Id.*

1776 "Speech of the Chief Rabbi of Ukraine and Kiev Moshe Reuven Azman in the British Parliament." *Kyiv Community Synagogue*, 5 Sept. 2018, http://sinagoga.kiev.ua/node/13422.

1777 Anatevka Jewish Refugee Community. "Our Friends Say Hi. Do You Recognize Them?" *Facebook*, 7 Sept. 2018, https://www.facebook.com/watch/?v=323183198432672.

1778 *Petro Poroshenko v. British Broadcasting Co.* [2019] EWHC 213 (QB), 7 Feb. 2019, https://www.bailii.org/ew/cases/EWHC/QB/2019/213.html.

1779 Shapiro, Ari. "On Libel and the Law, US and UK Go Separate Ways." *National Public Radio—Parallels*, 15 March, 2015, https://www.npr.org/sections/parallels/2015/03/21/394273902/on-libel-and-the-law-u-s-and-u-k-go-separate-ways.

1780 *Id.*

1781 *Id.*

1782 Hsu, Spencer S., Devlin Barrett, and Justin Jouvenal,. "Manafort Will Cooperate with Mueller as Part of Guilty Plea, Prosecutor Says." *Washington Post*, 14 Sept. 2018, https://www.washingtonpost.com/world/national-security/manafort-plans-to-plead-guilty-to-second-set-of-charges/2018/09/14/a1541068-b5c9-11e8-a7b5-adaaa5b2a57f_story.html.

1783 *Id.*

1784 *Id.*

1785 It cannot be ruled out that the plea and subsequent false cooperation by Manafort was entirely directed by Trump and his associates. By lying in his proffer statements, he destroyed himself as a witness against Trump.

1786 *Id.*

1787 *Id.*

1788 :Letter from Robert S. Mueller to Kevin Downing," *et al.* 13 Spet, 2018, p. 6 (Sept. 13, 2018). https://upload.wikimedia.org/wikipedia/commons/0/0e/Manafort_plea_agreement.pdf.

1789 "Salisbury Novichok Poisoning: Russian Nationals named as Suspects." https://www.bbc.com/news/uk-45421445.

1790 Brunt, Martin. "Super Recogniser Squad tracks Skripal Novichok Attackers." *Sky News*, 28 Aug. 2018, https://news.sky.com/story/super-recognisers-help-identify-skripal-suspects-11483995

1791 "RT Editor-in-Chief's Exclusive Interview with Skripal Case Suspects Petrov & Boshirov" *Russia Today* (Sept. 13, 2018). https://www.rt.com/news/438356-rt-petrov-boshirov-full-interview/

1792 *Id.*

1793 *Id.*

1794 *Id.*

1795 *Id.*

1796 "Skripal Poisoning Suspect's Passport Data shows Link to Security Services." *Bellingcat,* 14 Sept. 2018, https://www.bellingcat.com/news/uk-and-europe/2018/09/14/skripal-poisoning-suspects-passport-data-shows-link-security-services/.

1797 *Id.*

1798 "Skripal Suspect Boshirov identified as GRU Colonel Anatoliy Chepiga." *Bellingcat,* 26 Sept. 26, 2018, https://www.bellingcat.com/news/uk-and-europe/2018/09/26/skripal-suspect-boshirov-identified-gru-colonel-anatoliy-chepiga/.

1799 *Id.*

1800 *Id.*

1801 "Anatoliy Chepiga is a Hero of Russia: The Writing Is on the Wall." *Bellingcat,* 2 Oct. 2018, https://www.bellingcat.com/news/uk-and-europe/2018/10/02/anatoliy-chepiga-hero-russia-writing-wall/.

1802 *Id.*

1803 "Full report: Skripal Poisoning Suspect Dr. Alexander Mishkin, Hero of Russia." *Bellingcat,* 9 Oct. 2018, https://www.bellingcat.com/news/uk-and-europe/2018/10/09/full-report-skripal-poisoning-suspect-dr-alexander-mishkin-hero-russia/.

1804 *Id.*

1805 "Third Skripal Suspect Linked to 2015 Bulgaria Poisoning." *Bellingcat,* 7 Feb. 2019, https://www.bellingcat.com/news/uk-and-europe/2019/02/07/third-skripal-suspect-linked-to-2015-bulgaria-poisoning/

1806 "The GRU Globetrotters: Mission London."

1807 "Exhibit A to Registration Avenue Strategies Global LLC." 13 March 2018, https://efile.fara.gov/docs/6446-Exhibit-AB-20180313-5.pdf.

1808 Cohen, Adam. "Why Have So Many US Attorneys Been Fired? It looks a Lot Like Politics." *New York Times,* 26, Feb. 2007, https://www.nytimes.com/2007/02/26/opinion/26mon4.html.

1809 Kovensky, Josh. "EXCLUSIVE: Bud Cummins Tried to Interest US Law Enforcement in Ukraine Dirt on Bidens in 2018." *Talking Points Memo,* 24 Nov. 2019, https://talkinPGOintsmemo.com/muckraker/bud-cummins-ukraine-rudy-giuliani-yuriy-lutsenko.

1810 *Id.*

1811 *Id.*

1812 *Id.*

1813 "2017 November—General—Statewide." *Virginia Department of Elections,* 8 Dec. 2017, https://results.elections.virginia.gov/vaelections/2017%20November%20General/Site/Statewide.html.

1814 Chinni, Dante. "Inside the Data: What the Virginia Election Results Mean for '18.'" *NBC News,* 12 Nov. 2017, https://www.nbcnews.com/storyline/2017-elections/inside-data-what-virginia-election-results-mean-18-n820001.

1815 Barrón-López, Laura. "This Former CIA Officer Says She can beat Virginia Rep. Dave Brat." *Washington Examiner*, 30 May 2018, https://www.washingtonexaminer.com/news/campaigns/abigail-spanberger-the-former-cia-officer-challenging-rep-dave-brat.

1816 *Id.*

1817 Zurcher, Anthony. "Nancy Pelosi: The Remarkable Comeback of America's Most Powerful Woman." *BBC News*, 2 Jan. 2019, https://www.bbc.com/news/world-us-canada-46739947.

1818 Vozzella, Laura. "Saudi School Dominates TV Ads in Race for Suburban Richmond Congressional Seat." *Washington Post*, 18 Sept. 2018, https://www.washingtonpost.com/local/virginia-politics/saudi-school-dominates-tv-ads-in-race-for-suburban-richmond-congressional-seat/2018/09/11/1f8ad70a-b5d4-11e8-a2c5-3187f427e253_story.html.

1819 "NBC News/Wall Street Journal Survey." 3 Nov. 2018, http://media1.s-nbcnews.com/i/today/z_creative/181417NBCWSJNovemberPoll.pdf.

1820 Kornbluh, Jacob. "At 2018 Event with Parnas and Fruman, Giuliani said Democrats Will 'Start a Hundred Investigations' into Trump." *Jewish Insider*, 11 Oct. 2019, https://jewishinsider.com/2019/10/at-2018-event-with-parnas-and-fruman-giuliani-said-democrats-will-start-a-hundred-investigations-into-trump/.

1821 *Id.*

1822 *Id.*

1823 *Id.*

1824 *Id.*

1825 "Virginia's 7th House District Election Results: Dave Brat vs. Abigail Spanberger." *New York Times*, 28 Jan. 2019, https://www.nytimes.com/elections/results/virginia-house-district-7.

1826 "US House Election Results 2018." *New York Times*, 15 May 2019, https://www.nytimes.com/interactive/2018/11/06/us/elections/results-house-elections.html.

CHAPTER 9: THE DESPERATE CIRCUS

1827 Barrett, Devlin, Matt Zapotosky, and Josh Dawsey. "Jeff Sessions Forced out as Attorney General." *Washington Post*, 7 Nov. 2018, https://www.washingtonpost.com/world/national-security/attorney-general-jeff-sessions-resigns-at-trumps-request/2018/11/07/d1b7a214-e144-11e8-ab2c-b31dcd53ca6b_story.html.

1828 *Id.*

1829 "Whitaker Rejected Advice to Recuse from Russia Probe." *Politico*, 20 Dec. 2018, https://www.politico.com/story/2018/12/20/matthew-whitaker-recusal-russia-investigation-1071488.

1830 Blake, Aaron. "Barr Confirms He Shared his Mueller Memo with Lots of People around Trump." *Washington Post*, 15 Jan. 2019, https://www.washingtonpost.com/politics/2019/01/15/barr-confirms-he-shared-his-memo-with-lots-people-around-trump/.

1831 Safire, William. "Essay: The Patsy Prosecutor." *New York Times,* 19 Oct. 1992, https://www.nytimes.com/1992/10/19/opinion/essay-the-patsy-prosecutor.html.

1832 Johnson, Eliana. "The Real Reason Bill Barr Is Defending Trump." *Politico,* 1 May 2019, https://www.politico.com/story/2019/05/01/william-barr-donald-trump-mueller-report-1295273.

1833 "Viktor Shokin Was Denied Reinstatement as Prosecutor General." *CNT News Agency,* 24 Oct. 2018, https://unt.ua/news-polityka-vnutrishnya-polityka/24254-v-ktoru-shok-nu-bulo-v-dmovleno-v-ponovlenn-na-posadu-genprokuroru.html.

1834 *Id.*

1835 "Extraction Report, [Redacted]." p. 9.

1836 *Id.*

1837 Lafraniere, Sharon. "Manafort Breached Plea Deal by Repeatedly Lying, Mueller Says." *New York Times,* 26 Nov. 2018, https://www.nytimes.com/2018/11/26/us/politics/mueller-paul-manafort-cooperation.html.

1838 "Joint Status Report." *United States v. Paul Manafort, Jr.* Crim no. 17-201-1, 26 Nov. 2018, https://int.nyt.com/data/documenthelper/491-paul-manafort-plea-agreement-breach/49c0d15e0a829872d8c9/optimized/full.pdf#page=1.

1839 *Id.*

1840 Schmidt, Michael S., Sharon LaFraniere, and Maggie Haberman. "Manafort's Lawyer Said to Brief Trump Attorneys on What He Told Mueller." *New York Times,* 27 Nov. 2018, https://www.nytimes.com/2018/11/27/us/politics/manafort-lawyer-trump-cooperation.html.

1841 *Id.*

1842 *Id.*

1843 "Transcript: NPR's Full Interview with Trump Lawyer Rudy Giuliani." *National Public Radio,* 5 Feb. 2020, https://www.npr.org/2020/02/05/802423844/transcript-nprs-full-interview-with-trump-lawyer-rudy-giuliani.

1844 "Bart M. Schwartz." *Guidepost Solutions,* https://www.guidepostsolutions.com/our-experts/bart-schwartz/.

1845 Shorrock, Tim. "Giuliani's Love for His Country Is Equal to the Money He Makes." *The Nation,* 25 Feb. 2015, https://www.thenation.com/article/archive/giulianis-love-his-country-equal-money-he-makes/.

1846 "Individual Contributions: Bart M. Schwartz." *Federal Election Commission,* https://www.fec.gov/data/receipts/individual-contributions/?contributor_name=Bart%20M.%20Schwartz.

1847 "Transcript: NPR's Full Interview with Trump Lawyer Rudy Giuliani."

1848 Schreckinger, Ben. "'I'm the Real Whistleblower': Giuliani's Quixotic Mission to Help Trump in Ukraine." *Politico,* 27 Sept. 2019, https://www.politico.com/news/2019/09/27/giuliani-trump-ukraine-005098.

1849 Hettena, "What Happened to America's Mayor?"

1850 Schreckinger, "'I'm the Real Whistleblower.'"

1851 "Transcript: NPR's Full Interview with Trump Lawyer Rudy Giuliani."

1852 *Id.*

1853 *Id.*

1854 Hettena, "What Happened to America's Mayor?"

1855 Ward, "Exclusive: Giuliani Associate Willing to tell Congress Nunes Met With ex-Ukrainian Official to get Dirt on Biden."

1856 Cong. Rec. 115 H. 2320, 4 Mar. 2019, http://clerk.house.gov/foreign/reports/2019q1mar04.pdf.

1857 Ward, "Exclusive: Giuliani Associate willing to tell Congress Nunes met with ex-Ukrainian Official to get Dirt on Biden."

1858 Berman, Matt. "Rudy Giuliani Was with His Now-Indicted Ukrainian Friend at President Bush's State Funeral Service. Jeb Bush says it's 'Disappointing.'" *Buzzfeed,* 15 Oct. 2019, https://www.buzzfeednews.com/article/mattberman/rudy-giuliani-lev-parnas-bush-funeral.

1859 Ward, "Exclusive: after Private White House Meeting, Giuliani Associate Lev Parnas Said He Was on a 'Secret Mission' for Trump, Sources say."

1860 *Id.*

1861 Morin, Rebecca. "Trump, at Hanukkah Reception, Condemns Anti-Semitism." *Politico,* 6 Dec. 2018, https://www.politico.com/story/2018/12/06/trump-hanukkah-anti-semitism-1048013.

1862 Ward, "Exclusive: After Private White House Meeting, Giuliani Associate Lev Parnas Said He Was on a 'Secret Mission' for Trump, Sources Say."

1863 *Id.*

1864 *Id.*

1865 "Extraction Report, [Redacted]." p. 10.

1866 Belford, Aubrey, Tania Kozyreva, Andrew W. Lehren, Christopher Miller, and Emily R. Siegel. "Top Ukrainian Politician, Scandal-Scarred GOP Ex-Rep are Newest Names Linked to Trump Ukraine Project." *NBC News,* 5 Nov. 2019, https://www.nbcnews.com/politics/trump-impeachment-inquiry/top-ukrainian-politician-scandal-scarred-gop-ex-rep-are-newest-n1075196.

1867 *Id.*

1868 Kravets, Roman. "Yuriy Lutsenko: I Refused both Poroshenko and Zelensky to Shut Down Different TV Channels." *Ukrayinska Pravda,* 19 Nov. 2019, https://www.pravda.com.ua/rus/articles/2019/11/18/7232239/.

1869 "Extraction Report, [Redacted]." p. 11.

1870 *Id.*

1871 Goldman, Ada,m and Sharon LaFraniere. 'Mueller Says Manafort Lied about Contacts with Trump Officials." *New York Times*, 7 Dec. 2018, https://www.nytimes.com/2018/12/07/us/politics/manafort-special-counsel-lies.html.

1872 LaFraniere, Sharon, Benjamin Weiser, and Maggie Haberman. "Prosecutors Say Trump Directed Illegal Payments during Campaign." *New York Times*, 7 Dec. 2018, https://www.nytimes.com/2018/12/07/nyregion/michael-cohen-sentence.html.

1873 Zubkova, Dasha "Appeals Court: Sytnyk And MP Leshchenko Did No Act Illegally By Disclosing That Manafort's Name Is In Party Of Regions' 'Black Ledger.'" *Ukrainian News,* 16 July 2019, https://ukranews.com/en/news/642649-appeal-court-sytnyk-and-mp-leschenko-did-no-act-illegally-by-disclosing-that-manafort-s-name-is-in.

1874 "Extraction Report, [Redacted]." p. 13.

1875 *Id.*

1876 *Id.* p. 14.

1877 Kravets, "Yuriy Lutsenko: I Refused both Poroshenko and Zelensky to Shut Down Different TV Channels."

1878 Swann, Betsy. "Parnas Lawyer: Giuliani Delivered Graham Letter Calling for Sanctions on Ukrainian Officials." *Daily Beast,* 29 Jan. 2020, https://www.thedailybeast.com/parnas-lawyer-giuliani-delivered-graham-letter-calling-for-sanctions-on-ukrainian-officials?ref=home.

1879 Yarish, Ostap. "Giuliani Sends Letters to US Senate and Treasury Department Calling for Sanctions against Ukrainian Officials – Media." *Voice of America*, 29 Jan. 2020, https://ukrainian.voanews.com/a/giuliani-sanctions-graham/5265413.html.

1880 *Id.*

1881 Belford and Melkozerova. "Meet the Florida Duo Helping Giuliani Investigate for Trump in Ukraine."

1882 Extraction Report, p. 3.

1883 *Id.* p. 18.

1884 *Id.*

1885 *Id.* p. 115.

1886 *Id.* p. 117.

1887 Kent, George. p. 47.

1888 *Id.* p. 48.

1889 *Id.*

1890 *Id.* p. 49.

1891 Bump, Phillip. "How Ukraine's Top Prosecutor Went after Marie Yovanovitch, Step by Step." *Washington Post*, 15 Jan. 2020, https://www.washingtonpost.com/politics/2020/01/15/how-ukraines-top-prosecutor-went-after-marie-yovanovitch-step-by-step/.

1892 *Id.*

1893 "Memorandum of Interview of Viktor Shokin." p. 2, https://assets.documentcloud.org/documents/6557889/State-Department-Records-of-Giuliani-and-Ukraine.pdf

1894 *Id.*

1895 *Id.*

1896 Krasnolutska, Daryna, Kateryna Choursina, and Stephanie Baker. "Ukraine Prosecutor Says No Evidence of Wrongdoing by Bidens." *Bloomberg News,* 16 May 2019, https://www.bloomberg.com/news/articles/2019-05-16/ukraine-prosecutor-says-no-evidence-of-wrongdoing-by-bidens.

1897 Entous. "The Ukrainian Prosecutor behind Trump's Impeachment."

1898 Vogel, Kenneth P., Andrew E. Kramer, and David E. Sanger. "How a Shadow Foreign Policy in Ukraine Prompted an Impeachment Inquiry." *New York Times*, 28 Sept. 2019, https://www.nytimes.com/2019/09/28/us/politics/how-a-shadow-foreign-policy-in-ukraine-prompted-impeachment-inquiry.html.

1899 "Dep. of Marie Yovanovitch." p. 134.

1900 "Memorandum of Interview of Yuriy Lutsenko." 26 Jan. 2019, p. 1, https://assets.documentcloud.org/documents/6557889/State-Department-Records-of-Giuliani-and-Ukraine.pdf.

1901 *Id.*

1902 *Id.*

1903 *Id.*

1904 *Id.* pp. 1-2

1905 *Id.* p. 2.

1906 *Id.*

1907 "Dep. of Amb. Marie Yovanovitch." p. 43.

1908 *Id.*

1909 "Extraction Report." p. 28.

1910 "Iran's Zarif Calls Iran-Focused Summit in Poland a 'Desperate Circus'." *Reuters,* 11 Jan. 2019, https://www.reuters.com/article/us-iran-usa-summit-zarif/irans-zarif-calls-iran-focused-summit-in-poland-a-desperate-circus-idUSKCN1P528A?il=0.

1911 "Extraction Report." p. 151.

1912 "Dep. of Marie Yovanovitch." pp. 43-7.

1913 Ballhaus, Rebecca, and Alan Cullison, and Brett Forrest. "Giuliani Associates Urged Ukraine's Prior President to open Biden, Election Probes." *Wall Street Journal*, 8 Nov. 2019, https://www.wsj.com/articles/giuliani-associates-urged-ukraines-prior-president-to-open-biden-election-probes-11573247707.

1914 *Id.*

1915 *Id.*

1916 "Extraction Report." p. 30.

1917 Protess, Ben, William K. Rashbaum, and Michael Rothfeld. "Giuliani Pursued Business in Ukraine while Pushing for Inquiries for Trump." *New York Times*, 27 Nov. 2019, https://www.nytimes.com/2019/11/27/nyregion/giuliani-ukraine-business-trump.html.

1918 *Id.*

1919 "Extraction Report." pp. 30–33.

1920 *Id.*

1921 Protess, Rashbaum, and Rothfeld. "Giuliani Pursued Business in Ukraine while Pushing for Inquiries for Trump."

1922 *Id.*

1923 Polantz, Katlyn. "Mueller Believes Manafort Fed Information to Russian with Intel Ties." *CNN*, 8 Jan. 2019, https://www.cnn.com/2019/01/08/politics/manafort-russia-court-deadline/index.html.

1924 Ostrowski and Washington. "Lev Parnas in Palm Beach County: Unpaid Bills, Failed Business Deals."

1925 Vogel, Shane, Mazzetti, and Mendel. "Prosecutors examining Ukrainians Who Flocked to Trump Inaugural."

1926 *Id.*

1927 Stolberg, Sheryl Gay. "Gladiators of Impeachment: How 2 Lawyers Got the Case." *New York Times*, 2 Dec. 2019, https://www.nytimes.com/2019/12/02/us/politics/trump-impeachment-goldman-castor.html.

1928 *Id.*

1929 Desiderio, Andrew. "House Intel Hires Former Russian Mob Prosecutor to lead Trump Probes." *Politico*, 5 March 2019, https://www.politico.com/story/2019/03/05/house-intelligence-daniel-goldman-1204140.

1930 Samuelshon, Daniel. "Meet the Legal Minds behind Trump's Impeachment." *Politico*, 12 Dec. 2019, https://www.politico.com/news/2019/12/12/trump-impeachment-legal-083037.

1931 *Id.*

1932 "Letter from Robert S. Mueller III to Attorney General William Barr." 27 March 2019, p. 1, https://int.nyt.com/data/documenthelper/796-mueller-letter-to-barr/02499959cbfa313c36d4/optimized/full.pdf.

1933 Relman, Eliza, and Sonam Sheth. "Mueller Feferred 14 Criminal Matters to Other Prosecutors, but Only 2 of Them Are Public So Far." *Business Insider*, 18 April 2019, https://www.businessinsider.com/mueller-report-referred-criminal-matters-prosecutors-2019-4.

1934 @realDonaldTrump. "The greatest overreach in the history of our Country. The Dems are obstructing justice and will not get anything done. A big, fat, fishing expedition desperately in search of a crime, when in fact the real crime is what the Dems are doing, and have done!" *Twitter*, 5 March 2019, 9:11 a.m., https://twitter.com/realDonaldTrump/status/1102934716607578112.

1935 Ward, "Exclusive: Giuliani Associate Willing to Tell Congress Nunes Met with ex-Ukrainian Official to Get Dirt on Biden."

1936 *Id.*

1937 Perry, Rick. "The New American Energy Era: Secretary Perry Keynote Address at CERA Week." *US Dept. of Energy*, 13 March 2019, https://www.energy.gov/articles/new-american-energy-era-secretary-perry-keynote-address-cera-week.

1938 Butler, Desmond, Michael Biesecker, Stephen Braun, and Richard Lardner. "After Boost from Perry, Backers Got Huge Gas Deal in Ukraine." *Associated Press* 11 Nov. 2019, https://apnews.com/6d8ae551fb884371a2a592ed85a74426.

1939 *Id.*

1940 Perry, "The New American Energy Era: Secretary Perry Keynote Address at CERA Week."

1941 Butler, Desmond, Michael Biesecker, and Richard Lardner. "Profit, not Politics: Trump Allies Sought Ukraine Gas Deal." *Associated Press,* 7 Oct. 2019, https://apnews.com/d7440cffba4940f5b85cd3dfa3500fb2.

1942 *Id.*

1943 *Id.*

1944 *Id.*

1945 Waldman, Scott. "American Energy Exec Tried to Reveal Plot to Oust US Envoy." *Energy and Environment News,* 6 Nov. 2019, https://www.eenews.net/stories/1061472807.

1946 Whalen, Jeanne. "'The Head of Ukraine's Gas Company Has Been Shot at, Pilloried on TV and Attacked by Giuliani Associates. It's All in a Day's Work." *Washington Post,* 6 Nov. 2019, https://www.washingtonpost.com/business/2019/11/06/head-ukraines-gas-company-has-been-shot-pilloried-tv-attacked-by-giuliani-associates-its-all-days-work/.

1947 "Extraction Report." p. 38.

1948 *Id.*

1949 *Id.* p. 39.

1950 *Id.*

1951 *Id.* pp. 40–3.

1952 Solomon, "As Russia Collusion Fades, Ukrainian Plot to Help Clinton Emerges."

1953 *Id.*

1954 *Id.*

1955 *Id.*

1956 *Id.*

1957 "Sean Hannity Promotes John Solomon Report on March 20, 2019." *Media Matters for America*, https://www.mediamatters.org/media/3838456.

1958 Haines, Tim. "John Solomon: As Russia Collusion Fades, Ukrainian Plot to Help Clinton Emerges." *Real Clear Politics*, 21 March 2019, https://www.realclearpolitics.com/video/2019/03/21/john_solomon_as_russia_collusion_fades_ukrainian_plot_to_help_clinton_emerges.html.

1959 *Id.*

[1960] @realDonaldTrump. "'John Solomon: As Russia Collusion fades, Ukrainian plot to help Clinton emerges.' @seanhannity @FoxNews." *Twitter*, 20 Mar. 2019, 10:40 p.m., https://twitter.com/realDonaldTrump/status/1108559080204001280.

[1961] Heil, Andy, and Christopher Miller. "US Rejects Ukraine Top Prosecutor's 'Don't Prosecute' Accusation." *RFE/RL*, 21 March 2019, https://www.rferl.org/a/us-rejects-top-ukrainian-prosecutors-dont-prosecute-accusation/29834853.html.

[1962] Bolton, John. *The Room Where It Happened*. New York, Simon & Schuster, 2020, p. 409.

[1963] *Id.*

[1964] *Id.*

[1965] Dawsey, Josh, Tom Hamburger, Paul Sonne, and Rosalind S. Helderman. "Giuliani Consulted on Ukraine with Imprisoned Paul Manafort via a Lawyer." *Washington Post*, 2 Oct. 2019, https://www.washingtonpost.com/world/national-security/giuliani-consulted-on-ukraine-with-imprisoned-paul-manafort-via-a-lawyer/2019/10/02/7a6dc542-e486-11e9-b7da-053c79b03db8_story.html.

[1966] *Id.*

[1967] "Extraction Report." p. 127.

[1968] Davis, Aaron C., Beth Reinhard, and Paul Duggan. "GOP Figure Who Said He Tracked US Ambassador Was Previously Involuntarily Committed, Records Show." *Washington Post*, 16 Jan. 2020, https://www.washingtonpost.com/investigations/gop-figure-who-said-he-tracked-us-ambassador-was-previously-involuntarily-committed-records-show/2020/01/15/5fcd8b08-37c1-11ea-9541-9107303481a4_story.html.

[1969] *Id.*

[1970] "About Our Products." *Security Concepts International*, http://www.securityconceptsinc.com/products.html.

[1971] "Enclosure, Letter from Adam Schiff to Jerrold Nadler."14 Jan. 2020, p. 15, https://intelligence.house.gov/uploadedfiles/20200114_-_hpsci_transmittal_letter_to_hjc_-_new_evidence_attachment.pdf.

[1972] "Memorandum Opinion." *EPIC, et al. v. US Dept. of Justice* 19 cv 810 and 19 cv 957 at 3. (D.D.C.), 5 March 2020, https://assets.documentcloud.org/documents/6797022/Walton-Mueller-2020-03-05.pdf.

[1973] Mazzetti, Mark, and Michael S. Schmidt. "When the Mueller Investigation Ended, the Battle over Its Conclusions Began." *New York Times*, 1 May 2019, https://www.nytimes.com/2019/05/01/us/politics/mueller-letters-barr.html.

[1974] "Text of Letter Announcing AG Barr Received Mueller Report." *Associated Press*, 22 March 2019, https://apnews.com/719fb6dc299f43339ead6af26626459d

[1975] Ballhaus, Rebecca, Michael C. Bender, and Vivian Salama. "Trump Ordered Ukraine Ambassador Removed after Complaints from Giuliani, Others." *Wall Street Journal*, 9 Oct. 2019, https://www.wsj.com/articles/trump-ordered-ukraine-ambassador-removed-after-complaints-from-giuliani-others-11570137147?mod=searchresults&page=1&pos=1.

[1976] "Enclosure, Letter from Adam Schiff to Jerrold Nadler." p. 17.

[1977] *Id.*

1978 Dixon, Ken. "New Documents from House Investigators Show Hyde Monitored Ukraine Ambassador." *Middletown Press*, 17 Jan. 2020, https://www.middletownpress.com/middletown/article/New-documents-from-House-investigators-show-Hyde-14985210.php.

1979 Caygle, Heather, Andrew Desiderio, and Kyle Cheney. "Pelosi Tells Dems She'll Reject Highly Classified Briefing on Mueller Findings." *Politico*, 23 March 2019, https://www.politico.com/story/2019/03/23/pelosi-mueller-report-1233317.

1980 Howell Jr., Tom. "Adam Schiff Rejects 'Gang of Eight' Classified Briefing on Mueller Report." *Associated Press*, 24 March 2019, https://apnews.com/9807089fd83b246f85dc6fd2551fc504.

1981 "Memorandum Opinion." *EPIC, et al. v. US Dept. of Justice* 19 cv 810 and 19 cv 957, p. 3.

1982 "Letter from William F. Barr to Lindsey Graham." *et al.* 24 March 2018, p. 2, https://assets.documentcloud.org/documents/5779688/AG-March-24-2019-Letter-to-House-and-Senate.pdf.

1983 *Id.* p. 3.

1984 Gurman, Sadie, Aruna Viswanatha, and Byron Tau. "Mueller Doesn't Find Trump Campaign Conspired with Russia." *Wall Street Journal*, 24 March 2019, https://www.wsj.com/articles/top-findings-from-muellers-report-to-be-sent-to-congress-within-the-hour-11553454918.

1985 Tucker, Eric, Michael Balsamo, Chad Day, and Julie Pace. "Mueller Finds No Trump Collusion, Leaves Obstruction Open." 25 March 2019, https://apnews.com/ea617240fe264947a967f8d13ed9a9a5.

1986 Becket, Stefan, and Camilo Montoya-Galvez. "Mueller Did not Find Trump Campaign 'conspired' with Russia." *CBS News*, 25 March 2019, https://www.cbsnews.com/live-news/mueller-report-summary-william-barr-trump-russia-investigation-latest-updates-today-2019-03-24/.

1987 "Letter from Robert S. Mueller, III to William P. Barr." 27 March 2019, p. 1, https://int.nyt.com/data/documenthelper/796-mueller-letter-to-barr/02499959cbfa313c36d4/optimized/full.pdf.

1988 Lederman, Josh, and Anna Schecter. "Dutch Trump Superfan Who Claimed He Surveilled Ambassador Yovanovitch told People He Was DEA." *NBC News*, 29 Jan. 2020, https://www.nbcnews.com/politics/trump-impeachment-inquiry/dutch-trump-superfan-who-claimed-he-surveilled-ambassador-yovanovitch-told-n1124881.

1989 "Enclosure, Letter from Adam Schiff to Jerrold Nadler." p. 17.

1990 *Id.* p. 19.

1991 *Id.*

1992 *Id.* p. 20.

1993 *Id.*

1994 *Id.* p. 21.

1995 *Id.* pp. 22–24.

1996 Bolton, *The Room Where It Happened.* p. 409.

1997 "Dep. of Marie Yovanovitch." p. 61.

¹⁹⁹⁸ *Id.* p. 62.

¹⁹⁹⁹ *Id.* pp. 63–4.

²⁰⁰⁰ Solomon, John. "US Embassy Pressed Ukraine to Drop Probe of George Soros Group during 2016 Election." *The Hill*, 26 March 2019, https://thehill.com/opinion/campaign/435906-us-embassy-pressed-ukraine-to-drop-probe-of-george-soros-group-during-2016.

²⁰⁰¹ *Id.*

²⁰⁰² "Letter from Robert S. Mueller, III to William P. Barr." p. 1.

²⁰⁰³ *Id.*

²⁰⁰⁴ *Id.*

²⁰⁰⁵ "Letter from William P. Barr to Lindsey Graham." *et al.* 29 March 2019, pp. 1–2, https://assets.documentcloud.org/documents/5784092/March-29-Barr-Letter.pdf.

²⁰⁰⁶ *Id.*

CHAPTER 10 "I WILL DO BIG PRACTICE IN ENGLISH"

²⁰⁰⁷ "Zelenskiy Climbs in Opinion Poll, Tymoshenko Unchanged, Poroshenko Slides." *Kyiv Post*, 14 March 2019, https://www.kyivpost.com/ukraine-politics/zelenskiy-climbs-in-opinion-poll-tymoshenko-unchanged-poroshenko-slides.html.

²⁰⁰⁸ "Final Ukraine Results give Zelenskiy 30 Percent of Presidential Vote." *RFE/RL*, 4 April 2019, https://www.rferl.org/a/final-results-from-ukraine-presidential-election-give-zelenskiy-30-percent-of-vote/29860319.html.

²⁰⁰⁹ Kaleniuk, Daria. "I Respect that Poroshenko Admitted His Mistakes." *Kyiv Post*, 7 April 2019, https://www.kyivpost.com/article/opinion/op-ed/daria-kaleniuk-i-respect-that-the-president-admitted-his-mistakes.html.

²⁰¹⁰ "Email message from [Redacted] to S_All." 26 March 2019, https://www.documentcloud.org/documents/6557889-State-Department-Records-of-Giuliani-and-Ukraine.html#document/p39/a537060.

²⁰¹¹ Ballhaus, Bender, and Salama. "Trump Ordered Ukraine Ambassador Removed after Complaints from Giuliani, Others."

²⁰¹² Solomon, John. "Outline of Soros Reporting, Including Embedded Documents" "Received by Lev Parnas. 26 March 2019, https://assets.documentcloud.org/documents/6557889/State-Department-Records-of-Giuliani-and-Ukraine.pdf.

²⁰¹³ State Dept. Operations Center. "Re: S Calls Update" Received by SES-O_S-Calls. 29 May 2019, https://assets.documentcloud.org/documents/6557889/State-Department-Records-of-Giuliani-and-Ukraine.pdf

²⁰¹⁴ *Id.*

²⁰¹⁵ Wilkie, Christina. "Giuliani Associate Parnas Wants to Testify that Nunes Aides Hid Ukraine Meetings on Biden Dirt from Schiff." *CNBC*, 24 Nov. 2019, https://www.cnbc.com/2019/11/24/giuliani-ally-would-testify-that-nunes-staffers-hid-ukraine-meetings-from-schiff.html.

2016 *Id.*

2017 Kramer, Andrew E., and Michael Schwirtz. "The Ukrainian Prosecutor behind the Dossier Targeting Hunter Biden." *New York Times*, 15 Oct. 2019, https://www.nytimes.com/2019/10/15/world/europe/ukraine-prosecutor-biden-trump.html.

2018 *Id.*

2019 Sukhov, Oleg. "Leaked Memo Shows Prosecutors Accuse Biden of Getting 'Unlawful Benefit.'" *Kyiv Post*, 14 May 2019, https://www.kyivpost.com/ukraine-politics/leaked-memo-shows-prosecutors-accuse-biden-of-getting-unlawful-benefit.html.

2020 *Id.*

2021 Butsov, Yuiry. "Boomerang: The 'Manual' Prosecutor Hit Poroshenko." *Censor*, 28 March 2019, https://censor.net.ua/blogs/3119217/bumerang_ruchnoyi_prokuror_udaril_po_poroshenko.

2022 *Id.*

2023 Solomon, John. "Joe Biden's 2020 Ukrainian Nightmare: A Closed Probe Is Revived." *The Hill*, 1 April 2019, https://thehill.com/opinion/white-house/436816-joe-bidens-2020-ukrainian-nightmare-a-closed-probe-is-revived.

2024 Solomon, John. "Ukrainian to US Prosecutors: Why Don't You Want Our Evidence on Democrats?" *The Hill*, 7 April 2019, https://thehill.com/opinion/white-house/437719-ukrainian-to-us-prosecutors-why-dont-you-want-our-evidence-on-democrats.

2025 *Id.*

2026 Swan, Betsy. "Billionaire Ukrainian Oligarch Ihor Kolomoisky under Investigation by FBI." *Daily Beast*, 7 April 2019, https://www.thedailybeast.com/billionaire-ukrainian-oligarch-ihor-kolomoisky-under-investigation-by-fbi.

2027 Samuelsohn, Darren. "Mueller Obsessives Race to Get Redactions Lifted." *Politico*, 26 April 2019, https://www.politico.com/story/2019/04/26/mueller-report-redactions-1290339.

2028 *Id.*

2029 "Elections of the President of Ukraine." *Central Election Commission of Ukraine*, https://web.archive.org/web/20190424061802/https://www.cvk.gov.ua/pls/vp2019/wp300pt001f01=720.html.

2030 Zelenskyy, Volodymyr. "Volodymyr Zelenskyy's Inaugural Address." *The President of Ukraine*, 20 May 2019, https://www.president.gov.ua/en/news/inavguracijna-promova-prezidenta-ukrayini-volodimira-zelensk-55489.

2031 "First Conversation Had Between President Trump and President Zelensky of Ukraine." *Office of the Press Secretary, The White House*, 15 Nov. 2019, p. 2, https://www.justsecurity.org/wp-content/uploads/2019/11/ukraine-clearinghouse-memorandum-telephone-conversation-april-2019.pdf.

2032 *Id.* p. 3.

2033 *Id.*

2034 Bolton, *The Room Where it Happened*. p. 410.

2035 "Dep. of Jennifer Williams." p. 35.

2036 *Id.*

2037 Dale Perry is unrelated to former Energy Secretary Rick Perry.

2038 *Id.*

2039 Waldman, "American Energy Exec Tried to Reveal Plot to oust US Envoy."

2040 *Id.*

2041 Butler, Biesecker and Lardner, "Profit, not Politics: Trump Allies sought Ukraine Gas Deal."

2042 *Id.*

2043 Desmond Butler and Michael Biesecker, "Witnesses tell of Dealings of 2 Giuliani Allies" *Arkansas Democrat-Gazette* (Dec. 24, 2019). https://www.arkansasonline.com/news/2019/dec/24/witnesses-tell-of-dealings-of-2-giulian/

2044 *Id.*

2045 Bolton, *The Room Where it Happened.* p. 411.

2046 *Id.*

2047 *Id.* pp. 411–12.

2048 Tkach, Mikhail. "Kolomoisky Returned: 'I Decided to Live in Ukraine for the Next Five Years.'" *Radio Svboda,* 16 May 2019, https://www.radiosvoboda.org/a/schemes/29947380.html.

2049 Becker, Jo , Walt Bogdanich, Maggie Haberman, and Ben Protess."Why Giuliani Singled Out 2 Ukrainian Oligarchs to Help Look for Dirt." *New York Times,* 25 Nov. 2019, https://www.nytimes.com/2019/11/25/us/giuliani-ukraine-oligarchs.html.

2050 *Id.*

2051 "Dep. of Marie Yovanovitch." p. 112.

2052 *Id.*

2053 *Id.*

2054 *Id.*

2055 "Dep. of David Holmes." 15 Nove. 2019, p. 17, https://assets.documentcloud.org/documents/6552626/Holmes-Final-Version-Redacted.pdf.

2056 *Id.*

2057 Re, Greg. "Clinton-Ukraine Collusion Allegations 'Big' and 'Incredible,' Will Be Reviewed, Trump Says." *Fox News,* 25 Apr. 2019, https://www.foxnews.com/politics/trump-barr-will-look-at-incredible-possibility-of-ukraine-clinton-collusion.

2058 *Id.*

2059 Bolton, *The Room Where It Happened.* p. 414.

2060 *Id.*

2061 *Id.*

2062 *Id.*

2063 *Id.*

2064 Vogel, Ken. "Rudy Giuliani Plans Ukraine Trip to Push for Inquiries that Could Help Trump." *New York Times,* 9 May 2019, https://www.nytimes.com/2019/05/09/us/politics/giuliani-ukraine-trump.html.

2065 *Id.*

2066 *Id.*

2067 *Id.*

2068 *Id.*

2069 Perano, Ursula. "Trump Claims He Didn't Know about Giuliani Letter to Zelensky." *Axios,* 16 Jan. 2020, https://www.axios.com/trump-giuliani-letter-zelensky-ukraine-parnas-405ba89d-8538-4d8a-902d-a6ad0c228522.html.

2070 "The Trump-Ukraine Impeachment Inquiry Report." *House Permanent Select Committee on Intelligence,* 16 Dec. 2019, p. 58, https://intelligence.house.gov/uploadedfiles/the_trump-ukraine_impeachment_inquiry_report.pdf.

2071 *Id.*

2072 Protess, Ben, Andrew E. Kramer, Michael Rothfeld, and William K. Rashbaum. "Giuliani Associate Says He Gave Demand for Biden Inquiry to Ukrainians." *New York Times,* 10 Nov. 2019, https://www.nytimes.com/2019/11/10/nyregion/trump-ukraine-parnas-fruman.html.

2073 Creitz, Charles. "Giuliani Cancels Ukraine Trip, Says He'd Be 'Walking into a Group of People that Are Enemies of the US.'" *Fox News,* 11 May 2019, https://www.foxnews.com/politics/giuliani-i-am-not-going-to-ukraine-because-id-be-walking-into-a-group-of-people-that-are-enemies-of-the-us.

2074 *Id.*

2075 "Dep. of Jennifer Williams." p. 37.

2076 Wu, Nicholas. "What Giuliani Associate Lev Parnas Has Said about Trump, Pence, and Ukraine." *USA Today,* 17 Jan. 2020, https://www.usatoday.com/story/news/politics/2020/01/17/giuliani-associate-lev-parnas-what-he-said-trump-ukraine/4498122002/.

2077 Tkach, Mikhail. "Kolomoisky Returned: 'I Decided to Live in Ukraine for the Next Five Years.'" *Radio Svoboda,* 16 May 2019, https://www.radiosvoboda.org/a/schemes/29947380.html.

2078 Krasnolutska, Daryna, Kateryna Choursina, and Stephanie Baker. "Ukraine Prosecutor Says No Evidence of Wrongdoing by Bidens." *Bloomberg News,* 16 May 2019, https://www.bloomberg.com/news/articles/2019-05-16/ukraine-prosecutor-says-no-evidence-of-wrongdoing-by-bidens.

2079 Corn, David. "New Figure in Ukraine Scandal Was Taken into Police Custody at Trump Resort Last Year." *Mother Jones,* 14 Jan. 2020, https://www.motherjones.com/politics/2020/01/new-figure-in-ukraine-scandal-was-taken-into-police-custody-at-trump-resort-last-year/.

2080 *Id.*

2081 *Id.*

2082 *Id.*

2083 *Id.*

2084 *Id.*

2085 *Id.*

2086 *Id.*

2087 "Extraction Report." p. 53.

2088 Zavadski, Katie, and Jake Pearson, ProPublica, and Ilya Marritz. "A Brief Guide to Giuliani's Questionable Friends in Ukraine—'Trump, Inc.' Podcast." *ProPublica,* 2 Oct. 2019, https://www.propublica.org/article/trump-inc-podcast-rudy-giuliani-friends-in-ukraine.

2089 @RudyGiuliani. "With Omar Harfouch on the podium of the French Senate. *Twitter*, 21 May 2019, https://twitter.com/rudygiuliani/status/1130807191622094849.

2090 Helderman, Rosalind S., Tom Hamburger, Paul Sonne, and Josh Dawsey. "How Giuliani's Outreach to Ukrainian Gas Tycoon Wanted in US Shows Lengths He Took in His Hunt for Material to Bolster Trump." *Washington Post*, 15 Jan. 2020, https://www.washingtonpost.com/politics/how-giulianis-outreach-to-ukrainian-gas-tycoon-wanted-in-us-shows-lengths-he-took-in-his-hunt-for-material-to-bolster-trump/2020/01/15/64c263ba-2e5f-11ea-bcb3-ac6482c4a92f_story.html

2091 *Id.*

2092 "SAP Head Kholodnytsky, Trump's Lawyer Giuliani, and French 'Hunter for Corrupt Officials' Pratt Meet in France." *112 Ukraine,* 22 May 2019, https://112.international/politics/sap-head-kholodnytsky-trumps-lawyer-giuliani-and-french-hunter-for-corrupt-officials-pratt-meet-in-france-39982.html.

2093 *Id.*

2094 Miller, Christopher, Aubrey Belford, Veronika Melkozerova, Miriam Elder, Michael Sallah, and Ryan Brooks. "There's a Village in Ukraine Where Rudy Giuliani Is the Honorary Mayor. That's Not the Weird Part of this Story." *Buzzfeed,* 26 Oct. 2019, https://www.buzzfeednews.com/article/christopherm51/fiddlers-on-the-roof-ukraine-impeachment.

2095 "Dep. of David Holmes." p. 18.

2096 Buchman, Brandi, and Jack Rodgers. "Energy Department Releases Documents Relating to Perry's Ukraine Trip." *Courthouse News Service*, 20 Jan. 2020, https://www.courthousenews.com/energy-department-releases-documents/.

2097 Faseler, Hunter. "Reception and Lunch for International Delegations." Received by Richard Perry. 20 May 2019, p. 42, https://www.documentcloud.org/documents/6705330-DOE-Records-Regarding-U-S-Delegation-to-Ukraine.html#document/p7.

2098 *Id.* p. 37.

2099 Bolton, *The Room Where It Happened.* p, 416.

2100 *Id.*

2101 *Id.*

2102 "Dep. of Fiona Hill." pp. 55–59

2103 *Id.* p. 59.

2104 Fang, Lee. "Portland Executive Covertly Donates $1 Millon to Inauguration after Being Shamed over Trump Support." *The Intercept*, 21 April 2017, https://theintercept.com/2017/04/21/portland-executive-covertly-donates-1-million-to-inauguration-after-being-shamed-over-trump-support/.

2105 Bolton, *The Room Where It Happened.* p. 416.

2106 *Id.* p. 417.

2107 Whalen, "The Head of Ukraine's Gas Company Has Been Shot at, Pilloried on TV and Attacked by Giuliani Associates. It's All In a Day's Work."

2108 *Id.*

2109 *Id.*

2110 "Letter from Unknown to Richard Burr and Adam Schiff." 12 Aug. 2019, p. 7, https://assets.documentcloud.org/documents/6430359/Whistleblower-Complaint.pdf.

2111 "Text message from William Taylor to Kurt Volker." 29 April 2019, https://intelligence.house.gov/uploadedfiles/20191105_-_volker_additional_texts_final.pdf.

2112 "Text message from William Taylor to Kurt Volker." 26 May 2019, https://intelligence.house.gov/uploadedfiles/20191105_-_volker_additional_texts_final.pdf.

2113 "Text Message from William Taylor to Kurt Volker." 26 May 2019, https://intelligence.house.gov/uploadedfiles/20191105_-_volker_additional_texts_final.pdf.

2114 Bonner, Brian. "Ambassador William B. Taylor Returns to Ukraine to Lead US Mission." *Kyiv Post*, 18 June 2019, https://www.kyivpost.com/ukraine-politics/ambassador-william-b-taylor-returns-to-ukraine-to-lead-u-s-mission.html.

2115 "Deposition of Christopher Anderson." *House Permanent Select Committee on Intelligence*, 30 Oct. 2019, p. 15, https://assets.documentcloud.org/documents/6546423/Anderson.pdf.

2116 Johnson, Carrie, and Philip Ewing. "Robert Mueller, Long A Sphinx, speaks—Then Says It Was His Final Word." *National Public Radio*, 29 May 2019, https://www.npr.org/2019/05/29/582724398/special-counsel-robert-mueller-steps-down-after-leading-russia-inquiry.

2117 *Id.*

2118 *Id.*

2119 "DoD Announces $250M to Ukraine." *Department of Defense*, 18 June 2019, https://www.defense.gov/Newsroom/Releases/Release/Article/1879340/dod-announces-250m-to-ukraine/.

2120 Lipton, Eric, Maggie Haberman, and Mark Mazzetti. "Behind the Ukraine Aid Freeze: 84 Days of Conflict and Confusion." *New York Times*, 29 Dec. 2019, https://www.nytimes.com/2019/12/29/us/politics/trump-ukraine-military-aid.html?smid=nytcore-ios-share.

2121 Bolton, *The Room Where It Happened.* p. 418.

2122 Lipton, Haberman, and Mazzetti. "Behind the Ukraine Aid Freeze: 84 Days of Conflict and Confusion."

2123 *Id.*

2124 *Id.*

2125 "HSPCI New Parnas Evidence." p. 1, https://www.npr.org/2020/01/15/796593183/new-lev-parnas-documents-suggest-u-s-ambassador-was-under-surveillance-in-ukrain.

2126 *Id.*

2127 *Id.* p. 3.

2128 *Id.*

2129 *Id.*

2130 Lipton, Haberman, and Mazzetti. "Behind the Ukraine Aid Freeze: 84 Days of Conflict and Confusion."

2131 *Id.*

2132 *Id.*

2133 *Id.*

2134 *Id.*

2135 *Id.*

2136 Zubkova, "Appeals Court: Sytnyk And MP Leshchenko Did No Act Illegally by Disclosing that Manafort's Name Is in Party Of Regions' 'Black Ledger.'"

2137 "Dep. of David Holmes." p. 20.

2138 *Id.*

2139 "FARA Form 2 of Yorktown Strategies." 30 Dec. 2019, pp. 36–7, https://efile.fara.gov/docs/6491-Supplemental-Statement-20191230-4.pdf.

2140 "Dep. of Fiona Hill." p. 63.

2141 *Id.*

2142 *Id.* p. 65.

2143 *Id.* p. 67.

2144 *Id.* p. 67. *See also*, Bolton, *The Room Where It Happened*. p. 419.

2145 "Dep. of Alexander Vindman." 29 Oct. 2019, p. 27, https://assets.documentcloud.org/documents/6543468/Alexander-Vindman-Testimony.pdf.

2146 *Id.* p. 28.

2147 *Id.*

2148 Bolton, *The Room Where It Happened*. p. 419.

2149 "Dep. of Fiona Hill." p. 68.

2150 *Id.* p. 69.

2151 "Dep. of Alexander Vindman." p. 32.

2152 *Id.*

2153 "Dep. of Fiona Hill." p. 69.

2154 *Id.*

2155 "Dep. of Alexander Vindman." p. 35.

2156 "Dep. of Fiona Hill." pp. 69–70.

2157 *Id.* p. 70.

2158 "Dep. of Alexander Vindman." p. 36.

2159 *Id.*

2160 *Id.* p. 37.

2161 *Id.* pp. 37–38

2162 *Id.* p. 102.

2163 *Id.* p. 103.

2164 "Dep. of Fiona Hill." pp. 70–1.

2165 *Id.* p. 71.

2166 Bolton, *The Room Where It Happened.* p. 419.

2167 "Dep. of Fiona Hill." p. 71.

2168 Emma, Caitlin, and Andrew Desiderio. "White House Budget Officials Resigned Amid Frustration with Ukraine Aid Freeze." *Politico,* 26 Nov. 2019, https://www.politico.com/news/2019/11/26/democrats-trump-budget-ukraine-aid-074016.

2169 Entous, Adam. "What Fiona Hill Learned in the White House." *New Yorker,* 22 June 2020, https://www.newyorker.com/magazine/2020/06/29/what-fiona-hill-learned-in-the-white-house.

2170 Vogel, Kenneth P. "Behind the Whistle-Blower Case, a Long-Held Trump Grudge toward Ukraine." *New York Times,* 20 Sept. 2019, https://www.nytimes.com/2019/09/20/us/politics/whistle-blower-trump-grudge.html.

2171 *Id.*

2172 "Text message from Kurt Volker to William Taylor, Jr. and Gordon Sondland."22 July 2019, https://foreignaffairs.house.gov/_cache/files/a/4/a4a91fab-99cd-4eb9-9c6c-ec1c586494b9/621801458E982E9903839ABC7404A917.chairmen-letter-on-state-departmnent-texts-10-03-19.pdf.

2173 Zubkova, "Appeals Court: Sytnyk and MP Leschenko Did No Act Illegally By Disclosing That Manafort's Name Is In Party of Regions' 'Black Ledger.'"

2174 Belford and Melkozerova. "Meet the Florida Duo Helping Giuliani Investigate for Trump in Ukraine."

2175 *Id.*

CHAPTER 11 STRAY VOLTAGE

[2176] "Full Transcript: Mueller Testimony before House Judiciary, Intelligence Committees." *NBC News,* 25 July 2019, https://www.nbcnews.com/politics/congress/full-transcript-robert-mueller-house-committee-testimony-n1033216.

[2177] *Id.* at *passim.*

[2178] *Id.*

[2179] Davis, Julie Hirschfeld, and Mark Mazzetti. "Highlights of Robert Mueller's Testimony to Congress." *New York Times,* 24 July 2019, https://www.nytimes.com/2019/07/24/us/politics/mueller-testimony.html.

[2180] Bolton, *The Room Where It Happened.* p. 420.

[2181] "Dep. of Alexander Vindman." pp. 46-7.

[2182] "Text from Kurt Volker to Andriy Yermak." 25 July 2019, https://foreignaffairs.house.gov/_cache/files/a/4/a4a91fab-99cd-4eb9-9c6c-ec1c586494b9/621801458E982E9903839ABC7404A917.chairmen-letter-on-state-departmnent-texts-10-03-19.pdf.

[2183] "Memo of Telephone Conversation." *The White House,* 25 July 2019, p.1, https://www.whitehouse.gov/wp-content/uploads/2019/09/Unclassified09.2019.pdf.

[2184] *Id.* p. 2.

[2185] *Id.* p. 3.

[2186] *Id.*

[2187] *Id.*

[2188] *Id.* pp. 3-4.

[2189] *Id.* p. 4.

[2190] *Id.*

[2191] The transcript does not include a statement by Trump naming Burisma. Later testimony by two witnesses indicates that Zelenskyy did in fact say "Burisma." and that this word was edited from the call record.

[2192] *Id.*

[2193] *Id.*

[2194] *Id.* p. 5.

[2195] *Id.*

[2196] "Dep. of Tim Morrison." 31 Oct. 2019, p. 39, https://intelligence.house.gov/uploadedfiles/morrison_final_version.pdf.

2197 *Id.* p. 41.

2198 *Id.*

2199 "Dep. of Alexander Vindman." pp. 94–5.

2200 *Id.* p. 95.

2201 *Id.* p. 50.

2202 Duffy, Michael. "RE: Ukraine Foreign Assistance" Received by David Norquist, et al. 25 July 2019, https://assets.documentcloud.org/documents/6590667/CPI-v-DoD-Dec-20-2019-Release.pdf.

2203 *Id.*

2204 "Hearing Tr. Impeachment Inquiry, Laura Cooper and David Hale." 20 Nov. 2019, pp. 13–14, https://republicans-intelligence.house.gov/uploadedfiles/cooper_and_hale_hearing_transcript.pdf.

2205 "FARA Form 2 of Yorktown Strategies." 30 Dec. 2019, pp. 57–8.

2206 Miller, Greg, and Greg Jaffe. "At Least Four National Security Officials Raised Alarms about Ukraine Policy before and After Trump Call with Ukrainian President." *Washington Post,* 10 Oct. 2019, https://www.washingtonpost.com/national-security/at-least-four-national-security-officials-raised-alarms-about-ukraine-policy-before-and-after-trump-call-with-ukrainian-president/2019/10/10/ffe0c88a-eb6d-11e9-9c6d-436a0df4f31d_story.html.

2207 "Tr. Testimony of Alexander Vindman and Jennifer Williams." 19 Nov. 2019, p. 19, https://docs.house.gov/meetings/IG/IG00/20191119/110231/HHRG-116-IG00-Transcript-20191119.pdf.

2208 *Id.*

2209 "The Trump-Ukraine Impeachment Report." p. 106.

2210 "Dep. of David Holmes." pp. 22–23.

2211 *Id.* p. 24.

2212 *Id.*

2213 Barnes, Julian E., Michael S. Schmidt, Adam Goldman, and Katie Benner. "White House Knew of Whistle-Blower's Allegations Soon after Trump's Call with Ukraine Leader." *New York Times*, 26 Sept. 2019, https://www.nytimes.com/2019/09/26/us/politics/who-is-whistleblower.html.

2214 *Id.*

2215 *Id.*

2216 Barnes, Julian E., Michael S. Schmidt, and Matthew Rosenberg. "Schiff Got Early Account of Accusations as Whistle-Blower's Concerns Grew." *New York Times,* 2 Oct. 2019, https://www.nytimes.com/2019/10/02/us/politics/adam-schiff-whistleblower.html.

2217 *Id.*

2218 Hosenball, Mark. "Whistleblower Never Met or Talked with Schiff: Source." *Reuters,* 13 Nov. 2019, https://www.reuters.com/article/us-trump-impeachment-whistleblower/whistleblower-never-met-or-talked-with-schiff-source-idUSKBN1XN2O5.

²²¹⁹ Bolton, *The Room Where It Happened*. p. 423.

²²²⁰ *Id*.

²²²¹ *Id*.

²²²² Swan, Betsy, and Asawin Suebsaeng. "Parnas Attended Giuliani's Madrid Meeting with Zelensky Aide." *Daily Beast*, 21 Nov. 2019, https://www.thedailybeast.com/lev-parnas-attended-rudy-giulianis-madrid-meeting-with-zelensky-aide-andriy-yermak.

²²²³ "Extraction Report." p. 61.

²²²⁴ Helderman, Rosalind S., Devlin Barrett, Matt Zapotosky, and Tom Hamburger. "A Wealthy Venezuelan Hosted Giuliani as He Pursued Ukraine Campaign. Then Giuliani Lobbied the Justice Department on His Behalf." *Washington Post*, 26 Nov. 2019, https://www.washingtonpost.com/politics/a-wealthy-venezuelan-hosted-giuliani-as-he-pursued-ukraine-campaign-then-giuliani-lobbied-the-justice-department-on-his-behalf/2019/11/26/272105a2-0ec5-11ea-b0fc-62cc38411ebb_story.html.

²²²⁵ *Id*.

²²²⁶ Dawsey, Josh, Paul Sonne, Michael Kranish, and David L. Stern. "How Trump and Giuliani Pressured Ukraine to Investigate the President's Rivals." *Washington Post*, 20 Sept. 2019, https://www.washingtonpost.com/politics/how-trump-and-giuliani-pressured-ukraine-to-investigate-the-presidents-rivals/2019/09/20/0955801c-dbb6-11e9-a688-303693fb4b0b_story.html.

²²²⁷ *Id*.

²²²⁸ *Id*.

²²²⁹ Wood, "Where Did the Money come from for Rudy Giuliani's Ukraine Operations?"

²²³⁰ *Id*.

²²³¹ Swan, Betsy, and Asawin Suebsaeng. "Pro-Trump Network OAN Tried to Get this Ukrainian Millionaire a Visa Before His Arrest." *Daily Beast*, 10 Dec. 2019, https://www.thedailybeast.com/pro-trump-network-oan-tried-to-get-ukrainian-millionaire-oleksandr-onyshchenko-a-visa-before-his-arrest.

²²³² "Tr. Hearing of Kurt Volker and Tim Morrison." 19 Nov. 2019, p. 41, https://docs.house.gov/meetings/IG/IG00/20191119/110232/HHRG-116-IG00-Transcript-20191119.pdf.

²²³³ *Id*.

²²³⁴ "Letter from Eliot L. Engel and Adam B. Schiff to Members, House Intelligence Cmte, et al." 3 Oct. 2019, p. 6, https://foreignaffairs.house.gov/_cache/files/a/4/a4a91fab-99cd-4eb9-9c6c-ec1c586494b9/621801458E982E9903839ABC7404A917.chairmen-letter-on-state-departmnent-texts-10-03-19.pdf.

²²³⁵ *Id*.

²²³⁶ *Id*.

²²³⁷ *Id*.

²²³⁸ "The Trump-Ukraine Impeachment Report." p. 123.

²²³⁹ *Id*. p. 125.

2240 *Id.*

2241 "Letter to Richard Burr and Adam Schiff." 12 Aug. 2019, p. 1, https://assets.documentcloud.org/documents/6430359/Whistleblower-Complaint.pdf.

2242 Complaints from Intelligence Community whistleblowers intended for Congress are required to go through the Inspector General for the Intelligence Community first. *See* 50 USC. 5033(k) (2018).

2243 *Id.*

2244 *Id.* pp. 4–7.

2245 Dilanian, Ken, and Julia Ainsley. "CIA's Top Lawyer Made 'Criminal Referral' on Complaint about Trump Ukraine Call." *NBC News,* 4 Oct. 2019, https://www.nbcnews.com/politics/trump-impeachment-inquiry/cia-s-top-lawyer-made-criminal-referral-whistleblower-s-complaint-n1062481.

2246 *Id.*

2247 *Id.*

2248 "Letter from Michael K. Atkinson to Joseph Maguire."26 Aug. 2019, p. 1, https://assets.documentcloud.org/documents/6430363/Icig-Letter-to-Acting-Dni-Unclassified.pdf.

2249 *Id.*

2250 *Id.* p. 3.

2251 *Id.* p. 6.

2252 **Bolton,** *The Room Where It Happened.* p. 424.

2253 *Id.*

2254 *Id.*

2255 *Id.*

2256 Emma, Catlin, and Connor O'Brien. "Trump Holds up Ukraine Military Aid Meant to Confront Russia." *Politico,* 28 Aug. 2018, https://www.politico.com/story/2019/08/28/trump-ukraine-military-aid-russia-1689531.

2257 Letter from Eliot L. Engel and Adam B. Schiff to Members, House Intelligence Cmte. *et al.* p. 8.

2258 **Bolton,** *The Room Where It Happened.* p. 425.

2259 *Id.* p. 427.

2260 *Id.* p. 428.

2261 *Id.*

2262 "Dep. of William B. Taylor." 22 Oct. 2019, pp. 33–34, https://docs.house.gov/meetings/IG/IG00/CPRT-116-IG00-D008.pdf.

2263 *Id.* p. 34.

2264 Vazquez, Meagan. "Trump cancels Poland Trip to Monitor Hurricane". *CNN,* 29 Aug. 2019, https://www.cnn.com/2019/08/29/politics/donald-trump-poland-hurricane-dorian/index.html.

2265 "Letter from Eliot L. Engel and Adam B. Schiff to Members, House Intelligence Cmte. et al. p. 8.

2266 Bolton, *The Room Where It Happened* p. 430.

2267 Letter from Eliot L. Engel and Adam B. Schiff to Members, House Intelligence Cmte. *et al.* p. 8.

2268 *Id.*

2269 Dep. of William B. Taylor at 36.

2270 *Id.*

2271 Hearing Tr. of Gordon Sondland, p. 30-1. (Nov. 20, 2019). https://docs.house.gov/meetings/IG/IG00/20191120/110233/HHRG-116-IG00-Transcript-20191120.pdf

2272 The Trump-Ukraine Impeachment Report at 132.

2273 *Id.*

2274 Dep. of William B. Taylor at 35.

2275 Declaration of Gordon Sondland at 2 (Nov. 4, 2019). https://judiciary.house.gov/uploadedfiles/2019-11-04_declaration_of_sondland.pdf

2276 *Id.*

2277 "Remarks by Vice President Pence and President Duda of Poland in Joint Press Conference Warsaw, Poland" *The White House* (Sept. 2, 2019). https://www.whitehouse.gov/briefings-statements/remarks-vice-president-pence-president-duda-poland-joint-press-conference-warsaw-poland/

2278 *Id.*

2279 *Id.*

2280 Becker, Bogdanich, Haberman and Protess, "Why Giuliani singled Out 2 Ukrainian Oligarchs to help look for Dirt."

2281 Matt Zapotosky, Rosalind S. Helderman, Tom Hamburger and Josh Dawsey, "Prosecutors flagged Possible Ties between Ukrainian Gas Tycoon and Giuliani Associates" *Washington Post* (Oct. 22, 2019). https://www.washingtonpost.com/politics/prosecutors-flagged-possible-ties-between-ukrainian-gas-tycoon-and-giuliani-associates/2019/10/22/4ee22e7c-f020-11e9-b648-76bcf86eb67e_story.html

2282 *Id.*

2283 Witness Statement of Viktor Mikolajovich Shokin p. 1 (Sept. 4, 2019). https://cdn.factcheck.org/UploadedFiles/427618359-Shokin-Statement-1.pdf

2284 *Id.*

2285 *Id.* at 2.

2286 *Id.*

2287 *Id.* at 2-3.

2288 *Id.*

2289 *Id.* at 4-5.

2290 Editorial Board, "Trump tries to force Ukraine to meddle in the 2020 Election *Washington Post* (Sept. 5, 2019). https://www.washingtonpost.com/opinions/global-opinions/is-trump-strong-arming-ukraines-new-president-for-political-gain/2019/09/05/4eb239b0-cffa-11e9-8c1c-7c8ee785b855_story.html

2291 *Id.*

2292 Dep. of William B. Taylor at 38.

2293 "Letter from Eliot L. Engel and Adam B. Schiff to Members, House Intelligence Cmte. et al." pp. 8-9.

2294 "Dep. of William Taylor." p. 39.

2295 "Letter from Eliot L. Engel and Adam B. Schiff to Members, House Intelligence Cmte. et al." p. 9.

2296 Fandos, Nicholas. "Democrats Plan Vote to Formalize Procedures for Impeachment Investigation." *New York Times*, 8 Sept. 2019, https://www.nytimes.com/2019/09/08/us/politics/democrats-judiciary-procedures-impeachment-trump.html?searchResultPosition=6.

2297 *Id.*

2298 Fandos, Nicholas. "Democrats to Broaden Impeachment Inquiry into Trump to Corruption Accusations." *New York Times,* 8 Sept. 2019, https://www.nytimes.com/2019/09/08/us/politics/impeachment-investigation-trump.html.

2299 "Dep. of William Taylor." p. 39.

2300 *Id.*

2301 *Id.*

2302 *Id.*

2303 *Id.*

CHAPTER 12 A SCANDAL OF MAJOR PROPORTIONS

2304 **Bolton,** *The Room Where It Happened.* p. 432.

2305 "Letter from Adam Schiff, et al. to Pat Cipollone."9 Sept. 2019, p. 1, https://intelligence.house.gov/uploadedfiles/ele_schiff_cummings_letter_to_cipollone_on_ukraine.pdf.

2306 *Id.*

2307 *Id.* p. 2.

2308 *Id.* pp. 2-3.

2309 "Letter from Adam Schiff, et al. to Mike Pompeo." 9 Sept. 2019, pp. 1-5, https://intelligence.house.gov/uploadedfiles/ele_schiff_cummings_letter_to_sec_pompeo_on_ukraine.pdf.

2310 Letter from Michael K. Atkinson to Adam Schiff, *et al.* (Sept. 9, 2019). https://intelligence.house.gov/uploadedfiles/20190909_-_ic_ig_letter_to_hpsci_on_whistleblower.pdf

2311 Bolton, *The Room Where It Happened* p. 433.

2312 *Id.*

2313 *Id.*

2314 *Id.*

2315 *Id.*

2316 *Id.* p. 434.

2317 @realDonaldTrump. "I informed John Bolton last night that his services are no longer needed at the White House. I disagreed strongly with many of his suggestions, as did others in the Administration, and therefore...." *Twitter*, 10 Sept. 2019, https://twitter.com/davidaxelrod/status/1171458162429284352.

2318 "Letter from Adam Schiff to Joseph Mcguire." 10 Sept. 2019, pp. 1-2, https://intelligence.house.gov/uploadedfiles/20190910_-_chm_schiff_letter_to_acting_dni_maguire.pdf.

2319 *Id.* at 2.

2320 @rabrowne75. "The @StateDept notified Congress Wednesday that it will obligate $141.5 million in Foreign Military Financing for Ukraine. This is separate from the $250 million in Ukraine Security Assistance funds that has been held up by the Trump White House." 12 Sept. 2019, https://twitter.com/rabrowne75/status/1172151201577746432?s=20.

2321 Demirjian, Karoun, Josh Dawsey, Ellen Nakashima, and Carol D. Leonnig. "Trump Ordered Hold on Military Aid Days before Calling Ukrainian President, Officials Say." *Washington Post,* 23 Sept. 2019, https://www.washingtonpost.com/national-security/trump-ordered-hold-on-military-aid-days-before-calling-ukrainian-president-officials-say/2019/09/23/df93a6ca-de38-11e9-8dc8-498eabc129a0_story.html.

2322 "Letter from Adam Schiff to Joseph Mcguire." 13 Sept. 2019, p. 1, https://intelligence.house.gov/uploadedfiles/20190913_-_chm_schiff_letter_to_acting_dni_re_whistleblower_-_subpoena.pdf.

2323 *Id.*

2324 *Id.*

2325 Lippman, Daniel, and Tina Nguyen. "The Mystery of Rudy Giuliani's Spokeswoman." *Politico*, 10 Dec. 2019, https://www.politico.com/news/2019/12/10/christianne-allen-giuliani-079762.

2326 "Extraction Report." p. 63.

2327 Nakashima, Ellen, Shane Harris, Greg Miller, and Carol D. Leonnig. "Whistleblower Complaint about President Trump Involves Ukraine, According to Two People Familiar with the Matter." *Washington Post,* 19 Sept. 2019, https://www.washingtonpost.com/national-security/whistleblower-complaint-about-president-trump-involves-ukraine-according-to-two-people-familiar-with-the-matter/2019/09/19/07e33f0a-daf6-11e9-bfb1-849887369476_story.html.

2328 *Id.*

2329 "Transcript: Cuomo Prime Time." *CNN,* 19 Sept. 2019, http://transcripts.cnn.com/TRANSCRIPTS/1909/19/CPT.01.html.

2330 *Id.*

2331 *Id.*

2332 *Id.*

2333 *Id.*

2334 *Id.*

2335 *Id.*

2336 *Id.*

2337 *Id.*

2338 *Id.*

2339 *Id.*

2340 *Id.*

2341 *Id.*

2342 *Id.*

2343 *Id.*

2344 *Id.*

2345 *Id.*

2346 *Id.*

2347 *Id.*

2348 *Id.*

2349 Kramer, Andrew E. "Ukraine Pressured on US Political Investigations." *New York Times,* 20 Sept. 2019, https://www.nytimes.com/2019/09/20/world/europe/ukraine-trump-zelensky.html.

2350 Pierson, Brendan, and Karen Freifeld. "Giuliani Associate Paid $1 Million by Indicted Ukrainian Oligarch's Lawyer: Prosecutor." *Reuters,* 17 Dec. 2019, https://www.reuters.com/article/us-usa-trump-giuliani-parnas-oligarch/giuliani-associate-paid-1-million-by-indicted-ukrainian-oligarchs-lawyer-prosecutor-idUSKBN1YL26B.

2351 Przybyla, Heidi, and Adam Edelman. "Nancy Pelosi Announces Formal Impeachment Inquiry of Trump." *NBC News,* 24 Sept. 2019, https://www.nbcnews.com/politics/trump-impeachment-inquiry/pelosi-announce-formal-xmpeachment-inquiry-trump-n1058251.

2352 "Extraction Report." p. 64.

2353 *Id.*

2354 *Id.*

2355 Mettler, Katie, and Carol D. Leonnig. "'Transcripts' of Presidential Calls Are Nearly Verbatim but Not Exact. Here's How the Process Works." *Washington Post,* 25 Sept. 2019, https://www.washingtonpost.com/national-security/2019/09/25/transcripts-presidential-calls-are-nearly-verbatim-not-exact-heres-how-it-works/.

2356 "Engel Statement on September 23, 2019 Call with John Bolton." *House Committee on Foreign Affairs,* 29 Jan. 2020, https://foreignaffairs.house.gov/2020/1/engel-statement-on-september-23-2019-call-with-john-bolton.

2357 Obeidallah, Dean. "'SNL' Cold Open Reveals What a Difference Four Months Can Make." *CNN,* 30 Sept. 2019, https://www.cnn.com/2019/09/29/opinions/saturday-night-live-donald-trump-fortunes-obeidallah/index.html.

2358 *Id.*

2359 Fandos, Nicholas. "House Subpoenas Giuliani, Trump's Lawyer, for Ukraine Records." *New York Times,* 30 Sept. 2019, https://www.nytimes.com/2019/09/30/us/politics/impeach-giuliani-subpoena.html.

2360 "Subpoena Schedule." *House Permanent Select Committee on Intelligence,* https://oversight.house.gov/sites/democrats.oversight.house.gov/files/documents/20190930%20-%20Giuliani%20HPSCI%20Subpoena%20Schedule%20Only.pdf.

2361 "TRANSCRIPT: 1/16/20, The Rachel Maddow Show" *MSNBC,* 16 Jan. 2020, http://www.msnbc.com/transcripts/rachel-maddow-show/2020-01-16.

2362 *Id.*

2363 *Id.*

2364 *Id.*

2365 "Extraction Report." p. 133.

2366 "TRANSCRIPT: 1/16/20, The Rachel Maddow Show."

2367 DeYoung, Karen, Josh Dawsey, Karoun Demirjian, and John Hudson. "Impeachment Inquiry Erupts into Battle between Executive, Legislative Branches." *Washington Post,* 1 Oct. 2019, https://www.washingtonpost.com/national-security/pompeo-says-state-dept-officials-wont-show-up-for-scheduled-impeachment-depositions-this-week/2019/10/01/b350f8a2-e459-11e9-a331-2df12d56a80b_story.html.

2368 *Id.*

2369 Herb, Jeremy, Lauren Fox, Manu Raju, and Jennifer Hansler. "State Department Inspector General gives Congress Documents that Giuliani Provided." *CNN,* https://www.cnn.com/2019/10/02/politics/state-department-inspector-general-briefing-congress/index.html.

²³⁷⁰ "Letter from John Dowd to Nicholas A. Mitchell." 3 Oct. 2019, p. 2, https://www.justsecurity.org/wp-content/uploads/2019/11/ukraine-clearinghouse-2019.10.03.dowd-letter-to-committees.pdf.

²³⁷¹ *Id.*

²³⁷² "Extraction Report." p. 133.

²³⁷³ *Id.*

²³⁷⁴ Saul, Emily. "Giuliani Crony Igor Fruman Was Arrested Getting on Vienna-Bound Flight." *New York Times*, 1 Nov. 2019, https://nypost.com/2019/11/01/giuliani-crony-igor-fruman-was-arrested-getting-on-vienna-bound-flight/.

²³⁷⁵ Waas, "Ukraine Continued: How a Crucial Witness Escaped."

²³⁷⁶ Investigative reporter Murray Waas based his story on information provided by a source he described as a "former senior US diplomatic official." Waas's source also had their own opinions about the impeachment inquiry—recommending that the Democrats look into the escape of Konstantin Kilimnik from Ukraine to Russia.

²³⁷⁷ *Id.*

²³⁷⁸ Viswanatha, Aruna, Rebecca Ballhaus, Sadie Gurman, and Byron Tau. "Two Giuliani Associates Who Helped Him on Ukraine Charged with Campaign-Finance Violations." *Wall Street Journal*, 10 Oct. 2019, https://www.wsj.com/articles/two-foreign-born-men-who-helped-giuliani-on-ukraine-arrested-on-campaign-finance-charges-11570714188.

²³⁷⁹ Saul, "Giuliani Crony Igor Fruman Was Arrested Getting on Vienna-Bound Flight."

²³⁸⁰ Mazzetti, Mark, Eileen Sullivan, Adam Goldman, and William K. Rashbaum. "2 Giuliani Associates Arrested with One-Way Tickets at US Airport." *New York Times*, 10 Oct. 2019, https://www.nytimes.com/2019/10/10/us/politics/lev-parnas-igor-fruman-arrested-giuliani.html.

²³⁸¹ "Prosecutors' News Conference on Arrest of Giuliani Associates." *C-SPAN*, 10 Oct. 2019, https://www.c-span.org/video/?465164-1/prosecutors-hold-news-conference-arrest-indictment-giuliani-ukraine-associates.

²³⁸² "TRANSCRIPT: 1/16/20, The Rachel Maddow Show."

²³⁸³ *Id.*

²³⁸⁴ *Id.*

²³⁸⁵ *Id.*

²³⁸⁶ Klasfeld, Adam. "Denying Election Crimes, Giuliani Friends Raise Specter of Exec Privilege." *Courthouse News*, 23 Oct. 2019, https://www.courthousenews.com/denying-election-crimes-giuliani-friends-raise-specter-of-exec-privilege/

²³⁸⁷ "MP Andriy Derkach: 'NABU Leaks' Is the Key for Salvaging Ukraine-US Relations." *Interfax-Ukraine*, 10 Nov. 2019, https://www.google.com/search?q=andriy+derkach&rlz=1C1CHBF_enUS763US763&sxsrf=ALeKk02ApNOf8jdnNn0AjGZRO0mU5Mjomw%3A1597686264939&source=lnt&tbs=cdr%3A1%2Ccd_min%3A6%2F1%2F2019%2Ccd_max%3A2%2F7%2F2020&tbm=.

²³⁸⁸ *Id.*

²³⁸⁹ *Id.*

2390 *Id.*

2391 *Id.*

2392 Parnas's lawyer Joe Bondy would reveal Nasirov's involvement in January 2020. Sources told the *Wall Street Journal* Nasirov was involved in the original Hudson Holdings deal. Also in January, Bondy personally tweeted out video of Lev Parnas introducing Nasirov to President-Elect Trump at Mar-a-Lago. House impeachment managers chose not to charge on the peace efforts of 2016-17.

2393 *Id.*

2394 *Id.*

2395 Baker, Peter, and Nicholas Fandos. "Bolton Objected to Ukraine Pressure Campaign, Calling Giuliani 'a Hand Grenade.'" *New York Times*, 14 Oct. 2019, https://www.nytimes.com/2019/10/14/us/politics/bolton-giuliani-fiona-hill-testimony.html.

2396 Cheretsky, Victor. "Will Spain Extradite Fugitive People's Deputy Onyshchenko to Ukraine?" 24 July 2019, https://www.dw.com/uk/a-44786090.

2397 Ivanova, Tsvetkova, Zhegulev, and Baker. "What Hunter Biden Did on the Board of Ukrainian Energy Company Burisma."

2398 Fox, "Michael Cohen Is Now Even More Valuable than Before: The President's Former Attorney offers Dirt on Giuliani Associate Lev Parnas."

2399 *Id.*

2400 *Id.*

2401 *Kupperman v. House of Representatives*, Civil Case No. 19-3224 (RJL) (D.D.C. Dec. 30, 2019), p. 1, https://casetext.com/case/kupperman-v-us-house-of-representatives.

2402 Hawkins, Derek, and Tom Hamburger. "Former Top Trump Aide Asks Court to Rule on Whether He Must Testify in Impeachment Inquiry." *Washington Post*, 26 Oct. 2019, https://www.washingtonpost.com/politics/2019/10/26/former-top-trump-aide-asks-court-rule-whether-he-must-testify-impeachment-inquiry/.

2403 *Kupperman v. House of Representatives*, Civil Case No. 19-3224 (RJL) (D.D.C. Dec. 30, 2019), p.7.

2404 "Dep. of Catherine Croft." 30 Oct. 2019, pp. 39–40, https://assets.documentcloud.org/documents/6546394/Catherine-Croft-Testimony.pdf.

2405 Swan, Betsy, and Sam Brodey. "Impeachment Probe Eyes Mulvaney's Office in Early Effort to Hold up Ukraine Aid." *Daily Beast*, 31 Oct. 2019, https://www.thedailybeast.com/impeachment-probe-eyes-mulvaneys-office-in-early-effort-to-hold-up-ukraine-aid.

2406 Mazzetti, Mark, Eric Lipton, and Andrew E. Kramer. "Inside Ukraine's Push to Cultivate Trump from the Start." *New York Times*, 4 Nov. 2019, https://www.nytimes.com/2019/11/04/us/politics/poroshenko-trump-ukraine.html.

2407 *Id.*

2408 Bertrand, Natasha, and Mona Zhang. "Meet the Cannabis Lawyer Beating Trump at His Own Game." *Politico*, 24 Jan. 2019, https://www.politico.com/news/magazine/2020/01/24/joseph-bondy-lev-parnas-attorney-104004.

²⁴⁰⁹ Roston, Aram. "Exclusive: Giuliani Associate Parnas Will Comply with Trump Impeachment Inquiry-Lawyer." *Reuters*, 4 Nov. 2019, https://www.reuters.com/article/us-usa-trump-impeachment-parnas-exclusiv-idUSKBN1XE297.

²⁴¹⁰ Shear, Michael D., and Nicholas Fandos. "Republicans Argue Impeachment Case Falls Short of Proving Trump Misconduct." *New York Times,* 9 Nov. 2019, https://www.nytimes.com/2019/11/09/us/politics/republican-strategy-impeachment-trump.html.

²⁴¹¹ *Id.*

²⁴¹² "Letter from Devin Nunes to Adam Schiff." 9 Nov. 2019, p. 4, https://int.nyt.com/data/documenthelper/6436-nunes-witness-list-house-intel-committee/7913a874e301f2536a75/optimized/full.pdf#page=1.

²⁴¹³ "Memorandum from Republican Staff, Permanent Select Committee on Intelligence, et al. to Members, Permanent Select Committee. on Intelligence, et al." 12 Nov. 2019, p. 2, https://assets.documentcloud.org/documents/6546539/GOP-Memo.pdf.

²⁴¹⁴ On October 8, Trepak was appointed as deputy prosecutor general by President Zelenskyy. Oksana Grytsenko, "Ex-official who found Incriminating Evidence on Manafort named Deputy Prosecutor General" *Kyiv Post* (Oct. 8, 2019). Accessed at: https://www.kyivpost.com/ukraine-politics/ex-official-who-found-incriminating-evidence-on-manafort-becomes-deputy-prosecutor-general.html

²⁴¹⁵ *Id.* at 7.

²⁴¹⁶ "William B. Taylor and George Kent.Impeachment Inquiry of Donald John Trump." *House Permanent Select Committee on Intelligence*, 13 Nov. 2019, p. 9, https://docs.house.gov/meetings/IG/IG00/20191113/110188/HHRG-116-IG00-Transcript-20191113.pdf.

²⁴¹⁷ *Id.*

²⁴¹⁸ *Id.* p. 11.

²⁴¹⁹ *Id.* p. 12.

²⁴²⁰ "Gordon Sondland. Impeachment Inquiry of Donald John Trump." *House Permanent Select Committee on Intelligence*, 20 Nov. 2019, p. 12.

²⁴²¹ *Id.* p. 27.

²⁴²² *Id.* at *passim.*

²⁴²³ "Will Ferrell Appears as Gordon Sondland Next to Baldwin's Trump in 'SNL' Cold Open." *Global News Canada* 23 Nov. 2019, https://globalnews.ca/video/6210566/alec-baldwin-reprises-role-of-trump-on-snl-parodies-i-want-no-quid-pro-quo-remarks.

²⁴²⁴ *Id.*

²⁴²⁵ "Fiona Hill and David Holmes. Impeachment Inquiry of Donald John Trump." *House Permanent Select Committee on Intelligence*, 21 Nov. 2019, pp. 40–1, https://republicans-intelligence.house.gov/uploadedfiles/hill_and_holmes_hearing_transcript.pdf.

²⁴²⁶ *Id.*

²⁴²⁷ *Id.* p. 41.

²⁴²⁸ *Id.*

2429 *Id.* p. 81.

2430 *Id.*

2431 *Id.*

2432 *Id.* p. 82.

2433 *Id.*

2434 *Id.*

2435 *Id.*

2436 *Id.* p. 83.

2437 *Id.*

2438 *Id.*

2439 *Id.*

2440 *Id.*

2441 *Id.* p. 88.

2442 *Id.* p. 89.

2443 *Id.* p. 93.

2444 Bycoffe, Aaron, Ella Koeze, and Nathaniel Rakich. "Did Americans Support Removing Trump From Office?" *Five Thirty Eight*, 12 Feb. 2020, https://projects.fivethirtyeight.com/impeachment-polls/.

2445 *Id.*

2446 Bertrand and Zhang. "Meet the Cannabis Lawyer beating Trump at His Own Game."

2447 Helderman, Rosalind S,. and Colby Itkowitz. "Top House Democrat Says Ethics Probe of Nunes Is Likely over Alleged Meeting with Ukrainian about Bidens." *Washington Post*, 23 Nov. 2019, https://www.washingtonpost.com/politics/top-house-democrat-says-ethics-probe-of-nunes-is-likely-over-alleged-meeting-with-ukrainian-about-bidens/2019/11/23/0dde6b22-0e0a-11ea-97ac-a7ccc8dd1ebc_story.html.

2448 Saakov, Valery. "Onyshchenko Is To Be Extradited from Spain to Ukraine—Sytnyk." *Deutsche Welle*, 14 Nov. 2019, https://www.dw.com/uk/a-51236489.

2449 Myroniuk, Anna, and Jack Laurenson. "After 3 Years in Exile, Scandalous Millionaire to Return to Ukraine, Face Charges." *Kyiv Post*, 27 Nov. 2019, https://www.kyivpost.com/ukraine-politics/after-3-years-in-exile-scandalous-millionaire-to-return-to-ukraine-face-charges.html.

2450 Swan, Betsy, and Adam Rawnsley. "Ukrainian Fugitive Who Claimed to Have Dirt on Biden Firm Is Arrested." *Daily Beast*, 6 Dec. 2019, https://www.thedailybeast.com/oleksandr-onyshchenko-ukrainian-fugitive-who-claimed-to-have-dirt-on-burisma-is-arrested.

2451 Samuels, Brett. "Giuliani Draws Attention with Latest Trip to Ukraine." *The Hill*, 6 Dec. 2019, https://thehill.com/homenews/administration/473458-giuliani-draws-attention-with-latest-trip-to-ukraine.

2452 Vogel, Kenneth P., and Benjamin Novak. "Giuliani, Facing Scrutiny, Travels to Europe to Interview Ukrainians." *New York Times*, 4 Dec. 2019, https://www.nytimes.com/2019/12/04/us/politics/giuliani-europe-impeachment.html.

2453 Polityuk, Pavel, and Natalia Zinets. "Ukraine Lawmaker Met Giuliani to Discuss Misuse of US Taxpayer Money in Ukraine." *Reuters*, 5 Dec. 2019, https://www.reuters.com/article/us-usa-trump-impeachment-giuliani/ukraine-lawmaker-met-giuliani-to-discuss-misuse-of-u-s-taxpayer-money-in-ukraine-idUSKBN1Y918V.

2454 Vogel and Novak. "Giuliani, Facing Scrutiny, Travels to Europe to Interview Ukrainians."

2455 Duchon, Richie, and Alex Johnson. "House Judiciary Committee Publishes Full Impeachment Report." *NBC News*, 16 Dec. 2019, https://www.nbcnews.com/politics/trump-impeachment-inquiry/house-judiciary-committee-publishes-full-impeachment-report-n1102531.

2456 "H. Res. 755." 18 Dec. 2019, https://www.congress.gov/116/bills/hres755/BILLS-116hres755enr.pdf.

2457 Edmonsdon, Catie. "On Historic Impeachment Votes, Three Democrats Cross Party Lines to Vote 'No.'" *New York Times*, 18 Dec. 2019, https://www.nytimes.com/2019/12/18/us/politics/how-democrats-voted-on-impeaching-trump.html.

2458 *Id.*

2459 "Speaker Pelosi News Conference," *C-SPAN*, 18 Dec. 2019, https://www.c-span.org/video/?467571-1/speaker-pelosi-impeachment-managers-senate-trial-process.

2460 @realDonaldTrump. "[Image] In reality they're not after me they're after you." *Twitter*, 18 Dec. 2019, https://twitter.com/FactsareReal1/status/1208015083135217664.

2461 "Films of Derkach: the CIA Helped Poroshenko Fight with the Former People's Deputy Onyshchenko." *Glavred*, 22 June 2020, https://glavred.info/politics/poroshenko-i-bayden-cru-dopomagalo-poroshenku-borotisya-z-kolishnim-nardepom-onishchenko-poslednie-novosti-10181561.html.

2462 Sonne, Paul, Rosalind S. Helderman, Josh Dawsey, and David L. Stern. "Hunt for Biden Tapes in Ukraine by Trump Allies Revives Prospect of Foreign Interference." *Washington Post*, 1 July 2019, https://www.washingtonpost.com/national-security/for-months-trump-allies-hunted-for-tapes-of-biden-in-ukraine-now-theyre-turning-up/2020/06/30/f3aeaba8-a67b-11ea-8681-7d471bf20207_story.html.

2463 *Id.*

2464 *Id.*

2465 *Id.*

2466 *Id.*

Made in the USA
Columbia, SC
27 November 2020